*All About*
*HOUSE PLANTS*

# All About
# HOUSE PLANTS

THEIR SELECTION, CULTURE, AND
PROPAGATION, AND HOW TO USE
THEM FOR DECORATIVE EFFECT

## By Montague Free

*Revised and Expanded by Marjorie J. Dietz*
*Drawings by Ray Skibinski*

DOUBLEDAY & COMPANY, INC.
*Garden City, New York*

Copyright © 1979 by Nelson Doubleday, Inc.
Copyright © 1946 by The Literary Guild of America, Inc.
ISBN: 0–385–13532–7
Library of Congress Catalog Card Number 78–1197
All Rights Reserved
Printed in the United States of America
*Design by Jeanette Portelli*
15   14   13   12   11


**Library of Congress Cataloging in Publication Data**

Free, Montague, 1885–1965.
    All about house plants.

    Includes index.
      1.  House plants.  2.  Indoor gardening.
I.  Dietz, Marjorie J.    II.  Title.
SB419.F7  1979      635.9′65      78–1197
ISBN 0–385–13532–7

TO MY WIFE

# Contents

**Part 3**    *Types of House Plants*

**Part 4**    *Lists of Plants*

# Introduction to the
# Revised Edition

WITH TODAY'S HOUSES increasingly filled with greenery, it would seem that much has happened in the world of house plants since Montague Free's *All About House Plants* was first published in 1946. In fact, it might be asked why it deserves a revision, especially with the present abundance of books on the subject. But *has* so much happened? Montague Free himself, in his opening chapter of *All About House Plants,* noted that the list of recommended plants in a book first published in 1873 did not differ drastically from the list of plants he was writing about then—a situation somewhat parallel to what I have discovered today.

Yet the important reasons for reissuing *All About House Plants* are its unquestionable worth and validity for today's gardeners—beginners and experienced alike. Montague Free, every inch the knowledgeable professional in horticulture, also possessed a lifelong love for plants and their culture, unique qualities that made *All About House Plants* a lasting contribution to gardening literature and, not incidentally, the authoritative pacesetter for the many general house-plant books that have followed.

Although *All About House Plants* was ahead of its time, what Montague Free did not foresee was the tremendous impact on indoor gardening that the general use of artificial light would have. Nor could he foretell the effect of the crisis in our energy resources—an effect that has already reduced indoor temperatures in many of our houses and apartments. The resulting cooler environment benefits both plants and humans and widens the choice of plants that can be grown successfully indoors.

Perhaps it is best not to conjecture about what Montague Free would have said about the power of prayer over plants, the dialogues or empathetic relations between plants and growers, and like controversies! Yet since he accepted (albeit reluctantly) the parental role assumed by some toward their plants, just as he showed a patience for and tolerance of other foibles of human nature, it is quite likely he would have been more amused than saddened by such phenomena and would have realized that in time common sense would probably prevail.

Some of the plants recommended in the first *All About House Plants,* although rarely grown today, have been kept in the book, partly for the record and partly because their turn may come again. A former favorite among plants grown indoors is the Kenilworth-ivy, a rather fragile-appearing plant with a trailing habit and small purple-blue flowers. Following Montague Free's suggestions, I put a plant (rescued from a precarious, bruising existence near my back entrance, where it had survived the summer) in a small pot and placed it in my window garden. There it has flourished and is showing every prospect of reaching the substantial size, growing in its small container, predicted by Montague Free.

A practice nearly rejected for this revision was the sowing of sweet-alyssum seeds in eggshells for Easter favors. My first reaction was—"Now who would want to do that?" But this was quickly replaced by "What an intriguing idea!" And I, for one, plan to try it.

Of course since *All About House Plants* first appeared, new plants and varieties have been introduced; the botanical nomenclature of some plants has changed; and modifications in growing techniques and decorating trends have occurred. These changes have been taken into account for the revision.

I am indebted to Professor Joseph C. McDaniel, of the University of Illinois at Urbana, for helping me through the maze created by the nomenclature of the Christmas and Thanksgiving cacti.

MARJORIE J. DIETZ

*East Hampton, New York*

*All About*
*HOUSE PLANTS*

# 1

## PLANTS INDOORS

# CHAPTER 1

# What House Plants Bring to the Home

MY EARLY RECOLLECTIONS of house plants go back to a magnificent fuchsia and a "French" lavender which were my mother's pride and joy. My father used to knock out the ashes from his pipe into their pots (doubtless the ashes provided desirable potash!) and extinguish his matches by pushing them headfirst into the soil. These practices at times resulted in minor domestic storms. I used to suck the rather negligible amount of nectar from the fallen fuchsia flowers and enjoy the fragrance of the crushed leaves of the lavender. Fuchsias are still available in an ever-increasing number of varieties, but it is doubtful whether French lavender (which, in case you are interested, is *Lavandula dentata*) is very often grown as a house plant today.

But the cultivation of plants in homes goes back far beyond my boyhood—just how far it is difficult to say with any certainty. The early Greeks and the Romans grew plants in pots, and perhaps it is safe to assume that at times these were brought into their dwellings. Sir Hugh Platt in the *Garden of Eden,* printed in 1660, refers to the possibilities of growing plants in homes and says: "I have known Mr. Jacobs of the Glassehouse to have carnations all the winter by benefit of a room that was near his glassehouse fire." Apparently various citrus fruits were grown in England in the early 1600s and were accommodated during the winter in "orangeries"—which might be long rooms with many windows. The former orangery in the Royal Botanic Gardens at Kew (now used as a museum) is an example.

About a hundred and fifty years ago books began to appear on the cultivation of house plants in England and in France. In 1824 *The Greenhouse Companion—also the Proper Treatment of Flowers in Rooms,* by John Claudius Loudon, was published; and in 1842 Nathaniel Ward brought out his book

*On the Growth of Plants in Closely Glazed Cases*—the beginning of terrarium culture. In this country *The Parlor Gardener,* translated from the French and adapted to American use by C. J. Randolph, was published in Boston in 1861. Since that time books on house plants have appeared in increasing numbers, indicating great interest in this phase of gardening.

Although the plants recommended for house culture today are extensive and include some major, comparatively recent additions among tropical foliage plants and flowering plants such as African-violets and their relatives, it is surprising that the basic list has not changed more than it has in the last hundred years or so. According to a book called *Window Gardening,* edited by Henry T. Williams and in its sixth edition in 1873, many house plants that are in the front rank today were equally favored in 1873—begonia, cacti, English ivy, fuchsia, forced hardy bulbs, and geranium—all receiving considerable attention. Some of the plants recommended in *Window Gardening* are not rated very highly today because they are unfit for growing in our efficiently heated rooms (the trend toward lowering thermostats to conserve energy will improve indoor conditions for many plants, though), because fashions have changed, or because they are virtually unobtainable. Plants

*Various foliage plants decorate a city apartment window sill. Included are spider plant, philodendron, and ferns.*

falling in one or other of these categories are: calceolaria, carnation, cineraria, erica, and mahernia *(Hermannia verticillata).* The musk plant *(Mimulus moschatus),* which was among those recommended, in its fragrant form has been lost to cultivation. In my youth, almost every cottage window in England had its pot of musk, but with the loss of fragrance the chief incentive for growing it disappeared.

I was interested to notice that numerous winter-hardy plants were recommended for house culture. While a few of these, mostly early spring-flowering plants, are suggested in this book in Chapter 17, arborvitae, barberries, dianthus, honeysuckle, lychnis, mahonia, and peony, as recommended in 1873, are scarcely appropriate. A list of sixty or more so-called "alpine" plants is given—these to be kept outdoors or in a cold cellar during winter and brought into the house in March. Alpine-plant enthusiasts may see some merit in a suggestion such as this, especially if the plants are restricted largely to those very early species whose flowers, when produced outdoors, are likely to be marred by the weather sometimes experienced in late winter and early spring. Many alpines are diminutive plants whose charms can be fully appreciated only when they are inspected closely. Bringing them indoors gives us a chance to see them more nearly at eye level.

Some of the plants that are among the most important for house culture today are missing from these early works. African-violets and their relatives; the many species belonging in the pineapple family; peperomia; many species of philodendron and related aroids; the pickaback plant; snake-plant; and many others get no mention because they are comparative newcomers to the house-plant scene.

Incidentally, when thumbing over the pages of this old book, I came across an item that rather intrigued me—a turnip basket. This is made by scooping out the center of a turnip (presumably a rutabaga), starting from the root end, and leaving a shell about an inch thick. The hollow is filled with soil, morning-glory seed planted in it, and kept watered. Then the whole contraption is suspended by cords from a bracket in the window. The morning-glories climb up the cords, leaves grow from what is now the base of the turnip, providing an allegedly lovely combination. This is reminiscent of another practice of planting seeds of a dwarf variety of sweet-alyssum in eggshells to be used as Easter favors. This involves carefully decapitating the matutinal eggs and saving a sufficient number of shells so the seeds can be sown nine or ten weeks prior to the desired date of flowering.

Surely it is unnecessary nowadays to waste words in selling the proposition that the culture of house plants is well worth the effort required. The fact that there are so many house-plant addicts in large cities in apartments, offices, and other places of business where growing conditions are at their worst is sufficient evidence of the pleasure and interest they give. Perhaps they are valued even more in the city than they are in the country, for the greenness of their leaves and the brightness of their flowers bring relief from the everlasting bricks, mortar, stone, and asphalt.

*A seemingly endless procession of flowers above velvety leaves makes the African-violet a favorite among house plants.*

It has often been suggested that the culture of house plants provides a suitable occupation for invalids and others who are housebound. This is true enough; but it is also an absorbing hobby for the hale and hearty, who can expect dividends in beauty and interest if they tend their plants with knowledge and skill.

Growing plants indoors, especially if one is not content to string along with nothing but the old standbys, presents problems just as great as those one meets when growing hardy plants outdoors; and the thrill of accomplishment that is the result of solving them is eminently satisfying.

One gets a little closer to plants grown indoors and therefore gains a better insight into their idiosyncrasies, their beauty, and their adaptations to environment. One has the feeling he is something of a chemist when compounding soils and fertilizers; a budding naturalist when dealing with the bugs that may infest them; very much of a craftsman when he successfully performs the operations of making cuttings; and a creative artist when he sets up an indoor garden or terrarium.

With all these and other amenities it must be recognized that there is a responsibility to provide regular and intelligent care, and that there are certain limitations. Although there are a few plants that can exist for almost incredible periods in dim corners, most of the plants you will wish to grow demand a well-lighted situation, and some must have several hours of sunshine or bright light. The lack of humidity in the air may inhibit the culture of some plants unless they are grown in terrariums, and here spatial limitations enter the picture. Not all plants can adapt themselves to house conditions, though as shown later the number of tolerant kinds is large enough to satisfy any reasonable demands. Insufficient interest and lack of knowledge of the requirements of plants are perhaps the most potent limiting factors. Many plants

*An eggshell serves as a container for three rooted cuttings, thereby becoming a favor for an Easter breakfast table.*

*As this turn-of-the-century room shows, house plants are by no means a modern innovation. There is, however, a much wider selection of plants available today.*

demand cultural skill and meticulous attention to light requirements, watering, temperature, resting, and potting, as indicated in the following chapters.

On the other hand, the possibilities inherent in house-plant culture are tremendous. Although over three hundred genera and upward of a thousand species and varieties (this is an estimate—they haven't been counted!) are included in this book, even this extensive listing does not represent all the kinds that have been recommended for house culture from time to time in diverse places. And there are others, perhaps as yet untried as house plants, that would succeed if given a fair chance.

Where conditions are reasonably good from a plant standpoint it is possible, by making a suitable selection of varieties, to manage them in such a way that the house is never entirely devoid of flowering plants. They can be incorporated in a definitive decorative manner, or enjoyed as individuals without making any special attempt to display them effectively. They can be assembled in miniature gardenesque arrangements, grown in terrariums, or, under water, in aquariums. Many groups contain large numbers of species, cultivars, and varieties, which render them of great interest to the collector who wishes to specialize.

Plants that can be grown indoors, for part time at least, run the gamut from aroids to vegetables, from those that are found in deserts to denizens of the rain forests; and their natural habitats range from the Arctic to the Equator.

# CHAPTER 2

# *Give Them a Chance to Live*

MOST OF THE failures experienced with house plants are due to attempting to grow them under unsuitable conditions. In other words, the environment is at fault. The chief job, therefore, of the would-be grower of house plants is to provide the right growing conditions, and if the mountain will not come to Mohammed, why, Mohammed must go to the mountain—meaning that if the environment cannot be changed, plants must be selected which will endure the environment.

In certain plant families we find a number of subjects that are well adapted to growth under house conditions. Many of these belong in the lily family and include dwarf varieties of *Aloe; Asparagus* species grown for ornament and known as asparagus-fern; *Aspidistra,* known as cast-iron plant because of its toughness; *Dracaena,* in several species and varieties; *Gasteria* and *Haworthia,* interesting South African succulents; and *Sansevieria* (snake-plant), which, according to some, can be killed only by overwatering.

The Jack-in-the-pulpit family (aroids) is the one par excellence for providing candidates for home growing, though most of them, with the exception of calla-lilies and anthuriums, are regarded chiefly as foliage plants. There are many handsome and different kinds of *Philodendron* suitable for homes and air-conditioned offices. *Dieffenbachia, Aglaonema* (including the well-known Chinese evergreen), *Homalomena, Monstera, Scindapsus, Spathiphyllum,* and *Syngonium* are among other genera in this family that can "take it."

Desert plants, especially cacti and other succulents, are excellent whenever a sunny window is available and are particularly valuable in rooms where the air is excessively dry. Some of them, such as the Christmas cactus, mistletoe cactus, and orchid cactus, will endure some shade but need more atmospheric moisture.

*An eighteen-year-old jade plant. This succulent from South Africa is a good choice for dry, even drafty, rooms that are well lighted.*

Succulents, in addition to those mentioned above, include such well-known genera as *Crassula* (jade plant); *Kalanchoe,* a genus that includes the popular Christmas flowering plants as well as the curious air plant or "sprouting leaf"; and *Sedum,* all belonging in the same orpine family. *Fenestraria* and *Lithops,* "windowed plants" and living stones, and *Faucaria,* tiger's jaw, are a few of the many succulent members of the fig-marigold family that are grown as house plants by fanciers of this group.

Doubtless plants of this nature are able to survive because the impervious cuticle covering their leaves, which enables them to thrive under the hot desert sun and the lack of moisture, also enables them to get along in the dry air of the living room.

Other plants with tough constitutions are grape relatives such as *Cissus rhombifolia*, grape-ivy, and *C. antarctica*, kangaroo vine. Many plants in the pineapple family (bromeliads), especially *Neoregelia*, painted fingernail; *Billbergia; Cryptanthus;* and *Nidularium* will grow in dry air and with little light. *Pandanus, Ficus,* various citrus fruits, English ivy (if not kept too hot), and *Howea* (curly palm) also are excellent.

*Although tolerant of cool temperatures (down to 50° F. at night—60 to 70° F. during the day), the graceful Australian maidenhair fern* (Adiantum hispidulum) *requires a humid atmosphere to prevent its fronds from browning.*

In general those plants that have tough leathery leaves like those of the well-known "Brooklyn" rubber plant, and those whose leaves are shiny are best bets for the living room, though there are some excellent house plants with hairy leaves such as African-violets and episcias. These hairs serve much the same purpose as thickened and hardened skin in preventing loss of moisture by transpiration. The drawback to these hairy types is that they are too efficient as dust catchers.

It is fortunate for us that these plant "toughies," which can endure almost anything, are available, but if we restrict ourselves to them we are deprived of a large number of attractive plants that can be grown in the home if conditions are reasonably good. Therefore, if you are really interested in growing house plants, every endeavor should be made to change the environment to fit the plants which are likely to thrive under the conditions you are able to supply. Familiarity with the unfavorable conditions that make house plants miserable is helpful in enabling us to see just what has to be overcome and in devising means for setting things right.

*These house plants stand on moist pebbles in trays.*

*The asparagus-fern (not a true fern but related to the garden asparagus) is well suited to average indoor conditions.*

## TEMPERATURE, HUMIDITY, AND LIGHT

TEMPERATURE AND ATMOSPHERIC MOISTURE are most important. These two factors are linked because the higher the temperature of the air, the greater its capacity for moisture. High temperatures, with the resultant reduction in humidity, are responsible for many house-plant ills.

Humidify the air as much as possible. If you do this, you will find that you yourself will be comfortable at a lower temperature than is the case

*Hardly spectacular but dependable under varying indoor conditions, including dim light, is the foliage plant aspidistra, also known as cast-iron plant.*

when the air is deficient in moisture. Ventilation also is desirable whenever the weather permits, because it admits moist outdoor air.

LIGHT ESSENTIAL: Insufficient light often limits the variety of plants available for house culture unless artificial light—usually from fluorescent tubes— is used. Several plants, such as aspidistra, fiddle-leaf fig, and some of the philodendrons, are able to exist for months in dark corners. An example I knew of was snake plants set around a pool in the lobby of a neighborhood movie house (where there was practically no light except that provided by electricity on the dim side) that were able to last through the winter. But, for the most part, plants need to be kept as close as possible to windows, provided this does not involve setting them on top of an active radiator.

It is well known that country dwellers are able to grow to perfection a greater variety of house plants than those whose lot is cast in a big city.

They do not have to contend with the dust, noxious fumes, and air pollution that generally accompany city life. In many of the homes where the best house plants are grown, temperatures are maintained in a sensible range. Consequently, the rooms are only moderately warm, and the air, because of this, is comparatively humid.

ACCLIMATIZATION: The sudden transition from the excessively humid conditions of a greenhouse to the aridity of the average living room is sometimes disastrous. To overcome this, every effort must be made to raise the atmospheric moisture. It also helps to buy plants in the warmer months so they have a chance to adapt themselves to their new environment without the discomfiture attendant upon the dry air that usually accompanies artificial heat. Another reason for purchasing plants during the warm months is that there is no danger of their suffering from chilling during transit to the home.

Do not be too despondent if leaves start to turn yellow and fall off within a few days after the plants are received. Often this is just a passing phase— a sort of homesickness that is overcome after the plants become acclimated.

One way of helping to keep house plants healthy is to maintain them in a state of constant juvenility. This implies propagation by cuttings, air-layering, or seeds in your own home. If you are able to do this, you avoid the necessity of having to condition the plants to a sudden change.

And, lastly, it must not be forgotten that due attention must be given to watering, fertilizing, the use of right soil mixtures, resting, timing, pest fighting, and other factors previously mentioned which are concerned in good culture and may be looked on as part of the environment. These and other elements will be discussed in greater detail in subsequent chapters.

# CHAPTER 3

# *Real Gardens Indoors*

THE KIND OF indoor garden you create depends on the extent of your enthusiasm for house plants—whether you are basically a hobbyist who grows plants for their interest and intrinsic beauty and who probably possesses a touch of the collector's mania, often complicated with something akin to parental instinct; whether you are primarily a decorator who looks on plants as furnishings and transitory material to be discarded without a tear when it begins to look shabby; or whether your attitude toward house plants lies somewhere between these two extremes. This last category allows you the fascination of watching plants develop and gives the thrill of pride that comes from producing healthy, beautiful specimens. It also allows you to arrange plants attractively and to avoid jumbles of plants handled haphazardly without thought of their decorative effect.

## THE VERSATILITY OF INDOOR GARDENS

Usually the most satisfactory indoor gardens are those which contain both permanent plants (foliage plants such as schefflera, rubber plant, or flowering plants such as African-violets) and more transient material (paper-white narcissus, amaryllis, poinsettia). The first group provides background or serves as special accents, the latter contributes a change of scene and needed splashes of color.

Indoor gardens are no longer limited to window sills and can exist throughout the house. Not surprisingly, considering the pleasure that growing plants gives to those who care for them, indoor gardens or house-plant collections

*This contemporary plant room admits almost as much light as many green-houses. The Christmas cactus (foreground) is decorative in or out of bloom and the agave (rear) is outstanding in modern interiors.*

are increasingly seen in schools, offices, waiting rooms, showrooms, and other places of business. The reasons for this burgeoning of house plants beyond their traditional window-sill locations are various, but undoubtedly an important factor is the increase of light sources, both natural and artificial.

INCREASE OF INDOOR LIGHT: While most of us are not exactly dwelling in glass houses, the trends in architecture are certainly toward making the indoors much more exposed to light than in the past. The suburban "picture" windows, the "bubble" windows and other skylights that permit the entrance of light through roof areas, and the floor-to-ceiling walls of glass that barely separate interiors from outdoor living areas and garden all help to let in more natural light to brighten areas beyond the immediate window sills. Some houses are even planned and built to include specific places for plants: yesterday's Victorian conservatory is today's plant room.

For those rooms where natural light is lacking or inadequate, there is artificial light that permits the establishing of indoor gardens in all sorts of space or places formerly useless for growing plants, such as hallways, cellars, bathrooms, heated garages, unused fireplaces, sections of cabinets, book shelves, and walls. Most homeowners can make use of both natural and artificial light, thus greatly increasing the space available for their plants, while those in dimly lighted apartments can now rely on artificial light to grow a wide assortment of plants from African-violets to *Zebrina* (wandering Jew).

*Examples of transient plants which are valuable for their flowers in winter are a primrose* (Primula obconica) *and paper-white narcissus (right). The latter is fragrant.*

Fluorescent tubes are the most commonly used sources of artificial light, but track lights and other kinds of spotlights and lamps fitted with incandescent bulbs are also used. Fluorescent tube fixtures, some of which are specially designed to fasten under shelves or to suspend from ceilings, are available from local outlets and mail-order specialists. The most simple fixture is a table-top model, available in lengths from 24 to 48 inches, which, while strictly utilitarian, does approach grandeur when the space beneath it is filled with wax begonias and African-violets in full bloom. For those who are more particular about their furnishings, there are handsome as well as functional etagères, tables, carts, and cabinets—all with built-in light fixtures. As is the case with any well-designed and -built furniture, these can be expensive, so it behooves those who possess any craft skills at all to design and build their own special units. (See Chapter 11 for more information on light requirements, natural and artificial, of house plants.)

FLOOR GARDENS: Floor space is being increasingly utilized as a site for indoor gardens, a trend made possible by brighter, less cluttered modern interiors. Especially appropriate are the areas in front of or near large, low windows or sliding glass doors, but any site that is sufficiently lighted from natural or artificial sources and that fits into a room's arrangement can be used. Small plants are not properly appreciated much below eye level and, in addition, are a nuisance on the floor, but larger plants, some chosen for their foliage and bushy habit, others for their flowers as well, can be arranged for temporary or permanent display. In either case, some provision must be made to protect the floor from leaking pots. If you follow the pot-within-a-pot system in which the outside container lacks a drainage hole, there is no problem, but this method is most pleasing for a few plants or even one rather than for a group of plants that are supposed to give the effect of a garden indoors. Saucers under each individual pot also help, but sooner or later they are bound to overflow and again—an assemblage of pots in saucers may belie the effect of a garden.

More efficient are metal trays, usually custom-made, of varying widths and lengths with sides from 1½ to 2 inches in height. They serve a dual purpose of containing spillage after plants are watered and contributing to atmospheric humidity if they are filled with water and pebbles. The water level is maintained just below the surface of the pebbles so the pots do not stand continuously in water. Such trays, which when filled with plants are quite inconspicuous, can be made to fit your dimensions by local tinsmiths or metalworkers. Their shapes can be square or rectangular or, to fit into a corner, triangular. Smaller trays, of plastic or metal, are usually available from garden centers or mail-order sources.

Deeper than trays and difficult to move about once filled with soil and plants—something to think about if you are a frequent mover of furniture— are planters, modern versions of the traditional window box. As with the trays, these can be of various shapes, sizes, and materials and are sometimes built as permanent installations, although this last practice is more often encountered in showrooms and hotel lobbies. A popular use of planters has been to serve as room dividers, an illusion that is enhanced when a trellis is added on which to train vining plants. Planters have an advantage over trays in that pots are eliminated, accomplished by filling the planters with peat moss into which the pots can be plunged, or by setting the plants directly into a suitable growing medium. The peat moss maintains a cool, moist atmosphere around the potted plants, reduces the frequency of watering, and makes it easy to replace individual plants as need arises. But plants can certainly be transplanted directly into the planter, the practice most often used in window gardens (see below). However, some plants, as in any "permanent garden," will eventually outgrow their neighbors or quarters and require division or replacement.

## PLANTS AS ACCENTS

Quite the opposite of indoor gardens, which use a number of plants, is the use of a single specimen, the objective being to create an eye-filling, dramatic effect. Such a plant can be a beautifully grown African-violet or Boston fern displayed on a small table or pedestal, but more often it is a large, treelike house plant in a large pot or tub that rests on the floor.

*Hanging shelves make an indoor garden. These shelves, made of Plexiglas, are less obstrusive and admit more light than shelves of opaque material.*

This special use of a plant has been enthusiastically embraced by the more interior-decorative-minded growers who enjoy expeditions to garden centers and other plant outlets in search of just-the-right plant for a given situation. The single specimen can emphasize the mood or style of a room, complement a prominent piece of furniture, mark an entrance, attempt to alter the spatial effects of large or small rooms or rooms with high or low ceilings, or it can simply introduce a living element not unlike sculpture among inanimate objects. (The nuisance of the weight of these large tubbed plants does not seem to be a deterrent to their use or popularity, perhaps because when moving day comes around the tubs can be placed on coasters, available from garden centers and mail-order concerns.)

Some of these decorative specimens can be shrublike foliage plants, such as schefflera *(Brassaia actinophylla)* and the false-aralia *(Dizygotheca elegantissima)*, while others are more treelike, such as mature plants of the weeping fig *(Ficus benjamina)*, many palms, and the exotic-appearing dragon tree *(Dracaena draco)*. In very sunny areas, venerable specimens of cacti and

*Of the right scale for a sunny, narrow window ledge or shelf is the powderpuff cactus* (Mammillaria bocasana). *The brown hooks, barely visible in the mass of silky hairs, are not vicious, but are responsible for another common name, fish hooks!*

succulents can be arresting because of their unique silhouettes and growth habits. If any of these accent plants are to be on view for short durations, they will not suffer unduly if light is inadequate, since they will soon be returned to their permanent locations. However, a spotlight or some other form of artificial illumination can make them more dramatic in their setting and benefit their health, too.

**Permanent evergreen plants,** mostly of bold or massive character, some of tree form, for background and accent:

*Araucaria heterophylla* (Norfolk Island-pine)
*Aspidistra elatior* (Cast-iron Plant)
*Aucuba japonica* 'Variegata' (Gold-dust Plant)
*Brassaia actinophylla* (Umbrella Tree; Schefflera)
*Cibotium schiedei* (Mexican Tree Fern)
*Citrus* spp. and cultivars (Orange, Lemon, et cetera)
*Crassula argentea* (Jade Plant)
*Dieffenbachia* spp. and cultivars
*Dizygotheca elegantissima* (False-aralia)
*Dracaena* spp. and cultivars
*Ficus benjamina* (Weeping Fig); *F. elastica* (India Rubber Plant); *F. lyrata*
    (Fiddleleaf Fig); *F. retusa* (Indian-laurel)
*Laurus nobilis* (Bay Tree)
*Monstera deliciosa* (Swiss Cheese Plant)
*Nephrolepis exaltata* 'Bostoniensis' (Boston Fern)
Palms (especially *Howea forsterana, Chamaedorea erumpens,* and *Chry-*
    *salidocarpus lutescens*)
*Pandanus utilis* (Screw-pine); *P. veitchii* (Variegated Screw-pine)
*Persea americana* (Avocado)
*Philodendron* spp. and cultivars
*Pittosporum tobira*
*Podocarpus macrophylla maki; P. nagi* (Japanese-yew)
*Polyscias balfouriana* (Balfour-aralia); *P. fruticosa* (Ming-aralia)
*Rhododendron* cultivars (Evergreen Azalea)
*Rosmarinus officinalis* (Rosemary)

## HANGING PLANTS AND GARDENS

The Victorian vogue for hanging containers with plants of decumbent habit, or to use the older term, basket plants, is a welcome revival that intrigues the grower and that has become such an integral assist to the decorator that it seems doubtful it will ever again fade from fashion. Hanging plants are seen everywhere where light, natural or artificial, is sufficient for their needs. All kinds of containers are acceptable, many being designed especially

*The miniature wax plant* (Hoya bella) *shows to best advantage in a hanging container since its limp branches are more inclined to droop than climb.*

for suspension, but almost any pot can be placed in a macramé hanger or hung by wire or strong cord—the choice depending on your own taste and what is available. The majority of hanging plants can be moved outdoors in warm weather to decorate porches and terraces or can be hung from limbs of trees to provide a touch of the tropics.

The flaw to many hanging containers indoors is the dripping from drainage holes after watering. This can be circumvented by choosing containers without drainage holes (if the containers are large enough and the plants to be suspended are in smaller pots, it is a good practice to slip them inside the container); or choosing containers with molded-on saucers; or as a final resort, placing a saucer under the pot inside the hanger.

It should be remembered that plants in hanging pots tend to dry out faster than pots that rest on pebbles in water-filled trays.

The choice of plants for suspension is broad and goes far beyond the ones that were considered suitable in the past. The obvious candidates are any plants that normally trail or climb (see the section on Vines and Trailers in Chapter 17); many ferns, including the magnificent forms of Boston fern (*Nephrolepis exaltata* 'Bostoniensis'), whose drooping fronds showed to such advantage in the urns and on the pedestals favored by Victorians; and many kinds of orchids. Add to these almost any plant that is not starkly treelike in habit of growth: African-violets (although care must be exercised not to injure the brittle, long-stemmed leaves when arranging the plants in their hangers) and many of their relatives, including *Achimenes,* flame-violet *(Episcia),* and *Streptocarpus saxorum;* many begonias, especially those with long-petioled leaves, such as the popular 'Cleopatra,' and others with a semi-creeping or floppy habit such as *Begonia boweri* and its hybrids, *B. foliosa* and even many of the varieties of the common wax begonia *(B. semperflorens);* and such oddities as the strawberry-begonia *(Saxifraga stolonifera),* pickaback plant *(Tolmeia menziesii),* and the spider plant *(Chlorophytum comosum).* There are many cacti and succulents, beyond the cascading types, whose sculptural beauty is better appreciated when the plants are observed in space.

Several hanging containers of individual plants can be considered a "garden" but so, too, can containers filled with different plants—miniature or dish gardens. Terrariums and bottle gardens are joining them and are ideal for this purpose because many of them require less light (too bright sunlight can damage the shut-in plants) and need infrequent watering.

## WINDOW GARDENS

For all the invasion—but a benevolent one—of house plants and their gardens throughout the house, for most people the most accessible, the most practical and aesthetically pleasing places for plants indoors remain at the windows.

The number to grow depends first on the space available. A bay window, for example, offers infinite possibilities, but for those who lack such commodious quarters, there is space that can be gained from smaller windows in several ways: by combining hanging plants with stationary plants; by the addition of hanging shelves of glass or plastic that can accommodate plants in quite small pots; and by the widening of narrow sills to make room for two to three rows rather than one row of plants. This last possibility does not require any advanced carpentry skills and is easily accomplished by fastening a wider board to the sill. It can be painted to match the rest of the window's woodwork but this is not necessary if it is to be covered with the watertight trays mentioned earlier. It will probably be necessary to provide a leg at each end of the board—where it extends beyond the window ledge—

*A small lean-to greenhouselike structure, heated from the cellar, can be built around a window or opening in the foundation. It can be used for propagation, seedlings, and for bulbs that are being forced.*

for support, as trays filled with water, pebbles, and potted plants will be very heavy.

If you feel that with numerous pots on brackets at the sides of the windows, suspended from the top on a rod, with possibly more on glass or plastic shelves, you have enough in view, you may prefer using planters—window boxes—usually made to fit the window space. They ought to be 7 inches deep and as much wide—the wider the better within reason—to allow for flexibility in arranging plants. Drainage holes are desirable, and this requires a water-holding tray beneath them to catch the drips. Of course there are watertight planters, but care must be taken to avoid saturation of the soil or growing medium. If you are one of those who likes constantly to rearrange your indoor gardens, it will be best to fill the planter with peat moss, as recommended earlier, so plants can be left in their pots and simply plunged in—and pulled out—as needed. The peat moss is easy to handle and, if kept moist as it should be, reduces watering and increases humidity.

Other ways to enlarge a window garden include the use of plant stands of wood or metal, usually arranged toward the sides of the window but still placed where they receive sufficient light. As with hanging baskets, the plants and their stands can be particularly valuable for patio or porch decoration in summertime. Also offered by mail-order specialists in house-plant supplies are pole plant stands equipped with several adjustable, swinging arms with trays to hold the plants. Pole stands have the advantage of not blocking light even though they can hold several plants and are especially effective in front of very large windows.

The plants you choose for your window garden depend on your own interests, but even more on the quality and duration of light that will be available. (As a start, you might consult the lists of plants for various exposures and conditions in Chapter 20.)

Climbing plants can frame the window, although this practice is not as fashionable as it once was—and perhaps for good reason. Vines must be trained upward by fastening their stems to wire or by tape or thumbtacks, which soon makes them a more or less permanent fixture. Their leaves can become dust and soot catchers and in time can give a fussy, jumbled, if not junglelike, effect. Hanging plants, on the other hand, suspended from brackets at the sides of the windows or from horizontal rods at the top of the window are often more interesting and graceful and can be readily moved as occasion demands. However, it is perfectly possible to use a combination of the two—upward growing vines and those plants that trail downward or spread horizontally. Among the best climbing vines are the grape-ivies *(Cissus)*, cape-grape *(Rhoicissus capensis)*, English ivies *(Hedera helix)*, and nephthytis *(Syngonium podophyllum)*. A flowering vine grown from seeds and sometimes used indoors around sunny windows is the morning-glory, but since it climbs by twining, slender stakes or cord must be provided.

Trailing plants (see also the section on Hanging Plants and Gardens above) include hearts entangled *(Ceropegia woodii)*, English ivy, philodendron *(Philodendron scandens oxycardium)*, pothos *(Scindapsus)*, Swedish-ivy *(Plectranthus australis)*, German-ivy *(Senecio mikanioides)*, black-eyed Susan-vine *(Thunbergia alata)*, the various plants known as wandering Jew, and many kinds of gesneriads, many of which are summer performers.

Except when one is restricted to long-blooming flowering plants, such as African-violets and others, the content of the window garden will vary with the seasons. These frequent changes of material require the provision of another plant room or place, if possible, and preferably cooler in temperature, where hardy bulbs, azaleas, camellias, cyclamen, veltheimia, and the like can be brought along to the bud stage before putting them on display. The same area is used after the plants have finished flowering. Plants grown under fluorescent lights can be moved into a window for better appreciation, or elsewhere in the house, for that matter, and then moved back to their garden as their flowering wanes.

Of course one may make frequent purchases of plants in bud or bloom from the florist or garden center, such as poinsettia, kalanchoe, cineraria, or chyrsanthemum. If your financial state does not permit extensive splurges in the acquisition of plants, and if it is not possible to provide a room or interim space in which to grow or store plants when they are not in bloom or at their best, you will have to rely on those plants of long-flowering habit, such as African-violet *(Saintpaulia);* wax begonia *(Begonia semperflorens); B. scharffiana;* shrimp plant *(Beloperone guttata)*, an old favorite that blooms its head off if fading flowers are pinched off; and impatiens. There are more, particularly among the begonias, that you will soon discover by poring over catalogues of specialists and visiting garden centers and florist shops. Brightly colored foliage plants also play a part—coleus in winter, certain begonias, and caladiums in summer. There are many summer-blooming house plants that can also be grown and displayed on porches, breezeways, and terraces. They include gloxinias, achimenes, and many other gesneriads, tuberous begonias, fuchsias, and geraniums.

Most of the plants suggested above for the window garden are on the large rather than miniature scale, although in their young stages they may be contained in small pots. Hanging plant shelves of glass or plastic, supported by light metal hangers that attach readily to the sash frame, are ideal for plants in small pots. Browse through variety stores, garden centers, and hardware stores or mail-order catalogues of specialists in house-plant supplies for a unit that fits your needs.

These shelves offer a convenient eye-level place for miniature plants interesting enough to bear close inspection. Candidates for a sunny window include miniature geraniums *(Pelargonium)* and cacti and succulents in wide variety. For eastern and western exposures, there are miniature African-violets and certain orchids, some of the latter having incredibly small yet elegant blooms.

CACTI: Some of the cacti that have outstanding decorative quality are *Astrophytum myriostigma,* bishop's hood cactus; *Cephalocereus senilis,* old man cactus; *Chamaecereus sylvestri,* peanut cactus; *Echinocactus grusonii,* golden ball cactus; *Echinopsis multiplex; Espostoa lanata,* Peruvean old man; *Mammillaria bocasana; M. elongata,* golden lace cactus; *M. fragilis,* thimble cactus; *Opuntia microdasys,* rabbit ears cactus.

SUCCULENTS OTHER THAN CACTI: *Crassula lycopodioides; C. rupestris,* bead vine; *Echeveria secunda; Faucaria tigrina,* tiger's jaw; *Gasteria verrucosa; Haworthia margaritifera, H. truncata; Kalanchoe tomentosa,* panda plant; and any of the flowering stones (*Lithops* spp., et cetera); or the allied windowed plants—*Fenestraria* spp., et cetera.

Cacti and other succulents are suggested for the shelves partly because their cultural requirements are met by the light, airy, and dry environment.

There are a few things always to be kept in mind—things small in themselves, but which, if neglected, can detract immensely from any planned decorative effect: The pots in which the plants are growing should be a uniform color, scrubbed clean, or hidden; sickly plants should either be discarded or promptly removed to a room set apart to serve as a sanitarium—they have no place in what sets out to be an ornamental display; and yellowing leaves and faded flowers should be picked off as they appear. Almost invariably the best side of plants is that which is toward the source of light; consequently, when they are required to look well when seen from inside, it is necessary to turn them rather frequently—usually about once a week. Vines and plants too large to be given a weekly turnabout always appear at their best to the observer on the outside looking in, and there is nothing much that can be done about it.

## PLANT COLLECTING

The serious grower of house plants often discovers that certain groups have a special appeal—either because they thrive exceedingly well or because they have features that make them especially interesting. When this happens, this person is vulnerable to the collecting bug and any day is likely to become the willing victim of an absorbing hobby.

I once had a collector friend whose specialty was small succulents. His addiction to them led him to construct a small "greenhouse" over the cellar window on the south side of the house. The plants were inconveniently tended and admired by standing on a box in the cellar and thrusting head and shoulders through the window. One hopes that such devotion was repaid by the plants! Plants grown in such a situation add nothing to the amenities of the living room, and it is unnecessary to worm oneself into a frame over a cellar window to enjoy cacti and succulents, for they are more resistant to dry air than most plants, and they thrive in any sunny window or under artificial light.

Cacti and succulents, however, are too numerous to permit the formation of a comprehensive collection in a dwelling, so it is wise to limit oneself to a section within the group, or even to a single genus. If the objective is the cultivation of a large number of species and varieties—and a true collector may want to grow all available kinds within his limit—it is better to select a group whose members never attain any great size, or one in which the individuals can easily be maintained as small specimens by periodic propagation. Plants filling these specifications are found among the mammillarias, belonging to the cacti, many of which have the additional merit of flowering while still very small. Living stones and windowed plants, those strange inhabitants of the South African deserts, never get very large; neither do *Haworthia, Faucaria,* and selected species of *Crassula* and *Echeveria.* The tropical and subtropical sedums can easily be brought down to earth again, when old plants get too large, by making cuttings of their shoots, which root with ridiculous ease.

If sunny windows are not available, a collection of ferns could be installed; or one might make a hobby of many other plant groups by setting up fluorescent-light gardens.

A collection of begonias is almost never without some kinds in bloom— many of them producing their flowers over long periods—and most of them have leaves that are colorful, of interesting form, or otherwise attractive. Some begonias, however, may grow to considerable size and there is a natural reluctance to discard a beautiful well-grown specimen, so an extensive assortment is better not attempted unless there is plenty of room for it. Begonias are well suited to artificial-light gardens.

There are scores of species and varieties of the geranium *(Pelargonium),* including many fascinating miniatures that just fit a sunny window sill. Also there are the well-known scented-leaved group, the Martha Washington, the ivy-leaved, or the zonal geraniums. The last named, sometimes known as house geraniums, will produce flowers the year round if two lots of plants are maintained—the old plants to be set outdoors in the spring to bloom all summer. From these, cuttings are taken early (keep the flower buds picked off until the fall) and grown on to provide plants to bloom throughout the winter. This procedure will make it possible to avoid having plants of unwieldy size—the old ones, of course, are left in the garden in the north to freeze.

The bromeliads, a family to which the pineapple belongs (see the section on them in Chapter 17), are tremendously varied in leaf form and in habit of growth. Often their leaves are brilliantly colored, and the flowers of many species exhibit combinations of color found nowhere else in the plant kingdom. *Billbergia nutans,* for example, has blue-edged green petals, conspicuous golden stamens, and striking red bracts. These plants for the most part are well suited to house conditions.

The remarkable African-violet (*Saintpaulia* spp. and cultivars) is probably still the prime example of the collector's delight—it has created collectors virtually overnight, an accomplishment shared by few, if any, other plant groups. Not surprisingly, the popularity of the African-violet has focused new interest in other relatives, such as gloxinia *(Sinningia speciosa)* and other species of the same genus; achimenes and the cape-primrose (*Streptocarpus* spp. and hybrids); and produced a surge of enthusiasm for other members of the family (Gesneriaceae) that a few decades ago were hardly known to house-plant growers. Obviously, the opportunities for the collector abound in this family.

The majority of orchids was once considered too demanding in cultural requirements for most house conditions, and the enjoyment of growing them was reserved for greenhouse owners. This situation has changed radically and many kinds of orchids are being found in house-plant collections. Some growers have been overwhelmed by the madness for acquisition common to all collectors and are finding that there are enough possibilities among the orchid family to last their lifetime.

There may be those with the collecting instinct who desire more variety than is afforded by the cultivation of one group. Even though space is limited, they need not be deterred, for there is the possibility of making use of those plants that have a dormant period at different seasons so that growing space is occupied by one group while the other is resting. Fuchsias actively grow and blossom during spring, summer, and fall, and can be kept dormant in the cellar during the winter, during which time their place in the window garden can be occupied by a collection of winter-flowering bulbous plants such as *Lachenalia, Oxalis,* or *Veltheimia.* Or a collection of summer-flowering *Achimenes,* tuberous begonias, or gloxinias could be alternated with winter-flowering African-violets and orchids.

The collector does not, perhaps, have as much opportunity to produce decorative results as those who grow and display a greater variety of plant material, but there is sufficient compensation in getting to know a special plant group intimately and sharing much of this experience with others possessed by the same mania!

# CHAPTER 4

# *Terrariums and Bottle Gardens*

DRY AIR is one of the greatest obstacles to the successful culture of house plants. Growing them in terrariums enables us to overcome this handicap and permits the cultivation of a variety of plants that would be certain to die quickly if exposed to the air of the average living room. They are especially valuable for the city dweller because they enable him to maintain a moist atmosphere around his plants no matter how assiduously the superintendent attempts to reproduce in his apartment the climate of Death Valley.

Another name for terrarium is Wardian case, which commemorates Nathaniel Ward, a London physician who, more than a hundred years ago, discovered that plants could be grown in closed containers.

Ward greatly desired an old wall covered with a growth of ferns and mosses. There was no difficulty whatever about the old wall—it was already there—but the good doctor, residing in the dirt and smoke of London, could not make plants grow in it or on it. He was interested in all natural phenomena, and in the summer of 1829, wishing to see the emergence of an adult sphinx moth, he buried the chrysalis in soil contained in a glass jar which he then covered with a metal lid. Nothing is known about the fate of the chrysalis— Ward was too excited about a fern and a grass that appeared in the bottle and continued to thrive there with no attention and without additional water for nearly four years. There is no telling how long these two plants might have flourished if, during Ward's absence from home, the lid had not rusted and let rain into the jar, waterlogging the soil, causing the plants to rot.

The spontaneous growth of a plant belonging to a group which he had so far failed to grow in spite of all his efforts caused Ward to experiment with a variety of plants in all sorts of containers. He began with one of the most intractable of all plants under cultivation—a filmy fern *(Trichomanes radicans),* which grows wild in Killarney in Ireland but is the despair of most gardeners. It grew happily for four years in a wide-mouthed bottle covered with oiled silk, without any added water, and then became too crowded, necessitating its removal to a fern house. There, covered with a bell jar (thus continuing the principle of a closed container), it developed fronds 15 inches long—larger than those of specimens in its native haunts.

After experimenting with more than a hundred species of ferns and thoroughly proving the success of the system as far as this group is concerned, Ward constructed a glass case about 8 feet square which he placed outside a window on the north side of his house. In this case, which might easily be called an unheated greenhouse, he grew a great variety of hardy material including ferns and flowering plants, and also two palms. These flourished but, says Ward, "the atmosphere was too moist, and there was too little sun for them to ripen seed, with the exception of the *Mimulus,* the *Oxalis,* and the *Cardamine . . .*"

The "drawing-room case," which contained palms, ferns, club mosses, aloes, and cacti was very successful, and Ward says of it: "The palms have now been enclosed for fifteen years . . . they will continue for many years without outgrowing their narrow bounds." The association of moisture-loving ferns, et cetera, with desert plants is incongruous and presents cultural difficulties, but these were overcome by growing the former in the bottom of the case, and suspending the cacti and succulents from a bar near the roof where the only water available to them was that contained as vapor in the air.

Wardian cases, or terrariums, whichever you prefer, enable us to control the amount of atmospheric moisture around the plants grown in them. In those which are tightly closed the moisture evaporated from the soil and that transpired by the leaves condenses on the glass, runs down to the soil, and again becomes available for the use of the roots in a sort of perpetual-motion cycle.

The late W. A. Manda, a superb plantsman, once gave me a fish-bowl terrarium, tightly covered with a pane of glass, in which a variety of plants was growing. I left it on a southeast window sill with no attention whatever for nearly a year—just to see what would happen. As a result of neglecting to apply those curbs that are a part of routine care, one plant, *Fittonia verschaffeltii argyroneura,* had grown so vigorously that all the rest were smothered, but it was perfectly healthy and the terrarium was still presentable except for the depressing remains of the murdered plants.

Although many plants grow well in tightly closed cases, for our purposes a modification of the principle is desirable. When tightly closed, moisture often condenses on the glass, obscures the plants within, and defeats our objective of displaying decorative plants; also some plants object to an atmosphere in which the humidity is constantly kept at 100 per cent. So, except in special instances, it is desirable to provide some means of ventilation that can be increased or decreased according to circumstances.

*Former fish bowl becomes terrarium home for a clump of confederate violets* (Viola sororia). *The rhizomes were dug from the garden during a winter thaw and forced into flower on a cool, bright window sill.*

The plants in terrariums are protected from dust, temperature changes are gradual, and the plants are not exposed to drafts. All these are helpful factors when growing plants under the abnormally dry conditions of most living rooms. The terrarium should appeal especially to those who hate the daily chore of watering, because it almost entirely eliminates the need for such attention. Ward had a bottle containing ferns and mosses which were in perfect health after eighteen years of confinement without any fresh water. He expressed the opinion that it would be possible to fill a case with palms and ferns which would not require additional water for fifty or a hundred years. But this, of course, would be practicable only in a tight case in which the transpired and evaporated water is condensed on the glass and ultimately returned to the soil; and, as previously mentioned, such tight cases are not ordinarily desirable for our purpose.

## TYPES OF CONTAINERS

All sorts of containers have been used in which to grow plants on the principle of the Wardian case. They range from brandy snifters of normal or Gargantuan size through glass teapots, plastic "bubbles," kitchen canisters and similar whatnots to large fish bowls. Tropical fish fanciers have converted their aquariums into terrariums; and ordinary dirt gardeners have either bought terrariums with gleaming chromium frames or have made their own with less glamorous materials. Oversize, hermetically sealed test tubes with ferns in them, their roots growing in nutrient agar, are not unknown. There are bottle gardens, too, which may be set up in anything from a half-gallon wine jug to an acid carboy with a capacity of twenty-five gallons. When selecting wine or other glass containers to convert into a bottle garden, use those with clear rather than tinted glass.

An easy way to make a terrarium is to acquire a flat or box about 4 inches deep and of a convenient length and breadth. Unless there are cracks in the bottom, bore about six ½-inch holes to permit water to escape. Then have a glazier cut two pieces of glass about 16 inches wide (this dimension

*This terrarium was made of Lucite. Clear Plexiglas could also be used. The base is of outdoor plywood. The handle is a piece of driftwood. There is a layer of pebbles for drainage over which sphagnum moss and humus form a planting mix for ferns and panamiga* (Pilea involucrata).

will be the height of the terrarium—it can be varied in accordance with the size of the box so that it is in proportion). These two pieces should be the exact length of the inside dimension of the flat lengthwise. Two more pieces should be cut the same height and the width of the flat *less two thicknesses of the glass.* These are used to make the sides. One additional piece ¼ inch in excess of the inside length and breadth of the flat is cut to serve as a cover. The side and end pieces are fitted vertically in the flat, and soil, which will help to hold the glass in place, is put in.

Then the exposed joints of the glass are bound with tape, the plants are put in, and the top glass rested on the side walls. The final result is an efficient but not especially beautiful case. Unfortunately the flat top may become a repository for books and magazines placed there by unsympathetic members of the household.

A better-looking affair, which does not permit books, et cetera, to repose on it, can be made in the form of a span-roof greenhouse. This is an appropriate shape, because a terrarium in effect is nothing but a miniature greenhouse. A wooden frame holds the glass over the soil container (4 or 5 inches deep, of convenient length and breadth) made of planed boards. The frame is made of strips 1 inch square planed on all four sides and rabbeted (grooved) on two sides. It is attached to the base by lap joints or by overlapping brass strips fastened to box and frame by screws. If the first method is used, the boards of the soil container should be ½ inch thick; if the latter is used, a thickness of 1 inch is desirable.

*Three terrarium styles: the traditional "berry" bowl (center) and two newer types of acrylic. Too much bright sun will bake the contents of a terrarium, but fluorescent lights can save the day as they do not cause heat build-up.*

*Planting a terrarium with miniature sinningia hybrids (in pots and small plastic flat) and a plant of baby's-tears.*

The gable ends project about 1½ inches beyond the side walls. Two ³⁄₁₆-inch holes, an inch apart, are made in the projection to receive the whittled pegs that prevent the roof glass from sliding. When ventilation is necessary, the pegs are placed in the lowermost holes, allowing the glass to slip down to rest on them. If a completely closed case is desired, the glass is pushed up and held in place by putting the pegs in the upper holes.

Either of these terrariums can be used as a propagating case to raise new plants from cuttings or seeds.

Although plants can be grown in cases without any provision for under-drainage, it is much better to have some means for disposal of surplus water. Cases without holes in the bottom are not foolproof, because watering has to be done with great care to avoid getting the soil waterlogged; hence there should be from one to several holes in the bottom of the soil container.

In addition, a 1-inch layer of coarse sand or fine gravel should be placed in the bottom, first covering the holes with pieces of broken flowerpot to prevent the sand from sifting through. A thin layer of moss over the drainage is desirable to prevent fine soil from sifting down and clogging it. When the case is thus protected there is much less danger from overwatering. If it is decided to string along with a watertight case, a couple of inches of small pebbles mixed with a few lumps of charcoal will help to overcome the danger of waterlogging. (See Chapter 9.)

An open-textured soil is desirable, especially if the container is undrained. It should not be too rich, because if it is the plants will grow so quickly that they will soon raise the roof. A mixture of 2 parts fibrous loam, 2 parts coarse sand, and 1 part flaky leaf mold will suit most of the plants.

*Bottle gardens can be made from discarded wine bottles so long as the glass is clear to admit adequate light.*

Or try 1 part sterilized soil (it can be purchased in most garden centers), 1 part peat moss, and 1 part coarse sand. If acid-soil plants are to be grown, substitute acid peat moss for leaf mold and double the amount.

To plant, put in the drainage material and fill the box with soil, but do not pack it down; this last you will do as the plants are set in place. Then, if it is considered desirable to raise the level of one or more parts to give variation of contour, add small, well-shaped and pleasingly colored rocks and fill in behind them with soil.

The arrangement of the plants is the next item on the program. If the case has a flat top, it is usually better to concentrate the taller plants at either end, giving a sort of valley effect in the middle; if you are dealing with a peaked roof, the taller plants will be spaced down the center where there is more headroom and the completed terrarium turned from time to time to insure an equitable distribution of light.

It is helpful to place and replace the plants within the terrarium without removing them from their pots until you have a rough idea of the kind of arrangement most pleasing to you. Then remove the plants from their pots and scoop holes with the fingers large enough to receive the balls of soil. Press soil firmly around them as you proceed with the planting. Commercial terrariums are planted for immediate effect and almost always are over-crowded and cluttered with "waterfalls" of marble chips, miniature storks, gnomes, and so forth. Unless you dote on fiddle-faddles, it is better to pass them by and limit your accessories to lichen- or moss-covered rocks of interesting shapes and give the plants a little room in which to grow.

## BOTTLE GARDENS

Planting a garden in a bottle calls for nearly as much skill and patience as that exercised by an old-time sailor constructing a model of a full-rigged ship in a rum bottle. The manipulation of the plants with only a narrow opening through which to work is a delicate operation.

Great care is necessary to avoid spilling soil on the leaves or the inside of the container, because it is not easy to get it off once the plants are inside the bottle. Most, if not all, of the soil must be removed from the roots of the plants to enable them to pass through the opening; this means that the plant is set back to some extent and special care must be taken to spread the roots in the soil, to fill in between and over them, and finally to tamp firmly. The chances of success are improved if the bottle is provided with drainage holes. You may be successful in drilling two or three holes in the bottle.

Obviously a bottle garden cannot be planted without some tools; these, fortunately, can be made at home, although tools made for the purpose can usually be purchased through mail-order sources listed in classified ads of

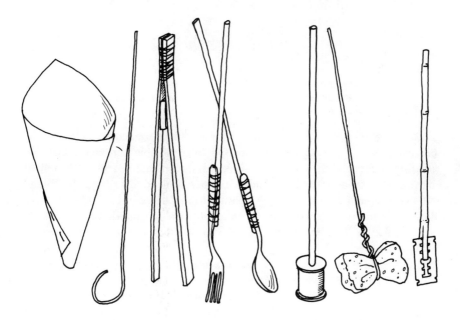

*Planting a bottle garden: Moist pieces of sheet moss (often available in garden centers or you may be able to collect your own) are poked with dowel into bottle to make a green lining.*

garden magazines. A funnel with a wide spout is needed to help get the soil in the bottle; this can be improvised from flexible cardboard fastened into funnel form with a stapler. Three hands are necessary if the job of pouring is to be done without undue exasperation—one to hold the funnel and two to manipulate the soil. A spatula to dig holes in the soil to receive the roots can be whittled from a piece of lath or something similar. Be sure to make it long enough to enable you to grasp the projecting portion easily. A tamper can be made by cutting a short section from a broom handle, drilling a hole through it, and inserting a thin plant stake or ¼-inch dowel of suitable length. Or use an empty thread spool fastened to a dowel.

Long tongs are needed to put the plants in position and hold them there while they are being planted. They can sometimes be obtained from dealers in aquarium supplies. If it is not possible to locate tongs of suitable size, a makeshift can be improvised from a bamboo plant stake by splitting it lengthwise and inserting a wedge at the upper end of the split to spread the legs.

Wind several turns of string and tie tightly near the upper limit of the split to prevent it from going too far.

To make your bottle garden, first put drainage material in the bottom. This can consist of coarse sand with the finer particles sieved out, or ⅛- to ¼-inch charcoal or small gravel. The amount to use depends upon the size of the container and whether or not it is provided with drainage holes. Half an inch will be sufficient for a half-gallon bottle if it is drained; otherwise use an inch, or even 2 inches.

The soil should be funneled in with care to avoid getting it on the sides. A mixture of equal parts loam, sand, and leaf mold, put through a ¼-inch

*The growing medium (first drainage gravel and charcoal, then soil) is poured into bottle with aid of funnel and plastic tube (a peashooter).*

sieve so it will pour easily through the funnel, is satisfactory, or concoct your own mixture from packaged soil mixes. While the soil should be moist, it should not be wet, lest it clog the machinery. From 2 to 5 inches of soil will be needed, depending on the size of the container. In large bottles it is usually desirable to arrange the soil in a slope (do this with the spatula), which gives a more pleasing effect and provides a greater depth of soil on one side to accommodate the larger plants.

As with regulation terrariums, it is desirable to arrange the plants outside the container before starting to plant in order to get a rough idea of the

*Add the tallest plants first. Fill in gaps between plants with bits of moss or pebbles. Plan before you plant!*

*After planting and "landscaping" are finished, clean the bottle's side with cloth fastened to wire.*

spacing. Obviously no plants can be used that are too large to pass through the bottle neck; with this limitation in mind a selection can be made from the lists of plants for terrariums at the end of this chapter.

The procedure in planting is to turn a plant out of its pot and shake enough soil from its roots to enable it to go through the needle's eye. Then, gauging the extent of the roots, make a hole in the soil large enough to receive them and gently insinuate the plant into the bottle. Hold the plant in position with the tweezers and scrape soil in between and over the roots with the spatula and make it firm with the tamper. Continue along these lines until planting is completed.

When all the plants are set they should be watered enough to make the soil moist, at the same time taking advantage of the opportunity to spray off any crumbs of soil that happen to rest on the foliage or the side of the container. This is fairly easy with an ordinary terrarium, but bottle gardens present some difficulty.

Probably the best tool for this purpose is a laundry sprayer. The great danger in applying water to terrariums and bottle gardens which have no drainage is that of using so much that the soil becomes waterlogged. To avoid this use no more water in spraying the foliage than is absolutely necessary, and examine the soil the following day to determine whether it was enough to moisten it all through.

CARE OF TERRARIUMS AND BOTTLE GARDENS: The frequency of future watering is determined mainly by the amount of ventilation given. As we have seen, it is possible to keep plants for years in cases without adding any water; but when enough ventilation is provided to prevent the condensation that obscures one's view of the plants, occasional watering is needed— it may be six or more months after the initial application.

The need, or otherwise, for watering should be determined after digging into the soil with a spoon, or by screwing an auger into it and pulling it straight up with samples of the lower soil sticking in the grooves. This last is the only convenient method of examining the lower stratum of the soil in bottle gardens. If the soil seems less than moist, it should be watered. When the case is well drained, the soil may have a thorough soaking, but in those which are watertight no more water should be given than is sufficient to make the soil moist. Should too much inadvertently be given, the case must be opened up widely to get rid of the surplus as fast as possible by evaporation.

No plant should be put into a terrarium if it is known to be infested with insects. This is especially important in bottle-housed plants because of the difficulty of getting at the insects to fight them. Solutions to the pest problem include the mixing of systemic granules, which should be used with caution and a light hand, in the basic soil mixture or a gentle burst of an all-purpose house-plant aerosol spray. Chances are you will not have to face this problem.

Dead leaves should be picked off and not left to decay and become a possible source of trouble. Aggressive plants must be pruned; or, if they become too obstreperous, removed entirely lest they smother their neighbors.

Generally the results are better if the cases are ventilated rather freely even though it necessitates watering more frequently. Ventilation is effected by tilting the covering glass or by sliding it down if the terrarium is of the span-roof type. The opening should be large enough to prevent moisture from fogging the glass. The amount of ventilation necessary will be conditioned to some extent by the weather. If the air in the home is not too dry, the side walls are sufficient to insure that little extra humidity and the top can be left off permanently.

The kinds of plants grown in the case will in part be determined by where it is placed (see lists of plants for various locations in Chapter 20). Placement in a sunny window where shade is provided by light draperies is generally satisfactory, though exposure to bright sunshine is not necessarily fatal. I had a terrarium in a window where it was fully exposed to the sun from

*Finally add water, allowing about a teaspoonful per plant. If the soil is already moist, use less or none.*

noon on, which was unattended for six months and was still in good condition. Some shade is preferable, however, to cut down fogginess of the glass, which is inevitable in bright sun. (An inexpensive soil thermometer available from mail-order seed firms can be used to check the temperature.)

## PLANTS FOR TERRARIUMS

The planted terrarium, offered by florists and garden centers, usually contains an indiscriminate mixture of tropical, subtropical, and hardy subjects, together with plants of the desert and rain forest, all of which are expected to dwell amicably together. Greater satisfaction may be expected, however, if the plants are selected thoughtfully with the idea of associating those with similar temperature and cultural requirements. The partridge berries, lichens, and mosses offered for sale in "fish" bowls around Christmastime cannot be expected to thrive permanently in an overheated apartment, though they might do well if kept outside the window instead of in the room. Plants of rapid growth and those that are subject to insect attacks should be rejected. Coleus is an admirable illustration of a plant that belongs in both these categories—it shoots up like Jack's beanstalk and almost invariably is infested with mealybugs.

In the lists below are a selection of plants that are suitable for culture in terrariums. Try to obtain plants in small (2¼- or 2½-inch) pots.

(For specific information concerning plants in the following lists, refer to Index.)

FOR ORDINARY ROOM TEMPERATURE: Abundant light is desirable but direct sun is not necessary.

*Acorus gramineus* 'Variegatus' (Miniature Sweet Flag)

*Aglaonema* spp. and cultivars (Chinese Evergreen)

*Alternanthera ficoidea.* These respond to pruning and may be kept to reasonable size.

*Anoectochilus* spp. (Jewel Orchid)

*Anthurium scherzerianum* (Flamingo Flower)

*Asparagus setaceus.* Will need pruning.

*Begonia boweri* and cultivars; *B. foliosa; B. imperialis; B. imperialis smaragdina; B. pustulata; B. rex-cultorum,* small cultivars, such as 'Dew Drop,' 'Granny,' et cetera, and many other small begonias.

*Billbergia nutans*

*Caladium humboldtii*

*Calathea roseopicta; C. zebrina.* Will soon grow too large.

*Cissus rhombifolia* (Grape-ivy). For large terrariums only and even then will need pruning.

*Codiaeum* (Croton). Small plants are very attractive but they quickly grow too large for small terrariums. Sunshine is necessary to keep their color.

*Cryptanthus bivittatus; C. zonatus* (Earth Stars)

*Dieffenbachia seguine.* Use small plants only—will ultimately grow too large.

*Dracaena; D. goldieana; D. sanderana; D. surculosa*

*Episcia dianthiflora* (Flame-violet)

*Fittonia verschaffeltii argyroneura* (Nerve Plant). Needs frequent pinching.

*Gesneria cuneifolia*

*Maranta arundinacea* 'Variegata' (Variegated Arrowroot); *M. leuconeura kerchoveana* (Prayer Plant)

*Pellionia daveauana*

*A water garden contains a sword plant* (Echinodorus *sp.*) *and whelk shell.*

*Peperomia obtusifolia; P. obtusifolia* 'Variegata'; *P. orba* (Princess Astrid Peperomia); *P. rotundifolia; P. rubella; P. sandersii.* These tend to rot if conditions are too wet.

*Philodendron scandens oxycardium* (Heartleaf Philodendron)

*Pilea cadierei* 'Minima'; *P. depressa; P. involucrata; P. microphylla* (Artillery Plant); *P. repens*

*Saintpaulia* (African-violet). Miniature cultivars only.

*Scindapsus pictus* 'Argyraeus' (Satin Pothos)

*Selaginella kraussiana* 'Brownii'; *S. pallescens*

*Sinningia concinna; S. pusilla;* and hybrids. (Miniature Sinningia)

*Soleirolia soleirolii* (Baby's Tears)

*Zebrina pendula.* Needs constant pruning.


## FERNS

*Adiantum capillus-veneris* (Southern Maidenhair); *A. raddianum; A. tenerum* ('Wrightii')

*Asplenium nidus* (Bird's-nest Fern)

*Davallia mariesii* (Ball Fern); *D. pentaphylla* (Dwarf Rabbit's-foot Fern)

*Nephrolepis* spp. and cultivars. (Boston Fern, etc.). Young plants only.

*Pellaea rotundifolia* (Button Fern)

*Polypodium aureum* (Rabbit's-foot Fern)
*Polystichum tsus-simense* (Holly Fern)
*Pteris cretica* and cultivars (Table Fern); *P. ensiformis* 'Victoriae' (Silver Table Fern)

FOR THE COOL WINDOW, plant room, or enclosed breezeway or sun porch, where the winter temperature does not go below 40° F. or much above 50° F.:

*Acorus gramineus* 'Variegatus' (Miniature Sweet Flag)
*Buxus sempervirens* 'Suffruticosa' (True Dwarf Box)
*Coprosma repens* 'Marginata' (Variegated Mirror Plant)
*Cymbalaria muralis* (Kenilworth-ivy)
*Daphne odora*
*Euonymus fortunei* cultivars; *E. japonicus* cultivars
*Ficus pumila* (Creeping Fig)
*Hedera helix* 'Itsy Bitsy', 'Needle Point' and other compact cultivars (English Ivy)
*Pittosporum tobira* 'Variegata'
*Pteris cretica* cultivars (Table Fern)
*Rhododendron*—Evergreen Azalea, in small sizes
*Saxifraga stolonifera; S. stolonifera* 'Tricolor' (Strawberry-begonia, Strawberry-geranium, Mother-of-thousands)

FOR A TERRARIUM OUTSIDE A NORTH WINDOW where the temperature may go below freezing. These plants could also be used in a cool room:

*Asplenium platyneuron* (Ebony Spleenwort); *A. trichomanes* (Maidenhead Spleenwort)
*Buxus sempervirens* 'Suffruticosa' (True Dwarf Box)
*Chimaphila maculata* (Spotted Wintergreen); *C. umbellata* (Pipsissewa)
*Drosera rotundifolia* (Sundew). Can be established in live sphagnum moss.
*Epigaea repens* (Trailing-arbutus)
*Euonymus fortunei* cultivars
*Gaultheria procumbens* (Wintergreen)
*Goodyera repens* (Rattlesnake-plantain)
*Hedera helix* cultivars. See also above.
*Hepatica americana* (Liverleaf)
*Lycopodium* spp. (Club-moss). Shoots will stay green over winter, may even root but will not thrive permanently.
*Mitchella repens* (Partridge Berry)
*Polypodium vulgare* (Common Polypody)
*Saxifraga stolonifera* (Mother-of-thousands)

Mosses and lichens in great variety, small evergreen ferns, seedling spruces, firs and hemlocks collected in woods and fields are admirable material for the "hardy" or natural terrarium. But be sure to avoid taking anything you "hadn't oughter" when scrounging for wildings.

# CHAPTER 5

# *Small Plant Arrangements —Gardens in Miniature*

THE ARRANGEMENT of plants in open containers is often known as "dish gardening," a rather horrible term that does not even correctly describe the product, which may be an idealization in miniature of a natural scene in woods, bog, swamp, or open meadow; a reproduction of a desert or wind-swept mountain landscape; a section of a garden scene; a model of a formalized garden; or an association of tropical plants.

Dish gardens can, of course, be bought ready-made from the garden center, but they may offend the fastidious because frequently they are cluttered up with foolish figures, windmills, wishing wells, bridges, or pagodas. Culturally they are seldom all that could be desired because of the association of incon-gruous materials—desert plants with moisture lovers, tropical plants with hardy kinds, and so on. They are put together to give an immediate effect with the plants jostling each other like people in a subway so that they have no chance whatever for future development. Anyone with the least bit of artistic skill, and perhaps even if he has none at all, is likely to get more satisfaction from a homemade product than from a hand-me-down, plus the pleasure that comes from the actual assembly and the joy of having created something.

Admittedly arrangements of this kind are often ephemeral—their length of life depending in large measure upon the sort of plants used in making them. Plants gathered from northern woods and kept in a dry room with a winter temperature of 75° F. cannot be expected to last long. When roots are massacred in the endeavor to jam too many plants into a container that is too small, the outlook is for a short life for the plants and not a very happy one. If plants requiring different soil and growing conditions are given the same quarters, some will survive and others succumb, so the good effect of the arrangement is quickly lost. Then, too, in many cases it is inevitable that some of the plants will grow much faster than others so the scale and balance of the composition are upset. Even so, an arrangement of living plants is much more lasting than an arrangement of cut flowers; and the fact that it does not endure forever is an advantage in that it gives an excuse for a change in make-up.

At the other extreme in longevity are dwarfed potted trees, known as bonsai, which can live for many, many years if given proper growing conditions and care. Miniature Japanese landscapes in trays are similar but usually can consist of more than one plant as well as mosses, certain kinds of grasses, rocks, pebbles, and sand—all skillfully assembled to reproduce a "living landscape" (known as *saikei* in Japanese). Traditional bonsai and miniature land-

*An arrangement in the Japanese manner uses a stiff, upright form of English ivy (Hedera helix 'Conglomerata'), driftwood, and a bonsai tray.*

*A miniature garden of plants (jade plant and cacti) that thrive under the same conditions.*

scapes consist of hardy plants that are no more suited to indoor conditions during winter months than the northern native plants mentioned above, but by substituting certain kinds of house plants (list follows at end of section) for the hardy material and adapting some of the techniques of bonsai, quite satisfactory results can be achieved. (Consult libraries and Chapter 21 for books devoted to bonsai.)

Receptacles for miniatures can be as varied as the plant arrangements. Almost any shallow (but not too shallow) container that will hold soil, with room for several plants, can be used. Wooden bowls, baskets lined with moss for temporary use, or a box constructed to fit the window space, are possibilities. Usually, however, pottery containers are most in favor. These may be of any shape—round, square, rectangular, elliptical. They should be at least 3 inches deep—4 is better—and it is best to have holes in the bottom to allow surplus water to escape. It is almost impossible to find a piece of pottery with this last feature, so it is usually necessary either to drill the desired holes laboriously or to rely on ample drainage material, exceptionally porous soil, and careful watering to avoid waterlogging.

Drainage material can consist of flower pots, soft bricks, or charcoal broken into ½-inch or smaller pieces; coarse sand; fine gravel of suitable size. To prevent the soil from immediately sifting into the drainage material, which is important when dealing with watertight containers, it can be covered with a piece of building material of the nature of "sheet rock," with holes bored through it and cut to fit. Sheet moss obtained from a florist, moss from the woods, or burlap will provide at least a temporary barrier between soil and drainage.

The character of the soil is of little importance for those arrangements that one knows ahead of time will be only transitory—anything that can be moistened to keep the roots from drying will do—but for those from which some degree of permanence is expected it is necessary to fit the soil to the subject. Woodland plants ordinarily will be dug up with a considerable amount of soil about their roots. This will form the bulk of soil in the container; any additional soil required could well be peat moss or leaf mold with a little sand to make it more porous. For the general run of plants a mixture of sand, loam, and peat moss or leaf mold in equal parts will be suitable, with addition of another part of broken charcoal for cacti and succulents. Purchased potting soil or soil-less mixes used according to directions on the container are also suitable.

Accessories for use above ground include small rocks of pleasing form and color, especially those that have lichens growing on them, and pieces of bark or dead branches, which often can be found supporting a growth of interesting fungi or beautiful mosses. Colored pebbles or shells, small figures and such, can be obtained from garden centers and variety stores, if you like them.

### SUITABLE PLANTS

If you have access to country roadsides, abandoned fields, or woodland areas, there is plenty of material that can be gathered during a fall walk that is especially adapted for use in plant arrangements for a cool window or room. Be careful to avoid trespassing where you are not wanted, and do not dig up anything that is on the list of plants needing conservation in your region, or any plant that does not occur in fair abundance. Using a stout trowel, dig the plants with as many roots as possible, retaining a ball of earth about each. Slip plants into plastic kitchen bags and, when enough plants are gathered, pack them closely together in an upright position in a box or carton. Sprinkle tops and soil with water if they have to be transported to any great distance.

The woodland will yield many plants of an evergreen nature that are well suited to our purpose. Young hemlocks, spruces, or firs will give the necessary height to the composition. To associate with them a selection can be made from hepatica, rattlesnake-plantain, pipsissewa, partridge berry, tea berry, small ferns, club-mosses, and true mosses. If the scale is small, one or other of the club-mosses *(Lycopodium)* can be used instead of the young trees, in which case still smaller material—tea berry, partridge berry, sporeling ferns, and mosses—will form the "undergrowth."

From roadsides and sunny abandoned fields you may be able to gather young red-cedars (common junipers) and ferns such as the ebony spleenwort, which provide an effective contrast with the low gray rosettes of pussy toes *(Antennaria).* A touch of color is given by that grayish lichen *(Cladonia)* with bright crimson apothecia (fruiting bodies), and other lichens on rocks or wood can be included for variety. With this and the preceding type of arrangement it is perhaps permissible, though it does savor somewhat of fakery, to make use of cut sprays of evergreens, which will last a considerable time when stuck into moist earth, especially if kept cool; and twiggy branches, which can be made to simulate deciduous trees—the twiggy branches of bridal wreath *(Spiraea)* can, by a stretch of the imagination, be likened to the branch system of an elm.

Shoots of boxwood, false-cypress, arborvitae, evergreen barberries, can be arranged in a gardenesque composition with considerable ease because all that needs to be done is to stick the sprigs in the moistened earth, or sand

*A large ceramic bowl filled with pebbles and water provides the needed humid atmosphere, and a fluorescent light fixture with two 20-watt tubes provides the light for this miniature garden. The plants—all in pots for arrangement flexibility—include a rex begonia 'Shirt Sleeves', a gesneriad (Chirita sinensis), a scented-leaved geranium (Pelargonium 'Little Gem') in flower, and a dwarf orchid, also in flower (rear center).*

in this case, in the container. This phase is perhaps more nearly akin to flower arranging than the making of a miniature garden.

One aspect of small plant arrangements that more nearly approaches the garden idea is the construction of model gardens. For years these were in evidence at flower shows (I remember seeing them at English flower shows where, to me, they were the most appealing feature). Usually the plants are artificially represented by pieces of sponge cut to shape, colored and fastened to small sticks to simulate trees. Toweling dyed green is used for the lawn, but sometimes natural material—used in the form of cut sprays— serves as trees and shrubs; while small, brightly colored flowers are dibbled in to represent flower borders. Those in which artificial material is used do not concern us here; and the kind that makes use of cut flowers is too ephemeral for most of us.

Model gardens of this kind, however, can be utilitarian in giving us a better idea of what a proposed garden will look like than can be gained from the most elaborate paper plan. Such a model could, for instance, represent a Tudor "knot" herb garden laid out in the intricate pattern beloved of Elizabethan gardeners, with sprigs of juniper, red-cedar, et cetera, representing the boxwood, lavender-cotton, germander, and rosemary used in the actual planting. In the knot gardens of Elizabethan times the spaces between the lines of plants forming the pattern were often surfaced with colored material which might be crushed brick for red; coal for black; sand for yellow

*An attractive foliage pattern results when four plants of the succulent haworthia are combined in a low clay bowl.*

or white. In making these models the surfacing material can be provided by mixing fine sand with dry colors obtained from a paint store. While these gardens of cut sprays are far from being permanent, they are fun to make; and, if the tougher evergreens are used, they may last in good condition for several weeks.

The most enduring and in many ways the most satisfactory dish or miniature gardens are those in which cacti and succulents are used. Under these conditions they are usually slow-growing, so the composition does not quickly become unbalanced. The plants are adapted to the dry air of the living room, although it has been discovered that even cacti can benefit from the humidity provided in a *partially* enclosed container. They can get along, as they have to do in a dish garden, without much soil about their roots, and there is sufficient variety in their appearance to permit making up interesting compositions. The pencil cactus *(Opuntia ramosissima),* when no more than 6 or 8 inches high, may resemble a branching giant saguaro and can be used as such along with much smaller cacti in an arrangement suggested by a scene in the Arizona desert. Cactus specialists can supply small plants in an infinite variety of form and color. Cacti collected from the wild should be avoided since they are difficult to establish and there is danger of some kinds being depleted.

Succulents are just about as enduring as the cacti and may be had in all shapes, sizes, and colors, ranging from the common-place jade plant to the intriguing panda plant with its fuzzy leaves tipped with tufts of rust-colored hairs which become dark brown with age. Relatives of the jade plant, such as the necklace vine, with each pair of leaves threaded on the stem; and *Crassula lycopodioides,* which looks like a club-moss, are effective in contrast. The plushlike leaves of the Mexican firecracker; the blue-gray rosettes of other kinds of *Echeveria;* the mottled leaves of some plants of *Kalanchoe, Gasteria,* and *Aloe,* provide material of exceptional interest. These cacti and succulents are grown mainly for the beauty of the stems, spines, and leaves, but sometimes they give an extra dividend of occasional flowers, often brilliantly colored.

Another type of arrangement is that made up of tropical material, which includes the variegated Ti plant *(Cordyline terminalis)* and the gold dust dracaena; any bromeliads that may be available; small philodendrons; and variegated wax-plant. Most of these are grown for their colored foliage; for flowers there are African-violets, especially the miniature varieties; *Kalanchoe blossfeldiana;* and wax begonias can be used. For green leaves the dwarf, small-leaved varieties of English ivy (even though not tropical) can be included, and that tufted mosslike *Selaginella* of brightest possible green known as *S. kraussiana* 'Brownii'. Many of these plants and others suitable for the purpose can be picked up at florists, garden centers that feature house plants, or other outlets. Do not, however, make the mistake of buying plants in large pots—the containers used for dish gardens usually are not big enough to hold them. Plants from 2-to-4-inch pot sizes are generally preferable.

As the days begin to lengthen, small pots of azalea, begonia, hybrid kalanchoe, primroses, and other plants in full bloom begin to make their appearance in stores. These can be combined with cut sprays of boxwood and other evergreens to make effective temporary dish gardens. By the time the flowers have faded, weather conditions may be such that it will be possible to remove the plants from the container and plant them separately outdoors.

Often the dish gardener has to be an opportunist and secure plants when they are offered for sale. He may combine them, even though they do not entirely fulfill the ideal of using none but congruous plants in a container; or hold them as pot plants until he is able to assemble enough of the right kind of material to suit his plans.


## ASSEMBLAGE

First gather all materials needed—plants, container, soil, drainage, et cetera—on a table or bench large enough to permit confortable working. Before removing plants from their pots, arrange them in the container to get a rough idea of how they can best be placed to make an artistic composition. (It is often possible to leave plants in their pots for temporary arrangements— disguise pot rims with sheet moss.) It will save time when it comes to actual planting if it is known in a general way where the plants are to go. Then remove the plants and put drainage material in the bottom of the container. If it is so shallow that there is not much room for soil, and if it is provided with drainage holes, a piece of broken flower pot over each hole to prevent soil from sifting through will be sufficient. If, however, it has no provision for the escape of surplus water, and if it is 3 inches or more in depth, put in ½ to 1 inch (or even more for deep dishes) of broken pots, bricks, or something similar. This should be covered with burlap, moss, or sheet rock to keep the soil from immediately clogging the drainage. Then fill the container with soil, *without pressing it down.*

The plants are removed from their pots by placing the fingers of one hand on the soil and turning the pots upside down and tapping the rims on the edge of the bench. Knowing just about where they are to go, it is easy to dig a hole in the soft soil with the fingers to receive the roots. If, as often happens, the ball of soil is too deep for the container, carefully tease out the roots until enough soil can be removed to make it fit. As the plants are set in place, pack the surrounding soil, which should be moderately moist, firmly about their roots.

When all the plants are placed, it is time to think about watering. This is a ticklish operation if the dish is watertight, and one where judgment must be exercised to give enough water to moisten the soil all the way through but not so much that it stands free in the soil. It is best to put on less than you think is necessary and then, the following day, dig down to the bottom of the soil with a kitchen spoon and notice its condition; give more water if needed. Containers with adequate drainage holes can be soaked until water runs through the bottom.

Subsequent care consists of placing the arrangement in the aspect most suited to it—a south window for cacti and succulents; an east or west window for the general run of plants; and a north window or a table or mantel away from direct sun for ferns and others that object to too much light. If your rooms are poorly lighted, consider growing dish gardens under fluorescent lights, showing them off only on special occasions. Winter-hardy plants should be kept in a cool room or porch.

Watering must be done thoughtfully. Except for cacti and succulents, most of which will not object if the soil becomes dry from time to time during the winter months, the plants demand moist soil. At first, comparatively little water will be required after the initial watering, but when the plants are established and the soil becomes filled with roots, more and more will be needed. It is a good plan to keep that kitchen spoon handy and dig down into the soil whenever there is any doubt as to its need for water.

*A miniature garden of succulents and cacti that should have a long life, providing it receives bright natural or fluorescent light and occasional watering (only when the lower leaves begin to shrivel).*

When some of the plants become overgrown, rip the arrangement apart and start all over again, reusing those that are suitable, and supplementing them with new material. Discard the unpresentable ones and pot up those that are healthy but too large.

## PLANTS FOR DISH GARDENS

Some of these are useful only at the very young stage—others are bound to quickly grow too large.

*Acorus gramineus* 'Variegata' (Miniature Sweet Flag)
*Aglaonema* spp. and cultivars (Chinese Evergreen)
*Asparagus densiflorus* 'Sprengeri' (Asparagus-fern)
*Begonia* spp. and cultivars of small-leaved types, such as *B. boweri, B. foliosa.* Consult catalogues of specialists for others.
Bromeliads
*Buxus sempervirens* 'Suffruticosa' (True Dwarf Box)
Cacti
*Chamaedorea elegans* (Parlor or Bella Palm)
*Cymbalaria muralis* (Kenilworth-ivy)
*Dieffenbachia* spp. and cultivars (Dumb Cane)
*Dracaena sanderana* (Ribbon Plant); *D. surculosa* (Gold-dust Dracaena)
*Euonymus fortunei; E. japonicus*
Ferns
*Ficus pumila* (Creeping Fig)
*Hedera helix* (English Ivy)
*Malpighia coccigera* (Miniature-holly)
*Maranta leuconeura kerchoveana* (Prayer Plant)
*Pandanus veitchii* (Variegated Screw-pine)
*Pelargonium* x *hortorum* (Geranium). Miniature cultivars.
*Peperomia* spp. and cultivars
*Phoenix roebelenii* (Pigmy Date Palm)
*Pilea involucrata* (Panamiga); *P. microphylla* (Artillery Plant)
*Portulacaria afra* 'Variegata' (Rainbow Bush, Elephant Bush)
*Rhododendron* (Evergreen Azalea). Small plants, even rooted cuttings.
*Rosa* cultivars of Miniature Roses
*Rosmarinus officinalis* (Rosemary); *R. officinalis* 'Prostratus' (Creeping Rosemary)
*Saintpaulia* (African-violet). Miniature cultivars.
*Saxifraga stolonifera* (Mother-of-thousands)
*Scindapsis* spp. (Pothos)

*Serissa foetida*
*Sinningia pusilla* and other miniature spp. and cultivars; high humidity needed for good results.
*Soleirolia soleirolii* (Baby's Tears)
*Streptocarpus saxorum*
Succulents
*Syngonium angustatum* 'Albolineatum'


## SOME HOUSE PLANTS FOR INDOOR BONSAI EFFECTS

Many can also be used in dish gardens and adapted versions of Japanese miniature landscapes.

*Araucaria heterophylla* (Norfolk Island-pine)
*Buxus* spp. and cultivars (Boxwood)
*Camellia japonica*
*Carissa grandiflora* (Natal-plum)
*Cissus rhombifolia* (Grape-ivy)
*Citrus* spp. and cultivars (Otaheite Orange, Calamondin, Meyer Lemon, et cetera)
*Crassula argentea* (Jade Plant)
*Dizygotheca elegantissima* (False-aralia)
*Eugenia uniflora* (Surinam-cherry)
*Euphorbia milii splendens* (Crown-of-thorns)
*Ficus benjamina* (Weeping Fig); *F. deltoidea* (Mistletoe Fig); *F. pumila* (Creeping Fig); *F. retusa* (Indian-laurel)
*Fortunella* spp. (Kumquat)
*Gardenia jasminoides* 'Prostrata'
*Grevillea robusta* (Silk-oak)
*Hedera helix* cultivars (English Ivy)
*Hibiscus rosa-sinensis* 'Cooperi'
*Lantana camara*
*Laurus nobilis* (Bay)
*Ligustrum japonicum* (Japanese Privet)
*Malpighia coccigera* (Singapore-holly, Miniature-holly)
*Myrtus communis* (Myrtle)
*Pelargonium* x *hortorum* (Geranium). Use miniature cultivars.
*Pittosporum tobira*
*Podocarpus macrophyllus maki* (Japanese-yew)
*Polyscias balfouriana* (Balfour-aralia); *P. fruticosa* (Ming-aralia)
*Psidium cattleianum* (Strawberry-guava)

*Punica granatum* 'Nana' (Dwarf Pomegranate)
*Rhododendron* cultivars (Evergreen Azalea)
*Rosmarinus officinalis; R. officinalis* 'Prostratus' (Rosemary)
*Serissa foetida*
*Trachelospermum jasminoides* (Star-jasmine)


## SUBMERGED GARDENS

Most submerged or aquatic gardens combine two hobbies—plants and fish. These live together in a co-operative relationship, each contributing to the other's welfare. The submerged plants give off oxygen, which enables the fish to breathe, while the carbon dioxide given off by the fish and their excrement provides the nutrients necessary for the welfare of the plants. By securing a proper balance between plant and animal life it is possible to set up an aquarium that will remain in good condition for years by merely adding water to replace that lost by evaporation.

However, it is quite possible to have an aquatic garden without fish. Such gardens can be quite easily set up in any sort of bottle or glass container. Wine bottles or jugs, food storage and confectionery jars, are examples of the containers suitable for a water garden and have the advantage of using less space than the usual tanks and fish globes. Select containers of clear glass—tinted glass shuts out light—and do not crowd the plantings.

PLANTS: One of the best plants for a water garden is *Vallisneria spiralis,* known as eel-grass or tape-grass, though it is not related to the true grasses. Its pale green translucent leaves may attain a length of 1½ feet. It is easy to grow and is particularly valuable for framing an aquarium. If a few plants are set at each end of the aquarium, the leaves will arch over and meet in the center. *V. spiralis tortifolia* is shorter, its twisted leaves reaching a height of 12 inches, making it a better choice for bottle gardens.

Other plants of similar appearance include submerged forms of various arrowheads *(Sagittaria).* The one listed as *S. graminea* grows a foot or more high and can be used at the back of the aquarium in between the *Vallisneria;* or as end plants in smaller aquariums. The ribbon arrowhead has small, narrow leaves; while the awl-leaf arrowhead *(S. subulata)* is still smaller, seldom exceeding 6 inches in height and is especially effective in bottles.

Several species of *Cryptocoryne,* which grow from creeping roots, are attractive water-garden plants. They do quite well in poorly lighted locations.

Then there is a group characterized by finely divided leaves arranged on the stems to give a plumelike effect. The most popular is *Cabomba caroliniana,* fish-grass, whose fanlike leaves are so brittle that they are broken if the fish get too rough with it. Pieces of *Cabomba,* which can be used in bottles, are commonly offered for sale in pet shops and variety stores. *Myriophyllum,* water-milfoil, is of similar habit and is said to be a favorite spawning ground for certain types of fish. Ditch-moss *(Elodea canadensis),* which may make shoots 3 feet long if the water is of sufficient depth, has undivided leaves arranged, usually in fours, along the stem and gives much the same effect as the preceding. This is another easy doer and is the plant known in England as "Babington's Curse" because it was introduced from America by a professor of botany of that name at Cambridge University. For a time it grew so rampantly that it impeded navigation on some of the waterways.

All of the plants mentioned are good oxygenators and hence are in great favor with fish fanciers. They have comparatively narrow leaves, however, and the plant lover will want to introduce subjects of different appearance to provide variety. One of these is *Ludwigia nutans,* which belongs in the same family as evening-primrose, though of entirely different appearance. It has small, roundish leaves which are green above with pinkish undersides, providing a different color note.

The above are grown solely for the effect of their foliage. If good light is available, a few aquatics with conspicuous flowers are worth a trial. These grow with their roots in sand or mud and float their leaves on the surface, and include floating heart *(Nymphoides peltata)* and water-poppy *(Hydrocleys commersonii)* with yellow flowers; and water snowflake *(Nymphoides indica),* which, as its name implies, has white flowers. Use these plants in large tanks only.

While most plants need to have their roots planted in sand or soil, there are some that will grow floating on the surface or partially submerged. One of the most interesting is bladderwort *(Utricularia* spp.), an insectivorous plant with tiny bladders on its leaves equipped with an ingenious mechanism for trapping minute aquatic animals. Their workings are described in detail in Darwin's book on insectivorous plants. Bladderworts grow wholly or partially submerged in the water, and while they do not add greatly to the appearance of the aquarium, do provide a talking point of interest.

Plants that grow floating free on the surface are for the most part ferns or their allies, such as *Ceratopteris thalictroides* (water fern), *Salvinia rotundifolia,* and *Azolla caroliniana,* which has been compared to floating branchlets of arborvitae. It is beautiful when examined under a magnifying glass. The easiest of the floaters to grow is duckweed, but it is messy-looking and unworthy of a place in the aquarium except as fish food. One of the most beautiful floating species is shell-flower or water-lettuce *(Pistia),* a relative of the calla-lily, which has rosettes of fluted leaves 2 or 3 inches across. It does best in a warmish aquarium.

Among aquarium plants those most likely to grow well and give the most satisfaction are the rooting, submerged plants. They can be obtained in great variety from water-garden and fish specialists, from pet stores (though usually in not so great a variety), and from variety stores.

When you have obtained plants from friends or dealers, spread them out in a large shallow pan of water, for their leaves are injured if exposed to air. Place from 1 to 2 inches of coarse, washed sand in the bottom of the aquarium or bottle and slope it to provide interesting contours. A small rock or two will help in achieving this end. Submerged wrecks, castles, et cetera, are not necessary! To avoid disturbing the sand, place a piece of wrapping paper over it before gently pouring in 3 or 4 inches of water.

The stronger-growing plants should be set at the rear and ends of the aquarium. Plant the rooted specimens first by making holes of sufficient size with a teaspoon to receive the roots, and then scraping the sand over to cover them. Some of the plants will be received as unrooted cuttings. These should be bundled in groups of three to five and their bases weighted by winding a piece of lead wire or a thin lead strip around them. They are then pushed gently into the sand. When all the plants are in place, add enough water to fill the aquarium or bottle, pouring very gently to avoid loosening the plants. When planting tall bottles, such as a wine bottle, use a plastic tube to guide the pebbles to the bottom. Then fill about half of the bottle with water. Use a dowel as a planting tool.

Do not use too many plants—they increase so quickly that if they are planted thickly you will soon be "unable to see the woods for the trees." When they begin to crowd each other, a certain amount of pruning is necessary. Whenever it is possible to do so without spoiling the artistry of the arrangement, the older portions of the plants should be selected for removal, leaving the young, vigorous shoots to carry on. A sharp wood chisel is a handy tool for cutting off the roots of the portion to be removed and the runners connecting old and new clumps; or you can sometimes purchase special tools from a dealer in aquarium supplies.

Weeds are always with us, even in aquariums. Certain objectionable algae make their appearance, growing either on the glass or free in the water. When this happens, the number of "scavengers" (such as snails) should be increased and the aquarium placed where the light is more subdued. Meanwhile the algae adhering to the glass can be scraped off by a safety razor blade affixed to a suitable holder; and much of that which is floating in the water can be removed by gently twirling something in the nature of a swizzle stick in among it.

It is not possible to go fully into the ins and outs of the culture of aquatics in a book on house plants, as it involves fish culture as well. Those who are specially interested should consult a book such as *Exotic Aquarium Fishes,* by W. I. Innes, which deals with plants as well as fishes.

# 2

## CULTURE

# Introduction

FOR SUCCESSFUL GROWTH, house plants must have proper care, and this involves regular attention to their requirements. It does not imply that they cannot be left untended for a day or two if proper precautions are taken, but it does mean that, whenever possible, they should be looked over carefully with an eagle eye every day to be sure that all their needs are supplied. The plants should be studied and those that require a rest period provided for; watering must be done thoughtfully; temperature, humidity, ventilation, and light requirements attended to. If you are one of those who are able to keep plants growing healthily year after year, repotting must be done in proper soil whenever it is needed and fertilizers supplied at the right time.

Provision must be made for summer and vacation care; and pruning, pinching, and propagating carried out at the right seasons. Remember to watch out for insect pests! If you can catch them in their early stages, life will be much simpler for both you and and the plants.

All these subjects are considered in detail in the pages that follow; but first acquire the right philosophical attitude toward your plants. Inevitably some will languish and reach a stage when they are no longer useful, beautiful, or interesting. When this happens, throw them out without any compunction, for a plant that becomes debilitated under house conditions can seldom be restored even if the unfavorable factors are rectified; it is better to start with a new healthy plant if you are determined to grow that kind.

I had a friend who refused to keep dogs because she became so attached to them that when the time for parting came (a dog's life being not so very full of years) she was so anguished that her life seemed unbearable. Such suffering can deprive one of much of the joy of living. Remember that hackneyed old saying, "It's better to have loved and lost . . . !" So, with plants, reconcile yourself to an occasional loss and take pleasure in those that thrive.

# CHAPTER 6

# *Soils and Potting Mixtures*

PLANTS in the home should be grown in containers as small as possible consistent with maintaining them in a vigorous, healthy condition. Large pots filled with soil are heavy and a nuisance to handle, although the use of plastic and various kinds of fiber pots has reduced this problem somewhat. Plants that are overpotted are usually unhealthy because of waterlogged soil that is difficult to avoid when there are not enough roots to quickly use the water supplied by an overzealous gardener. A plant in a pot too large for it is evidence of poor culture and distressing to look at because of lack of balance. But small pots entail a restricted root run and a small bulk of soil, which must be abundantly supplied with nutrients. The uninitiated might think these could easily be supplied by mixing liberal quantities of concentrated fertilizer with any kind of soil. This will not do, though, because some, or all, of the fertilizing ingredients are "quickly available" and when used too freely go into solution at a strength that "burns" the roots in contact with them. Then, too, the soil must be in *the right physical condition*— sufficiently porous to allow water to pass through it freely, and well supplied with decayed organic matter which will hold some moisture and at the same time help keep the soil open so that it is well aerated.

While it must not be thought that a special soil mixture has to be made up for each kind, plants do vary in their soil requirements and the successful grower does his utmost to supply their needs. Some grow best in a rather heavy clay loam; others need an open sandy soil; some cannot thrive unless the mixture consists largely of decayed organic matter—which must have an acid reaction for certain types and be neutral for others. While some house plants will thrive in soil used just as it is dug from the vegetable or flower garden, many of them will not; and in some regions the soil is utterly unsuited as a potting medium without amelioration of some kind, either because it packs down too hard in the pots or because it has other objectionable features.

For these reasons the grower of house plants should follow the practice of the professional grower of pot plants and keep on hand various ingredients which can be combined to make the right kind of growing medium for different plants and purposes. He will also need drainage material to facilitate the escape of surplus water from the pots—pieces of broken pot to put over the hole in the bottom, with smaller pieces, cinders, or clinkers, for a covering layer ½ to 1 inch deep, depending on the size of the pot.

The base for most potting mixtures is loam, which is a naturally occurring mixture of clay (20 per cent or less), silt (30 to 50 per cent), and sand. When sand predominates, it is known as sandy loam. When making up a potting mixture with clay loam, more sand must be added to give the necessary porosity than would be needed with a sandy loam. When the loam is very sandy, it is unnecessary to add sand for most plants.

An old practice for obtaining loam was to visit a fertile pasture and cut 4-to-5-inch thick slabs from the surface. These were stacked upside down in a neat pile with a layer of cow manure about 2 inches thick between each layer of sods. If the stack was made in the spring, it was in excellent condition for use in the fall. This was the "fibrous loam," beloved of professional gardeners and used frequently in their soil-mixture formulas. In fact, this practice is still followed by some English gardeners. The small amount needed for home potting can conveniently be handled by placing the sods in a slatted crate of suitable size rather than in an open pile. Today the cow pasture has been replaced by subdivisions, but it is no problem to use loam taken from the vegetable or flower garden, with dehydrated cow manure as a filling for the sandwich, at one-fourth the rate suggested above.

To provide the necessary organic matter, flaky leaf mold is preferred for most plants. (Peat moss is a suitable substitute and can be purchased at garden centers.) This consists of leaves in which decay is sufficiently advanced so that the integral parts crumble easily, but in which the texture is flaky rather than powdery. Leaf mold can be prepared on a small scale by gathering tree leaves in the fall and packing them wet in a crate so that air has access to the pile. Maple leaves will be ready for use in about a year; oak leaves take longer to decay. A leaf mold crate can be kept in perpetual operation (until the wood rots) by raking out the leaf mold from the bottom (remove the lowermost slat to make this possible) and adding fresh leaves to the top whenever they are available and there is room. Or the contents of the crate may be turned out and the more decayed, crumbly leaves put aside for immediate use while the remainder is returned to decay further.

The decayed material from a compost pile—maintained today by most frugal gardeners—is also a source of humus and a good substitute for leaf mold. Leaf mold from oak leaves or pine needles is good for plants that

*This unusual dracaena* (D. goldieana) *from tropical Africa requires a potting soil with high humus content.*

require an acid soil; or peat moss, the most generally available source of humus, can be used. If these sources of humus-forming materials have to be used for sweet-soil plants, and the base soil also is acid, pulverized limestone should be added to the mixture. About ½ pound of pulverized limestone should be sufficient to neutralize the acidity of a bushel of peat moss.

Coarse river or bank sand is used to give the desired porous texture. Sea sand is often of too fine a texture and must be washed before using to remove salt. This is not difficult to do; the presence of salt should not deter anyone from using sea sand provided it is sufficiently coarse. All that has to be done is to put the end of a hose in the bottom of a bucket, fill the bucket with sand, and then turn on the water and let it run for ten minutes or so, occasionally stirring the sand. This will also get rid of the clay or silt if any is present. Builders' sand, obtained in coastal cities, is sometimes washed with sea water to remove silt. Such sand also should have a stream of fresh water passed through it before using it for plants.

Fertility can be added to the soil by using organic manures. These are preferable because their fertilizing constituents are slowly liberated. If you have access to dried cow manure gathered from a pasture, it is the ideal material; or you can use thoroughly rotted horse manure. However, the processed commercial product is all that is available to most of us and can be used at half the rate recommended for that collected from a pasture. Most garden centers and mail-order catalogues now offer slow-release plant foods that can release nutrients over a long period. Always follow directions on container.

Either superphosphate or bone meal (bone meal also contains a modicum of nitrogen) is used to augment the supply of phosphorus in the mixture. Raw bone meal contains a slightly higher percentage of nitrogen (2 to 6 per cent) and less phosphoric acid (15 to 27 per cent) than steamed bone meal (1.65 to 4 per cent nitrogen; 18 to 34 per cent phosphoric acid). The latter is more quickly available than the former and might be preferred when it is undesirable to increase the nitrogen supply. However, the differences between the two forms are so slight that no one is justified in worrying over which kind to use. Bone meal is usually the choice of organic gardeners while superphosphate is used by the general run of gardeners. It is the source of phosphorus in most commercial or inorganic fertilizers, such as 5-10-5, and is widely available.

To aid in making the soil right for those plants that demand a light, very porous mixture, we can use the following: mortar rubble (bits of cement) broken into pieces ¼ inch in diameter and smaller, for those cacti and other plants that need lime as well as porosity in their soils or use broken pieces of charcoal); broken flowerpots or soft bricks similarly hammered into small pieces for acid-soil plants; and broken charcoal, especially for bromeliads, orchid cacti, *Anthurium,* orchids, et cetera.

Here are some mixtures that can be used for various purposes and types of plants. There is nothing sacred about them to prevent anyone from making any change that seems according to common sense. The variability of the ingredients in different sections of the country precludes any hard-and-fast recommendations. It would be as well, however, not to increase greatly the amount of manure or phosphorus without first trying it out on a small scale.

FOR SEED SOWING AND POTTING CUTTINGS JUST REMOVED FROM ROOTING MEDIUM: Equal parts of loam, leaf mold or peat moss, and sand passed through a ½-inch sieve or crumbled to remove clods of soil and organic material and thoroughly mixed, will serve for most plants. If loam is sandy, reduce the proportion of sand; if of a clayey nature, increase it so that a handful of the moist mixture when squeezed into a ball readily falls apart when pressure is released. For acid-soil plants, such as azaleas—though house-plant growers are not likely to be raising them from seed—substitute peat moss for leaf mold and double the amount. For those that require a soil rich in humus—African-violet, begonia, gloxinia—double the amount of leaf mold or peat moss.

The Boston fern and its many named forms is an excellent foliage plant that adapts well to varying indoor conditions. This is the dwarf Boston fern known as 'Compacta.'

Several different kinds of house plants have been arranged as an indoor garden. Included are the long-lasting poinsettia (foreground) and amaryllis.

The bottle garden (left), once planted, requires little from its creator except enjoyment. A bonsai tray (below) becomes a miniature garden, Japanese-like in its seeming simplicity. The little flowering plant is the sinningia 'Bright Eyes'. These planter boxes (right) are on wheels and deep enough to hold large plants in their pots so the display can be easily changed. Bark chunks hide the pots and help retain moisture around the plants. The tree at left is the ming-aralia.

*The Norfolk-Island-pine, here decorated for the holiday season, is an elegant evergreen of pyramidal shape. It does best in good light and cool rooms, but will tolerate warmer temperatures for a time.*

*Marjorie J. Dietz*

Another plant that needs a cool temperature is the cymbidium orchid. The spectacular flower sprays are especially long-lasting. As with the Norfolk-Island-pine, plants in bloom can be brought into warmer rooms for display.

*Marjorie J. Dietz*

*Charles Marden Fitch*

*African-violets (left) are justly popular for their nearly ever-blooming habit. Interest in them has brought attention to other relatives — the gesneriads. Contrast in flower size is shown by two sinningias (above): the spectacular, large-flowered gloxinia, and the miniature sinningia, 'Doll Baby'. Both are essentially summer bloomers. Gaining in popularity is another gesneriad — the columnea or goldfish plant (right). Most columneas are drooping or vine-like in habit and are shown to advantage in hanging containers. Columneas tend to rest in winter, the best flower displays appearing in spring through fall.*

*An unbeatable combination for a cool, sunny window are salmon-pink geraniums and amaryllis.*

*A pot of the tulip 'Keizerskroon' provides indoor cheer in the middle of winter.*

*For fragrant flowers, there are paper-white narcissus, easily forced in water and pebbles. The double-flowered narcissus on the right is 'Cheerfulness,' also forced here in water and pebbles. Kalanchoe is their bright-flowered companion.*

*Two durable foliage plants are the familiar heartleaf philodendron and striped dracaena* (Dracaena deremensis *'Warneckii'*).

FOR TRANSPLANTING SEEDLINGS: Same as the above, with the addition of superphosphate or bone meal, ¼ cupful to a peck, plus 1½ cups of dried cow manure. For acid-soil plants use superphosphate instead of bone meal (because of its lime content) and increase organic matter as indicated above.

PACKAGED SOIL POTTING MIXTURES AND SOIL-LESS OR SYNTHETIC MIXES: For apartment and city dwellers who do not have access to garden soil and for gardeners in general who are interested in convenience, these purchased mixtures are the answer. The packaged potting mixtures can be found in garden centers and flower shops as well as gardening departments of variety stores. Some have been especially formulated for cacti or ferns and African-violets; others are general-purpose mixtures. Some are very satisfactory but a few seem to lack "body" and nutrients and appear to be composed mostly of humus. The reader is advised to experiment with the different brands until one is found that proves to be satisfactory.

These potting mixtures can also be improved by "beefing" them up with varying amounts of soil-less mixes. It is difficult to suggest an exact recipe because of the different compositions of various brands of these potting soils, but a ratio of half potting soil and half soil-less mix should be safe. Again, the reader is urged to experiment.

The soil-less mixes, available under several trade names such as Jiffy Mix, Redi-Earth, Pro-Mix, Super-Soil, were developed at Cornell University and the University of California and have played an important part in the increase in both indoor and outdoor container gardening, as practiced by commercial growers and home gardeners alike. The mixes, which are sterile (making them very useful as growing media for seeds), are composed of peat moss, vermiculite and/or perlite, sometimes sand, and usually fertilizers. You may be familiar with the appearance of these soil-less mixes since many commercial house-plant growers are using them. (Some mixes do not contain fertilizers—read and follow directions on the package.)

Their advantages are sterility, light weight, and convenience. They retain moisture well and at the same time are supposed to drain sufficiently to prevent waterlogging, which can be so detrimental to the roots of potted plants. Nevertheless, some caution should be taken when watering plants in the soil-less mixes or when they are used in combination with garden soil or purchased potting soil mixtures: Usually much less frequent watering is necessary and care must be taken not to oversaturate the growing medium (see Chapter 10).

## MIXTURES FOR POTTING ESTABLISHED PLANTS

When transferred from one pot to another of larger size without root disturbance:

GENERAL-PURPOSE MIXTURE: Chrysanthemums, fuchsias, geraniums, palms, screw-pines, and similar plants: 4 parts loam, 2 parts sand, 1½ parts dried cow manure, 2 parts leaf mold or peat moss, with ½ cup bone meal (or about ¼ cup superphosphate) to each peck of mixture. If the loam is clayey, increase quantity of sand; if sandy, reduce it. Loam that is reasonably free from stones does not need sifting. Use a spade to chop the lumps into pieces of walnut size. If put through a screen, much of the desirable fibrous material will be held back by the sieve. The leaf mold should be passed through a ½-inch sieve for small pots; a 1-inch sieve for pots 6 inches and over. This is to remove sticks and stones. The manure should be crumbled or rubbed through a ¼-inch mesh sieve.

FOR BULBS: Daffodils, hyacinths, tulips: 6 parts loam, 4 parts sand, 3 parts leaf mold, with ½ cup bone meal or ¼ cup superphosphate to each peck. For amaryllis, *Lachenalia, Veltheimia,* and the like add 1 part thoroughly rotted or dried manure to the mixture.

FOR PLANTS REQUIRING A HUMUSY MIXTURE: African-violets, begonias, ferns, et cetera; 4 parts loam, 4 parts leaf mold or peat moss, 2 parts sand, 2 parts dried manure, with ½ cup bone meal (or ¼ cup superphosphate) and 2 cups broken charcoal (¼ inch and smaller) to each peck of mixture. The last item is not essential, but does help make the mixture light and well aerated, which is desirable.

A variation of the above might be 2 parts top soil or loam, 1 part peat moss, 1 part perlite, and 1 part Jiffy Mix.

FOR ACID-SOIL PLANTS: Azaleas, camellias, gardenias, et cetera: 4 parts loam, 3 parts sand, 3 parts peat moss, 1 part leaf mold, 1 part thoroughly rotted or dried manure.

FOR CACTI AND SUCCULENTS: Equal parts loam, sand, leaf mold, mortar rubble (or broken bricks, charcoal, or flower pot chips), with ½ cupful of bone meal to each peck. One successful grower of cacti uses double the amount of leaf mold.

FOR JUNGLE-TYPE CACTI, SUCH AS THANKSGIVINGS AND CHRISTMAS CACTUS, ORCHID CACTUS: 4 parts loam, 2 parts sand, 3 parts peat moss, 1 part leaf mold, 1 part thoroughly rotted or dried manure, 1 part mortar rubble, 1 part broken charcoal.

FOR MOST BROMELIADS, MANY ORCHIDS, AND *ANTHURIUM SCHERZERIANUM:* Pot should be ⅓ full of drainage material. For potting, use redwood chips, fir bark, or a combination of both 6 parts, ½ inch-charcoal 1 part. Most of the mail-order orchid specialists sell potting mixes for terrestrial and epiphytic orchids.

A sufficient supply of soil for immediate needs should be kept under cover at all times so that necessary potting is not held up by rain, preventing soil from being brought in. (One might very well find it convenient to catch up with potting on a rainy day.) In the fall enough soil should be brought indoors to last through the winter. It will be needed for seed sowing and potting in late winter when it is impossible, because of snow or frozen ground, to bring in soil from outdoors. The purchased potting and soil-less mixes are a big help at this time of year.

# CHAPTER 7

# *Fertilizers*

SOME house plants, such as bromeliads and cacti, thrive on what a vegetable grower would consider a very inadequate supply of nutrients. Others, like the Chinese evergreen, can get along very well for long periods on just plain water and air. But most plants require a substantial ration of mineral nutrients, supplied initially by the soil in which the plants are potted (when water is applied and the minerals are slowly dissolved, forming what is known as the soil solution). Usually there comes a time when the available nutrients become depleted, or are present in insufficient quantity, so that something must be done to keep the plants well fed and happy. This something means either repotting in new soil or in a larger container or adding fertilizers to the growing medium. Often the latter is preferable because of the undesirability of using excessively large pots under house conditions.

It must be recognized, however, that fertilizers are not a cure-all, and improperly used may do more harm than good. Do not get the notion that because a teaspoonful is beneficial a tablespoonful will be three times as effective. If the first amount is the optimum for a particular plant in, say, a 6-inch pot, tripling the amount is likely to result in a concentration of salts in the soil solution in sufficient amount to "burn" the roots. If any erring is done, let it be on the side of too little rather than too much.

Never give fertilizer to a plant that is suffering because of waterlogged soil; it is in no shape to make use of additional nutrients, which, if supplied, will only accentuate the trouble.

Do not attempt to force a plant to grow by giving fertilizer during its resting period.

Usually a plant potted in fertile soil will not need additional fertilizer until the pot becomes crowded with roots, which could take a year. Examine the roots by turning the plant upside down and tapping the rim of the pot on a bench or table, holding the ball of soil with one hand so it does not fall to the floor. If the ball is covered with a network of roots, you can assume that fertilizer will be beneficial.

If most or all of the leaves of the plant are yellowish, if it is not making vigorous growth during the season it should be active, and if its poor health is not attributable to unsuitable growing conditions (too hot, too cold, insufficient light, waterlogged soil, dryness at roots, or desiccated air), then, in any of these circumstances, giving it additional fertilizer may be very helpful. Also it should be kept in mind that plants growing in a soil-less mix will need more frequent fertilizing.

## WHAT TYPE TO USE?

In order to use fertilizers intelligently it is desirable to know something of the role played by the various ingredients. There are many soil elements necessary for plant growth. They include nitrogen, phosphorus, potash, calcium, sulphur, magnesium, iron, copper, zinc, boron, manganese, sodium,

*Bromeliads can exist for long periods without fertilizer. Here bromeliads decorate a brick patio wall during warm weather.*

and aluminum. The merest trace of some of these is enough, and with the exception of the three first named, they occur in sufficient quantity in most soils. It is with nitrogen, phosphorus, and potash, therefore, that we are most concerned.

Nitrogen promotes strong growth of shoots and leaves and it is an essential constituent of the green coloring matter (chlorophyll) of plants. An excess of nitrogen, especially if associated with a deficiency of phosphorus and potash, may result in growth of leaves and shoots to an extent that prevents flower production; also it is believed that such an excess results in a flimsy development of cell walls which makes them an easy mark for invading fungus enemies. Fertilizers rich in nitrogen can be used to advantage for those plants that we grow primarily for their leaves—palms, ferns, et cetera; and for flowering plants whose leaves are yellowish and whose shoot growth is weak.

Phosphorus is concerned in flowering and the production of fruits and seeds. It promotes strong root development, stiffens plant stems, and makes them more woody.

Potash also has a stiffening influence on the stems of plants and may help them to resist disease. In common with phosphorus it helps to prevent the characteristic rank growth likely to ensue when there is an overbalance of nitrogen. Usually there is no deficiency of potash in soils abundantly supplied with organic matter.

## SOURCES OF SUPPLY

Giving an excess of one fertilizing element will not make up for a deficiency of any of the others; therefore, it is usually best to use what is known as a "complete" fertilizer—one containing nitrogen, phosphorus, and potash. Animal excrement is complete in the sense that it contains these three elements, but they are not well balanced because of insufficient phsophorus. Nevertheless, a time-honored liquid manure can be made by steeping a bag of cow manure in water and diluting the liquor to a pale amber color before using it about every two weeks during the period of active growth. It is usually satisfactory if bone meal or superphosphate have been mixed with the potting soil.

There are, however, obvious objections to the use of animal manures in the house. Many of us do not have access to such materials and do not have a convenient place in which to store the brew; some squeamish souls object to the odor in the living room. Animal manures used in a dry state have the same disadvantages, perhaps in lesser degree; but if you are willing to overlook them, dried and pulverized cattle and sheep manure can be used at the rate of 1 level tablespoon to a 6-inch pot, scratched into the surface and watered in. Use poultry manure at half this rate.

Cottonseed meal is a complete fertilizer of vegetable origin with only small proportions of phosphorus and potash. It is used at the rate of 1 teaspoonful for a plant in a 6-inch pot. It has an acid reaction and is useful for fertilizing azaleas and similar acid-soil plants.

Fish emulsions are available under several brand names and are excellent organic sources of the necessary elements. For rate of dilution, follow recommendations on the bottle.

Commercial fertilizers are a convenient means of supplying additional nutrients to the soil of potted plants. Those in which nitrogen, phosphorus, and potash occur in the ratio of 1–2–1 are good general-purpose types. If extra phosphorus is needed, one with a ratio of 1–3–1 would be desirable. Fertilizers commonly offered for sale with these ratios will be recognized as those with an analysis of 5 per cent nitrogen, 10 per cent phosphorus, 5 per cent potash; and 4 per cent nitrogen, 12 per cent phosphorus, and 4 per cent potash, respectively. These can be used dry at the rate of 1 level teaspoonful to a 6-inch pot; or in liquid form, made by stirring 2 tablespoonfuls in 1 gallon of water. Apply every four to six weeks when the plant is actively growing. Fertilizers more concentrated than these are available, and if used, the rate of application must be correspondingly reduced. For making liquid fertilizers, completely soluble forms of dry fertilizers, obtainable from garden centers or from mail-order house-plant specialists, are preferred. (See also Chapter 6.)

Those gardeners who also run an outdoor garden will probably have fertilizers on hand suitable for use on house plants. Those whose gardening is restricted to the indoors can buy many types of fertilizers especially packaged and formulated for house plants at garden centers or through mail-order sources. There are also fertilizers designed to meet the needs of different groups of plants, such as African-violets or orchids.

When nitrogen only is considered desirable, either nitrate of soda or sulphate of ammonia can be used at the rate of a tablespoonful to a gallon of water. Other sources of nitrogen are dried blood or the animal manure liquid fertilizers mentioned above.

Phosphorus can be supplied through the medium of 20 per cent superphosphate at the rate of 1½ tablespoonfuls to 1 gallon of water.

Wood ashes can be used to supply potash to plants that do not require an acid soil; they contain lime, which has an alkalizing action. The potash content is variable (2 per cent to 10 per cent), which makes it difficult to give specific rates of application, but 2 tablespoonfuls to 1 gallon of water should be about right. For acid-soil plants muriate of potash (about 45 per cent potash) can be used—1 teaspoonful to 1 gallon of water.

It is impossible to lay down hard-and-fast rules as to the time and frequency of application of fertilizers. Good gardeners, by observing the plant, can tell when to start using them and, just as important, when to stop. If a plant is growing satisfactorily, leave well enough alone, and refrain from taking a chance of upsetting the apple cart by overfertilizing. Much depends on the potting soil—if it was good initially and slowly gives up its nutrients over a long period, little or no additional fertilizer may be needed.

# CHAPTER 8

# *Pots and Potting*

PLANTS can be, and are, grown in any kind of container that will hold a sufficient quantity of soil or growing medium, but some are preferred over others for certain purposes. Those most generally used are the standard clay pots, which are pinkish in color and somewhat porous, and plastic pots of varying colors and weight. The standard pot is as broad as it is long while the tub is generally three-quarters as tall as wide; the height of cyclamen pots is about four fifths their diameter; azalea pots are three fourths; bulb and seed pans are about half as tall as they are broad. Standard pots are obtainable in sizes ranging from 1¼ to 24 inches, but these extremes are seldom seen. Sometimes earthenware pots are made with holes around the sides or extra holes in the bottom in addition to the usual drainage hole. These are especially suitable for plants such as some orchids and bromeliads, which require an exceptionally well aerated rooting medium.

There has been some controversy concerning the merits of porous pots vs. plastic pots. The advocates of porous pots point out that the soil is likely to be better aerated; there is less danger of the soil becoming waterlogged; and, under house conditions, the loss of moisture from the sides of the pots is an advantage in helping to humidify the air. Their opponents maintain that the need for frequent watering is diminished by the use of impervious pots and that plants grow better in them. They are also considerably lighter in weight than clay pots. Plants can be grown well in both types, but when the air is dry perhaps plastic pots are better.

You can also use fancy ceramic pots and bowls, even treasured antique teapots or wash basins. Plants can be grown in such watertight containers but their use involves extra care to avoid waterlogging the soil unless they are used for temporary display of plants remaining in their original pots.

*Scrubbing pots before storing.*

In the tropics, sections of bamboo 2 or 3 inches in diameter, each containing a node, are commonly used as flower pots. Hollowed-out logs, wicker baskets, and, for orchids, wooden "baskets" are sometimes used. Square or round wooden plant tubs are preferable for plants of large size.

"Strawberry pots" made of earthenware and equipped with "pockets" on the sides to hold soil that is in contact with the soil in the body of the pot are much used, suitably planted, for patio or terrace. They also have possibilities for indoor decoration provided a size is chosen that is in proportion with the space available for it. The usual practice, and it is a good one, is to use at least a few plants of trailing or semitrailing habit in the side pockets.

In greenhouses, plant rooms, or outdoors on the terrace hanging baskets made of wire and lined with sheet or sphagnum moss, obtained from a florist or garden center, are commonly used. They are not totally satisfactory for most interiors because of the difficulty of keeping the soil moist, which involves much sloshing of water around, and flood on the floor. Indoors, use pottery or plastic containers furnished with a saucer to catch any water that may run through the drainage hole; or use a hanging jardiniere in which an ordinary flower pot is placed—but watch out that water does not collect in the bottom of it.

Pots not in use should be stacked neatly according to size, indoors or out. If they are dirty, they should be washed with water and a scrubbing brush and allowed to dry before using.

## HOW TO POT AND REPOT

I will always remember the thrill that came to me when in training at Kew Gardens in England I was first allowed, officially, to repot a plant. This occurred only after spending about two years in the humble but important job as crock boy, whose responsibility was "crocking" the pots—putting in drainage material—for the journeyman gardeners who did the actual job of potting. I later came to realize that potting plants is not a mysterious process which can safely be revealed only to those who have undergone an extensive apprenticeship.

Actually, it is far more difficult to learn *when* to pot than *how* to do it. Generally speaking, the best time to transfer ("shift" is the technical term) those plants that are permanently grown in pots is at the close of the resting season, usually in late winter. Young plants that are actively growing (as in the case of those raised from seeds or cuttings, or small plants dug from the flower border in the fall) should be transferred to larger pots at any season whenever the roots become so crowded that growth is likely to be checked.

Therefore, keep a close watch on your plants at all times, especially in winter when the lengthening of the days brings about a recrudescence of activity. When new leaves are beginning to form near the soil level, as in the case of ferns and aspidistra; or new shoots start at the tips of the branches of the shrubby plants; or new leaves push forth with greater vigor on the dracaena—in other words, whenever there are signs of renewed activity after a period of quiescence—examine the plants to determine whether or not repotting is necessary. This is done by turning the plant upside down and, putting the fingers of one hand on the surface soil, tapping the rim of the pot on bench or table to remove the ball of roots—not by holding the pot with one hand and yanking at the plant with the other! If the roots are matted together and obviously crowded, a shift into a larger pot is probably needed.

Sometimes, however, it is desirable to repot into a smaller container than a larger one. This situation occurs when roots are unhealthy and do not fully occupy the soil, a condition brought about by previous overpotting coupled with too much water, and possibly the presence of earthworms which clogged the drainage. Whether or not to spend time on such a plant in an attempt to save it depends upon its condition, its value (sentimental or otherwise), and whether you get pleasure from nursing sick plants and restoring them to health. If the plant's efforts at making new growth are feeble, it is better to put it in the trash can and forget about it; but if it seems to be making a real attempt at growing, and there is a possibility that it may regain its vigor, this is what should be done:

Carefully shake all soil away from the roots, taking pains to avoid injuring any that show signs of vigor. With a sharp knife remove dead and injured roots, making the cut through healthy tissue back of the injured portion. Select a pot large enough to contain the roots without overcrowding and prepare it by putting at least an inch of flower pot chips in the bottom to ensure free drainage. Put the roots in the pot, hold the plant at the right level with one hand, and sift the soil in between the roots with the other. Jiggle the roots as you are putting in the soil to avoid bunching them, using a lean mixture of equal parts sand, soil, and leaf mold or peat moss that is moist and crumbly—not soggy. (If you are using one of the soil-less mixes, follow directions on the package about watering.) When the pot is filled to the rim with soil, tap it on the bench and then press the soil down with the fingers. This will leave just about enough room for watering, which should be sufficient to soak the soil thoroughly; then do not water again until the soil is nearly dry. Ample air is necessary for free root action, so subsequent watering should be aimed at keeping the soil no more than moist until plenty of new roots are formed, at which time normal watering may be resumed.

Plants need repotting when the pot is crowded with roots and the available plant-food nutrients in the soil are exhausted, but in the case of house plants, where small pots are desired because of the ease of handling them, it is

*Cacti and succulents in a strawberry jar, an earthenware pot with open pockets for plants in addition to the top opening.*

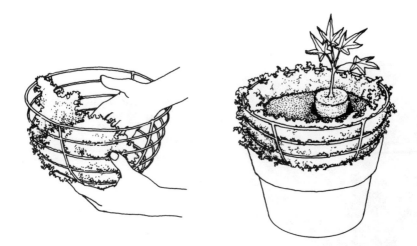

*Wire baskets for hanging plants can be used outdoors or on terraces or in plant rooms, but they are too drippy for most interiors. The wire basket is lined with moss, then filled with the growing mixture. Standing the basket on a clay pot helps steady it during the planting operation.*

worthwhile to consider, first, whether the plant cannot be kept in health by an operation known as "top-dressing." This merely requires the loosening and removal of soil on the surface and replacing it with a 50-50 mixture of loam and rotted or dry manure, to which superphosphate or bone meal has been added at the rate of 1 tablespoon to a 6-inch pot of soil. Before the top-dressing is added, the plant can be removed from its pot and if the drainage has become clogged the trouble remedied before returning the plant to the pot. Subsequent supplementary feedings with liquid nutrients (fertilizers dissolved in water) are usually desirable for pot-bound plants. If, however, the pot is so full of roots that no soil can be removed from the surface, then one can be reasonably sure that a shift into a larger pot is in order.

A modification of the top-dressing procedure is to remove a good deal of the old soil and to replace the plant in a pot of the same size. Only the experienced plantsman can surely tell whether this should or should not be done: knowing which plants can endure the inevitable root injury and respond to the treatment comes only from extensive handling of plants over several years. The plant to be operated on is turned out of its pot, the drainage material is removed, and, with gentle pinching, kneading, and rubbing motions, the soil ball is reduced until it is small enough to go back into the pot with enough room between it and the pot to permit new soil to be packed around it with a dowel used as a "potting stick." A "potting stick" is a 12-inch label, a portion of a lath, a dowel, or something similar that is used to pack down soil.

The first step in proper repotting is to provide clean pots of suitable size. If new clay pots are used, it is best to soak them for ten minutes in water

Begonia *'Sophie Cecil' needs repotting.*
*Here the plant is supported at its*
*base, prior to being turned upside down*
*for gentle removal from the pot.*

*The begonia being set in its slightly larger*
*new pot. The planting hole was formed by holding*
*the old pot and molding the soil around it.*

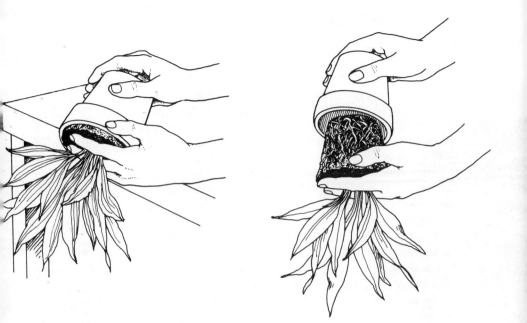

*How to remove a plant from a pot: With left hand holding plant securely at its base, knock the rim of the pot sharply against the edge of a bench or table.*

and then allow them to dry before using. Such a treatment is not necessary with plastic pots. The pot into which the plant is to be shifted should not be much larger than the old one. Usually ½ to 1½ inches of clearance between the ball of earth and the side of the new pot is sufficient. The use of too large a pot results in the soil remaining too wet and less thorough aeration. Adequate drainage is secured by covering the hole on the bottom of the pot with a piece of broken flowerpot with the concave side downward; this in turn is covered with a layer ½ to 1 inch thick of flowerpot chips, small stones, or something similar. On top of this, organic materials such as moss, flaky leaf mold, or coarser parts of the compost are placed to a depth of ¼ inch. This is to prevent fine soil from sifting through and clogging the drainage. Professional gardeners, especially commercial ones, often make only sketchy provision for drainage, but good drainage is an insurance against waterlogging that the home gardener cannot afford to neglect.

The next step is to take the plant from its pot, rub off the loose surface soil, and remove the old drainage material if the latter is not too firmly embedded in the crowded roots. Place the plant in the new pot, first putting in a little soil, tamped down on the drainage, if it is necessary to bring the old ball of earth to the correct height. This should be about 1 inch below the rim, more or less, depending on the size of the pot, to provide for convenient watering.

Having set the plant at the correct level, soil is filled in around the roots and settled somewhat by jarring the pot on the bench. It is desirable that the new earth should be packed to the same density as that in the old ball. When the soil is uniformly packed with the potting stick, finish off by pressing down the surface soil and leveling it with the tips of the fingers; after which give the pot a slight jar on the bench to smooth the surface.

When potting cacti and other plants of a spiny nature, handle them with kitchen tongs, being careful to avoid bruising; or make cornucopias of stiff paper and slip them over the thumb and finger, holding them in place with a dab of quick-setting adhesive.

After potting is completed, thoroughly soak the soil with water applied by means of a watering can with a fine mist. Do not water again until the soil shows signs of becoming dry. Great care should be taken to avoid overwatering until new roots grow.

Repotting plants that have to be divided seems more nearly akin to plant propagation (see Chapter 15).

LOOSE-ROOT POTTING: When potting seedlings removed from a flat or seed pan, the technique is somewhat different. Usually these go into comparatively small pots, and a single piece of broken pot over the hole on the bottom provides sufficient drainage. The pot is filled to the rim with soil. Then, with a dibber or with a finger, make a hole large enough to accommodate the roots; set the roots in it; tap the pot and press down the soil with the fingers. When repotting rooted cuttings (which are likely to have a larger root system, more difficult to be "dibbled" in), the technique is similar to that of repotting into smaller pots previously described. A little soil is placed

*Amaryllis (top) and cacti are common examples of plants which should not be grown in too large pots. Nor do they require frequent repotting. Cacti need a coarse potting mixture that drains quickly.*

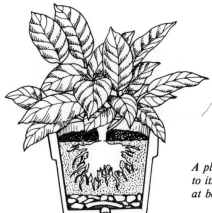

*A plant in good proportion
to its pot with pieces of crock
at bottom for drainage.*

over the drainage, then the plant is set in place. Fine soil is sifted between and over the roots with a throwing motion of the hand, and, when the pot is filled to the rim, the soil is pressed down with the fingers in such a way that it is made firm *about the roots*—not just on the surface.

When the soil surface becomes packed and hard as a result of overhead watering or covered with a growth of moss or algae, it should be loosened with a pointed stick or table fork.

There is a widespread notion among beginners that repotting into a larger pot is a panacea for all the ills that befall potted plants. This is not so, and if a plant fails to thrive because of overwatering, poor drainage, or unsuitable soil, repotting it into a larger pot only accentuates the trouble.

# CHAPTER 9

# *Watering*

THE QUESTION "How often should I water my house plants?" is one most frequently asked and most difficult to answer because so many different factors are involved. Among these are:

1. The nature of the plant. For example, cacti, succulents, and other desert plants need less water than palms, ferns, hydrangeas, cyclamens, et cetera.
2. When growth is active, more water is needed than when the plant is at rest.
3. If the pot is filled with roots, all absorbing moisture, the soil dries out more quickly than when roots are few compared with the bulk of soil, as, for instance, in the case of newly potted plants.
4. Some soils are able to hold more moisture than others and in consequence are slower in drying. A plant in sandy soil, therefore, other things being equal, will need watering with greater frequency than one in heavy loam with plenty of humus mixed with it. The soilless mixes tend to require less water.
5. Ordinary clay flowerpots are porous, and the soil loses its moisture through their sides as well as from the surface; therefore, it dries out more rapidly in them than it does in plastic pots or other containers that are impervious to moisture.
6. Humidity of the air, which is influenced by conditions outdoors as well as those within the house, affects the need for water; less is called for when the air is moist.
7. Sunshine, shade, and artificial light influence moisture. Plants tran-

spire more moisture when exposed to sunshine or when growing under artificial light; therefore, more water is needed at their roots.

8. Plants growing in a cool room need less water than those grown in a warm room because the moisture-holding capacity of cool air is less than that of heated air, and the loss of moisture by evaporation from the soil and by transpiration from the leaves is consequently reduced.

9. Low temperatures outdoors in winter are often accompanied by low humidity. The use of artificial heat to raise the temperature indoors reduces the relative amount of moisture of the indoor air still more and increases the need for copious watering.

*Methods of wick-watering to keep the soil evenly moist for a long period from one application. Water is drawn up through wick, which has been pushed through drainage hole and unraveled at bottom of pot. The tray will hold several small pots embedded in peat moss kept moist by the wicks.*

With all these points in mind it can readily be seen that plants cannot be watered properly in measured amounts by clock or calendar but only by applying water when it is needed. Some plants may require watering two or three times a day under certain weather conditions; others two or three times a week; and some can be left for a month or even longer without watering. The important thing is to give the plants daily attention and water those that call for it.

## WHEN DO PLANTS NEED WATERING?

The good gardener uses the senses of sight, touch, and hearing to determine whether his plants need watering. If he sees that the plant is wilting, he is reasonably sure that moisture is lacking; a glance at the soil surface may confirm the diagnosis—it will be lighter in color when dry. It is not wise to let the plants get to the wilting point before watering them, so before this happens the soil or growing medium should be examined by looking at it and by touching it. If it looks moist and feels moist, probably no watering is required, but sometimes if the soil did not get a good soaking at its previous watering it may be moist on top and bone-dry below. This is where the sense of hearing comes into play. Tap the pot; if the sound is dull, no water

*Plastic bags help retain moisture when plants must be left untended. Small plants can be covered by the bags, as shown. The pots of larger plants can be slipped inside the bags and their tops closed around the stem of the plant with wire ties so the soil surface is enclosed by plastic.*

is needed. But if the pot gives off a ringing note, the soil below is likely to be dry. This can be confirmed or disproved by turning the plant out of its pot and examining the soil with the eyes. Don't get the notion it is necessary to evict every plant every day! A look at the root ball once or twice during the season is likely to be sufficient to give you the knack, so that you have a good idea of the moisture conditions of your soil, with your plants, under your system of watering.

Tapping the pots can be done with the knuckles or with a small wooden mallet. When I was a journeyman gardener, we thought we shouldn't use anything but the knuckles, but anyone in fear of developing calluses on them can easily make a mallet by cutting 2 inches off the end of a broom handle and boring a ¼-inch hole through it to receive a small plant stake about 18 inches long to serve as a handle.

Experienced gardeners can tell from the weight of a lifted pot whether or not water is needed—it is heavy when wet, light when dry.

All this sounds like an awful lot of bother, but it really is not so bad. After you have been watering the plants for a few days you quickly learn which are the habitually thirsty ones and water them accordingly. You will also learn to take into account weather conditions outdoors, knowing that less watering is needed on dull, humid days than on bright, sunshiny ones. Temperature will also be considered and less water given when it is low and little or no artificial heat is being used.

## WHEN AND HOW TO WATER

In general, watering should be done in the morning when the temperature is rising, because transpiration is more rapid during the hours of daylight and the need for water is greater in consequence; furthermore, it is considered undesirable for plants or soil to be too wet when the temperature is falling. This, however, should not deter anyone from watering a plant at any hour if it is obviously suffering from a lack of water.

While millions of plants are successfully grown in greenhouses using water that may be many degrees lower than the air temperature, just as it comes from the hose, it would seem to be desirable for the water to be of room temperature or a few degrees higher to avoid chilling the roots. Although there seems to be no clear-cut evidence that watering with cold water is harmful to plants in general, we do know that ring-spot of African-violets (and many of their relatives among the gesneriads) is caused by water of lower temperature than the air coming in contact with the leaves. Some growers of house plants attribute their success to the practice of using the tea left over from breakfast for watering purposes. One can congratulate them on their success, express commiseration for their inability to drink coffee or their lack of liking for it, and wonder whether the tempered liquid or the tannic acid contained in it is responsible for the good growth of the plants! If the water from the faucet is "hard," it is desirable to use rain water for acid-soil plants.

Many people ask whether plants should be watered from the surface or from below. The answer is that the good grower is likely at times, under certain circumstances, to use both methods. Surface watering is easier and in general satisfactory provided there is sufficient room between the surface of the soil and the rim of the pot to hold enough water to moisten the soil throughout. Unfortunately there is a tendency among beginners to fill the pot too full of soil when repotting so that the only way to do an adequate job of watering is to apply water to the surface several times until it runs through the drainage hole in the bottom; or submerge the pot for half its depth in a vessel of water and leave it there until moisture shows on the surface. Even when there seems to be sufficient room to water satisfactorily from above, it is a good plan, in the case of pot-bound plants, to subirrigate them, say once a week, to ensure thorough soaking of the ball.

WATERLOGGING: Most plants cannot thrive in a waterlogged soil which, because the pore spaces are constantly filled with water instead of air, deprives the roots of the oxygen they need to function.

Adequate drainage material in the bottom of the pot and the prompt eviction of earthworms which may clog the drainage are among the means of avoiding a waterlogged soil; careful watering is another. Standing flowerpots in water-tight jardinieres is a source of danger unless great care is taken to make sure that water does not collect in the container and partially submerge the flowerpot. It is very difficult to maintain the correct moisture conditions in flowerpots without drainage holes. This type is usually of glass or glazed pottery, which makes matters worse because there is no loss of moisture except from the surface of the soil. Consequently a single overwatering may be sufficient to cause ill-health or death of the plants because there is no way whereby the surplus water can be removed quickly. Of course the pot could be stood upside down for an hour or two, but this is not always convenient; and often the grower does not realize in time that the soil is waterlogged.

WICK-WATERING: This is a method whereby water is conducted by capillarity from a reservoir through a wick, preferably of fiber glass, to the soil. Wicks of various sizes for use with different-size pots are obtainable from mail-order firms dealing in garden supplies and possibly elsewhere. The wick is cut long enough to permit the end to be teased out so that it will approximately cover the bottom of the inside of the pot and reach the water in the container below. It is easier to install the wicks when repotting is done (no drainage material is necessary or desirable), but they can be supplied to plants already potted by turning them out of their pots, removing the drainage material, replacing it with soil, inserting the wick through the drainage hole, spreading it out, and replacing the plant.

Devices for implementing wick watering will occur to everyone. By raiding the kitchen I was able to obtain an enameled baking pan and a metal contraption for the bottom of a roasting pan which is perforated with ½-inch holes

*Yet another method for the care of house plants when you go away: Several plants are enclosed in a plastic tent.*

through which the wicks are passed. By resting this on the baking pan four or five 3-to-4-inch pots can be accommodated. Or all this improvisation can be avoided by purchasing plastic pots of various sizes equipped with a deep saucer and necessary wicks.

When wick-watering first came into the limelight, I thought that perhaps it might be the foolproof method we were looking for, but it does not seem that way—at least not to me. When dealing with a variety of plants of different sizes it is difficult to fit them with wicks of the right capacity to deliver just the amount of water needed. I found that some of mine were getting too much water, especially during dull weather. Of course this can be adjusted by not filling the reservoir when each plant has a separate source of supply, but when a variety of plants is supported over one reservoir, this cannot be done. Occasionally the wick does not deliver enough water, and the supply has to be supplemented by ordinary surface watering, so even with a wick device you have to use your head.

The method is well adapted for use with plants such as gloxinia and African-violet whose leaves are better kept dry; and undoubtedly some plants, especially those that need to be kept constantly moist, thrive better when watered by capillarity. I had a wick-watered pickaback plant, growing in a 3-inch pot, which attained a diameter of 15 inches. I doubt if it would have reached this size with ordinary watering. The wick method also affords a means of applying nutrient solutions to the sand or other media in which the roots are growing.

Even with this method of watering, the plants need fairly frequent attention to replenish the water in the reservoirs, unless they are large and cumbersome. I found that the African-violet in a 4½-inch pot normally uses up a margarine tub (¾ cup—6 ounces) full of water every two days.

The so-called "self-watering" window or planter box works on much the same principle and is satisfactory if care is taken to avoid getting the soil too wet. The water-holding part beneath the false bottom should be allowed to dry up from time to time.

The practice of occasionally standing house plants outdoors when it is raining is a good one *provided* the temperature is not much lower than it is in the house and the rain does not become a torrent that beats down the plants and oversaturates the soil.

To do a real job, watering must be done thoughtfully, taking into consideration the weather, the kind of plant, and whether or not it is undergoing its resting period (see Chapter 12). It might seem that with all this meticulous attention the care of plants would tie one down as much as keeping a cow. However, it is not quite so bad as all that. They can be left without attention over weekends if all are well watered before departing at noon on Friday and the really thirsty ones are "bedded down" in the pebble-laden watertight trays, plunged in peat moss in a window box, provided with fairly large drip saucers filled with water, or watered by the wick method. Turning the thermostat down will help, too.

For longer periods—even up to two weeks or so—plants will keep very well if their pots are slipped into plastic kitchen bags. The plants should be watered first. The plastic bags can be rather loosely fastened at the base of the plant with wire ties or the plastic can merely be folded or tucked in around the base of the plant. The surface of the soil or growing medium should be covered by the plastic. Of course, small plants—pot *and* plant— can be enclosed in a bag. A bamboo stake or two will help to hold the bag upright and prevent the plastic from clinging to the foliage. Very large billowing plants, especially ferns in wire baskets that tend to dry out quickly, can often be totally encased in plastic. The bags used by cleaners are useful for these large pots.

# CHAPTER 10

# Growing Plants
# Without Soil
# —Hydroponics

IT HAS ALWAYS seemed to me that growing plants without soil by using nutrient solutions is more trouble than growing them in soil by the old-fashioned method. But hydroponics, or "water culture," may appeal to those who get a kick from mixing chemicals.

Growing plants in nutrient solutions is no new thing, and interest in it among both commercial growers and home gardeners wanes and then rises—for no apparent reason. Some plants thrive exceedingly well when grown directly in the solution; and it will surprise many to learn that certain cacti, which we ordinarily think of as resenting wet feet, will grow with their roots constantly immersed in liquid. Many plants grow better when their roots are in sand, gravel, or vermiculite watered with the solution.

Other advantages claimed for this method of culture are that it eliminates soil-borne insect pests and diseases and that it enables one to control the kind and quantity of nutrients offered to the plants. Most of these claims have been proven false. Considerable knowledge of a plant's requirements is necessary, however, before one improvises on the standard solution.

Among the drawbacks when growing plants directly in the solution are the necessity for aerating the solution twice daily by pumping air through it; changing the solution every three weeks to obviate the danger of a concentration of salts in excessive quantity due to evaporation of liquid, and to ensure that no element is lacking; and the difficulty of supporting certain plants in a sightly manner. There are some, such as Chinese evergreen, dieffenbachia, English ivy, and wandering Jew, which need no special support; but others, such as ferns and plants of similar habit, must be held up by

*Gynura, often called velvet plant because of its soft-textured leaves, will root in and thrive in water. This plant has formed a healthy root system after ten days in water and fertilizer diluted to 1/4 strength.*

excelsior or something of a similar nature packed around the base of the plant and confined within a hardware cloth cage made to fit over the solution container. And then there is the necessity for frequently testing the solution with a soil indicator to determine whether it is too acid or too alkaline.

When growing plants in a supporting medium such as coarse sand, pebbles, or gravel, which usually is the best method for the home gardener, the medium should be flushed at weekly intervals with plain water to remove any possible accumulation of excess salts.

## SOLUTIONS

The easiest way to indulge in hydroponics is to buy the necessary chemicals ready-mixed and needing nothing more than the addition of water according to the directions on the package. In fact, hydroponic kits are available that include container, seeds, and enough nutrients for six months.

A book, *Chemical Gardening for the Amateur,* by Charles H. Connors and V. A. Tiedjens, explains, in addition to many other formulas, one in which the necessary materials can be obtained by rummaging around the kitchen (and bathroom). Here it is:

Saltpeter ..................................... 1 teaspoonful
Epsom salts ................................. 1 teaspoonful

Baking powder (a brand that does not
    contain alum) ............................ 2 teaspoonfuls
Washing Ammonia .......................... 1 to 4 teaspoonfuls
Water ..................................... 1 gallon

A formula suggested years ago by Dr. J. W. Shive, which I have used successfully, is made with salts of the ordinary fertilizer grade, as follows:

Nitrate of soda................................ 1 teaspoonful
Superphosphate ............................... 2 teaspoonfuls
Epsom salts .................................. 3 teaspoonfuls
Muriate of potash ............................ 1 teaspoonful
Water ....................................... 5 gallons
    The ingredients are dissolved separately by shaking each in a pint or so of water. Allow the sediment to settle, pour off, mix the clear liquids and add enough water to make 5 gallons.

Certain minor elements are needed by plants in very small quantities. These are likely to be present in fertilizer grade chemicals, but to make sure, 1 teaspoonful (half the usual rate) of trace element stock solution, made up as follows, can be added to 5 gallons of culture solution:

Ferrous sulphate .............................. 1/2 teaspoonful
Boric acid ................................... 1/4 teaspoonful
Manganese sulphate .......................... 1/4 teaspoonful
Zinc sulphate................................. 1/4 teaspoonful
Water ....................................... 1 pint

There are many variants of culture solutions, using different salts to supply the necessary nitrogen, phosphorus, potash, et cetera; if you want to go more fully into this, a book on soil-less culture, such as *Hydroponic Greenhouse,* by Joel Hudson, or *Home Hydroponics and How to Do It,* by Lem Jones, is what you need. (See also Chapter 21.)

## TECHNIQUES

Plants with fairly stiff stems, of the nature of philodendron, dieffenbachia, and Chinese evergreen, can be supported directly in the solution contained in glass or pottery vases, or preserving jars if your tastes are not too fancy. On the theory that roots, like those whose deeds are evil, prefer darkness, the containers should be opaque, but I notice that the roots on ivy shoots growing in water in a clear-glass container are just as abundant and apparently as healthy as those nearby in a crockery marmalade jar. It should be remembered in this connection that the roots are sometimes decorative and it is interesting to watch them grow.

*An example of a modular hydroponic garden available in various sizes for both home gardeners and commercial use. When necessary, fluorescent lights can be added.*

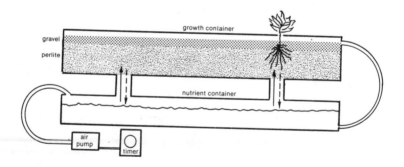

*Diagram shows how this hydroponic unit works: Air is forced into the reservoir container, pushing nutrients up vertical tubes (solid arrow) into growing medium (gravel and perlite). After one hour, timer shuts off pump and solution runs back into reservoir by gravity (dotted arrow).*

While some plants grow satisfactorily in a solution that is not artificially aerated, it is considered desirable to bubble air through the solution daily for all plants thus grown. (Aquarium pumps can be used in tanks.) For most plants, the solution should be slightly acid, showing between pH 5 and pH 6.5. To make sure it is not too acid or too alkaline, it should be tested occasionally with a soil indicator. If above pH 6.5, showing too much alkalinity, add a few drops of vinegar until the correct reaction is reached. If below pH 5, indicating that the solution is too acid, add a few drops of a solution of bicarbonate of soda. Discard the solution every three weeks and use a fresh mix. If you are a thrifty soul and do not like to see fertilizer go to waste, pour the rejected solution on lawn or garden soil.

For most house plants it will be desirable to use a more substantial medium than water to support the plants. This can be sand, gravel, fine cinders, or sphagnum moss. The three first named dry out rather quickly and consequently need frequent applications of solution; sphagnum dries out slowly, does not perhaps provide such a good aeration, is a difficult medium in which to pot the plant without injuring or bunching the roots, and not all plants grow well in it.

The containers used should be of nonporous material with drainage holes in the bottom—glazed flowerpots, earthenware crocks or jars or tanks (if of wood or metal, their insides must be painted with a waterproof asphalt) are satisfactory. Soil should be carefully washed from the roots to avoid injuring them before potting the plants in the selected supporting medium. Sand is the easiest material to work in between and over the roots. Flood with water and tap the pot on the bench to settle the sand firmly around the roots.

Future watering will be done with nutrient solution. It can be poured from a watering can or teapot in the usual manner of watering; the surplus that runs through the drainage holes can be collected from the drip saucers beneath the pots and used over again.

In the "continuous-drip" method the solution is applied drop by drop by means of a mechanical contrivance. This is excellent from the standpoint of results, but it involves the use of three containers per plant instead of the usual two—one to contain solution, one to hold the plant, and one to catch the drips from the plant container. Personally, I wouldn't want too many such contraptions around.

At weekly intervals the sand should be flushed with clear water to prevent accumulation of excess salts. A convenient way to do this is to stand the plants in the bathtub (leave the drain open!) and apply a copious amount of water to the sand from the sprinkler nozzle on the bath hose.

Growing plants in nutrient solutions has definite possibilities for the production of first-class plants. It does not eliminate the necessity of observing other rules of good cultivation—the provision of correct temperature, ample light, and keeping the plants free from insect and fungus pests.

*Home-contrived hydroponic system: Continuous-drip method applies nutrient solution to plant grown in gravel or sand. Solution caught in receptacle under pot is returned to upper tank to be used over again.*

*Method of providing support for plants grown in nutrient solution: A section of wire mesh is placed over the container (with a hole cut for the plant's stem if necessary) and a collar of wire mesh is packed with excelsior, sphagnum moss, wood shavings, or the like.*

PLANTS IN WATER: There are a number of plants capable of forming roots and thriving for long periods when their stems are kept in ordinary water from the faucet. The most familiar examples are Chinese evergreen and English ivy varieties (one of the best ivies for this purpose is *Hedera helix* 'Hibernica' Irish ivy). Others that can be used are wandering Jew in several varieties; various members of the Jack-in-the-pulpit family such as philodendron, dieffenbachia, syngonium, and pothos.

There are various woody evergreens, the shoots of which last a long time if their bases are kept in water, and which can be used to advantage in wall vases and similar containers. Some of them will form roots when so treated and may then be potted in soil to become permanent occupants of the home. Among those amenable to this treatment are conifers such as the giant arborvitae *(Thuja plicata)* and redwood burls *(Sequoia sempervirens)*, both from the Pacific states. The last named should be set in a shallow bowl of water. Then there are shrubs such as boxwood *(Buxus)*, oleander *(Nerium)*, rhododendron, the so-called huckleberry *(Vaccinium ovatum)*, and skimmia *(Skimmia japonica)*.

Certain bulbs can be brought to the flowering stage in water. See pages 208–15.

## VEGETABLES AS HOUSE PLANTS

Northern gardeners will find that a raid on the vegetable bin in winter will yield material with decorative and interesting qualities which will grow when placed in water.

A sweet-potato vine will remain in good condition for many months and its culture is simplicity itself. Just obtain a fat, sound, unblemished tuber and insert it, root end down, in a suitable container—a good-looking pickle jar, a quart-size Mason jar, or something fancier.

The potato should lodge half in and half out of the bottle neck. If the opening is too large, your ingenuity will enable you to devise a means of wedging the tuber in the right position. Whenver there is any doubt as to which end should be upward (usually it is the fatter part), lay the tuber on a bed of moist peat moss, in a warm place. This will cause growth to start and enable you to determine how to place it.

Today many of the sweet-potatoes sold in supermarkets are kiln-cured or have been dipped in a chemical to prevent sprouting and so are incapable of growth. Either use home-grown stock or pick out a specimen that is showing signs of life. (Or you might try washing off the chemical.) The water in the container, in which a lump of charcoal is placed, should touch the base of the potato. Use toothpicks inserted in the potato to suspend it at the proper level in the container.

Water added to replace that used by the plant and lost by evaporation should be of room temperature or a little warmer. The shoots should be a

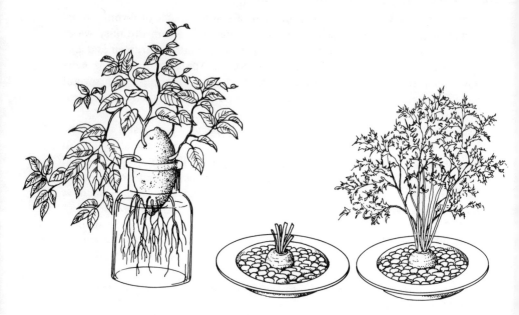

*The tuber of the sweet-potato (left) makes a presentable vine when grown in water. Ferny foliage is the result when a carrot is set in pebbles and water. Use only the top 2–3 inches of the carrot.*

foot or more long in about six weeks and may attain a length of 6 feet. Probably too many shoots will grow, and you will want to remove all but three or four of the strongest ones when they are still small.

Beet roots may be treated in the same way as sweet-potatoes, but carrot and rutabaga should be sliced off with a horizontal cut, 2 or 3 inches from the top, and stood in a saucer of water. Or you may prefer to embed them in pebbles in a water-holding bowl, which makes a more stable arrangement. Avocado seeds will sprout in water. For information on it, the pineapple, and a few other fruits, see pages 106–109.

# CHAPTER 11

# Environment: Temperature, Humidity, and Light

MOST BEGINNERS fail to realize that their rooms are too hot, not too cold, for the great majority of plants suited to house culture. This is probably not so much a matter of temperature, as such, as it is of humidity, which is lowered whenever the air temperature is raised by artificial heat, unless the burner is equipped with an extraordinarily efficient humidifying device. Even tropical plants, which we think of as delighting in heat, get along better in a bedroom (if the thermometer falls no lower than 50° F.), where the relative humidity is higher because of the lowered temperature, than they do in a living room consistently maintained at 67° F. or higher, with consequent aridity. It seems they accept the lowered temperature as the lesser of two evils. Therefore, if you want to succeed with house plants, keep the temperature as low as possible, consistent with your own comfort. Try to avoid letting the thermometer go above 72° F., and allow the temperature to drop 10 or 15 degrees at night. Because of the high cost of fuel and our increasing awareness of the need to conserve energy resources, maintaining lower indoor temperatures no longer seems so unusual.

Of course care must be taken not to overdo things. In those sections where winter readings of zero and below are commonplace, the temperature of the air *near the windows* where many plants are kept may fall dangerously low at night. To avoid damage, supplementary heating devices should be used as suggested later in this chapter, or newspapers may be slipped in between the plants and the window glass; or the plants may be temporarily transferred to a warmer part of the room.

There are a few plants that are likely to suffer or not grow so well if the temperature falls below 60° F. Poinsettias may drop their leaves (although

*The tips of the leaves of this dracaena are being cut off because they have become brown. This condition is usually from too low atmospheric moisture.*

the new hybrids seem to be able to adjust to temperature extremes without suffering), African-violets stop blooming, and the leaves of the gardenia become yellowish if kept too cool.

When growing plants that need really cool conditions during the winter (40° to 50° F.), keep them in a nonheated room or sun porch, bringing them into the living room only occasionally or when they are in bloom. Doing this will take care of their temperature and humidity requirements most of the time; and the plants should not be greatly harmed by deviations from this procedure during the short periods they are on display.

HOW TO MAKE THE AIR HUMID: Plants transpire an enormous amount of moisture, and the sides of the pots (if they are of the porous kind) and the surface of the soil give up their quota of water vapor. So the more plants you grow the more humid the air becomes and the easier it is to grow more plants. It's a good idea to purchase humidity indicators so you can see for yourself how dry many rooms can be. The majority of house plants do best in a relative humidity between 50 and 70 per cent.

If you can do so without injuring curtains, drapes, and furniture, spray the leaves (except the fuzzy ones) with water at least once a day. Provide watertight trays in which to stand the plants. I use shallow rectangular enameled trays found in the kitchen. If you wish a more fancy arrangement, you can have metal trays constructed to fit the window space or buy plastic trays available in garden centers. Place water in them and then fill with pebbles to support the pots so that the plants do not stand directly in the water. Or use plant saucers with pebbles and water in the same way.

If your house is heated by steam or hot water, place evaporating pans on the radiators and *keep them filled with water* whenever the heating plant is operating. If the house is heated by hot air, be sure that the humidifying device on the oil burner is in working order. There are various kinds of sprayers that deliver a mistlike spray. Keep them filled with water and spray the plants on sunny dry days.

More expensive but worth it for their great efficiency are room humidifiers which can hold from 3 to 8 gallons or more of water. Such electrically operated humidifiers improve the atmosphere for plants, furnishings, and people.

Growing plants in closed glass cases offers a means whereby those plants that demand high humidity can be successfully managed. (See Chapter 4.) Using a glass screen to enclose, or partially enclose, a bay window is an extension and modification of this method. If this is done, care must be taken during cold snaps to avoid letting the temperature fall too low. Keep a thermometer in the enclosed space and if the mercury approaches the critical point, start up a small electric heater, with a pan of water on it; or even keep a few light bulbs operating to raise the temperature.

VENTILATION: "Fresh" air is not essential for plants in the same way that it is for human beings. I have before me a plant of wandering Jew growing happily in a quart Mason jar in which it was "canned" six months ago. Since its incarceration it has grown to more than ten times its original size and looks much healthier—a good indication that some plants, at any

*An attractive way to display a plant and maintain humidity around it is to enclose it in a glass dome. Here an African-violet 'Pocono Mountains' and* Caladium humboldtii *stand on moist perlite within the dome.*

rate, can get along without a "change of air." Even so, it is desirable to admit outside air to the rooms in which plants are growing as freely as possible, whenever the weather permits it.

During the months when artificial heat is used the air indoors is usually drier than that outside, so free ventilation may help to maintain the humidity that is desirable. It is also a measure of insurance against harmful concentrations of artificial (not natural) gas within the home and likely to improve the health of the human occupants as well as that of the plants. Avoid, however, admitting air in such a way that cold blasts blow directly on the plants. Sometimes this can be done by opening windows from the top, or a window well away from the plants, or even one in another room if the communicating door is opened.

Artificial gas and coal gas have injurious effects on most plants. African-violets refuse to bloom, Jerusalem-cherries drop their fruit and leaves, and some kinds just look unwell. The wax begonia will drop its foliage and sulk,

*This indoor garden of foliage plants stands on moist pebbles in a watertight floor tray.*

and baby's tears may have its leaves blackened and soon die. Natural gas is not injurious because it doesn't contain substances harmful to vegetation.

By the way, ripening apples give off ethylene gas which may cause yellowing or bleaching of foliage, so they should not be kept in quantity in rooms containing plants.

*A former fish aquarium has become an open "terrarium" for a collection of succulents. They receive the essential light from two 40-watt Wide Spectrum Gro-Lux fluorescent tubes which are about 8–12 inches above the foliage.*

*A wall-mounted light fixture provides illumination for African-violets, coleus, and begonias. A wedged louver hides the three 40-watt fluorescent tubes.*

*A table-top fixture provides light for orchids and other house plants in a city apartment.*

LIGHT: Many of the plants we grow in our homes are native to tropical forests where they became habituated to a dim light. Some of the bromeliads, *Sansevieria, Philodendron,* many ferns, palms, and foliage plants in general can survive for long periods and sometimes even thrive in poorly lighted rooms; but most house plants need the best lighted positions available, because, as every photographer knows who takes pictures indoors, the intensity of the light there is much less than it is in the open, or even under trees.

Plants react to insufficient light by producing pale, anemic leaves on long stalks reaching out toward sunshine and stems which are lankier than normal. When this condition is noticed, every endeavor should be made to provide better illumination.

South, east, and west windows should be chosen for those that demand the most light—cacti and succulents in general, and the majority of flowering plants—while "foliage" plants such as ferns, philodendrons, ivy, and peperomia can be relegated to the north windows. City dwellers, especially, should be careful to keep their plants as near as possible to the source of light, because so much is shut off by the pall of smoky haze which covers urban areas a considerable part of the time.

Those who are really serious in their desire to grow house plants will avoid the use of heavy window drapes, using only thin curtains which let most of the light through, and placing the extreme sun lovers between the curtains and the glass. But be careful not to overdo it. Plants whose skins have been "tenderized" by the dull days of winter may be scorched by full exposure to the sun when the days begin to lengthen. Yellowing of the entire plant or a scalded appearance of the leaves (similar to that seen on tomato fruits exposed by excessive pruning of the leaves) in the spring may mean that a little shading is necessary.

ARTIFICIAL LIGHT: Overcoming the lack of sunshine indoors by the use of artificial light is a common practice today that allows many people to grow a wider range of house plants than was formerly possible. Although artificial light simulates sunshine, it does not follow that 4 or 5 hours of artificial illumination are the equivalent of the same hours of sunshine. Artificial light—the source is usually from fluorescent tubes, which are more economical to operate and which do not emit the heat generated by incandescent bulbs—must be on for about 12 to 16 hours daily for healthy growth and flower production.

The plants that respond best to artificial light are those that would normally receive less than full sun in their natural environment. The "stars" of many light gardens are African-violets *(Saintpaulia)*. The positive response of the African-violet to fluorescent lights has probably contributed to its enduring popularity and has spurred the current interest in many of its relatives in the gesneriad family. Orchids and begonias are two other large plant groups that thrive—and flower—under artificial light. However, most kinds of plants respond in some favorable measure, including foliage plants, especially those with color variations in their leaves.

Although incandescent bulbs are less satisfactory, mostly for the reasons mentioned above, they too have their uses, especially for flooding large plants

*A functional light garden for a basement or plant room has been made with an inexpensive steel shelf frame which supports two 40-watt fluorescent lights.*

or indoor gardens with light, or spot-lighting a group of plants at night. The heat drawback to incandescent bulbs has been diminished somewhat by the introduction of cool beam bulbs. Some benefit in growth is possible from an ordinary table lamp fitted with a 75-watt bulb for a plant that is kept a safe distance (about 12 inches) from the bulb.

For a time it was thought that combining incandescent bulbs with fluorescent tubes gave better growth results, but it is now generally believed that the wide-spectrum tubes, especially formulated for plants, give as good results and, in the long run, are cheaper. Several types of fluorescent tubes are available, usually in lengths from 18 to 48 inches and in various wattage. (Fluorescent lights also come in U, panel, or circular shapes.) A basic light garden can be established under a table-top fixture which contains two 40-watt tubes, one a "warm white" type, the other "cool white." The fixture can be lowered or raised, according to the heights of the plants beneath it. Keep the plants close to the tubes; about 4 to 8 inches is recommended for flowering plants and no more than 12 inches or so for most foliage plants. If plants are not thriving or flowering properly and appear to be "stretching" toward the light, they are probably too far from the source. Also, the greatest light intensity from fluorescent tubes exists toward their centers so plants located at the ends receive less light.

In growing plants under lights, it is important to maintain sufficient humidity. Standing the plants on pebbles in water-filled trays is about the easiest method.

Garden centers, hardware and electrical supply stores usually have an array of equipment that can be adapted to light garden use. In addition many house-plant specialists feature specially designed carts and cabinets, all equipped with lights, that can make attractive light gardens.

# CHAPTER 12

# *Rest Periods for House Plants*

THERE ARE practically no perennial plants that go through life without a resting period, and those who grow plants in their homes must take this into consideration if they want them to remain healthy and bloom freely.

Plants are said to be "resting" when active growth ceases. In some plants the resting period is not very obvious, but in others it is so conspicuous that—accompanied as it is by the complete loss of leaves or, in some cases, by the death of the aboveground portions—it is visible even to the least observant. When either of these conditions occurs, the plant is said to be "dormant," but this often is a misnomer, for there may be significant changes going on in the cells of the seemingly inactive plant. Also, it should be remembered that even though there are no signs of life *above* ground, the roots and underground structures may be growing vigorously, as in the case of tulips and other bulbous and tuberous plants, in the fall.

It is easy to imagine that the resting habit of plants in their natural environment was brought about, in part at least, by unfavorable growing conditions at certain seasons. It is helpful to the plantsman to know the native country of the plants being grown, and something of its climate, because this knowledge often provides a clue to the kind of treatment desirable under cultivation.

Unfavorable conditions for growth may be drought or low temperature. In the tropics and desert regions the resting period is usually associated with the dry season; in temperate climates, with the onset of winter; and some plants (such as the hardy spring-flowering bulbs) rest, or even become dormant, early in the summer, start into growth again in late summer insofar as the underground parts are concerned, and become more or less "dormant" again when the soil above or about their roots is frozen. A knowledge of

*Crown-of-thorns requires less water during the winter months, even while it is blooming.*

the habits of these hardy bulbs is important, for they cannot successfully be forced into bloom in the house except when they are kept cool and moist during the period of root formation. Other bulbous and tuberous plants—such as *Oxalis tetraphylla,* achimenes, gloxinia, and tuberous begonias—have the habit of actively growing and flowering during the summer, presumably because conditions in their native habitats are unfavorable for growth during the period corresponding to our winter.

But while it seems reasonable to suppose that unfavorable growing conditions are largely responsible for the acquisition of the habit of resting periodically, and certainly the cold of winter by inhibiting growth brings about an enforced rest with many plants, this is not the entire story. Even though conditions are apparently just right, there comes a time when active growth ceases and the plant, as it were, marks time. Thus we find with plant life generally a sort of rhythm, in which a cycle of growth is followed by a period of rest, the duration of which may be only a few weeks, but which may last for six months or longer.

The scientific explanation is that the rest period is caused by "the inhibition of enzyme activity due to an overaccumulation of the products of their work." In other words, an excess supply of carbohydrates in the plant tissues checks the work of the enzymes which make continuing growth possible.

Thus plants insist on their rest period even though conditions are suitable for continued growth. When I was a student gardener at England's Kew Gardens, this was vividly illustrated by an occurrence that had me worried for several weeks. I had charge of a section of the large Palm House, which, because of its size, accommodated a variety of tropical trees other than palms. One of these was completely leafless—enjoying its rest period—at the time I took over. It soon came out in full leaf, but after a few months shed them, leaving me aghast in the expectation of being fired for horticultural malpractice. But in a few weeks it again put on an entirely new suit and Montague Free once more was able to go about his chores without a sense of impending doom. The probable explanation was that the tree came from a part of the tropics that has *two* dry seasons, and so ingrained was the resting habit that when the proper time arrived it just quit, regardless of the facts that it was adequately supplied with water at the roots and that it was high summer.

Now, it may be argued, if plants take their rest regardless of cultural practices, it is unnecessary to bother about making any changes in routine. But it so happens that unless the change in environment (or its equivalent), associated in nature with the rest period, is provided, then the plant may fail to grow properly when the time comes to resume activity; or it may refuse to produce flowers.

Blueberry *(Vaccinium)* and trailing-arbutus *(Epigaea repens)* are not house plants, but are such familiar garden plants that a brief account of Dr. F. V. Coville's experiments with them may illustrate the need for certain environmental changes. Blueberry plants brought into a greenhouse at the end of summer and kept there at growing temperature dropped their leaves and became dormant. Furthermore, they failed to start into growth the following spring, and some remained dormant for a full year! But Dr. Coville found that if the plants were kept at low temperatures (a few degrees above freezing was sufficiently low) for two or three months, growth would proceed normally when the plants were again given warmth. Trailing-arbutus, with several clusters of flower buds, kept in a warm greenhouse over winter, was able to open only a single flower the following spring; while a similar plant, kept outdoors all winter, bloomed profusely.

English ivy when grown outdoors in northern gardens is subject to freezing temperature during winter and properly located can endure zero without much damage. It is not surprising, therefore, that it often fails to thrive when kept in an apartment where the winter temperature ranges between 70° and 80° F. I once stayed at a remote little hotel in Nova Scotia which had a remarkable ivy growing in a 12-inch pot. Its shoots were long enough to train twice around the lounge, which was larger than the average living room. The room was heated by an old-fashioned stove, and my guess is that, during the night at any rate, the temperature in winter dropped nearly to the freezing point, and that this, by approximating natural conditions, was largely responsible for the exuberant growth.

The finest pot-grown specimen of emerald-feather *(Asparagus densiflorus* 'Sprengeri') that I have ever seen—not excluding those grown by professionals in greenhouses—was exhibited by a farmer's wife at a county fair where I

*The poinsettia 'Annette Hegg' is an example of a modern poinsettia* (Euphorbia pulcherrima). *This plant was retained after the holiday season and brought into bloom the following Christmas, as shown.*

was judging house plants many years ago. It was simply magnificent, and I have no doubt whatever it was grown in a house that had no central heating and consequently was exposed to chilly conditions during winter which contributed the necessary factor of rest to ensure vigorous growth come spring.

Azaleas and camellias are accustomed to cool conditions in winter and, for the most part, are not harmed by exposure to a few degrees of frost. Knowing this—and remembering Dr. Coville's experiment with trailing-arbutus—it is easy to understand why the common practice of keeping azaleas or camellias in a room in which the temperature is seldom below 70° F. results in blasted flower buds and general ill-health.

Therefore, these and other plants listed in Chapter 20 should be kept as cool as possible, but not (except for thoroughly winter-hardy plants) subjected

*After flowering, it was allowed
to gradually dry out.*

After this rest period, it was cut back, fertilized, and watered. If all goes well during summer and fall—that is, the plant is watered as necessary, fed occasionally, and kept in bright light—the blooming cycle should again be repeated for Christmas. Since poinsettia is a "short-day" plant, flowering will be delayed well beyond the holiday period unless the plant is kept in the dark for about 12 hours daily, beginning about October 1 in the North, until buds set in mid-November.

to freezing during the winter months. One benefit of the sky-rocketing costs of oil is that thermostats are being set lower but, admittedly, in many homes it is still difficult to provide the necessary cool conditions. Often a room can be set aside, heating it only when the temperature approaches 32° F.; and sometimes an unheated sun porch or enclosed breezeway is available. When neither of these can be provided, the next best plan is to keep the plants in a room in which the night temperature is low, trying, however, to avoid too much difference (no more than 30 degrees) between day and night. It is probably unnecessary to say that the plants should not be exposed to a freezing blast from an open window. This may involve a daily shift, because they must be kept close to the window during the day to take full advantage of the small amount of sunlight available during the winter in northern climates.

It is necessary to make a distinction between those plants—primroses, cyclamen, freesia, et cetera—that *grow* best at a low temperature and those that need it for resting. The former (which may be brought into the coolest, lightest part of the living room when their flowers show color) will need every possible attention in the matters of feeding and watering; the latter should not be given any fertilizer and only enough water to prevent the soil from becoming dry.

While some plants need low temperatures during part of the year, others must be kept dry. This is particularly true if flowers are expected from certain bulbous and tuberous plants, and subjects such as wax-plant and poinsettia.

When I was a gardener in England we found that *Iris tingitana* (a bulbous species from North Africa) in our section of the country would not produce flowers except when the bulbs were dug up, after the foliage had died down, and exposed to sunshine for several weeks to ripen them thoroughly. This was required because of the difference in the climate of England and Africa. It is not necessary to be so drastic with the bulbous and tuberous plants that we grow in our homes, but most of them should be dried off during some part of the year. Failure of amaryllis to bloom can often be attributed to incomplete ripening of the bulbs because the soil was not kept on the dry side during fall and early winter. (It must not be thought that this is the only cause for nonflowering of amaryllis—loss of interest in the plant as soon as the flowers have faded, resulting in lack of proper care during the time the leaves are active in manufacturing food for the bulb, is another reason for their failure.)

Calla-lilies, too, should have a rest, and under house conditions this is given by withholding water from the soil after their winter and spring season of growth. Sometimes calla-lilies are planted in the garden to continue their growth in summer. If this is done, the plants must be dug up early in the fall and the tubers kept dry for three months or so before again starting them into growth. Calla-lilies are much more flexible than some plants in their resting habits. I knew of one English garden in which they were planted outdoors under a foot of water and left there, year in, year out! This was definitely the reverse of the usual procedure, but apparently low temperatures during the winter took the place of the customary drying off. It is said that under some conditions calla-lilies will keep on growing indefinitely.

To have it bloom freely, the wax-plant *(Hoya carnosa)* must be kept on the dry side during winter, giving only enough water to prevent the leaves from shriveling, Poinsettia may be deprived of water entirely from mid-January to mid-April, although the new hybrids have a remarkable characteristic of retaining their blooms in perfect condition for months and months if watered.

Some of the plants commonly grown in our houses do not have a long or pronounced resting season, and close observation is necessary to determine when growth ceases. Many of the so-called foliage plants—pandanus, dieffenbachia—belong in this group. Plants of this nature are successfully grown by those who are entirely unaware that plants require rest; so we can assume that seasonal variations in temperature (which occur even indoors) are sufficient to provide the conditions requisite for a short nap.

Many differences are exhibited in the growth cycles of various plants, and these are important to the gardener whether he grows plants indoors or out. As previously mentioned, hardy spring-flowering bulbs have two periods of active growth and two dormant. During the winter they are inactive and cease growing during the hot days of summer. Sometimes flowering coincides with active shoot growth (as with fuchsia, impatiens, and calla-lily); and sometimes it comes toward the end of the growing season—for example, with tulips. On the other hand, flowering may *precede,* or go along with, the beginning of active shoot and leaf growth—some azaleas, amaryllis, and meadow saffron are typical examples.

Knowing how and when to give plants the conditions requisite to their resting stage is an essential part of a good gardener's skill. Admittedly it is a somewhat complicated business but, by following some general rules, by "doing as you are told," and by close observation of your own plants, the problem can be solved.

The first important principle to remember is that the time for resting comes *after* a period of active growth, which may be long or short according to the subject; so, when the plant is no longer putting out new shoots or leaves and when flowers have faded, give it less water at the roots and a lower temperature (if cessation of growth comes at a time when it is possible to do this). *Refrain from giving any fertilizer.* However—especially with plants grown for their foliage—avoid reducing the water supply to the extent of causing the leaves to wilt.

Those plants that have bulbs or tubers—for example, amaryllis, nerine, freesia, achimenes, veltheimia, and gloxinia—should usually be kept completely dry during part of the year. The "drying-off" process *should be gradual* and spread over several weeks, beginning when growth ceases and leaves begin to turn yellow. Plants (such as clivia) that do not have a well-defined bulb should be watered carefully, giving only enough to prevent the leaves from wilting or shriveling.

The rest period of plants of temperate climates should be accompanied by cool conditions through at least part of the winter.

Potted plants brought in from outdoors in the fall have usually been growing vigorously all summer. Cool conditions in the house, which in the homes of cost-conscious families commonly precede the use of artificial heat, give them the rest they need. With the exception of subjects such as poinsettia, which still have to complete their growth, no attempt should be made at this time to force them into growth by fertilizing or watering them heavily. This applies also to mature bedding plants that are cut back and potted, such as begonia, geranium, and impatiens. On the contrary, self-sown *seedlings* of begonia, flowering tobacco, marigold, et cetera, dug up from the flower border and potted, should be kept growing by fertilizing them as soon as they have made some new roots. Repot them into larger pots when necessary. Unlike the mature plants, these seedlings are just entering upon a period of active growth, instead of just concluding such a period.

## RESTING HOUSE PLANTS

### Dry or Dryish in Winter

| *Plant* | *Special Treatment* |
| --- | --- |
| Bromeliads—Pineapple Family: *Aechmea* spp.; *Ananas comosus,* Pineapple; *Neoregelia spectabilis,* Painted Fingernail; *Billbergia; Cryptanthus; Nidularium; Vriesia;* et cetera. | These should be kept fairly dry at the roots, but the foliage should be sprinkled daily and the center water "cups" kept filled. Water freely when flower spikes start to grow. |
| Cacti, desert forms: *Aporocactus; Cereus; Echinocereus; Ferocactus; Mammillaria; Opuntia;* et cetera. | Slight watering every few weeks usually sufficient to prevent shrivelling. Keep soil moist when growth begins. Temperature 50° to 60° F. |
| Cacti, tropical forms: *Epiphyllum,* Orchid Cactus; *Rhipsalidopsis,* Easter Cactus; *Rhipsalis,* Mistletoe Cactus; *Schlumbergera* (syn. *Zygocactus*), Christmas Cactus) | Keep on dry side during fall and early winter. Give enough water to keep leaflike stems from shriveling. Moist air desirable. Easter cactus requires a cool period (about 50° F. at night) to develop buds for spring bloom. Christmas cactus needs cool treatment in fall for holiday bloom. |

| | |
|---|---|
| *Ceropegia woodii,* Hearts Entangled, Rosary Vine | Water weekly. If shoots die back, keep dry until late winter. |
| *Clivia miniata,* Kafir-lily | Give only enough water to keep leaves from wilting. Keep cool (45° to 50° F.). |
| *Euphorbia milii splendens,* Crown-of-thorns | Water about every two weeks from mid-November to early January. |
| *E. pulcherrima,* Poinsettia | Gradually dry off when leaves begin to fall. Cut back, usually toward spring with modern hybrids. Then resume regular watering. Water about every two weeks from mid-November to early January. |
| *Fuchsia* | Keep cool (50° F.) and give only enough water to keep wood plump from October to December. Prune in late winter; water normally; give temperature of about 65° F. and sun. |
| *Hippeastrum,* Amaryllis | Keep dry October to January. Moisten soil when growth begins; water freely when leaves or buds form. |
| *Hoya carnosa,* Waxplant | Give only enough water to keep leaves from shriveling. |
| *Sansevieria trifasciata,* Snake-plant | Water at weekly intervals during winter or as soil dries out. |
| Succulents: *Agave; Aloe; Crassula; Echeveria; Gasteria; Haworthia; Kalanchoe; Pedilanthus; Sedum;* et cetera. | Give enough water to keep leaves from shriveling. *Pedilanthus* may be kept completely dry in December and January. Water winter-flowering species *(Kalanchoe blossfeldiana)* until blooms fade, then keep on dry side for two months. |

Tuberous plants and bulbs, grown primarily for summer blooms, which are kept dry in winter include:

| | |
|---|---|
| *Achimenes* | Leave tubers in soil completely dry from time tops die (early fall) until early spring; temperature 60° F. |
| *Begonia* (tuberous) | Store tubers in dry peat moss until early to midspring. |
| *Caladium* | Keep tubers dry from fall to early spring, then start growing for summer display. |
| *Oxalis rubra, O. tetraphylla* | Dry off for three or four months. Store in cool (50° F.), dry place. |

| | |
|---|---|
| *Sinningia speciosa,* Gloxinia | Dry tubers off in their pots; or remove tubers and keep in dry peat moss in plastic bags until late winter to early spring. |
| *Smithiantha zebrina,* Temple Bells | Treatment as for *Achimenes,* except that growth and flowers may continue through fall and into early winter. |

## Dry in Summer

| | |
|---|---|
| *Anemone coronaria,* Poppy-flowered Anemone | Gradually dry off as foliage withers. Repot and keep soil moist in fall. |
| *Freesia* x *hybrida,* Freesia | Gradually reduce water as leaves begin to turn yellow. Keep bulbs dry in their pots until fall. |
| *Ipheion* (syn. *Triteleia*) *uniflorum,* Spring Star-flower | When leaves die down, keep dry until early fall. |
| *Ixia* spp., Corn-lily | Treat same as *Freesia.* |
| *Lachenalia* spp., Cape-cowslip | Keep dry, in their pots, from withering of leaves until late summer. |
| *Nerine sarniensis,* Guernsey-lily | Dry May to August. Expose bulbs in their pots to sun. Do not disturb roots. |
| *Oxalis bowiei; O. cernua* (Bermuda-buttercup); *O. hirta; O. lasiandra; O. purpurea.* | Winter to spring-flowering oxalises should be kept dry in their pots from late spring until early fall. *O. bowiei,* and others, if flowered in summer, will not bloom the following winter unless dried off for at least two months. |
| *Ranunculus asiaticus,* Persian Ranunculus | Treat same as *Anemone.* |
| *Saintpaulia,* African-violet | Keep a little on dry side in summer during hot, humid weather. |
| *Sparaxis* spp. | Treat same as *Freesia.* |
| *Veltheimia viridifolia* | Dry in summer. Start watering when new growth begins in early fall, and keep in cool sunny window. |
| *Zantedeschia aethiopica* (Calla-lily); *Z. elliottiana* (Golden | For house culture, best dried off in summer. If planted outdoors, should be dug in fall |

Calla); *Z. rehmannii* (Pink Calla)

and tubers dried for three months before potting. Purchased tubers of *A. elliottiana* should be exposed a few weeks in warm room before potting.

## Cool in Winter *

*Araucaria heterophylla,* Norfolk Island-pine

Water only when soil is dry.

*Asparagus densiflorus* 'Sprengeri', Aspargus-Fern

Reduce water supply.

*Cyclamen persicum,* Florists' Cyclamen

Water normally.

*Camellia japonica,* Camellia

Keep soil moist. When the days are appreciably longer, this and the following plants can be kept at living-room temperature (65° to 70° F.). When growth begins, water freely; repot and fertilize as necessary.

*Cymbalaria muralis,* Kenilworth-ivy

*Cyrtomium falcatum,* Holly Fern

*Ficus pumila,* Creeping Fig

*Hedera helix* cultivars, English Ivy

*Ligularia* (syn. *Farfugium*) *tussilaginea* 'Aureo-maculata,' Leopard-plant

*Osmanthus fragrans,* Sweet-olive

*Pteris cretica,* Table Fern

*P. serrulata,* Brake Fern

*Rhododendron,* Evergreen Azaleas

* Night temperatures of 40° to 50° F. are best, with warmer daytime temperatures in the 60° range tolerated.

## CHAPTER 13

# *Pinching, Pruning, Training*

SOME PINCHING and pruning are necessary to keep shrubby plants in ship-shape condition; and training, combined with pinching and pruning, is called for by those of climbing or trailing habit.

PINCHING is the term applied when the tip of a growing shoot is removed. Usually it is done with the thumbnail and finger. It promotes a compact, bushy habit of growth by checking the strong shoots and stimulating into

*Pinching, pruning, disbudding techniques:* Pinching *is done to induce the formation of side shoots, resulting in a branching, bushier plant;* pruning *controls the shape of the plant or is done to stimulate new growth from the base;* disbudding *produces larger, more perfect individual flowers by reducing the number the plant has formed.*

growth shoot buds that otherwise would have remained dormant. The removal of *flower* buds to force the plant to conserve its energies until the time we desire it to bloom is another form of pinching.

PRUNING is done with a sharp knife, scissors, or pruning shears and consists of cutting back the branches to a greater or lesser degree according to the subject and the purpose in view. It may be desirable to prevent the plant from growing to unwieldy size, to promote the formation of strong flower-bearing shoots, or to improve its shape.

TRAINING usually implies the provision of a support to which the shoots are attached by tying or otherwise, and is sometimes combined with pruning and pinching to produce the required form, as in indoor bonsai subjects. Disbranching chrysanthemums (done when the branches are no more than an inch or so long) to make them grow to a single stem, and the product of "standard" plants (those with a single straight stem of considerable height and a branching head at the top, as sometimes is done with geranium, heliotrope, and fuchsia) are other forms that training takes.

## PRUNING AND PINCHING

Pruning cuts should be made just above a leaf that has in its axil a bud pointed in the direction we wish the bush to develop; or, when a branch is removed and not merely shortened, close to the parent branch or trunk from which it grows. The object of this is to avoid ugly-looking stubs.

Following are some of the plants arranged alphabetically, that need, or are improved by, pruning and/or pinching:

*Abutilon,* Flowering-maple. Prune old plants in fall by cutting back shoots of the current season about one-half. Young plants and the new shoots of old plants should have tips pinched out if necessary to promote bushiness.

*Camellia japonica,* Camellia. Ordinarily needs little pruning beyond shortening any shoots that spoil the symmetry of the bush. This should be done immediately after flowering.

*Campanula isophylla.* Cut back flowering shoots to pot level when all flowers have faded. To prolong the blooming season, prevent seed formation by picking off old flowers.

*Chrysanthemum frutescens,* Boston Daisy, Marguerite. Old plants may be cut back one-half when flowering is over; but a better plan is to raise young plants annually from cuttings inserted in a cold frame in June or July.

*C.* x *morifolium,* Chrysanthemum. If bushy plants are required, pinch out tips of shoots whenever they attain a length of 6 inches until mid-July. When one-, two-, or three-stemmed plants are desired, they are "disbranched" by removing all side shoots as soon as they are large enough to handle, once the required number of main shoots has been produced. Larger flowers are produced by disbudding—that is, by removing all but the strongest bud on each shoot. A modification of this procedure is to remove the weakest buds in a spray.

*Dieffenbachia,* Dumb Cane. Sometimes becomes too tall and has too much bare stem showing, necessitating decapitation to bring it to earth. This procedure involves air-layering, which is more akin to propagation and is treated in Chapter 15.

*Dracaena,* Corn Plant. Same treatment as Dieffenbachia.

*Euphorbia pulcherrima,* Poinsettia. Old plants should be cut back to within 6 inches of the pot in April and repotted. If a propagating case is available (see Chapter 15), it is better to root cuttings obtained from the cut-back plants rather than to keep the old plants.

*Ficus elastica,* Rubber Plant. Handsomest when grown to a single stem, but sometimes people develop a strange affection for this plant and keep it even after it has gawky branches. Removal of the growing point from "wild" shoots will make them branch. Misplaced branches may be cut out in their entirety. This should be done outdoors in spring so that the oriental rug is not gummed up by latex dripping from the cut ends of the shoots.

*Fuchsia* x *hybrida,* Fuchsia. Start old plants into growth in midwinter, January or February in most northern regions. As soon as buds show green, cut back to the strongest point and remove all dead wood. To promote bushi-

*Flowering-maple* (Abutilon pictum *'Thompsonii') needs an annual pruning to maintain shapeliness.*

*Pruning results in stockier, more uniformly shaped plants. Dark bands on plant at left indicate where pruning cuts should be made to achieve bushy growth on plant at right.*

ness of old and young plants the tips of shoots may be pinched out as soon as they have made six or eight pairs of leaves. Excessive pinching of new growth will delay flower production.

*Gardenia jasminoides,* Cape-jasmine. If plant is getting too large, prune back one-third before it is set outdoors in spring. When new shoots attain a length of 6 inches, pinch out tips until August. When plants are no larger than is needed, only prune to shorten any shoots that spoil symmetry.

*Hedera helix,* English Ivy. When a bushy plant is required, obtain the "self-branching" types, such as 'Hahn's Self-branching,' and pinch out tips occasionally. The Irish ivy (*H. helix* 'Hibernica'), commonly grown, does not branch freely even when pinched back. Specimens that have grown too large for their quarters should be discarded and replaced by other ivy varieties that are more compact.

*Heliotropium arborescens,* Common Heliotrope. Old plants dug up from the garden to serve as house plants should be cut back about two-thirds. They are not very satisfactory, however, when so treated, and it is better to raise young plants from seeds or cuttings in the spring and keep all flower buds picked off until they are brought in during the fall. Shapeliness may be induced by pinching out tips of wayward shoots.

*Hibiscus rosa-sinensis,* Chinese Hibiscus. Cut back one-third in early spring; or if it is still blooming then, wait until it is put outdoors later. Thin out weak wood and prune to make bush as shapely as possible.

*Hoya carnosa,* Waxplant. Needs little pruning. "Wild" shoots, if any, may be checked by pinching out their tips. Avoid cutting off the spurs (stubby growths) on which the flowers are produced; from them come additional crops.

*Hydrangea macrophylla,* French Hydrangea. Cut back, leaving only two pairs of leaves on each shoot, as soon as flowers fade. Remove weak, spindling shoots entirely.

*Lantana camara,* Lantana. Plants that have spent a season in the flower border may be dug up, potted, and cut back three-fourths, but they will be a sorry sight for many weeks. Young plants raised from cuttings or seeds in midspring, which have had their flower buds pinched off until fall, are much more satisfactory.

*Pelargonium* x *domesticum,* Lady Washington Geranium. Cut off all weak shoots in late summer to early fall. Shorten those remaining to improve shape. If it is desired to reduce their size, they may be cut back rather severely at this time. Young plants may be made into compact specimens by pinching out tips of shoots if it seems necessary.

*P.* x *hortorum,* House or Zonal Geranium. Old plants dug up from the border should be cut back about one-half, having in mind the production of a shapely plant. It takes several months for these cut-backs to develop into presentable plants so it is best to raise new plants from cuttings in spring for winter flowering. Pinch out tips of 6-inch shoots to induce bushiness, and remove all flower buds until fall.

*Philodendron scandens oxycardium,* Heart-leaf Philodendron. Treat as recommended for *Syngonium.*

*Rhododendron hybrids,* Evergreen Azalea. Prune for shape immediately after flowering but do not cut back any more than is absolutely necessary. Pinch out the tips of shoots that outstrip their neighbors.

*Rosa chinensis* 'Minima,' Fairy Rose and other miniature roses. In January cut back resting plants one-half and remove any weak twigs.

*Scindapsus aureus (Epipremnum aureum)* and *S. pictus* 'Argyraeus.' *See Syngonium.*

*Syngonium podophyllum,* Nephthytis. Bareness at the base may be deferred for a while if the tips of one or two of the shoots are pinched out when they are about 8 inches tall. This will temporarily check those shoots and induce branching by stimulating lower buds into growth.

*Tibouchina urvilleana,* Princess Flower. Rest by keeping cool (40° F.) in winter. Prune in February by shortening one-half all strong shoots of preceding year and removing weak twigs. Young plants should be pinched to induce the required amount of bushiness and then allowed to grow freely.

*Tradescantia fluminensis,* Wandering Jew. Used mainly as "droopers." If potted in good soil, growth may be so lush as to give an effect of heaviness. This can be corrected by thinning out some of the shoots, cutting them off near the pot. The cut-back stubs will produce new shoots which will take the place of older shoots that have become shabby. Even with this treatment

*Chrysanthemums show progressive reduction in size of individual blooms as number of stems per plant increases.*

a pot of wandering Jew will not last in good condition indefinitely, so it is desirable from time to time to start a new pot of cuttings from terminal shoots—an easy matter.

*Zebrina pendula,* Wandering Jew. *See Tradescantia.*

While it is hoped that the foregoing tips will be helpful, it should be remembered that pruning and pinching are not matters of rule of thumb, but things that must be done with thoughtful consideration. Plants do not always behave as we desire—environmental conditions may affect their performance. So study your plants and use common sense in conjunction with the specific instructions given above.

## TRAINING

It has already been intimated that training in part is a matter of pinching and pruning. In the case of climbers and trailers it may also involve the provision of suitable supports to which the shoots are attached by ties or otherwise.

Philodendrons, nephthytis, scindapsus, hoya, some orchids and others that attach themselves to their supports by aerial roots should be provided with rough material on which to climb. This may consist of unbarked length of a red-cedar trunk about 2 inches in diameter; an inch-square plant stake on which narrow strips of virgin cork have been nailed; or a plant stake wrapped with moss or osmunda fiber held in place with thin copper wire. The supports, which are installed when the plants are potted, should extend to the bottom of the pot, and the soil must be packed firmly around them to make them rigid. Supports of this kind are inclined to be top-heavy and need a weighty base to keep them from toppling. Therefore they are not satisfactory in pots of less than 6-inch size.

*Use sharp scissors to cut out dead flowers and foliage of plants in terrariums. Potted plants can also be kept presentable by means of such minor surgery.*

*Pinching tips of fittonia.*

*Supports for vines in pots can readily be improvised. Use wire or three flexible bamboo sections (right) and a small hoop. Use wire ties to fasten the bamboo stakes together at their tips and to the hoop.*

While these plants are able to attach themselves to supports of this nature by their air roots, it is usually desirable to give them a helping hand, in the beginning at least, by tying in the shoots with thin twine. If the situation is such that daily spraying may be practiced, the air roots will be considerably encouraged.

Morning-glories, which climb by twining, can best be accommodated by sticking three slender bamboo stakes in the soil at equal distances around the edge of the pot. About halfway up the length of the stakes install a hoop—of wire or an embroidery hoop of sufficient size will do—and fasten it with ties. Then bring the tops of the stakes together and tie them and you will have a contraption looking something like the sketch.

Sometimes a simple wood trellis is the best solution to the problem of attractively supporting and displaying climbers and trailers. Usually this is handled by making a wood base to which the trellis is fastened and on which the potted plant is stood. A base of 1¼-inch material about 8 inches square will satisfactorily hold a trellis up to 30 inches in height. The uprights of 1½- by ½-inch material, planed on four sides, can be attached to the base by wood screws, reinforced by angle irons. The crosspieces can be ¼- by 1-inch strips nailed to the uprights. The trailing shoots can be trained by tying them unobtrusively to the uprights and crosspieces, or by simply winding them back and forth behind and in front of the support. Plants that can be effectively displayed on a trellis such as this or on any other that your imagination and artistic taste may lead you to construct, include English ivy, kangaroo vine, sweet-potato, grape-ivy, Madeira vine.

# CHAPTER 14

# *Summer Care*

ON THE WHOLE, the plants that make the most successful go of it in our homes are those that are grown outdoors and store up enough vigor to endure a period of arduous service indoors before we get them. The hardy spring-flowering bulbs are an example of this type. Other successful plants, such as tuberous begonias and gloxinias which are dormant in winter, can be grown in summer in well-ventilated rooms where the air is not desiccated by artificial heat. Those that can be spared from their job of indoor decorating may be given a recuperative summer vacation outdoors to keep them going through the winter.

When the weather becomes settled and warm in midspring, it is time to take stock of the situation and get as many plants as possible outdoors. But first dispose of those that have outlived their usefulness—which have grown too big for the niche they occupy and which cannot be reduced in size by pruning. The big Boston fern, or dracaena, which is almost touching the ceiling, and the ungainly rubber plant should be deposited in the trash can or given to someone who has more room, unless there is a place for them on a partly shaded terrace or porch. If they are needed for propagation or can be brought down to usable size by air-layering (see Chapter 15), you may want to keep them a little longer.

If the loss of these plants and the temporary departure of others on vacation outdoors leave too many gaps in your decorative scheme, fill the voids with such summer-blooming subjects as achimenes, fuchsias, and gloxinias which, along with African-violets, are better off indoors in most sections. If placed outdoors, it should be in a well-lighted situation protected from hot midday sun and drying winds. Some terraces are suitable but usually a partially enclosed breezeway or porch is preferable.

While most of the plants that have served throughout the winter are benefited by a summer outdoors, it is not simply a case of putting them out
and letting it go at that—there are certain preliminaries and precautions to
be observed.

First look over the entire stock with an unprejudiced eye. Discard any
that you think are too far gone to recover and any whose ornamental quality,
even when healthy, is of dubious value and which have no compensating
features of interest to make it worthwhile to retain them. (Personally, I would
place in this category spider-plant *(Chlorophytum)*, tree aloe, and several
others whose only claim to consideration is their ability to thrive as house
plants.)

Then decide whether any plants need repotting in larger pots—because
they *should* be kept in pots of adequate size. Do not plant them out where
their roots can run freely in the garden soil. If this is done they are likely
to grow with such abandon that it will be impossible to get them back into
pots of reasonable size in the fall without ruthlessly chopping off the major
portion of the root system, which is likely to set them back so far that
they will never again be satisfactory as house plants. Poinsettias, especially,
are rampant growers when planted out, and as they drop their leaves on
the slightest provocation, they are likely to look like ruinous wrecks a week
or less after they are brought indoors.

Any pruning of shrubby plants that may be necessary to promote symmetry
or to achieve a reduction in size should be done before eviction proceedings
are started. In some cases it is desirable to do the cutting back a few weeks

*In putting house plants outdoors for the summer, take care to provide them
with congenial conditions. Cacti and most succulents like full sun, ferns and
most foliage plants, shade; the rest prefer varying degrees of sun. Exposure
at first to outdoor light should be gradual or the plant's leaves are bound
to be injured. If pots are to be sunk in the ground, keep pot rims slightly
above soil level and put in a layer of pebbles or broken crocks at the bottom
of the hole to prevent roots from reaching soil.*

*It's a good idea to spray all plants with a general-purpose insecticide before bringing them indoors at summer's end.*

ahead of the time when it becomes safe to set them outdoors. The flowering shoots of hydrangea, for example, should be cut back to the second pair of leaves as soon as the flowers have faded so that the new shoots have time to grow and ripen before the plants are brought in during early winter; any azalea shoots that are greatly outstripping their neighbors should be checked by pinching out their tips.

Hunt down any existing insect pests before putting the plants in their summer quarters. It is possible at this time to lay the pots on their sides and squirt water or an insecticide on the undersides of the leaves, making it much easier to get at the beasts now than after the pots are plunged in earth.

## LOCATION

Sometimes it is possible to provide an outdoor bed for house plants in a location, sheltered from violent winds, that affords the variety of conditions desirable for the different kinds—shade for palms, ferns and foliage plants in general; partial shade for azaleas, Christmas cactus, and orchid cactus; and full sun for desert plants (cacti and succulents), amaryllis, and geraniums. Such a spot can often be found in the vicinity of a high-headed tree or shrub with foliage that is not too dense or on a terrace or patio that is convenient to the house. In other gardens it may be necessary to spot the plants here and there in the flower or shrub borders, but in general it is better to group them together for convenience of care. A neighbor summers her plants on the rail/of a north porch by embedding the pots in peat moss contained in window boxes. It is desirable to provide some such anchorage as this to prevent the pots from being blown over by high winds, and the peat moss, incidentally, helps to keep the soil moist. In a situation such as this the plants are not exposed directly to the sun but get plenty of light from skyshine.

Remember that the light is much more intense outdoors than it is in the house, and even the sun lovers should be accustomed to it gradually by shading them for a week or so; otherwise they are bound to sunburn. Those that are fully in the open can be shaded by throwing squares of cheesecloth over them for a week or two or by rigging up a screen made by nailing laths an inch apart on a frame of furring strips. The plants that are in the dappled shade cast by the leaves of trees or shrubs will probably need no extra attention.

To lessen the need for watering and make it possible for the owner to go on a summer vacation, the pots should be buried to their rims in soil; or, if a special bed is provided, in peat moss or sand. The bases of the pots should rest on a 2- or 3-inch layer of pebbles to provide free drainage, to discourage roots from emerging through the drainage hole, and to repel earthworms.

House plants cannot be entirely forgotten in summer. Although they can to some extent take care of themselves when their pots are plunged to the rim in soil out of doors, if they are neglected the results may be disastrous, particularly if watering is not taken care of during a dry spell or insects and other pests are allowed to obtain a foothold.

Spraying plants with water from the hose is one of the best prophylactic measures against insect pests and those irritating mites commonly known as red spiders. To be effective, however, the water must be applied in a spray with considerable force and directed particularly toward the undersides of the leaves and to the leaf axils where pests are likely to congregate. In order to kill two birds with one stone, so to speak, and to avoid giving the plants more water than is good for them, the spraying should be done when the soil is on the dry side.

Early morning is a good time to apply the spray, on the general principle that it is undesirable to wet the leaves when the temperature is falling. A thorough weekly spraying with plain water is usually all that is required, but if mealybugs gain a foothold it may be necessary to use a good contact spray diluted according to directions. Plant lice also will succumb to this spray, or they may be killed by hitting them with a strong soap solution— 2 ounces of soap flakes or powder to 1 gallon of water. If red spiders are abundant, dusting the foliage lightly with dusting sulphur, plus the weekly spraying with water, should control them adequately. White flies may become troublesome, especially if you have fuchsias, but an aerosol containing res-methrin gives reliable control.

The normal summer rainfall will reduce the need for watering, and most of the house plants will come through in fairly satisfactory shape if they take potluck with the rest of the plants in the garden (which ordinarily are watered with hose or sprinkler whenever a prolonged dry spell is experienced). Better results, however, may be expected if they are given a little closer attention and watered whenever they need it, for after all, their roots are confined and cannot range deeply in search of moisture as can those of plants that are unrestricted.

It may be desirable to provide additional soil fertility for actively growing plants during the vacation period. This can be done by steeping a bag of dried manure in water, diluting the liquor to the color of pale amber and watering them with this, when the soil is moist, once every 4 or 5 weeks. Or liquid commercial or fish fertilizer may be used (see Chapter 7).

While light shade is preferable for most of our house plants during the summer months, we must take care that it doesn't become too dense for their welfare. If shade is provided by overhanging trees or shrubs, a little selective snipping with pruning shears may be necessary to ensure that it does not become too much of a good thing.

Pruning the plants themselves during the summer is not likely to be an onerous job; all that is necessary, usually, is to keep an eye on those of a shrubby nature and pinch out the tips of shoots that are growing wildly and spoiling their symmetry. Such pinching back will make the plants more compact. Flower buds should be removed from young plants of geranium, heliotrope, et cetera, if they are expected to bloom during the winter.

It is particularly important to give good cultural conditions during summer to winter-flowering bulbous plants of the amaryllis type. Unfortunately all too many gardeners lose their interest in them as soon as the flowers have faded in late winter or early spring. Forgetting, or not knowing, that the leaves that follow the flowers are responsible for building up the bulb to sufficient size and strength to produce another flower stalk the following spring, some of us dump it in an out-of-the-way corner and either neglect to water it at all or remember it only spasmodically. It is far more essential to be careful in watering, fertilizing, and providing abundant light during the time that the leaves are active than it is during the short period when the flower stalk is being produced. Therefore, those who have the welfare of their amaryllis at heart will, when the plants are placed outdoors for the summer, remove the loose, worn-out topsoil and replace it with a mixture of ⅔ rich loam, ⅓ rotted or dried manure or compost, and bone meal or superphosphate at the rate of a teaspoonful for each plant. Water them during droughty periods, bring them indoors in the fall, and then keep the soil almost dust dry until they start growth in late winter.

## IN THEY COME!

Vacation time for house plants is over in most northern sections right after Labor Day. It is important to get them under cover before they are exposed to equinoctial storms, for gales can play havoc with tender foliage. Exceptions include cymbidium orchids and Thanksgiving and Christmas cacti which need cool fall nights to form buds. (Poinsettias and large foliage plants are particularly susceptible in this respect.) Perhaps the most potent single factor in making plants miserable in the home is the dryness of the air. Therefore, if we bring them into the house before it is necessary to use artificial heat for our own comfort, they are enabled to adapt themselves to a changed mode of living without having to endure the additional discomfort of heat without humidity.

The roots should not be injured or disturbed any more than is necessary. There will be no difficulty about this if the advice to leave the plants in their pots with a substratum of drainage material is followed, and if they are turned occasionally to remind the roots to stay in the pot where they belong.

Young plants started from cuttings will not be too difficult to handle even though they are planted in the soil rather than in pots, because their root systems will be small enough to be dug up intact. But if large plants were turned out of their pots in spring and planted directly in the ground, you may have a problem. In this last case either an excessively large container must be used to accommodate all the roots or the root system must be drastically reduced with resultant injury to the top of the plant because of the inability of the roots to supply sufficient moisture to the leaves. In such situations it is better to dig up the plants in late summer, pot them in containers large enough to accommodate most of the roots, and reduce the top if it can be done without spoiling the shape of the plant. Then stand the pots in a shady situation outdoors for two or three weeks before bringing them into the house. During this period the tops should be sprayed with clear water two or three times a day.

If the calla-lilies were planted out to carry on in the flower border during the summer, they should be dug up and potted. Give them a thorough soaking and then gradually reduce the supply of water until the soil is completely dry. Keep them this way for three months to give them a complete rest before starting them into growth indoors. Easter and other true lilies, which were kept watered after the fading of the flowers and planted out when danger of frost was over, may bloom again in the fall but will not be suitable for further growth indoors. Leave them where they are and mulch heavily with leaves; if the winter is not too severe, they may come up again the following spring.

Before bringing the plants indoors, the outsides of all pots should be cleaned by scrubbing them with a brush and water. If the plants are still actively growing, the topsoil should be removed down to the roots and replaced with a mixture of ⅔ garden soil and ⅓ thoroughly rotted or dried manure or rich compost plus bone meal or superphosphate at the rate of a teaspoonful to each 6-inch pot.

It will eliminate a great deal of trouble and contribute to the welfare of the plants in the days to come if they are thoroughly cleaned of any insect pests before they are brought into the house. You can spray insecticides and slosh water around out of doors with a freedom that would not be tolerated in the house, where damage to furnishings is often a prime consideration. Therefore, better look your plants over carefully, and if there are any signs of aphids, mealybugs, white flies, or red spider mites, get after them right away. (See Chapter 16.)

It is a good plan to become hard-boiled at moving time and consign to the compost pile all those plants that because of ill-health are no longer decorative. If they did not recover during their vacation outdoors, they are not likely to improve when brought inside. Those that are retained should be given locations near windows, sunny or shady according to their preferences, and be accorded routine daily care.

# CHAPTER 15

# *Propagation*

GOOD GARDENING, both indoors and out, always involves keeping an eye on the future, which explains why it is an excellent idea to look over the house plants critically from time to time to decide whether anything needs to be done to make them more presentable and useful. Perhaps the rubber plant has lost its symmetry or has grown too large for its quarters. The dracaena may be hitting the ceiling (or almost) and the dieffenbachia looking as leggy as a young colt. These faults can be corrected by air-layering.

The strong-growing climbing members of the Jack-in-the-pulpit family *(Syngonium, Philodendron, Monstera),* after a few seasons of growth in the home, may be bare below and reaching up into the air above the supports; the geraniums and Boston fern may be getting far too large; so, remembering that juvenility rather than senility is an asset so far as house plants are concerned, we make preparations to start new plants by means of cuttings.

Asparagus-fern *(Asparagus densiflorus* 'Sprengeri') is a useful house plant, but it is also a voracious feeder and, after a while, unless potted annually into larger and larger pots, its "leaves" become yellowish and unattractive. Young plants of this, in common with many other house plants, can be more effectively raised from seeds than from cutting or layers. All these operations involve some form of plant propagation.

An operation of absorbing interest, plant propagation at home not only affords us an opportunity to correct the faults of many of our plants but also gives us a chance to increase our stock of special favorites and raise new plants in an environment to which they are already accustomed. The use of fluorescent lighting is an aid in propagation, since areas that were formerly too dark for successful growth of seedlings and cuttings can be made into "nurseries," leaving the best natural-lighted spaces free for mature plants or those ready for display.

## EQUIPMENT

Fortunately very little is needed in the way of equipment, and much of it is probably already in the house. It may consist of nothing more than sand and peat moss, flowerpots, small seed flats made from milk cartons (these fit well on narrow window sills if you don't have a fluorescent light setup) or those accumulated from the produce departments of supermarkets (these molded trays, sometimes known as "market paks," are 7½ by 5½ inches and can also be purchased at garden centers or from mail-order seed houses) and clear plastic bags used for food storage. The plastic bags used by cleaners are handy for enclosing larger flats used for cuttings or seeds. Or if the terrarium is not working, it can be pressed into service as a propagating case. Or such a case can be made from a wood flat: Make a curved framework of wire (two strands cut from a straightened coat hanger will serve if nothing better is at hand) and enclose with plastic. Molded plastic bread or shoe boxes can also be converted into propagating cases. Of course you can buy specially designed propagating cases but they will be more costly.

Optional supplies that are not absolutely necessary but that can be useful and time-saving include bags of vermiculite or perlite, or a soil-less mix (see Chapter 9), a heating cable (for gentle heat for a flat in a cool room or window), the "one-step" peat pellets that magically become small pots when soaked in water.

If there is no room in the house for your propagation experiments, they can be carried on outdoors at a suitable season in a cold frame. Or cuttings can be inserted in sandy soil in a shaded spot and covered with a preserving or discarded food jar. Such subjects as geraniums, Christmas and orchid cacti can be rooted without any covering.

Actually nothing is needed in the way of equipment for the propagation of house plants that is not already included in the regular supplies of anyone at all interested in plants.

## AIR-LAYERING

Air-layering, mossing, or, if you want a fancy name, *marcottage,* are terms applied to the method whereby roots are produced on shoots while they are still attached to the parent plant. When this is done, a rooted plant of considerable size and vigor can be produced in a comparatively short time without the loss of leaves that would ensue if the shoot were treated as a cutting. While air-layering can be done at any time, roots seem to be emitted more freely in the spring. In any case it is preferable to carry out the operation

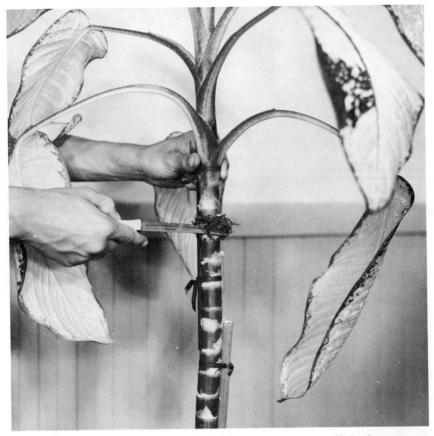

*Air-layering a dieffenbachia (dumb cane): Insert moist unmilled sphagnum moss in cut.*

when the plants are indoors because there is less likelihood that the moss in which the roots are produced will be allowed to become dry, although enclosing the moss in plastic reduces this danger.

The operation is a simple one, consisting merely of cutting a notch, extending one third of the way into the stem at the point where it is desired to have the roots form. In the case of a rubber plant this would be from 9 to 15 inches below the growing tip; in dracaena and dieffenbachia, just below the lowermost leaf; and the same goes for monstera and strong-growing philodendrons, except that, because there is a limit to the size of the portion that can be successfully layered, the cut should not be more than 2 feet from the tip. The wound should be wrapped with a large double handful of wet moss, preferably unmilled sphagnum moss, which can be obtained from garden centers or mail-order sources, tied firmly in place. The moss must be kept constantly moist, so it is desirable to cover it with polyethylene (a food-storage plastic bag serves well after being slit) to prevent undue loss of water by evaporation. An opening must be left at the top so that additional water can be applied to the moss as needed.

*Add additional moist moss around cut.*

*Moss is enclosed in plastic which is fastened with wire ties, here having their ends cut off for neatness.*

In about eight weeks (sometimes longer) the moss should be filled with roots, at which time the layer may be cut off and potted up in the usual way without, however, disturbing the moss surrounding the roots. The old plants are then thrown away; or, in the cases of dieffenbachia and dracaena, the stub left behind can be used for propagating purposes, if additional plants are needed, by cutting it into lengths of 2 to 3 inches. These pieces should be partly buried, horizontally, in a flat box of moist sand or sand and peat moss and kept, if possible, in a temperature between 70° and 80° F. A propagating case or plastic-covered box will provide ideal growing conditions. In the course of time a young plant will be produced. The thick fleshy stems of Chinese evergreen and monstera can be similarly treated. The essential point is to make sure that a growth bud is included in each specimen. This can be done by making sure that each piece contains a leaf scar.

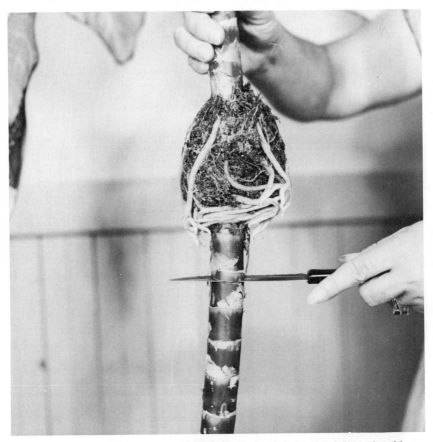

*Several weeks later roots have formed, and after being severed from the old stem, the new plant can be potted.*

## CUTTINGS

Cuttings of most plants can be rooted with greater assurance of success if the air around them is saturated with moisture. This limits loss of water from the leaves by transpiration and enables them to carry on until enough roots are formed to supply their needs. The saturated atmosphere is provided by putting the cuttings in a tight propagating case, either purchased or made at home, as described above; in a terrarium or a converted aquarium; or by covering them with glass tumblers or something similar. Any of these will retain the moisture evaporated from the leaves and the wet rooting medium instead of allowing it to become dispersed in the surrounding air. (It is rarely necessary to water the rooting medium again in these enclosed cases.)

ROOTING MEDIA: The cuttings may be inserted in soil suited to the plant, with a layer of sand on top (as described later); in sharp, gritty sand; in a 50-50 mixture of peat moss and sand, which perhaps, is most generally useful for the majority of plants; or in perlite, a silica derivative that can be obtained

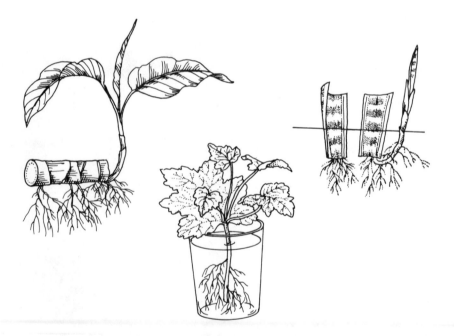

*Rooted cuttings: A rooted stem cutting of dieffenbachia (top left) after being removed from propagating flat. Chinese evergreen and monstera can be increased in similar manner. Leaf section cuttings of sansevieria (top right) are made about 4 inches long and inserted half their length in the rooting medium. Leaf of pickaback plant* (Tolmiea menziesii) *(bottom) rooting in water. New plant is developing from base of leaf blade.*

*Stem cuttings: Tip cutting of philodendron (top left) shows roots at the joints even before it is put in rooting medium. Impatiens (top right) cutting ready for insertion. It and wandering Jew (bottom left) root quickly from tip cuttings. An easily contrived propagating case (bottom right) is made by stretching a plastic bag over a bent wire in a pot.*

at garden centers (use it alone or mix with peat moss, soil, or sand). The soil-less mixes, some of which contain perlite, can also be used for cuttings, either alone or mixed with sand. (Their only drawback is that they are so efficient at retaining moisture that there is a danger of saturation which may rot the cuttings.)

Whatever the medium used, it should be packed firmly in the container because it is most important to bring the bases of the cuttings in close contact with it. Stem cuttings are inserted by making a hole (1, 2, or 3 inches deep, depending on the size of the cutting) with a dibber (small stick or pencil), the blunted point of which should be at least equal in size to the base of the cutting. When inserting the cutting, make sure the base touches the bottom of the hole and then pack the sand or medium closely around it with the dibber. After all the cuttings have been set, give a thorough soaking with water to help settle the sand around them.

FUTURE CARE: Virtually no watering will be needed in a closed container because no moisture is lost to the outside air, but keep an eye on the rooting medium anyway and add water but only if it begins to approach dryness.

While the cuttings of some plants can get along satisfactorily without any ventilation, it is a good plan to remove the covering for about ten minutes every morning and wipe away the condensed moisture on the glass or plastic to prevent supersaturation. If any evidence of mildew or decay shows up, remove affected leaves and ventilate more freely. Any dead or fallen leaves should be promptly removed.

Except when they are set in soil, the cuttings should be removed as soon as they have roots 1 or 2 inches long and potted up in a soil mixture suited to them but containing a little more sand than usual. (See Chapter 6.) This is to avoid their becoming stunted from lack of nutrients. (Most of the soil-less mixes contain some fertilizer which will last for a few weeks or so.) Such lack may retard their growth even if they are planted in fertile soil as soon as the condition is noticed. While it is important to pot up the cuttings as soon as they have roots 1 or 2 inches long, you should not dig them up every day to see if they have reached this stage! When you think the time has arrived when they should have roots, give one or two of the cuttings a gentle tug—if they do not come up, they probably have roots, which can be determined by carefully digging them up with a stout-bladed kitchen knife. If they have no roots or if the roots are not long enough, put them back immediately, not forgetting to make the medium firm around them. The time needed for rooting varies greatly according to the subject. Coleus and wandering Jew may be sufficiently rooted in two or three weeks; shrubby plants ordinarily take much longer.

The best time to make and insert the cuttings varies somewhat with the subject; in general they are most likely to be successful between spring and fall, provided young but not sappy shoots are available. Consult the table at the end of Chapter 17 for special cases.

When potting up the cuttings, use flowerpots large enough to contain the roots without crowding them but *no larger.* Use the soil mixture recommended for cuttings in Chapter 6 and the potting technique described for cuttings in Chapter 8. Water them thoroughly and keep somewhat shaded from direct sun, although such plants can be placed at once under fluorescent lights without harm resulting. Follow this procedure until they begin to form new roots, which will be in about two weeks, then give them the aspect suited to their needs. Spraying them daily with clear water during the time they are getting settled in their new pots helps them to recover from the shock of transplanting.

Many plants readily form roots from cuttings placed in jars of water. These include English ivy, wandering Jew, Chinese evergreen, oleander, pandanus, and pineapple. Special care must be taken to avoid bunching the roots of plants treated in this way when potting them in soil.

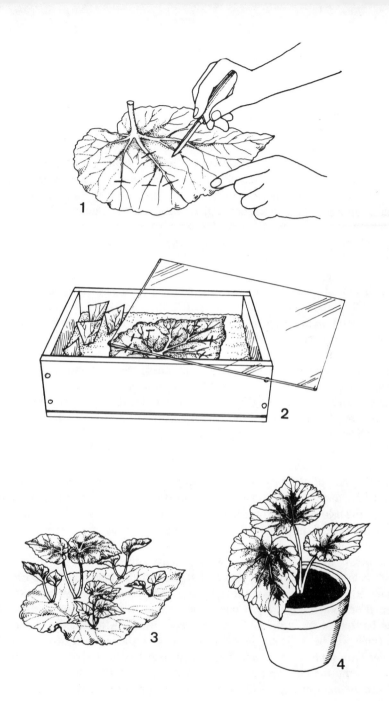

*Propagation of rex begonias from leaves: 1. Turn leaf upside down and cut through veins. 2. Place leaf right side up in a propagating flat in sand and peat moss. Triangular sections of leaves containing veins can also be inserted in upright position, as shown. 3. Young plants appear where veins were cut. 4. Young plant after being potted.*

One of the commonest complaints regarding pandanus as a house plant is that if it grows, it quickly gets too large for the window space. If your plant is approaching this stage, make ready to discard the old plant by rooting one or more of the suckers or offsets that grow at its base. These should be removed when their leaves are 6 to 8 inches long. Hold the shoot near its attachment with thumb and finger and press down. It usually comes free quite easily, and you may find that one or two roots have already started. If it does not readily part from its parent, help matters along by pushing a sharp knife or wood chisel between its base and the trunk.

The next step is to draw the leaves together in one hand and cut the tips off with a sharp knife or scissors about 4 inches from the base. The main object of this is to make it possible to cover the entire cutting with a plastic bag after the base has been inserted 1 inch deep in sandy soil in a 4-inch pot. If a larger bag is available, or if you have a propagating case that will contain the leaves entirely, it is not necessary to cut them back. If you don't want to go to all this trouble, just put the base of the cutting in a jar of water!

Among the easiest house plants to root are coleus, wandering Jew, impatiens, ivy, philodendron, and geranium. These can be handled by inserting them in sand, but they are so amiable that some of the steps can be eliminated and the cuttings rooted in the pots in which they are to grow by the following procedure: A flower pot should be prepared by putting in a ½-inch layer of pebbles or flower pot chips for drainage. Then fill it to within ½ inch of the rim with a mixture of 2 parts each of sifted soil and leaf mold and 1 part sand. Press down with fingers, make the surface level, and cover with ¼ inch of clean sand. As the cuttings are inserted, a small amount of sand falls to the bottom of the hole and provides a well-aerated cushion on which the base of the cutting rests—air is necessary for root formation. Preferably the tips of the shoots should be used, 3 to 4 inches long in the case of impatiens and wandering Jew and 8 to 10 inches long for ivy and philodendron. The basal cut should be made with a sharp knife or razor blade, about ¼ inch below the junction of leaf and stem, and the lowermost leaf or leaves removed. Make a hole in the soil or growing medium with an unpointed pencil or something similar, insert the cutting so that its base is pressed on the bottom of the hole, and pack the soil firmly. After all the cuttings are in (nine will be sufficient in a 6-inch pot) give the soil a thorough soaking, cover with a plastic bag, and put in a shaded but light spot until rooted, at which time the covering can be removed and, after a few days, the plants placed in natural light sufficiently intense for their needs. Or place them under fluorescent lights. If small covers are used, put fewer cuttings in small containers to correspond. Geraniums do not need any cover other than something such as cheesecloth or newspaper to shade them from bright sunshine. Avoid sappy shoots, using none but those with firm wood. Cuttings of nephthytis, strong-growing philodendrons, and monstera may be up to a foot in length. Obviously these cannot be accommodated under a tumbler or plastic bag—they need the room afforded by a propagating case. As a matter of fact, if you are planning to raise any considerable number of plants from cuttings, it is far more convenient to do so in a propagating case than it is to bother with numerous individual containers.

LEAF CUTTINGS: Some plants root with great facility from leaf cuttings; for example, pickaback plant, peperomia, African-violet, streptocarpus, gloxinia, snake plant, and rex begonia. In the case of the pickaback plant, cut off mature leaves with about 2 inches of leafstalk and insert in the rooting medium so that the blade of the leaf is touching the surface. This plant will also quickly root if the leafstalk is placed in a small jar of water with the blade barely touching the surface. With peperomia, gloxinia, and African-violet the procedure is much the same except that it is not necessary for the leaf blade to touch the surface, because the new plants are formed at the base of the leafstalk. The leaves of some plants (see rex begonia p. 156) also root without any leaf stem or petiole. They include African-violet, hoya, peperomia, kalanchoe, sedum, and crassula.

With snake plant the usual way is to cut the leaves into lengths of about 4 inches and, keeping them right side up, insert them for about half their length in the rooting medium. An interesting thing about this method is

*Pot-in-pot (or "Forsyth" cutting pot) for propagation: The center pot's drainage hole is plugged with a cork; water gradually seeps out to keep rooting medium moist. Cuttings are of crown-of-thorns (Euphorbia milii splendens).*

that the striped leaves of the parent are not reproduced in the progeny. If you want to retain the longitudinal stripe, the plants must be propagated by division of the rhizome or main root "crown." Except for the pickaback plant, which will root with facility even though uncovered, it is desirable to treat all these as described for stem cuttings.

There are two ways in which rex begonias may be handled—one involves using an entire leaf; the other, pieces of the leaf. Proceed by obtaining a box about 9 inches square and 5 inches deep (or use one of the plastic propagating frames sold at garden centers or by mail-order houses). Make two or three ½-inch holes in the bottom for drainage, put in a layer of peat moss, then fill it to within 2 inches of the top with sand. A 50-50 mixture of peat moss and sand is sometimes used. (This suffices also for stem cuttings of dieffenbachia, et cetera.) If you have a propagating case or terrarium not fully occupied, it can be used instead.

In the spring choose a mature but not a fading leaf and cut it off with about 1 inch of leafstalk attached. Turn it upside down on the table and with a sharp knife cut through all the main veins just below the place where they divide. Turn it right side up, make a hole in the sand to receive the stalk, and then place the leaf so that it is lying flat on the sand. Cover the box with a pane of glass or plastic and wait until plantlets grow from the leaf. The plantlets, if dug up and potted, will grow along to make nice specimens for next winter. The other method of dealing with rex begonia is to

*This dwarf gloxinia* (Sinningia *hybrid*) *has just finished flowering. The older growth (right) can be cut off and discarded or the older leaves can be rooted to obtain more plants. The new growth from the tuber (left) will soon produce another crown, ready to flower. After the older growth is cut off, the tuber can be repotted in a slightly larger (1–2-inch) pot.*

*An African-violet prepared for division by cutting off the old, yellowing leaves.*

*These individual plantlets came from a single clump of African-violet —itself grown from a single leaf—and will be placed in 2½-inch pots.*

cut the leaf into triangular pieces, 2 or 3 inches high, each containing a good-size vein. The end nearer the vein should be inserted to a depth of ½ inch in a plastic-tumbler-covered pot, a propagating case, or a box similar to that just described.

Several ferns (*Asplenium bulbiferum* as an example) develop plantlets on their fronds. These may be detached and potted when they have two or three leaves; or the frond may be laid on moist sand and the plantlets allowed to grow there for a while by the method described for entire leaves of rex begonia.

ROOTING CUTTINGS OUTDOORS: If you are cramped for room indoors, it is good to know that cuttings of many varieties of house plants can be successfully rooted outdoors. A shaded cold frame is excellent for the purpose. The cuttings may be inserted in a suitable medium contained in pots or flats or directly in the soil of the cold frame if it is sufficiently porous. A cold frame is very useful for handling those cuttings that are too large to be accommodated in the indoor propagating case.

If your garden does not boast of a cold frame (by the way, a very useful adjunct for many gardening operations), the cuttings can be inserted in a shaded spot in soil made porous, if necessary, by mixing sand with it. The cuttings can be covered with preserving jars or something similar; or, in the case of geraniums and cacti, merely shaded from sunshine. Or convert an ordinary wooden flat into a propagating case, as described above.

Rooting may be accelerated by using one of the root-inducing chemicals, and you may be interested in experimenting with them. They are obtainable from garden centers with directions for use. It must be remembered, however, that these chemicals are not a substitute for good gardening, and the requirements of suitable cutting material, care in making the cuts, proper environment, et cetera, must be fully met.


## GROUND-LAYERING

Some plants produce runners very much like those of the strawberry, which, when properly treated, will make excellent vigorous youngsters to carry on the family line. Examples of runner-forming house plants are strawberry-geranium, or mother-of-thousands *(Saxifraga stolonifera);* Boston ferns; that plant with striped leaves known to many as spiderplant *(Chlorophytum)* which increases by means of plantlets produced on the ends of its flower stalks. Two others that produce runners are episcia (flame-violet) and neomarica.

One way of handling these runner makers is to fill a 3- or 4-inch flowerpot with a mixture of half loam and half leaf mold or peat moss, with a little sand if the loam is sticky, and then pin the runner with a hairpin in the center of the pot of soil. As soon as roots have formed, the runner can be severed from the parent plant to lead an independent existence.

Another method, excellent in the case of Boston ferns, is to plant the pot outdoors in the spring, dig up the soil around it, and mix in a 3-inch layer of sifted leaf mold or peat moss and sand in which the runners will root. The runners, by the way, are those fuzzy, stringlike growths that originate in profusion around the base of the Boston fern. (Many beginners are bothered by them, not knowing whether they should be cut off or left to grow. If they seem to you to make the plant look untidy, they can be cut off unless they are needed for propagation.) When the runners have made two or three leaves, they should be dug up, potted in 3-inch pots, and kept in a shaded spot (preferably in a cold frame) and well watered until they are established. You will find, in all probability, that these young plants are more satisfactory for your purpose; and, if the old plant is scale-ridden, they afford an excellent means of bypassing this pest.

## DIVISION

The habit of growth of some plants is such that division constitutes the proper method of propagating them. The best time to do this is when new growth is just beginning—usually during late winter. African-violet *(Saintpaulia), Aspidistra,* and *Pteris* are good examples to illustrate the methods of division.

If you carefully examine an African-violet that has been growing in the house all winter, you will see, in all probability, that it has split up into several crowns, each producing a tuft of foliage. If at this time flowering is on the wane, it is a good plan to turn the plant out of its pot, gently loosen the soil ball, pull the crowns apart without any more root injury than is absolutely necessary, and pot them up in individual pots. These separated plants are likely to develop into far better flowering plants than the old plant potted on without division. The African-violet is one of those plants that grow better in a rather loose soil, so don't press it down too firmly.

*Aspidistra,* or cast-iron plant, will remain in good health year after year if progressively repotted into a pot of larger size. This is all very well, but after a time it becomes a veritable white elephant capable of being moved by no one but the strong man from the circus. Therefore, lest it become unwieldy, the aspidistra should be divided every three or four years at a

Begonia *'Cleopatra' leaf sprouts new plantlets—soon to grow into an attractive clump.*

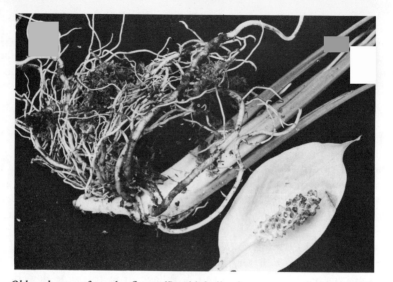

*Older clumps of spathe flower* (Spathiphyllum) *are propagated by division. A cut "flower" (actually a whitish spathe, the true flowers being arranged along a club-shaped spadix) is shown at right.*

time when the new leaves can be seen as tiny pointed spears at the base of the plant. Turn the plant out of its pot and slam it on a bench to loosen the soil. With a knife cut through the rhizomes (horizontal stems) at the points selected for division and pull off sections containing from three to nine leaves, according to the size of plant you wish to retain. Some ruthless gardeners merely chop the plant into sections of the required size with a spade, but considerable wreckage is likely to result unless the job is skillfully done. If the operation is purely propagational, the smaller sizes are preferred; but if the objective is one or two larger plants of immediate good appearance, then use the nine-leaf divisions. Repot these in pots large enough to contain the roots without crowding and make the soil quite firm. The old leaves will tend to point every which way as a result of rhizome displacement. This can be corrected when potting by manipulation of the rhizomes—wedging them with soil so that the leaves are vertical; or by temporarily holding them upright with thin plant stakes.

The roots of *Pteris, Adiantum,* and other ferns grow into such dense, fibrous masses completely filling the pot that usually the best plan is to slice off first about 2 inches from the bottom of the root ball with a stout knife or a hatchet, and then with vertical cuts separate the remainder into pieces of the desired size. While this method destroys many roots, it is perhaps less harmful than to attempt to tease out the matted roots with the fingers. This, however, is done commercially when a large increase is sought and the stock plant is separated into individual crowns.

In all cases when division involving much root disturbance is practical, care must be taken to avoid overwatering during the period preceding the formation of new roots. Shade from bright sunshine must be given for a few weeks, and, if possible, a daily overhead spraying with clear water.

## PROPAGATION BY SEEDS

So far only "vegetative" methods of propagation have been discussed—that is, securing new plants by using some part of an existing plant other than seeds. Some house plants, such as *Asparagus densiflorus* 'Sprengeri,' *Cordyline indivisa, Kalanchoe blossfeldiana,* and certain cacti produce better plants or can be handled more conveniently if seeds are used.

The small fiber trays or flats mentioned earlier in this chapter, small flower pots, or bulb pans can be used to hold the medium in which the seeds are sown. They must be drained by putting in the bottom a half inch or so of broken flower pots, pebbles, or coarse cinders as described in Chapter 9.

The soil should be porous enough to allow water to pass through it freely and at the same time retentive enough to eliminate the need of frequent watering. A mixture of equal parts by bulk of loam, leaf mold, and sand fills these specifications.

The gardener is likely to be plagued by pre-emergence or post-emergence damping-off caused by various fungus organisms, especially when seedlings are raised indoors. If you have experienced trouble in the past, if your seeds failed to germinate, or if the seedlings decayed and toppled over at the ground line, it would be well to sterilize or partially sterilize the soil before planting.

For partial sterilization watering the soil with boiling water is usually effective. The soil mixture is passed through a ¼-inch or ½-inch sieve and the pots filled with it and prepared for sowing. They are then watered twice (to do a good job) with boiling water applied by means of a watering can with a fine sprinkler attached to the spout to avoid disturbing the surface. Or use the same applicator you use for misting foliage to raise the humidity. When the soil has cooled, the seeds may be scattered on the surface, pressed in with a tamper, and covered with dry sand.

*Five-month-old African-violet seedlings ready for 1½–2-inch pots.*

Another quite simple method for sterilizing soil is by means of the kitchen oven, following the same procedure as you would in baking a potato. Place the soil in baking pans and add a potato. When it is cooked through, the soil mixture should be sufficiently baked.

Another means of circumventing the damping-off organisms is to sow the seeds in sphagnum moss or in sharp sand, both of which must be watered with nutrient solution. Use one of the formulas in the section on soil-less culture (Chapter 10) diluted 1 part to 5 parts water until seedlings have made the first true leaf, then increase the concentration to 50-50; after a week or two, use at full strength.

By far the most convenient way to obtain sterilized soil today is to use one of the soil-less mixes, such as Jiffy Mix or Redi-Earth. However, remember they lose their sterilization if they are mixed with unsterilized soil. These mixes require much less water than most growing media, so care must be taken to avoid soggy rather than merely moist conditions.

FILLING THE POTS: The pots should be "crocked" (see Chapter 9) and the drainage covered with ¼ inch of moss or the rough material rejected

*Coffee "beans" (unroasted!) may take a month or more to germinate, holding the outer seed coat on new leaves for several weeks. Seedlings are good terrarium plants for a year or so if pinched to restrict growth.*

by the sieve when screening the soil. (It is unnecessary to screen the soil-less mixes.) Then fill the pots more than full of soil and strike off even with a piece of lath. If very fine seeds are to be sown—begonia, gloxinia—the top inch of soil should be passed through an ⅛-inch sieve. With a circular tamper (made from a ½-inch section of a branch about 2 inches in diameter screwed to a 3-inch length of broom handle) or a flat-bottomed tumbler, press the soil down so that it is about ½ inch from the pot rim. Put the labels in place close to the pot edge and sow the seeds thinly. Try to allow at least ⅛ inch between small seeds and ¼ inch between those of fair size. If this is done, there is less danger of damping-off. Gently press the seeds into the soil with a tamper.

After the seeds are sown, stand the pots in a baking or roasting pan containing about 2 inches of water and allow them to stay there until moisture shows on the surface. Very small seeds will need no soil covering, but the pots should be covered with a pane of glass or a plastic sheet or bag until the seeds begin to germinate, when it should immediately be removed or tilted to admit air. Larger seeds should be covered with sand or growing medium to a depth equal to twice their diameter. This can conveniently be accomplished by putting sand in the flour sifter and turning the handle to dispense a sufficient amount of sand. (Be careful to remove all grit from the sifter before making a pie.) Needless to say, all this work should be done in a place where there is no danger of spilled sand, soil, and water spoiling rugs or waxed floors.

The pots may be stood on a layer of pebbles in an empty terrarium or aquarium; or they may be put in a flat or shallow box with moist peat moss between them. Spray gently with water to settle the sand and shade with newspaper. If your seed containers must be kept in a cool room (below 65° F.), you may want to use a heating cable, which can be coiled beneath trays. Such cables are available from mail-order garden supply firms.

Keep close watch on the pots and water them whenever the soil shows signs of becoming dry. This can be done by partially immersing them in a pan of water or by overhead spraying, which must be done carefully to avoid disturbing the surface. As soon as the seeds germinate, move them to a light and more airy location but shade with newspaper or cheesecloth from bright sunshine for a few days, gradually reducing the amount of shade until they are fully exposed. Fluorescent lights are a tremendous aid in raising house plants—or all kinds of plants, for that matter—from seeds. No shifting of flats or pots is necessary as it is in a sunny window, but it is important to keep the seedlings close to the tubes. Lower the fixture, or use wood blocks or inverted flower pots to raise the seed containers to 4 to 6 inches beneath the tubes.

When the seedlings make their first true leaf (as distinguished from the initial or cotyledonary leaves) they should be pricked off (transplanted) 2 inches apart in flats or into small pots, thus giving them room in which to grow.

*In the small plastic box are sporlings of a staghorn fern species (Platycerium grande).* Larger plants are seen in the flats in the background.

Here are some of the house plants that can easily be raised from seeds:
*Asparagus densiflorus* 'Sprengeri' (emerald-feather); *A. setaceus,* asparagus-fern (use the cultivar 'Nanus'—it is better adapted to house culture). The seeds of citrus fruits, especially grapefruit, are useful for providing a pan of greenery if the seeds are planted about an inch apart. (Don't raise oranges, grapefruit, et cetera, from seeds if your objective is flowering or fruiting plants—they are too long-winded—buy plants.) *Cordyline indivisa* (blue dra-caena) is best raised from seeds, and the seedlings are useful for providing variety in fern dishes or miniature gardens. Seeds of all of these should be soaked overnight in lukewarm water just before sowing them. Cacti in great variety can be sown if you are interested in them. Almost every seedsman offers packets of mixed seeds, but if you want named kinds, you will probably have to go to a specialist. The soil mixture should be made very porous, which can be done by adding to the standard mixture ¼ part of old mortar or flower pot chips broken up to pass through a ¼-inch sieve.

Better plants of *Kalanchoe blossfeldiana* and black-eyed Susan vine *(Thunbergia alata)* are produced by raising them annually from seeds; and annuals such as marigold, and sweet-alyssum must, of course, be raised from seeds. Other house plants or pot plants for both indoor and patio decoration to grow from seeds include begonias, particularly wax *(Begonia semperflorens);* coffee plant *(Coffea arabica);* coleus; crossandra; cyclamen; geranium; many gesneriads, including gloxinia, miniature sinningias; impatiens, primroses such as *Primula obconica* and *P. malacoides.*

## RAISING FERNS FROM SPORES

Any clean container can be used. Suitable are flowerpots (squat or shallow pans, since a deep layer of the growing medium is unnecessary), plastic or glass food containers, or seed flats which should be disinfected with 1 part clorox to 9 parts of water and then rinsed in clear water. Add a layer of drainage material, about ½ inch deep, of pebbles, vermiculite, or crocks. The growing medium can be an equal mixture of peat moss and fine sand; 1 part humusy soil, 1 part peat moss, and 1 part fine sand; or the fine-textured commercial mixes that are recommended for African-violets. The mixture should be put through a ¼-inch mesh sieve and then pasteurized by having boiling water poured through it. Allow to drain and when it has cooled, place over the drainage material in a layer about 1 to 2 inches deep. The spores may then be sown.

Spores are produced in cases in lines or dots, usually on the underside of the frond. Sometimes they are formed along the margins of the frond, which seems to roll over. It is important to collect the spores at the right time, which is when the spore cases are beginning to split open. Examination with a magnifying glass may be necessary in some cases to determine this. (A few seed houses offer fern spores with directions for their planting.)

Two methods may be followed in sowing the spores: 1. Cut the spore-bearing frond into ½-inch pieces and lay them, spore side down, on the surface of the prepared soil in the seed pan. The spores will drift out and sow themselves. When the spores have been discharged, remove the portions of frond. 2. Or gather fronds bearing ripe spore cases and place them in paper bags or wrap in paper and keep in a warm, dry place. In a few days the dustlike spores will be shed and they can be scattered thinly on the surface of the soil.

Immediately after the spores have been sown, cover the seed pan with a pane of glass or stretch a sheet of plastic over it and stand it in a saucer, which must be kept constantly filled with water. Never attempt overhead watering until leaves are visible. Cover the seed pan with newspaper to keep out light.

When the spores germinate, they first form a flat, delicate plate of green tissue (the prothallium) on the underside of which the reproductive organs are formed. At this stage, the covering (not the glass) can be removed to admit some light (never sunlight). After fertilization is effected, the young plantlets begin to grow, and when this happens, the glass covering may be removed and the seed pan watered from overhead if more convenient.

# CHAPTER 16

# *House-plant Enemies*

I ALWAYS told my classes in house-plant culture, with tongue in cheek, that there was no excuse for the presence of pests on house plants. Actually there is a good deal of truth in the assertion. If plants are properly grown and not subjected to the hot, dry air that provides favorable conditions for an epidemic of red spider mites; if they are given prophylactic treatment by thoroughly spraying them at weekly intervals with plain water; if vigilance is exercised to avoid bringing infected plants in contact with healthy ones; and if a close watch is kept and measures taken to control disease and insects before they make much headway—then little trouble need be experienced.

## CONTROLLING DISEASES

Usually house plants are not much bothered by fungus diseases, presumably because the hot, dry air is more inimical to pathogenes than it is to higher plants. When leaf spots that seem to be of fungus origin are noticed, pick off the affected leaves immediately and discard them. If this does not stop the disease, or should the entire plant be affected, the best plan is to discard the plant and start afresh. Of course you can spray with a fungicide, hoping to prevent the spread of the disease. Bordeaux mixture is standard and easily obtainable but leaves a disfiguring residue and you may prefer to use ammonia-cal copper carbonate or one of the newer fungicides available in garden centers.

Mildew, which looks like a grayish-white powder on the leaves, can be checked by covering the plant with a thin film of dusting sulphur or a spray of benomyl, usually sold under the trade name of Benlate. Benomyl is one of the newer general-purpose fungicides and, being a systemic, is absorbed into the plant's entire system, where it acts on susceptible fungi.

Wilts and root rots are usually controlled by discarding affected plants; by modifying cultural practices to provide free ventilation; by thoroughly aerating the soil by making it porous; and by the avoidance of overwatering. (See the list at the end of this chapter.)

## FOLIAGE PROBLEMS

Yellowing of the foliage may be caused by insufficient nitrogen in the soil, to be rectified by repotting or feeding with a nitrogenous fertilizer; by over- or underwatering; by getting cold water on the leaves (in the case of African-violet); by too much sun; or, in the case of gardenia, by alkaline soil, which can be remedied by incorporating acid peat moss in the potting mixture or by watering occasionally with iron-sulphate solution. (See list.)

Unusual pallor of the leaves, especially when associated with abnormal lengthening of the stems, may be due to insufficient light. The remedy is obvious—a better-lighted position.

## INSECT PESTS

I was always a great believer in the Saturday morning bath as a means of keeping those plants that can stand it free from red spider mites and some other insect pests. But plants with fuzzy foliage (African-violets, achimenes, gloxinias and most other gesneriads, and some succulents) are catlike in objecting to water on their fur; some begonias, fine-leaved ferns, and any fragile plants are likely to suffer mechanical injury if sprayed with water forcibly enough to dislodge insects.

Usually the best way to spray house plants with water is to put them, or hold them on their sides, in the bathtub, shower, or sink and than direct water on *both* sides of the leaves and particularly in the angles formed by the leaf and stem, with the purpose of washing the insects down the drain.

In addition to the use of plain water, insects can be fought with insecticides of various kinds. House plants ordinarily are not bothered by leaf-eating insects, and if they do put in an appearance they are usually few in number so that they can be picked off by hand. If the plants are attacked by too many leaf-eaters, such as caterpillars, for manual control, the foliage can be sprayed or dusted with carbaryl (available as Sevin) according to directions.

Sucking insects are attacked with contact insecticides (sprays or dusts) which must be applied so as to hit the insects. A handy, nonpoisonous one that is effective against plant lice (aphids) is soap, such as Ivory Flakes, and water—1 to 2 ounces of flakes or powder to a gallon. Try the weaker solution first.

*One way to avoid infestations of red spider mites on dracaena is to sponge the foliage weekly with water.*

A more effective spray than the soap-and-water mixture results when a teaspoonful of 40 per cent nicotine sulphate (usually available as Black Leaf 40, and although less objectionable than some of the newer chemicals, it is also poisonous and must be used carefully) is added to a gallon of soapy water. Rotenone and other contact sprays can also be added to the basic soapy water solution and used in accordance with directions on the package or bottle.

These liquid insecticides can be used as dips rather than sprays. Of course a dip is only convenient when the plants are not too large. A plastic dishpan makes a satisfactory receptacle for this purpose, as does a discarded roasting pan. (Needless to say, any containers used for this purpose should be retired from kitchen or culinary duties, since the chemicals used in them are likely to be highly poisonous.)

Fill the pans with the insecticide, mixed according to directions on package or bottle. Then make a wad of newspaper and with it cover the soil of the pot to prevent it from spilling into the mixture, hold it in place with one hand, invert the plant, and gently swish it through the insecticide, making sure all plant parts are covered. It's wise to protect your own hands with plastic or rubber gloves. Lay the plant on its side to drain for a few hours out of the sun.

Incidentally, if you are so unlucky as to find African-violets infested with mites (see list), the dip method of control is an exception to the rule mentioned earlier about wetting furry-leaved plants. Mites, both cyclamen and broad, tend to gather in the crowns of African-violets, and the most efficient way to reach them is by submerging the plants in the dip bath. (Use tepid rather than cold water.)

When the plants are too large to be dipped, the insects can be sprayed with a hand sprayer or insecticide "bomb" or can whose contents are under pressure. Remember that most of the insects that concern us must be hit with the insecticide, so direct the spray to the locations where they usually congregate—the tips of the shoots, underside of leaves, and junction of leaf and stem. If using a pressurized can, observe the directions carefully and, above all, don't spray the plants too closely.

Always spray the plants thoroughly with clear water a few hours, or a day, after they have been treated.

Among the important insects affecting house plants are the following:

MEALYBUGS: There are several species of these ubiquitous pests, but it is not important to be able to distinguish among them. They are oval, varying in size from ⅙ to ¼ inch long, covered with a mealy, waxy material which sheds insecticides. They fall into two groups—long- and short-tailed. Those in the first group have four extra-long filaments at their rear ends; the others

*When in doubt, use a magnifying glass which will pick out the tiny red spider mites. The plant is* Dracaena surculosa (*formerly* D. godseffiana).

have bodies margined with leglike filaments of equal length. The short-tailed species lay eggs (300 to 600 of them!) in a cottony sack; the others give birth to living young. They attack almost every kind of plant, being especially partial to African-violet, fuchsia, and gardenia. The weekly spraying with water, properly done, helps to keep them down. Prompt action as soon as they are discovered is essential. When they are few in numbers, the egg masses can be removed with thumb and finger and the adults touched with a camel's-hair brush or cotton swab on a toothpick which has been dipped in alcohol. This last is probably the best method of dealing with them when they attack African-violets or when they shelter behind the spines of cacti.

SCALE INSECTS: These are related to mealybugs but differ considerably in appearance. They may be flattened or hemispherical; round, oval, or scurf-like; one species looks like a short, thin line made with a pen dipped in India ink. (Sometimes the spore cases on the fronds of certain ferns are mistaken for scale insects.) When mature they are immobile, and are covered with scalelike armor which usually resists insecticides at strengths not injurious to plants. They are vulnerable when they are young and running around, either to a water spray which knocks them off the plants, or to contact

*A frond of holly fern showing spores—not to be confused with scales.*

*Podocarpus is especially susceptible to scale infestations, here being attacked with a paint brush dipped in rubbing alcohol.*

insecticides such as malathion (but do not use this insecticide on ferns or begonias). Mature insects are usually best removed manually, using a softish brush, a rag, or a sponge wet with a mixture of the insecticide and soapy water. Or use the dip method described earlier. Be careful in the use of these methods, for the cuticle of some plants is easily marred by harsh treatment.

WHITE FLIES: These are tiny white flies that look like miniature moths; the nymphs congregate on the undersides of leaves. Fuchsia, lantana, and nicotiana are especially subject to attack. This is a particularly difficult pest to control because the adults fly off as soon as they are disturbed by spraying. The best remedy is to spray with resmethrin, a synthetic pyrethroid, usually available in pressurized cans. The spray must be repeated every four or five days until the infestation is cleaned up.

PLANT APHIDS: Known also as green-flies, black-flies, and lice, these insects are winged or wingless according to the stage of development. In common with some scale insects, they secrete a syrupy substance known as honeydew, which gives the leaves a varnished appearance and on which a black mold may grow, to the detriment of the appearance of the foliage. They are soft-bodied insects and usually succumb readily to contact insecticides; but it is very desirable to get rid of them when they first appear before they have a chance to cause much damage. Often their feeding causes the leaves to curl and wrinkle, making it much more difficult to reach them with a spray.

MITES: The most common mites are red spider mites. These are not true insects. They are minute—barely visible without the aid of a magnifying glass—and often the first observed indication of their presence is injury manifested by a speckled yellowing, browning, or graying of the leaves or stems (in the case of cacti). Examination of infested leaves with a hand lens is likely to disclose a silken web, crawling with eight-legged mites, up to $\frac{1}{60}$ of an inch long, red, green, yellow, or black in color. Hot, dry air favors their development; therefore, every effort should be made to humidify the air and keep the temperature at reasonable levels—below 70° F. A thorough spraying with water once a week is helpful. Once they have obtained a foothold, other measures must be taken. Badly infested plants, unless very valuable, should be discarded. If the leaves are large enough to wash with a wet soapy sponge, many of them can be removed by this means. Spraying with Kelthane or dipping the plants in a soapy water solution containing this insecticide is an effective control.

Other kinds of mites that may infest certain house plants are the cyclamen and broad mites. They are most common on African-violets, gloxinias and other relatives, and cyclamen. Unlike the red spider mites, these mites do not form the tiny webs that are visible to the naked eye, and you need a microscope, not a magnifying glass, to see these pests at all. However, their damage is readily apparent (see list). Fortunately Kelthane and other miticides give quite efficient control.

MISCELLANEOUS INSECTS: Tiny black flies may often be seen hovering around the plants. Harmless to plants and only mildly annoying to humans, they come from maggots in the organic matter in the soil. Watering the soil with nicotine, a teaspoonful to a gallon (no soap), will most likely kill the maggots; and spraying the adults with a contact spray will probably put them out of business. I have never tried it, never having been sufficiently bothered by them.

Often complaints are made concerning small white jumping insects, which appear either on the surface of the soil or in the water contained in the plant saucer. These are springtails, which are innocuous, living as they do on decaying organic matter. To get rid of them, try the measure suggested above for plant aphids.

EARTHWORMS: There are some who advocate the introduction of earthworms to flowerpots for their alleged beneficial effects on the soil. Personally, while I recognize their value as tillers of the soil in field and garden (they can be decidedly obnoxious when infesting a fine lawn, though), I have always regarded them as a minor nuisance when operating within the confines of a pot where they may disturb the plant roots and indirectly cause waterlogging by depositing their "casts" in the drainage. If your plants are not thriving as they should and there are worms in the pots, I would advise ejecting them by watering the soil with lime water; or, if acid-soil plants are affected, with mustard water made by mixing a teaspoonful of powdered mustard in a quart of water.

In the list that follows, you will find the major house plants and their pests and remedies.

## Battle Plans for Bugs and Blights

### AFRICAN-VIOLET
*(Saintpaulia)*

Mealybugs

Oval, white, soft, cottony insects which suck sap.
*Remove with soft brush dipped in alcohol; or spray with malathion; discard badly infested plants.*

Mites

Stunted, deformed leaves and flowers due to cyclamen mite; glassy leaves, to broad mite; yellowing, to red spider mite.
*Discard deformed plants; spray with or dip plants in Kelthane; or spray with a systemic such as Cygon or try the dry systemic granules added to the soil; space pots so leaves do not touch; wash hands with soap before touching healthy plants.*

Chlorosis

Irregular yellow mottling on leaves.
*Do not wet leaves; keep out of bright sun.*

### AMARYLLIS
*(Hippeastrum)*

Red fire disease

Red spots on leaves, flowers, and bulb scales; flower stalks and foliage bent and deformed.
*Remove and burn infected parts; spray with ferbam; discard badly infected bulbs. Make sure new bulbs are healthy.*

Bulb flies

Maggots of greater or lesser bulb fly eat out centers and destroy basal plate.
*Discard infested bulbs; or treat with hot water at 110° to 111.5° F. for four hours.*

Mealybugs

May infest bulb scales and leaf bases.
*Scrub off with nicotine sulphate and soap solution; spray with malathion or Cygon.*

### ASPIDISTRA

Leaf spots

White spots, brown margins on leaf blades, stalks; pale spots on leaves.
*Remove and burn infected leaves.*

Chlorosis

Yellow leaves, possibly due to too strong light.
*Try location out of direct sunshine.*

Fern scale

White male, brown female scales.
*See Ferns and Bromeliads.*

## AZALEA
### (Rhododendron)

Red spider mites

Leaves yellow, webby, mealy on underside.
*Grow at low temperature, high humidity; syringe foliage. Spray with Kelthane.*

Lace bugs

Leaves stippled whitish; brown spots underneath.
*Spray with nicotine sulphate and soap.*

Chlorosis

Yellowing from too alkaline soil; iron unavailable.
*Use plenty of acid peat in potting soil; sprinkle soil with Green-Garde, available at garden centers.*

## BEGONIA

Mealybugs

White, dusty bugs in axils of leaves and branches.
*Spray with nicotine-soap before blooming or syringe with pure water, or remove with toothpick swab dipped in alcohol.*

Aphids

Serious injury, from melon aphids and others, if numerous.
*Syringe with water, or spray with nicotine-soap solution; during blooming use rotenone, pyrethrum, or resmethrin.*

Leaf nematodes

Discolored russet areas in leaves, which curl up and drop.
*Keep plants well separated; avoid handling or wetting foliage; dip leaves in hot water (115° to 118° F.) for three minutes.*

Mites

*See African-violet.*

Blight

Grayish mold on leaves and flowers.
*Avoid syringing; remove infected parts.*

Leaf drop

Foliage loss from too heavy, wet soil, hot, dry air, or drafts.
*Use porous soil; cool room, high humidity. Do not overwater.*

## BROMELIADS

Scale

Some bromeliads are prone to scales, firm-shelled sucking insects that are mostly stationary.

*Wipe off with rag or sponge dipped in nicotine-soap or malathion solution; or spray with malathion or rotenone-pyrethrum, according to directions. Mild infestations can be picked off with cotton-tipped swabs dipped in alcohol. See Fern.*

## CACTI

Mealybugs

White, fuzzy insects at base of spines causing yellowing.

*Remove with pointed brush; try mist spray, nicotine sulphate, or pure water (plant on side); or spray with malathion; wash off later with water.*

Root mealybugs

Live in soil on outer roots; may kill plant.

*Remove from pot, wash off soil and insects; repot in clean soil.*

Scale

Grayish, circular, hard-shelled insects.

*Scrape off with soft brush, rag, or swab dipped in alcohol; or spray with malathion.*

Red spider mites

Mealy cobwebs over yellowish surface.

*Spray of water with plant on side or spray with Kelthane.*

Rot

Decay starting around wounds or depressed areas.

*Do not water from above or overwater; cut out infected parts.*

## CALLA-LILY
### (Zantedeschia)

Root rot

Leaves streaked, flowers malformed and brown.

*Destroy infected plants and soil.*

Soft rot

Base of stem and rhizomes decayed.

*Discard infected plants.*

Aphids

Occasionally numerous on leaves.

*Spray with nicotine-soap solution or malathion.*

## CITRUS

Scales
Various kinds of scales, especially the soft brown.
*See Ferns and Bromeliads.*

Mites
*See African-violet. Grow plants in a cool, airy atmosphere. Hot, dry locations invite infestation.*

White fly
Minute, white four-winged flies and pale-green oval nymphs. Plants turn yellow, wilt, eventually die if not controlled.
*Spray frequently with resmethrin in pressure can; older remedy is nicotine-soap solution. Always hit undersides of foliage.*

## COLEUS

Mealybugs
White cottony insects at leaf and branch axils.
*Spray with nicotine sulphate and soap or spray with or dip plants in malathion; wash off with water, or remove with cotton swab on toothpick dipped in alcohol.*

Black leg
Stalks black, water-soaked at base; plant wilts, may die.
*Destroy infected plants; use fresh soil for new cuttings.*

White fly
*See Citrus.*

## CRASSULA

Mealybugs
Neglected plants often covered with bits of white fluff.
*See Coleus.*

Mites
Leaves rusty brown, rough; finally die.
*See Cyclamen.*

## CYCLAMEN

Cyclamen mites
Leaves deformed, curled; blooms distorted; plant stunted due to cyclamen mites too small to see with naked eye.
*Spray with nicotine-soap solution or Kelthane; space so that leaves do not touch; dip small plants in Kelthane.*

Rot
Soft, slimy rot at crown; plant wilts.
*Water from below; do not wet crown.*

Yellowing

Yellowing and drooping after plant leaves grower.

*Keep in cool room or window (not over 60° F.) and place pot in saucer with an inch of water.*

## DIEFFENBACHIA

Leaf spots

Orange spots with bacterial ooze, or reddish-brown spots with decidedly darker borders; the first infection often entering through open wounds.

*Avoid syringing plants; space far apart; control mealybugs and avoid wounds.*

## DRACAENA

Red spider mites

Cause yellowing of leaves and general debility of infested plant.

*Sponge foliage weekly; spray with Kelthane.*

Leaf spots

Brown areas, yellow margins, black dots in center, or tip blight.

*Cut off and burn infected parts; keep foliage dry.*

## FERNS

Scales
  Soft brown
  Fern

Low, convex, reddish-brown scale.
Males white, conspicuous, females ocherbrown.

  Florida wax
  Hemispherical

Convex, oval scales.
Large, convex, brown scales on fronds and stem.

*Dip fronds in nicotine sulphate–soap solution or spray with pyrethrum-rotenone pressure can; rinse thoroughly with water three to four hours after treatment; keep plant out of sun temporarily; discard badly infested plants.*

Mealybugs

Long-tailed types sometimes on fronds.
*See Scales.*

Nematodes

Reddish to black bands from midrib to border of fronds caused by microscopic eelworms.

*Remove and burn infested leaves or plants.*

Florida fern caterpillar | Fronds stripped at night by green or black, white-striped caterpillars.
*Spray or dust with rotenone or pyrethrum.*

Anthracnose | Tips of Boston fern turn brown and shrivel.
*Keep foliage dry; remove infected leaves.*

Tip blight | Loss of color; ash-gray spots with purple margins.
*Same as above.*

Sooty mold | Dark fungus growing in honeydew secreted by scales and mealybugs.
*Control insects.*

## FUCHSIA

White flies | *See Citrus.*

Mealybugs | White, cottony insects often present in leaf axils which suck sap, causing yellowing and general debility of plant.
*Control as for white fly. See also African-violet.*

Sooty mold | Growing in white-fly honeydew.
*See Ferns.*

## GARDENIA

Chlorosis | Yellow leaves due to soil too alkaline, iron unavailable, too wet or too dry, too low humidity.
*Keep pH of soil around 5.6; temperature 62° F.; pot in sandy loam with 1/3 peat moss; if yellowing persists, water with ferrous sulphate (1 ounce to 4 gallons water) or Green Garde or Greenol Liquid Iron, following directions on container.*

Bud drop | Buds yellow and drop off just before opening; due to high temperature plus lack of sun.
*Cooler temperature in winter.*

Mealybugs | *See Coleus.*
White flies | *See Citrus.*
Sooty mold | *See Ferns.*

## GERANIUM
### (Pelargonium)

White flies | *See Citrus.*

Mites | Young leaves curled, spotted, look scorched.
*See Cyclamen.*

| | |
|---|---|
| Black leg stem rot | Cuttings rot at base, stems of older plants turn black. |
| Rust | Raised powderlike spots.<br>*Take cuttings only from healthy plants; use fresh or sterilized medium for rooting. Use Benlate.* |
| Blight | Gray mold over water-soaked areas in leaves and blossoms.<br>*Avoid overwatering; keep tops dry; spray with zineb.* |
| Oedema | Water-soaked spots, turning corky—physiological disease.<br>*Do not overwater in cloudy weather when transpiration is reduced.* |

## GLOXINIA
### *(Sinningia)*

| | |
|---|---|
| Mealybugs | *See African-violets.* |
| Mites | *See African-violets.* |

## IVY
### *(Hedera)*

| | |
|---|---|
| Red spider mites | Leaves yellowish, cobwebby, and sticky. Very common.<br>*Prevent by weekly bath in cool water; if established, dip foliage in nicotine-sulphate solution or Kelthane; grow at cooler temperature.* |
| Scale | Oleander scale (males white, females buff) or soft brown scale.<br>*See Bromeliads.* |
| Leaf spots | Greenish, water-soaked spots turning brownish.<br>*Avoid high temperatures and keeping the foliage too wet.* |

## JERUSALEM-CHERRY
### *(Solanum)*

| | |
|---|---|
| Gray mold | Grayish yellowing of leaves and fruit, which shrivels.<br>*Provide better aeration; avoid syringing.* |

## KALANCHOE

| | |
|---|---|
| Stem-rot wilt | Blackened stems, rotting flower stalks, wilting.<br>*Use porous soil; avoid nitrogenous fertilizer; do not plant too deep or overwater.* |

Powdery mildew

Gray-white mealy growth on leaves and stem.
*Spray with or dip in benomyl.*

## NARCISSUS
### *(Paper-white)*

Blind buds

Buds do not develop, or blast, due to starting too early, growing at too high temperature, insufficient water.
*Start after October 15, root in dark, then bring to light in cool room; keep roots covered with water.*

Rot

Bulbs decay.
*Do not let water cover top of bulb.*

## ORCHIDS

Many kinds can be attacked by scales.
*See Bromeliads and Ferns.*

## PALM

Scales

*Many species on leaves.*
*Keep leaves sponged off with soapy water.*
*See Bromeliads and Ferns.*

Leaf spots

Gray or brown spots.
*Cut out infected parts.*

## PEPEROMIA

Ring spot

Foliage disfigured with concentric zonal markings, probably caused by a virus.
*Discard infected plants; keep free from insects; propagate from healthy plants.*

## PHILODENDRON

Dying leaves

Possibly due to root injury or too dry air.
*Grow in water with piece of charcoal or in soil watered regularly.*

Scales

*See Bromeliads and Ferns.*

## PICKABACK
### *(Tolmiea)*

Mealybugs

*See Coleus.*
*Grow in cool room.*

## POINSETTIA
### *(Euphorbia)*

Mealybugs
Common on underside of leaves and in axils.
*Remove with toothpick; wash with water. See Coleus.*

Root aphids
Yellow-green cottony lice infest roots.
*Loosen earth ball and immerse in nicotine-soap solution at 110° F.*

Leaf drop
Leaves yellow and drop.
*Keep Christmas plants in warm, light, humid room; do not place by cold windows at night.*

## PRIMROSE
### *(Primula)*

Blight
Gray mold on leaves and flowers.
*Keep foliage dry; remove infected parts; spray with benomyl or zineb.*

## RUBBER PLANT
### *(Ficus)*

Anthracnose
Tip burn and scorching of foliage.
*Pick off and burn infected leaves. Do not let water stand on foliage.*

Scales
Several species on leaves.
*Keep leaves wiped off. See Bromeliads.*

Mealybugs
At base of leaves and undersides, with sooty mold growing in honeydew.
*Wipe off or spray. See African-violet.*

## SCHEFFLERA
### *(Brassaia)*

Scales
*See Bromeliads and Ferns.*

Mites
*See African-violet.*

## SNAKE PLANT
### *(Sansevieria)*

Leaf spot
Sunken reddish-brown spots, yellow borders.
*Destroy diseased leaves; avoid syringing.*

## STRAWBERRY-BEGONIA
### *(Saxifraga)*

Mites
*See African-violet.*

# 3

## TYPES OF HOUSE PLANTS

CHAPTER 17

# Flowering Plants
# and Other Plants of
# Unique Ornamental Value

THE SUCCESSFUL CULTIVATION of flowering plants provides a thrill of accomplishment that one does not get in so large a measure from foliage plants. Except for the few constantly in bloom, they provide a change in the decorative scheme and add a note of gaiety to the ensemble. The annual show put on by the exquisitely beautiful though evanescent flowers of the apostle plant *(Neomarica),* and the spectacular blooms of amaryllis and orchid cactus, give us something to look forward to. Some flowers, while not especially ornamental—for example, those of hearts-entangled *(Ceropegia)*—intrigue us with their interesting structure; and some, such as the fragrant-olive *(Osmanthus),* please us with their scent.

With the exception of African-violet, which will bloom in a north window, and a few others, such as spider plant and *Spathiphyllum,* flowering plants demand the light afforded by artificial light or by east, south, or west windows, though sometimes it is necessary to shield them from undiluted sunshine, especially in spring and summer.

For convenience in dealing with cultural details, it has been desirable to group them to some extent as follows: (1) perennials—those that may be kept year after year; (2) annuals and those that, though perennial, are best renewed each year; (3) bulbs, corms, and tubers; (4) cacti and succulents; (5) orchids; (6) those that are definitely shrubby in habit; (7) those grown primarily for their fruits; (8) vines and trailers, including some plants known more for their foliage than flowers; (9) "gift plants," many of which are not adapted to permanent culture in the house; and (10) house plants throughout the year, with timetable.

Begonia boweri *'Nigromarga' is a creeping miniature begonia pretty in or out of bloom. Its sprays of white flowers usually appear in spring.*

## 1. PERENNIALS (LONG-LIVED PLANTS)

**Anthurium:** Surely the record for "long-lastingest" must be held by the inflorescence of *A. scherzerianum.* I once received a plant in a 3-inch pot at the end of September with a bloom that did not fade until a new one started at the end of December! This species is comparatively small—about a foot tall—with a deep red spathe and a coral-colored, curly spadix decorated with tiny circles of white pollen. Its ease of culture and tolerance of house conditions make it well worth growing. It needs a well-drained pot and a coarse soil mixture of redwood bark, peat moss, charcoal, and sand, with plenty of moisture and indirect sunshine.

Other anthuriums—those spectacular kinds known under the generic title of flamingo flowers, whose showy spathes look as though they had been varnished—are not easy to grow but are worthy of a trial by those who have warm, *moist* air in their houses at all times. These grow much larger than *A. scherzerianum*—up to 3 feet high and as much across.

**Begonia:** In more ways than one, the begonia heads the list of house plants that may be looked on as permanent and faithful bloomers as well as outstanding foliage plants. The genus is a large one with the estimated number of species ranging between 1,200 and 1,300; the number of named varieties, strains, and hybrids produced by crossing and otherwise runs into the thousands. It is a group that offers splendid opportunities for the keen plantsman and collector. One specialist has created an indoor begonia garden in one room of his house by installing fluorescent lights in the ceiling and mirrors on the wall to reflect additional light. Begonias attract all kinds of indoor gardeners, including those who are most interested in the decorative possibilities of plants.

The begonias form a fascinating group, exceedingly diverse, and all exhibiting definite characteristics that enable you at once to say, "This is a begonia." Some begonias are so small they can be grown comfortably in a terrarium; others, tall and multistemmed, are decidedly bushlike in habit while there are some that are treelike, with single upright, thickened stems supporting only a handful of leaves. And most begonias are prized as much for their foliage as for their flowers. Many kinds make superb subjects for baskets and other hanging containers because of their long-petioled, beautifully colored and sculptured leaves. There is much the same variety among the flowers of begonias as among their foliage: Some are small, others large and spectacular, yet all tend to be borne in abundance and over long periods in summer and winter. Some begonias can be classed as virtually ever-blooming.

There are so many begonias of interest that it is impossible to do more than sketch in the highlights and offer a sampler of some of the proven kinds. Many, many desirable species and varieties must go unmentioned.

Begonias are often grouped according to their root characteristics, which can be fibrous, tuberous or rhizomatous. Among the latter is a dainty beauty from Mexico, *B. boweri*, certainly one of the highlights among the many begonias that have appeared in recent years. Much of *B. boweri's* charm is in its foliage—each leaf, bright green with black patches radiating from the veins, is edged with prominent erect hairs that with a stretch of the imagination seem to resemble eyelashes. This has naturally led to the plant being commonly designated as the "eyelash begonia," hardly the most appealing name for a plant with so many outstanding characteristics. Its small white flowers, in abundant clusters in winter and spring, are another attraction of this begonia, but it must be admitted they are not freely produced unless the plants receive plenty of winter light, either from sunny windows or under artificial tubes. Young plants of *B. boweri* remain low and compact but as the plants mature the leaf petioles lengthen, making the plants ideal subjects for baskets and other hanging containers. The height of mature plants is still not much above 6–7 inches. Several kinds exist, some of which are small enough to include in terrariums. A few are: *B. boweri* 'Nigromarga', 2–3 inches tall; 'Bow-Arriola', dark green, star-shaped leaves; 'Bow-Joe', pink flowers and chocolate-brown leaves. Some gardeners have complained of cultural difficulties with *B. boweri*. As with most begonia troubles, these are probably due to overwatering and too hot and dry an atmosphere. (See end of this begonia section for culture tips.)

Another very popular rhizomatous begonia these days is the hybrid 'Cleopatra'. It is larger in every way than the more miniature *B. boweri* and its offspring, and has proved to be a sturdy survivor of varied indoor wintry climates, including low humidity and temperatures ranging for periods as low as 55° F. 'Cleopatra' has long-petioled, maple-shaped leaves, 4–5 inches across, that assume a wide range of reddish tints, their translucent quality being shown to advantage when the plants are suspended in hanging containers in a sunny winter window. In late winter and spring, 'Cleopatra' puts forth a bountiful floral display with many clusters of bright pink flowers rising well above the foliage.

The angel wing begonia is a common name applied to several begonia species and their many forms and hybrids. One of the best known is *B. corallina,* which has tall, canelike stems, oblique leaves about 5 inches long, and coral-red flowers in clusters. Among its well-known hybrids are 'President Carnot', 'Corallina de Lucerna', and many others, some of which have leaves marked with silvery spots.

*B. dregei* is an example of a begonia with a semituberous root. It has small, bronze-green maplelike leaves and succulent, freely branching stems rising to a height of 3 feet with conspicuous swellings on the older portions. The white flowers are produced profusely in winter. This species should be rested by keeping the soil definitely on the dry side after growth and flowering are completed—usually in late spring.

The beefsteak begonia (*B.* x *erythrophylla* [syn. *B. feastii*]) is one of the very common house plants in rural districts, but it is tough enough to withstand most interiors provided it isn't roasted to death. It has thick, almost round leaves, green above and red beneath, with white whiskers on the margins. The flowers are pink, carried effectively above the foliage in winter. There is a hybrid known as *B.* x *erythrophylla* 'Bunchii', which has the edges of the leaves crested and ruffled, and one *B.* x *erythrophylla* 'Helix', in which the lobes are spiraled like a snail's shell.

A favorite for hanging baskets is the small-leaved *B. foliosa,* which has a naturally pendulous habit. The tiny leaves, almost fernlike, crowd the branches at the ends of which, equally tiny, pale pink flowers are borne. Its root system is fibrous. Another long-popular, small-leaved, fibrous begonia is *B. fuchsioides.* Its tiny leaves, pointed and very glossy, cover the arching stem, which can reach 24 inches. When the plants are clothed with the numerous bright red, nodding flowers, the effect is that of a small, dainty fuchsia.

The specific name of the star begonia, *B. heracleifolia,* means "having leaves like the cow-parsnip," which is good enough so far as it goes because in general outline they do resemble that coarse perennial herb. But you should imagine a much refined cow-parsnip, with smaller leaves marked with silver, red, or black-green in some of the varieties; and white or rose-colored flowers on stalks which may be from 2 to 4 feet long and produced from February to April. This is one of the toughest of the begonias. I have known a plant in a 4½-inch pot with leaves 8 inches in diameter to produce two flower stalks that attained 2 feet in spite of the cramped quarters occupied by the roots.

A spring-blooming kind, *B. manicata,* is remarkable for the striking fleshy red hairs arranged in collars around the leafstalks. The pink flowers are displayed in airy, elegant panicles on foot-long stalks and are very effective.

There is a cultivar, 'Aureo-maculata', the leaves of which are blotched with white and yellow; and 'Crispa', whose leaves have crested and ruffled edges.

Although it produces interesting pink and green flowers in spring, *B. masoniana,* the iron cross begonia, is more renowned for its unique foliage, rounded and bold with a puckered texture and marked with a red-brown pattern that gives this rhizomatous species its common name. Plants rarely grow above 10 inches and like the rex begonias, require a fairly humid atmosphere and temperature warmer than most begonias, between 60° and 65° F. at night.

*B. metallica* is a handsome plant about 4 feet high when well grown. Its leaves are glossy olive-green above with metallic purple veins and red beneath. The flowers, borne in clusters, are large and light pink in color. It has long been known as an excellent house plant.

One nurseryman's catalogue lists over one hundred named forms of *B. rex,* the painted leaf begonia. This does not by any means represent all the forms of this extraordinarily variable species, which includes a series in which the leaf lobes are spiraled like the end of a snail's shell and a series of intriguing miniatures. The flowers of the rex begonias are nothing much in comparison with the leaves, which are among the most decorative of any in the plant kingdom. They often have a metallic sheen, and exhibit an array of colors, arranged in broad, irregular zones, impossible to describe accurately.

These rex begonias will not prosper in hot, dry rooms. They require a moist atmosphere and good air circulation, a temperature no lower than 60° to 65° F. at night and bright light but not direct sunshine. Try them under artificial light or in a north window, standing the pots on pebbles in water-filled trays. Water the pots sparingly in winter when the plants require a resting period, and avoid overwatering at other seasons—something to remember about any begonia.

*B.* x *ricinifolia* is a hybrid, very vigorous, with large leaves which, arising from a prostrate rootstock, are less deeply lobed than *B. heracleifolia* (one of its parents), and are bronzy green. They resemble those of *Ricinus,* the castor-oil plant. The rose-pink flowers are displayed in panicles a foot or more across on stems up to 4 feet tall, in winter and early spring.

One of the most beautiful begonias is *B. scharffii,* which has large rose-pink flowers in hanging clusters and is almost never out of bloom, though most floriferous in summer. It is an upright grower with hairy olive-green leaves, red on the undersides. *B. scharffiana,* an entirely different plant with white flowers, is reputed to be difficult to grow.

The best known of all is the wax begonia *(B. semperflorens).* Always a favorite, it is now at the apex of popularity and is widely planted in the summer in gardens among both annual and perennial plants or in containers, planters, or beds near or on terraces and patios. It is just as popular indoors on sunny window sills or under fluorescent lights. The wax begonia is a perennial that may live in good condition for five or more years, but it is so readily grown from seed (see Chapter 15) that it is often treated as an annual, the plants being used in summer, then discarded when cold weather arrives.

Hybridizers continue to introduce new strains and cultivars with varying characteristics, some having double flowers and others bronze foliage. Some are especially compact and dwarf in habit, others may be taller, but all share the same near ever-blooming flowering characteristic. Among the recommended wax begonia cultivars are: 'Firefly', double scarlet flowers and bronze foliage; 'Thimbleberry', dark red flowers and dark red foliage; 'Snow White', double white flowers and green foliage; 'Curly Locks', yellow and pink flowers, thimble-shaped, with dark bronze foliage; 'White Christmas', double white flowers and bright green leaves; 'Christmas Candle', fluffy-doubled rose-red flowers and bright green leaves; 'Butterfly' strain, red, rose, or white flowers, 3 inches across.

The calla-lily begonia belongs in the *B. semperflorens* group. This is the begonia whose variegated white and green leaves have a remote resemblance in form to a calla-lily. It was once considered very temperamental and only grown successfully in farmhouses and cool-summer regions. Certainly summer coolness is a factor in its successful culture, as with many other begonias, but many gardeners are having success with these plants today, perhaps because they have learned not to overwater them—in summer outdoors or in winter indoors. Calla-lily begonias also need good light—filtered sunshine or very bright light in summer, and indoors during the winter, as much direct sun as possible. 'Charm' is one of the best calla-lily-type begonias, having pink flowers that contrast well with the quite large variegated green, yellow, and white foliage.

The spectacular and floriferous hybrids of the Christmas begonia group, resulting from a cross between *B. socotrana* and *B. dregei,* sold around Christmas, are discussed in Section 9 of this chapter.

*B.* 'Templinii' has clustered pink flowers from January to March and leaves that are blotched with white, yellow, and red, and have ruffled margins. This is reputed to be a sport of *B. phyllomaniaca,* a species characterized by an amazing production of tiny plantlets on the leaves and stems.

The popular summer-flowering garden race of tuberous begonias, to which the name *B.* x *tuberhybrida* has been applied, is discussed in Section 4 of this chapter.

Begonias will grow in a variety of soils provided only that they are porous. One very successful grower in California recommends 2 parts loam, 1 part peat moss, 1 part dehydrated (dried) cow manure, 1 part sand, with a sprinkling of commercial fertilizer and fine charcoal. Another grower suggests a rather heavier soil for kinds such as *B.* x *erythrophylla, heracleifolia, manicata,* x *ricinifolia,* et cetera, namely: equal parts loam, leaf mold, sand with ⅛ part by bulk of dried cow manure and a pint of bone meal to each bushel. Or you could use the mixture for begonias suggested in Chapter 6.

While the soil must be made sufficiently firm to hold the plants upright, it should be left looser than for the general run of pot plants. The pots *must be well drained*—put a concave piece of broken pot over the hole in the bottom, and on that a layer, ½ to 1 inch deep, depending on the size of the pot, of crocks broken into pieces of about ½-inch size. This will help to prevent fatal waterlogging. Except for tuberous and semituberous varieties (which should be kept dry, or nearly so, during their resting periods), the soil should be watered thoroughly only whenever it is beginning to get dry.

Shade the large-leaved begonias from bright sunshine except in the depth of winter; avoid exposing them to drafts and violent fluctuations of temperature. If they are placed outdoors in summer, it should be in a situation sheltered from strong winds. Wax begonias endure more sun than other begonias and in fact demand it indoors in the winter if they are to continue flowering.

**Beloperone guttata** (or more correctly these days—*Justicia brandegeana*), **the Shrimp Plant,** can be a welcome introduction to the house-plant scene because it is virtually ever-blooming. It is about 18 inches tall, and its leaves are ordinary, but its inflorescence is showy. The flowers are white, spotted with purple. The chief effect, however, is made by the long-lasting reddish-brown bracts beneath which the flowers originate. (Bracts are leafy or membranous organs, often brightly colored, usually associated with inflorescence. The conspicuous parts of dogwood and poinsettia are bracts.) The chief defect of the shrimp plant is its tendency toward gawkiness and bare legs. This can be overcome to some extent by raising new plants annually from cuttings (at any time) and pinching out tips of shoots in the early stages to promote bushiness. It needs sunshine, a well-drained pot, general potting mixture, and plenty of water at the roots.

**Bromeliads** or **Air-pines:** For many years I was a voice in the wilderness advocating, without much effect, the use of bromeliads as house plants. The interest in these plants has now burgeoned and there is an active Bromeliad Society with chapters in many regions. These relatives of the pineapple are extraordinarily interesting and infinitely varied, ranging from the soft, slender droopiness of the Spanish-moss to the harsh uprightness of some of the *Hohenbergia* species. Some grow in soil; others perch themselves on rocks, trees, or even telegraph wires. Practically all have decorative foliage, and the inflorescences of some exhibit color combinations unique in the vegetable kingdom. Here, for example, are some flower descriptions culled at random: rose-colored bracts with blue flowers *(Aechmea fasciata);* pink bracts, green petals edged with blue *(Billbergia nutans)* (I might add that this species has conspicuous golden anthers providing another note in color contrasts); violet-purple flowers edged white with inner leaves bright red (*Neoregelia carolinae* 'Tricolor').

In general, bromeliads belong to the group known to botanists as xerophytes. That is, they are especially adapted to survive periods of drought. Although bromeliads need some sunshine or artificial light to bloom, they will withstand dim light for a time and all kinds of neglect (though this is not advocated in their culture!). I have seen offsets of several species of *Cryptanthus* inadvertently knocked off the plants, kicked around on the greenhouse floor, finally to come to rest in the gravel under the benches where they rooted and prospered. Many kinds do well under house conditions though doubtless there are some, Spanish-moss, for example, that will refuse to thrive. I had a specimen of *Neoregelia carolinae* which I kept for a time in an unheated, poorly lighted basement room; then it was placed in a sunny window and given the reasonably good conditions of the plant room; then it took a long trip in a cold car to be photographed in a decorative window arrangement. Then it was put in the dry living room where it developed the typical brilliant crimson coloration on the central leaves which was followed by the production of its lavender flowers.

This is a large family of about two thousand species and many hybrids; obviously only a few can be mentioned here: *Quesnelia* (syn. *Aechmea*) *marmorata,* Grecian vase, has stiff, recurving, mottled leaves in vaselike form. Originating from the center, the pendulous inflorescence carries pale pink bracts and blue-petaled flowers. *Aechmea fulgens* has pale green spreading leaves from a basal rosette and numerous blue-tipped flowers with red calyxes arranged on a stiff panicle which remains ornamental over an extended period. Many other *Aechmea* are equally worthy of cultivation, including the popular hybrid x 'Foster's Favorite', which has blue flowers with coral-red "berrylike" calyxes.

Some of the billbergias have their leaves arranged to give an almost tubular effect; in common with many bromeliads the clasping bases are constructed to hold water. *Billbergia nutans,* the parent of many hybrids, has already been mentioned. A hybrid of *B. saundersii* has green leaves, suffused with reddish tones, mottled pale green and white, with faint gray bars on the undersides. They are abruptly recurved at the tip. The flowers have green petals tipped with blue attended by brilliant red bracts. The billbergias are among the most free-blooming of the bromeliads.

As might be guessed from the name, *Cryptanthus,* this genus is not noteworthy for its floral display, but some species make up for it by their bizarre foliage. Mention has already been made of their toughness. Several species are rugged enough to survive commercial made-up "dish gardens."

*C. bivittatus,* a practically stemless kind, has leaves with undulating spiny margins striped with brownish green and pinkish cream. It seems to do equally well in a sunny window and in rather dense shade. *C. zonatus* ought to be called "zebra plant" from the crinkly leaves marked with transverse bands of white, green, and brown. These have a tendency to extend themselves horizontally and recurve as though trying to clasp the pot in which they are growing. A very striking plant.

*Guzmania zahnii,* which I have never seen in bloom, has curving leaves up to 2 feet long, gracefully arranged in a rosette. They are almost translucent and have longitudinal pencilings of bronze and red, which give a delightful effect when the leaves are seen against strong light. In my experience this was not so amenable as a house plant as some of the other bromeliads and probably needed more atmospheric moisture than I was able to supply.

*Neoregelia carolinae* has already been mentioned. Other noteworthy species are *N. marmorata,* with leaves almost a foot long, marbled with red-brown patches. Its head of pale violet flowers is produced down in the center of the rosette. Painted fingernail *(Neoregelia spectabilis)* looks as though someone had dipped a thumb in red ink and pressed it on the tip of each leaf. This makes a rosette of foot-long curving leaves slightly undulated along the margins and barred on the reverse with narrow bands of silvery scurflike hairs. This is another species that was pushed around from pillar to post in my house without any apparent ill effects.

Spanish-moss *(Tillandsia usneoides)* has several relatives with long 1½-foot slender, tapering leaves gracefully arranged in rosettes. These epiphytes do not always do well as house plants, requiring more humid conditions than most of us can provide. However, some years ago I gave one, *T. fasciculata,* to a friend who reported excellent results. *T. lindenii* has tapering green leaves and a spectacular inflorescence. The carmine bracts are closely imbricated (overlapping) to form a flattened structure that reminds one of a cock's comb. The large purple flowers emerge in succession from the bracts, alternately from side to side over a long period.

*Vriesia carinata* has an inflorescence somewhat similar to the above, but more loosely constructed, and the bracts are scarlet at the base and yellowish at the tip; the flowers are pale yellow. The leaves are thin and pale green. *V. hieroglyphica* is grown chiefly for its foliage strongly marked with dark hieroglyphs. Vriesias seem to require less bright light than some bromeliads, and even do quite well in north windows.

Many bromeliads hold water in considerable quantities in their leaf bases, which makes them worthy of consideration as humidifiers and enables them to be used as "living vases." Care should be taken when inserting cut flowers to avoid injury to the leaves of the "vase."

I have had best success with those bromeliads that grow on trees and rocks by growing them in pots filled ⅓ with broken flowerpot pieces (they resent stagnant water around their roots, which must have access to air); and using orchid peat (osmunda fiber) mixed with a few lumps of charcoal as a potting medium. Substitutes are flaky leaf mold or peat moss, mixed with shredded fir bark and equal parts coarse sand, perlite, and charcoal broken into ¼-inch pieces.

During winter they should be kept on the dry side at the roots, but the leaf bases of those equipped to hold water should be kept filled. Occasional overhead spraying is good. It is believed that certain cells in the leaf bases are capable of absorbing nutrients contained in the water they hold. Don't, however, try to help them along by adding commercial fertilizer to the water. This was once done to a collection under my charge (without first consulting me) with disastrous results. In many species the old rosette is useless after flowering and should be discarded, and the young plants developing around it potted up separately to carry on.

The terrestrial species (*Ananas* [pineapple], *Bromelia, Cryptanthus, Dyckia, Hechtia,* et cetera) should be potted in sandy soil with about ⅓ leaf mold or peat moss and ⅙ rotted or dried cow manure. Avoid overwatering them during winter. These, with a few exceptions, are less appealing than the epiphytic kinds. *Bromelia* is too spiny to be handled comfortably. The *Dyckia* species, though their flowers are interesting, have stiff and rather forbidding leaves. *Hechtia argentea,* however, even though spiny, is so spectacular with its dense rosette of silvery, recurving leaves, 1 inch wide and up to 2 feet long, that it is worth a trial if it can be obtained. It is reputed to be difficult of culture even in a greenhouse. *Ananas comosus,* the pineapple of commerce, has several varieties in which the leaves are variously striped with white or

*Neomarica or apostle plant with its irislike fan of foliage and flower. The stem usually needs a wire stake to hold it upright.*

yellow, some with reddish tones. These are well worth growing and can be purchased in full fruit. (See how to grow a pineapple plant in Section 7 of this chapter.)

**Impatiens—Patience Plant:** The names "patience plant" and "patient Lucy" are interesting examples of how the original meaning of a plant name can be reversed. The vernacular names are derived from the botanical name *Impatiens,* coming from the Latin meaning "impatient," referring to the sudden bursting of the seed pods. More a reflection of this trait is another common name, "busy Lizzie." Although patience plant has for many years been a favorite house plant because of its long-blooming habit, ease of culture, and tolerance, it is even more popular today because of the excellent hybrids that have been introduced. (Consult seed catalogues for named hybrids and strains.) Patience plant has also benefited from the current boom in bedding plants (along with coleus, wax begonia, and others) and has become an important "summer" house plant for use on or near terraces and patios and any area that has become an outdoor extension of the living room. Many varieties are suitable for hanging containers and all are invaluable in boxes and planters.

The botanical classification of *Impatiens* has been changed in recent years. Two former species, *I. holstii* and *I. sultanii,* are now incorporated in *I. wallerana,* but other species, some only recently discovered in New Guinea and elsewhere, are also being used by hybridizers. The result is that today there are more different forms than ever of patience plant, with flowers ranging in color from white through pink to scarlet and purple, including many with bicolored flowers. There are also varieties with variegated or bronze-colored foliage. Some of the new foliage types may grow up to 3 feet or more, but the kinds used as house plants remain much lower—from 6 to 12 inches or so. When the plants become too large for their quarters, they may be cut back.

It's easy to grow patience plants from seeds or cuttings—at almost any season of the year. Because of the way the plants disperse their seeds, self-sown seedlings can appear in all sorts of unexpected places, including pots of other house plants. Many of these seedlings are well worth saving. Use a general-purpose mixture for potting with the addition of a cupful or so of pulverized limestone to each bushel of soil if it is on the acid side. Avoid overpotting—large plants can be produced in small pots. Give a sunny situation during the winter months; in summer half-shade is desirable for the best flowers. Impatiens does not do well in dense shade.

**Neomarica** (syn. **Marica**)—**Apostle Plant:** The apostle plant, or twelve apostles, is so called because the individual fans or tufts commonly contain twelve leaves. These are sword-shaped, about 2 feet long, light green, and very decorative. It is a much more effective plant when only one "fan" is allowed to develop in each pot. The species most commonly grown, and the best, is *N. northiana.* The exquisite but ephemeral irislike fragrant flowers are 3 to 4 inches across and pure white, with the inner segments marked with violet. The other species sometimes grown in the house is *N. gracilis,* smaller in all its parts. Its white flowers are marked with yellow, brown, and blue. Old plants of either species may be divided after flowering; or the plantlets that sometimes develop on the flowering stems may be used for propagation. Seldom attacked by insects, *Neomarica* needs nothing more than routine care and general-purpose mixture for potting.

**Pelargonium—Geranium:** The semishrubby plants commonly known as geraniums, but generically as *Pelargonium,* fall into four groups, any one of which contains enough variety to make it worthy of the consideration of the "collector." These are (1) show pelargonium *(P. domesticum),* also known as Lady Washington geraniums and pansy-flowered geraniums; (2) house geraniums *(P. x hortorum),* also known as bedding and zonal geraniums; (3) ivy-leaved geraniums *(P. peltatum);* (4) scented-leaved geraniums, represented by many species.

The Lady Washington types are *not* perpetual bloomers. The showy flowers, often conspicuously marked with black or dark-colored blotches, are produced mostly in the spring at the tips of the shoots rather than several inches back, as is the habit of the next group. There are many cultivars ranging in color from salmon pink ('Edith North') to amaranth red ('Easter Greeting'). Other good ones are 'Mme. Layal', pink, white, purple, and black; and 'Fifth Avenue', black-blotched, deep red, free-blooming over a long period.

Cuttings may be taken after flowering and grown outdoors until September, when they should be brought indoors and kept in a sunny window. During the early stages of growth, selective pinching of the tips of shoots should be practiced to promote bushiness and a shapely plant. Do not carry on with this beyond late winter lest you destroy potential flowering shoots. Keep cool during the winter (50° F.) and be careful to avoid overwatering. In February and March, when they begin to grow, a sprinkling of complete fertilizer (1 teaspoon to 6-inch pot) on the surface will be helpful (or use a special house-plant fertilizer according to direction). After flowering, the plants may be placed outdoors and rested by keeping them on the dry side. In August or early September, prune them into shape and cut out weak shoots. Repot them in general-purpose mixture; if the pot becomes crowded with roots, shift into a larger size pot in January.

There is a bewildering selection in the zonal or house geraniums with single or double flowers; some with handsomely colored foliage, and many of dwarf (8–10 inches) and miniature (6–8 inches) stature, the second group being well suited to limited window or fluorescent light shelf space. Good varieties include: 'Apple Blossom', semidouble pink and white; 'Beauté Poitevine', salmon; 'Little Darling', miniature with deep pink flowers; 'Little John', miniature with double salmon flowers; 'Robin Hood', semidwarf with double red flowers; 'Rosebud', double pink (also in this flower form are 'Scarlet Rosebud', 'Magenta Rosebud', 'Apple Blossom Rosebud'); 'Tiny Tim', single red; 'Tu-Tone', pink. A good point in favor of these diminutive geraniums is that they can remain in small (2¼–2½-inch) pots for many years, requiring only an occasional pinch of fertilizer. A drawback to them is that they may require daily watering, simply because their pots are so small.

Standard-size zonal geraniums that have stood the test of time include the following with colored foliage: 'Happy Thought', green and cream, with dark zone—flowers scarlet; 'Mme. Salleron', a dwarf, compact sort with white-edged leaves; 'Mrs. Pollack', leaves bronzy-red, crimson, and yellow, double red flowers; 'Wilhelm Languth', leaves edged white, scarlet double flowers.

Although one often sees ancient plants of this group completely filling sunny windows, usually it is a better practice to raise new plants from cuttings (see Chapter 15) annually in spring and keep them growing along, but removing all flower buds until fall so they will be vigorous producers of winter blooms.

The zonal geraniums are easily raised from seeds sown in pots indoors in early spring, but the progeny is likely to be inferior to named cultivars unless you select the 'Carefree' strain, a recent development in geraniums hybridized for growing from seeds. If you should happen to get a superior form, it is easy to perpetuate it by cuttings. Sometimes plants that have served a season planted out in the flower beds are dug up in the fall, cut back, potted up, and brought in the house. These are seldom, if ever, satisfactory for winter bloom under the arduous conditions they encounter in the average house. They are not so good-looking as cut-back plants, and it takes them months to grow out of their stumpy awkwardness.

For potting, use general-purpose mixture; make it quite firm in the pot; avoid overpotting, but when roots become crowded, shift into a larger size— preferably not over 6 inches, however. When they have filled the ultimate pots with roots, fertilize with complete fertilizer or your favorite house-plant fertilizer every four to five weeks. Keep in a sunny window in a cool room (45° to 50° F. at night), and water only when soil is beginning to get dry, then give a thorough soaking.

The ivy-leaved geraniums are characterized by a trailing habit and glossy, almost succulent leaves. They are not so easy to grow as the other types and on the whole not so free-flowering, but under favorable conditions they may have blooms from late winter until fall. They are more likely to succeed where the air is not so dry and in regions where the summers are cool. In England they have always been favored plants to trail over the edges of large outdoor vases in summer. There are many hybrids of ivy-type geraniums. The following are reputed to be free bloomers: 'Apricot Queen', salmon shades; 'Charles Turner', rose pink; 'Intensity', orange-scarlet; 'Kotinka', double red; 'Mexican Beauty', blood red; 'Mrs. Banks', white; 'Snowdrift', double white flowers of "rosebud" form; 'Sybil Holmes', pink, "rosebud" type. 'Sunset-ivy' ('L'Élégante') has variegated leaves and pink flowers. These plants may be displayed in hanging pots or baskets in a sunny window or used on a terrace or patio for summer color.

The scented-leaved pelargoniums are a varied group in leaf size and structure, in flowers and in fragrance. As a rule their flowers are not so large or so showy as those in the preceding groups. They are grown partly for their foliage but chiefly for their fragrance—the rose geranium, one of the oldest of house plants, was used to adulterate attar of roses. Sprigs of the small-leaved kinds were used in finger bowls, and single leaves of the large varieties are still used for the same purpose.

Many species and cultivars of scented pelargoniums are obtainable from a few specialists dealing in them. A selection of outstanding kinds follows: *P. capitatum,* rose-scented, large leaves on trailing stems; flowers rose purple; *P. crispum,* lemon-scented, small leaves on compact little bushes; several varieties available, including 'Prince Rupert', with foliage variegated green and white, and 'Limoneum', with showy purple flowers; *P. denticulatum,* large, finely cut leaves prompting the appellation "skeleton leaf," pine-scented, with lilac-colored flowers. *P. graveolens,* one of the old-time rose geraniums, has large, deeply lobed and toothed leaves; flowers pink or pale purple. There are several forms of this, distinguished in part by their varying scents. *P. odoratissimum,* the nutmeg geranium, has rounded leaves about 1½ inches across and small white flowers. There is a form with variegated leaves and one with apple fragrance. *P. tomentosum* has long-stalked, peppermint-scented leaves, so clothed with hairs on both sides that they are velvety to the touch. The flowers are small and white.

Pelargoniums in general need what the professional gardener calls a buoyant atmosphere, promoted under greenhouse conditions by free ventilation and the use of artificial heat with ventilators open on dark and muggy days in winter. Go easy on spraying and avoid wetting the leaves when the air is very humid as this favors the fungus diseases that sometimes attack them.

**Saintpaulia—African-violet:** The African-violet (*Saintpaulia* species and cultivars) is probably America's favorite house plant, and almost everyone who grows any indoor plants at all has at least a few specimens; there are many who make a hobby of collecting as many of the different ones available as they have space for. The African-violet is not a "violet" at all (that is, it is not related in any way to the true violets, which belong in the genus *Viola*), but is related to the gloxinia, achemenes, and streptocarpus.

The African-violet's free-flowering habit, ease of culture and propagation, ability to stand the high temperatures common to many houses and apartments, and the fact that it thrives even in a north window (although flowering results are much better in brighter exposures or under artificial lights) are reasons enough for its popularity.

The species *S. ionantha,* the source of most of the thousands of named African-violets now available, has single violet-colored flowers, but today the varietal range includes a dazzling array of flower forms and colors. The only colors lacking are yellow and orange. The typical African-violet plant is a rosette of attractive spoon-shaped, hairy-textured, almost succulent, leaves, but the natural tendency of the plants to mutate combined with accomplishments of hybridizers has resulted in an equally wide range of plant forms, including miniature, semiminiature, and trailing varieties. In fact there are so many varieties and the scene changes so much each year as new introductions take the place of old favorites that it seems foolhardy to list specific varieties. The reader is urged to consult the catalogues of specialists listed in Chapter 21.

African-violets will grow almost anywhere in the house, provided the temperature doesn't drop much below 65° F. at night and hovers around 68° to 70° F. and higher during the day. A relatively high humidity is important as it is for most house plants. African-violets should have at least 40 per cent, but 50 or 60 per cent is better. While they will bloom in a north window, east or west aspects are preferable, and in winter in the North the brightness of a south window can be tolerated for several hours. As the winter wanes, protection from hot sun can be provided, if needed, by thin curtains or taller plants that diffuse the light.

The rise in popularity of the African-violet and the use of artificial (mostly fluorescent) light as a substitute for sunlight seem to have gone hand in hand. This is understandable in view of the African-violet's generally compact, low-growing habits which make them suitable for the often restricted space available in many indoor light gardens and their favorable response to artificial light in increasing flowering. African-violets grown under artificial light require about 12 to 14 hours of exposure daily and should be as close to the light source as 6 to 10 inches.

Use the humusy soil mixture recommended for these plants (see Chapter 6) and add enough ground limestone, if necessary, to make its reaction pH 6 to 6.5, or about 1 tablespoon to 4 quarts of the mixture. When potting or repotting, avoid making the soil too firm. They may be divided or repotted into larger pots in the spring—usually the former is preferred. Because of their low stature, they are more effective and there is a better balance between pot and plant when they are kept in squatty, tub-shaped pots 4 to 5 inches in diameter. If they are repotted annually, there is little need for additional fertilizer, but when the pots are filled with roots, a 5–10–5 fertilizer could be applied to the surface soil and scratched in every four or five weeks, using at the rate of ½ teaspoon to a 5-inch pot. Or use, according to directions, one of the fertilizers formulated for flowering house plants.

African-violets should be kept moist at the roots and never allowed to become bone-dry. Yet a waterlogged growing medium should be avoided. They are well adapted to wick-watering. Doubtless you have read or have been told that water should never be allowed to touch the leaves of African-violets, but this is an exploded notion. They are not harmed by overhead water *provided* the water temperature is not lower than that of the air. I have seen them growing in a greenhouse where they were almost constantly wet with spray from a fountain.

They are not immune to pests, so keep a close watch, especially for mealybugs, and scotch them before they have a chance to get around to laying their eggs. Mite-infested plants—manifested by curling leaves—had better be discarded. (See Chapter 16.)

New plants may be raised from seeds sown in the spring (flowering is prolonged if seed formation is prevented by snipping off faded flowers; so if plenty of flowers is the objective, let someone else attend to seed production), by leaf cuttings, which root easily in moist sand or in water, and by division. (See Chapter 15.)

The African-violet is one of the few house plants that are not benefited by being placed outdoors in summer, and it does not seem to require a resting period. A summer sojourn where the plants are protected from wind, heavy rainfall, and bright sun should do no harm, though.

## SOME OTHER GESNERIADS—CLOSE AFRICAN-VIOLET RELATIVES:

The African-violet family (Gesneriaceae) includes many other genera with fibrous rather than tuberous or rhizomatous roots that are catching on with house-plant enthusiasts. (The gloxinia, achimenes, and other tuberous-rooted gesneriads are discussed in the section on summer-flowering bulbs later in this chapter.)

*Aeschynanthus:* Sometimes called the "lipstick vine" because of the bright red, two-lipped, tubular flowers typical of some, but not all, species. It would take an expert to figure that this essentially trailing or pendulous plant is related to the African-violet. The very showy flowers, in shades of or combinations of red, orange, yellow, often with touches of brown and green, usually appear in late winter and spring, although some flowers may appear at other times. Out of bloom the aeschynanthus makes a handsome, robust foliage plant, especially as a mature specimen billowing from a hanging basket. Immature trailers and some species that are more arching than pendulous in habit make satisfactory pot plants in east or west windows—or even south windows in winter—or under artificial light. All others are best displayed in hanging containers.

*A. evrardii* has variegated foliage and an erect growing habit; its flowers are red and orange and mostly produced in summer. *A. radicans* is a trailer with red-tinged, fleshy-textured foliage on wiry stems and dark red flowers in late spring and summer. *A. obconicus* has dark red, bell-shaped flowers and large, waxy leaves; its habit is arching, making it suitable for a stationary pot or as a suspended plant. *A. speciosus* has heavy, 48-inch trailers clothed with waxy leaves and bright yellow-red flowers. These plants are epiphytes and should be grown in an open, humusy mixture. The trick is to keep the growing medium reasonably moist but not soggy and the atmosphere humid. During the winter, less water is required while the plants rest. At this time a somewhat cooler temperature (60° F. at night) can be tolerated.

*Columnea:* Another fibrous-rooted gesneriad that quite closely resembles aeschynanthus, requiring about the same growing conditions and also being much used as a hanging plant. Columneas are generally more free-blooming,

Episcia *'Moss Agate'* has green leaves marked with silver veins. The flowers are brilliant orange-red. Episcia grows well under fluorescent lights.

some kinds rating as ever-bloomers, others tending to bloom most prolifically in spring and summer. With one's imagination roaming freely, it is possible to see why they are called "goldfish plants," as the two-lipped, tubular flowers of some kinds do resemble an open-mouthed goldfish. (The flowers of another gesneriad, *Nematanthus,* also share this resemblance.) These flowers are exceptionally showy in red, orange, yellow, or pink shades. The leaves of columnea vary from glossy to very hairy. Many hybrids and species are offered by specialists, and most general house-plant nurseries always list a few. Some recommendations include *C.* x *banksii,* scarlet flowers in spring and small, wax-textured leaves, red on their undersides; *C.* 'Canary', canary-yellow flowers covered with white hairs from fall to spring, and an interesting foliage arrangement, the dark green, glossy leaves being arranged in pairs, one always being larger than the other; *C.* 'Cayugan', bright red-orange flowers covered with red hairs in winter and spring; *C.* 'Yellow Dragon', yellow-orange flowers in winter on trailing stems; 'Christmas Carol', bright red flowers from late fall to late winter.

*Episcia:* Members of this genus are sometimes called "flame-violets" because of the shape and color of their flowers, and "peacock vines" in reference to their richly colored and textured leaves which vary in green and copper shades, overlaid with patterns of silver and pink. The tubular or bell-shaped flowers, equally rich-colored in a range from red through purple, in some cases with the lobes attractively fringed, appear mostly in spring and summer, making them good companions for their relatives, gloxinia and achimenes, on terraces and in other sheltered outdoor-living areas. The plant habit is spreading and cascading and suited to both hanging or stationary containers.

Episcias have two important requirements: warmth and humidity. Temperatures around 68° to 72° F. are needed to prevent the plants from slipping into dormancy. The humidity should range between 50 and 75 per cent (use a hygrometer, offered in many house-plant mail-order catalogues or in hardware stores, to check the atmosphere around your house plants). Obviously episcias do well in the moist air of a terrarium, but most do too well, spreading rampantly, their stems taking root wherever they touch the growing medium, and soon overcrowding every other plant. The solution here might be to devote the entire terrarium space to one stunning episcia specimen rather than attempting a balanced planting of different kinds of plants. A few of the more desirable episcia hybrids and species include 'Acajou', with orange-red flowers and mahogany leaves marked with a metallic silver-green; 'Chocolate Soldier', orange-red flowers and dark brown leaves marked with silver; 'Pink Brocade', red-orange flowers and beautiful variegated pink foliage; *E. dianthiflora,* pure white, fringed flowers in summer and small, velvety-textured leaves, their midribs marked with purple; *E. reptans,* dark blood-red flowers, attractively fringed, and dark green quilted leaves, the veins marked with silver.

*Streptocarpus* (**Cape-primrose**): In this genus is a curious species, *S. wendlandii,* which forms one huge leaf, corrugated and hairy, that may reach 3 feet or more in length and about 1½ feet in width. The many small, violet-blue flowers are carried above the leaf on 20-inch stalks. Some of the desirable traits of this unusual species will be found in the 'Wiesmoor' hybrids, a seed strain that will bloom in six to eight months from time of sowing. The resulting plants are described as having large trumpet-shaped flowers, some fringed and ruffled, on strong stems, and rosettes of foliage, considerably more compact than the wonder leaf produced by *S. wendlandii.* Another hybrid strain is based on *S. rexii,* the original Cape-primrose which was introduced in Europe in 1824 from South Africa. The plants bloom for long periods, producing large trumpet-shaped flowers on 6-inch stalks in a wide color range from deep reds, purples, and violet-blue to pinks and white.

A quite different species from the preceding is *S. saxorum,* which has small, fleshy gray-green leaves on succulent stems that are upright when young but which eventually elongate into a trailing habit. This becomes a fine plant for baskets and hanging containers. It seems too bad that this species has become stuck with the common name of "false-African-violet," probably because its pretty light blue flowers, borne on slender stems from the leaf axils, show a very slight resemblance to that relative. *S. saxorum* is attractive enough not to be encumbered with the name of another plant—even though it is a relative.

The Cape-primroses are easier to grow than some of the gesneriads, having about the same requirements as African-violets. Blooming may slow or stop in hot, humid summer weather, at which time watering should be reduced. As growth picks up in the cooler days of autumn, crowded plants can be carefully divided—their root system is sparse—and repotted in a humusy, quick-draining mixture. Except for summer, the plants are prolific with their flowers. Shy bloomers are probably not getting enough light—natural or artificial.

The above represents only a smattering of the vast gesneriad family. (Some others will be discussed in Section 3 of this chapter.) Since growing one kind often leads to a desire to try other family members, it is suggested that so-inclined readers join two societies for up-to-the-minute information on growing techniques and varieties. They are The African-violet Society of America, P.O. Box 1326, Knoxville, Tenn. 37901, and the American Gloxinia and Gesneriad Society, P.O. Box 174, New Milford, Conn. 06776.

## 2.   ANNUALS AND OTHERS TREATED AS ANNUALS

We now come to those plants that usually give better results if they are renewed annually. Some of these are true annuals—that is, they die when they have performed their function of seed production—but others (some of them shrubs) are perennial in nature.

Personally I must confess I have never been any too successful in deliberately raising annuals for house use. This can be attributed to lack of interest (a reprehensible idiosyncrasy, no doubt) and to procrastination, which resulted in starting the seeds when the days were approaching their shortest. However, even at that, sweet-alyssum and garden balsam *(Impatiens balsamina)* grew and bloomed freely, even though they were not transplanted from the 3-inch pots in which they were sown.

My best success with annuals was with seedlings dug up from the flower border early in the fall, notably with flowering tobacco *(Nicotiana)*. Those who have a garden in which such plants as wax begonia (not an annual), sweet-alyssum, patience plant, marigold, nicotiana, and torenia are grown will find it profitable to hunt around and in between the plants with a view to picking up seedlings originating from self-sown seeds. Of course if you are meticulous in weeding, you may not find any, but if you, like me, have always bitten off more than you could chew, and in consequence had only time to hit the more conspicuous spots with the hoe, you are likely to find plenty from which to choose. In fact, such seedlings can even turn up in planters and pots used on the terrace.

Medium-size plants are preferred because they can be dug up with the root system nearly intact, resulting in almost no check to growth when the plants are potted up. Nicotianas about 6 inches in diameter; begonias, sweet-alyssum, marigolds, and torenia of 3 to 4 inches in size will be about right. Pot them in well-drained pots large enough to receive the root ball, water thoroughly, and stand them in a shady place for a week or so before bringing them indoors. Then give them a sunny window indoors and pot them in larger pots when the roots become crowded.

You can, if you wish, make a seedbed outdoors and sow the seeds of these, and others mentioned below, in spring to early summer, but you will have the trouble of caring for them and will miss the pleasure that comes from getting something for practically nothing.

*Antirrhinum majus:* You may be tempted to dig up small snapdragons from the border, but these are likely to be more successful for winter blooming in a greenhouse. Seeds may be sown in July and should be grown as cool as possible—50° F. at night is sufficient.

*Browallia speciosa:* This is a semitrailing plant, usually about a foot tall, though it may get larger, with freely produced violet-blue flowers, in the cultivar 'Major' up to 2 inches across. The seeds may be started any time from June to August.

*Exacum affine:* Sometimes known as Persian-violet, it makes a pretty little pot plant when well grown. Its small blue flowers have prominent yellow stamens and are pleasantly fragrant. Seeds can be sown anytime, but for winter and spring bloom, sow in early summer. Pinch to form bushy growth. These are plants for a sunny window; they might do well under fluorescent lights.

**Forget-me-not** *(Myosotis sylvatica):* Once commonly grown as a house plant, and while its numerous, small blue flowers with yellow eyes have charm, the plants today can hardly stand up to the more showy, glamorous African-violets and other favorites. However, those who are always searching for something different to grow indoors may wish to try the forget-me-not. (Personally I have always preferred it outdoors blooming with spring bulbs or naturalized in an open woodland.) The seeds may be sown in midsummer for winter bloom.

All of these annuals and near-annuals should be grown in the general-purpose mixture and shifted into larger pots as their roots become crowded. All need a sunny site and, except for exacum and nicotiana, which prefer warmth, at least 70° F., should be given cool temperatures, between 55° and 65° F.

Other annuals—more often grown in greenhouses for winter bloom, such as candytuft, calendula, and stock—may tempt the adventurous to experiment with them if favorable growing conditions (coolness, ample light and space) are available. I once took a chance on stock, but all it did was writhe snakily about, producing plenty of good foliage but none of the fragrant flowers I desired.

For trailing and climbing annuals, see Section 8 of this chapter.

*Flowers for spring: cineraria (left) and tulips, embellished with cut sprays of pussy willow.*

## PERENNIALS AND WOODY PLANTS RAISED ANNUALLY

**Chrysanthemums—***Chrysanthemum* x *morifolium* **cultivars:** When intended for display in the house, these are handled to best advantage by letting them spend most of their time outdoors or in a cold frame.

The so-called hardy varieties may be grown in the garden in the usual way by digging up old plants as soon as the ground is workable in the spring and pulling off strong-rooted shoots and planting them 1 to 1½ feet apart in rich soil. When the flower buds begin to show, those plants destined for indoor decoration or late summer or fall display on a terrace should be thoroughly watered a day in advance of digging them up with a good ball of soil about their roots. Plant them in pots just large enough to hold the root ball, soak thoroughly, and keep shaded for a few days. Then bring them into a cool plant room or window to open their flowers. This procedure affords us a chance to enjoy late-blooming varieties which would be cut by severe frost if left outdoors. When the flowers have faded, the plants should be cut back and, in their pots, plunged in sand or peat moss in a cold frame if they are wanted for propagation purposes.

If you are ambitious to produce enormous flowers 6 or more inches in diameter, it is better to grow the plants in pots almost from the start. You can find a bewilderingly plentiful offering of large-flowered varieties in mail-order catalogues (see Chapter 21), and since varieties are constantly changing, no recommendations are given here. However, the improvements in modern varieties are truly astounding. For one thing, far less growing time from cutting or division to blooming has been achieved, a boon to the home gardener in northern climates where fall frosts come early. Some varieties also produce large flowers without disbudding.

A convenient way to get a start is to buy rooted cuttings in late spring to early summer and pot them in 3-inch pots in general-purpose mixture. They must have abundant light and free ventilation.

The plants must be shifted to larger pots whenever the roots become crowded, until they receive their final potting (make soil very firm) in pots 6 to 10 inches in diameter in late summer. During the time they are outdoors the pots should be plunged in sand, peat moss, or in rows in the vegetable or cutting garden to reduce the need for watering, which must be carefully attended to. When the pots are plunged after the final potting, put an inch or two of pebbles beneath the pot for drainage and turn the pot every week or so to discourage roots from emerging through the drainage hole. When the plants become pot-bound, they may be fed at weekly intervals with half-strength liquid fertilizer (see Chapter 7), never applying it, however, when the soil is dry. As soon as the flower buds show color, stop feeding. Bring them indoors when frost threatens and keep them in a sunny, cool room.

To get large flowers, the plants must be restricted to one, two, or at most three shoots; and no more than one flower bud should be allowed to develop on each. If two stems are allowed to develop, the flowers will be smaller than if the plants are restricted to one, and still smaller if they carry three stems. If plants with more than one stem are required, the tip of the shoot is pinched out when the plant is potted and two or three of the strongest shoots are allowed to develop. All side growths on these are rubbed off as soon as they are visible. If single-stem plants are needed, obviously only one shoot is allowed to develop. Some growers pinch out the tip of the main shoot or shoots every time the plant is potted up until the beginning of summer, in order to reduce the height of the tall varieties. Continue removing side branches from the main stem or stems. A flower bud ("first-crown" bud) may make its appearance in early summer, but unless this is a very early flowering variety, it will not develop into a good flower and it must be removed by pinching, together with *all but one* of the side branches developing around it. The shoot that is left will produce the "second-crown" bud. If this appears in midsummer or later, retain it for flowering production, removing all the remaining flower buds and auxiliary shoots. This is a simplified procedure designed to eliminate the necessity for keeping a chart (as is done by many professional gardeners!) telling the exact date for taking and the kind of bud—first crown, second crown, or terminal—desirable for each variety.

Not many have the facilities—or the patience—for raising large-flowered chrysanthemums. This much abbreviated account of their culture is included for the few who may wish to try them and as a matter of academic interest to others. And of course you can go to your local florist or garden center and purchase budded or flowering plants that will keep for a long time in a cool room.

**Heliotrope**—*Heliotropium arborescens:* If you happen to have a plant of heliotrope that is really fragrant and want it to bloom in the house in early winter, you should insert cuttings in a shaded cold frame in early summer, pot them in general-purpose mixture when rooted, and keep the flowers pinched off until September. (Heliotrope can also be raised from seeds, but the plants so often lack the fragrance that is the chief reason for growing them.) When brought indoors early in September, give them a sunny window and keep the night temperature down to 50° F. Spray the foliage on sunny days. When they stop blooming, rest them by giving less water at the roots. Plant outdoors as soon as danger of frost is past and start the circle over again with cuttings in early summer. The old plant will bloom all summer, but it will suffer greatly if dug up, potted, and brought indoors in the fall and will not be nearly so satisfactory for winter bloom as young plants handled as described above.

**Lantana**—*Lantana camara:* These shrubs, related to the *Verbena* of summer gardens, with showy, flat-topped, varicolored flower heads 2 inches or more in diameter, are handled in much the same way as heliotrope. They are basically summer bloomers but can be free-flowering and good-tempered in a sunny window garden.

**Primrose**—*Primula:* There are three species of primula, each with many varieties, which can be used as house plants provided the necessary cool conditions, 50° to 65° F., can be given them during the winter. These are Chinese primrose, fairy primrose, poison primrose (*P. sinensis, P. malacoides,* and *P. obconica* respectively). A hybrid between *P. floribunda* (buttercup primrose) and *P. verticillata* (Arabian primrose), known as *P. x kewensis,* is another possibility requiring the same culture as those mentioned above. Its flowers are fragrant.

The fairy primrose gives a graceful, airy effect with myriads of flowers arranged in tiers on slender stalks. Colors range from white through rose to red. The poison primrose, so called because the leaves irritate the skin of sensitive persons, has large leaves and large flowers in umbels, white to red and purple shades. The Chinese primrose has lobed leaves, flowers of many colors, which are arranged in superimposed umbels. Under suitable conditions, such as a cool window or plant room with some sun, all these primroses remain in bloom for many weeks.

For winter bloom the seeds are sown from January to March in a temperature of 60° to 65° F. The seedlings are transplanted to flats, adding ½ part rotted manure to the seed-sowing mixture. They are subsequently potted up, using the humusy mixture recommended for begonias but without charcoal. During the summer they should be kept in a partially shaded area out of direct hot sunshine and where they get plenty of air. Bring them indoors before frost and give a temperature as near as possible to 50° F.; 45° will not harm them. Plenty of light is needed, but shade lightly from bright sunshine except in the depth of winter in the North.

All are perennials, but better results are obtained by raising them annually. For those who don't want to raise their own plants, it is usually possible to buy budded plants in winter from florists and greenhouse operators.

*Senecio* x *hybridus*—**Florists' Cineraria:** Among the showiest of florists' plants, with flowers up to 4 or 5 inches across in some of the exhibition strains, cinerarias demand growing conditions that are beyond the facilities of the average indoor gardener. They must be grown cool; and never, never allowed to become dry.

Cinerarias fall into two main groups: the dwarf, large-flowered kinds and the type that has smaller flowers. In both, the color range extends from white and blue to deep crimson and salmon. Often two colors are arranged on the flowers in well-defined zones.

Most people today prefer to buy budded plants from their florist, but for those who wish to try, this is the method: For autumn and winter flowering, the seeds are sown in May; for spring bloom, in August and September. They must be kept as cool as possible at all times. We used to grow ours during summer in a cold frame set on the north side of a building where they got no direct sun (but plenty of skyshine) except in early morning and evening. Brought indoors before frost, and given a light, airy situation, during the winter they were provided with a night temperature of 45° F., rising to 55° during the day. This just about outlines the kind of environment they need. Use general-purpose potting mixture and avoid allowing them to become pot-bound, until they are in their flowering-size pots, which may be from 5 to 7 inches according to size of plant. Feed with liquid fertilizer when pots are full of roots.

### 3.  BULBS, CORMS, TUBERS, AND HARDY PLANTS FOR FORCING

In this very general and heterogeneous grouping we have some of the most showy of all house plants. For convenience in handling cultural details they are segregated as follows: (1) hardy spring-flowering bulbs, (2) hardy spring-flowering nonbulbous plants, (3) tender spring-flowering bulbs, (4) summer-flowering bulbs—the name "bulbs" in every case being stretched to include corms, tubers, pips, et cetera.

*HARDY SPRING-FLOWERING BULBS:* It is a big advantage when we can use as house plants those that have been grown outdoors and are kept in the house only for a comparatively short time to enable them to bloom a little in advance of their outdoor season. The hardy spring-flowering bulbs

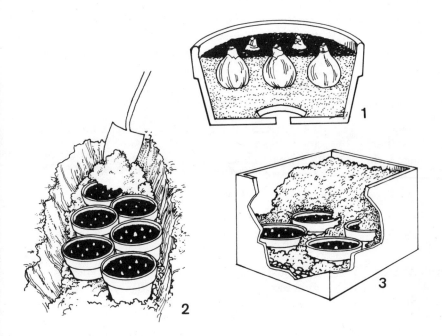

*Forcing hardy bulbs, such as daffodils and tulips: Bulbs are planted close together in squat bulb pot. Pots can be stored outdoors in a trench and covered with peat moss and soil; after the soil freezes about 1/2 inch deep, add a layer of straw or leaves to prevent further freezing. Or use a wooden crate large enough to accommodate the pots and fill around and on top of the pots with moist peat moss.*

possess this feature beyond all others because normally they are produced under ideal conditions in regions especially suited to their culture. Stored within the confines of the bulbs are all the makings for the successful production of roots, leaves, and flowers, and they will do this provided they are given a reasonable chance. Usually they are inexpensive, so that we don't feel too bad about discarding them when their blooms have faded. If putting them on the compost pile is too great a shock to your notions of thrift, you can continue to water them until the leaves wither naturally; or until it is warm enough to plant them outdoors in the perennial border or other appropriate place. Treated thus, they will probably bloom the following spring—almost certainly in two years—but only if they are left outdoors; bulbs forced one year are not satisfactory for forcing the following season. Always purchase best-quality bulbs for indoor culture—you start off with two strikes against you if you use inferior bulbs.

The kinds most favored for indoor culture, in order of their importance, are: daffodil or narcissus, tulip, hyacinth, crocus, grape-hyacinth, and scilla. There is a host of "lesser bulbs" including snowdrop, winter-aconite, et cetera, with which the adventurous and those who like variety will experiment.

A list of cultivars suitable for indoor culture, of the three principal kinds, is given below. It can be augmented, if necessary, by using the forcing varieties recommended by dealers in their catalogues. Those daffodils *(Narcissus)* that will not survive severe freezing are included among the "tender" bulbs.

## DAFFODILS

| 'Cheerfulness' | 'Flower Record' | 'Silver Chimes' |
| 'Dutch Master' | 'Ice Follies' | 'Spring Glory' |
| 'February Gold' | 'King Alfred' | 'Verger' |

## TULIPS

(F = Fragrant)

| *Single Early* | *Darwin and Darwin Hybrids* | *Cottage* |
| 'Bellona' F | 'Clara Butt' | 'Bronze Queen' |
| 'Brilliant Star' | 'Diplomat' | 'Golden Harvest' |
| 'Couleur Cardinal' | 'Gudoshnik' | 'Rosy Wings' |
| 'De Wet' F | 'Jewel of Spring' | |
| 'Dr. Plesman' F | | |
| 'Prince of Austria' | *Early Double* | *Late Double* |
| 'White Hawk' | 'Peach Blossom' | 'Livingstone' |

*Triumph*

| 'Apricot Beauty' | 'Orange Wonder' |
| 'First Lady' | 'Paul Richter' |

## HYACINTHS

| 'Borah' | 'Lady Derby' | 'Ostara' |
| 'City of Haarlem' | 'La Victoire' | 'Salmonetta' |
| 'Delft Blue' | 'L'Innocence' | 'Snow Princess' |

Roman hyacinths, which produce several smaller spikes with fewer flowers from each bulb, are preferred for early bloom. By potting them in late August or early September and bringing them into warmth at three-week intervals they may be had in bloom from November to spring. They should not be exposed to severe freezing. Similar are the multiflora hyacinths which can be forced into bloom in January.

If you have trouble locating Roman or multiflora hyacinths, most mail-order concerns that specialize in spring-blooming bulbs offer specially prepared hyacinths with standard-size blooms that can be forced into bloom as early as Christmas. Commerical growers who force these hardy bulbs into bloom to obtain flowers for cutting commonly plant the bulbs thickly in shallow boxes (flats), but this method is not likely to appeal to the average home gardener who doesn't have a greenhouse and who would do better to stick to ordinary flowerpots and bulb pans. The pots and their contents may be subjected to freezing during the preliminary treatment, so you will not want to expose fancy, expensive containers to the hazards of breakage and to possible injury to the finish from contact with the soil. If the appearance of the ordinary flowerpots offends your artistic eye, they can be slipped inside jardinieres or something similar during the time they are in bloom and on display.

It is well to adapt the container to the bulbs. For tall, strong-growing daffodils and Darwin tulips, use 6-inch standard pots, which will take about three daffodil bulbs or five or six tulips. For hyacinths use 4½- or 5-inch pots for single bulbs; or plant three in a 6¾-inch pot, which in height is between the standard pot and the bulb pan. For smaller bulbs—crocus, scilla, grape-hyacinth, and netted iris *(Iris reticulata)*—the regulation bulb pans in 6-to-8-inch size are satisfactory. These can also be used for tulips and daffodils, but to my mind the proportions between plants and container are not so good. As a rule a space of 1 to 1½ inches should be allowed between the bulbs.

The fact that many bulbs can be brought into bloom by growing them in water, pebbles and water, peat moss and fiber—all of which are deficient in nutrients—is an indication that the quality of the soil, provided it is porous, is less important with these hardy forcing bulbs than it is with most plants.

*For fragrant flowers, grow paper-white narcissus in pebbles and water and hyacinth bulbs in special hyacinth glasses.*

Nothing you can do between the time of planting the bulbs and their blooming will increase the number of flowers they will produce. Good soil and good growing conditions, however, will improve the size and quality of the flowers; so, if possible, use the soil mixture suggested in Chapter 6. This, perhaps, is a good place to point out that improper handling (sometimes, but rarely, before you get the bulbs) may result in the blasting and nondevelopment of the flowers.

Planting can be done any time in the fall up until December in the New York City area and regions with similar climates, but usually the earlier the bulbs are in the soil the better it is for them. Hardy daffodils and winter-aconites especially are likely to be harmed if left out of the ground too long.

Don't mix varieties requiring differing periods for development in the same pot, because the appearance of the late ones will be marred by the presence of fading leaves of the early ones and the pot as a whole will never be at its best.

The pots and pans should be scrubbed with water and a stiff brush and allowed to dry before using. New pots should be soaked in water for a few hours or they will take too much moisture out of the soil.

Put a piece of broken pot over the hole in the bottom of the pot, cover this with a handful or two of the coarser parts from your soil mixture, and then put in enough soil, pressed down *lightly,* so that when the bulbs are placed in position their noses are about ½ inch below the rim of the pot. Gently press the bulb into the soil, but *not* with a screwing motion—such treatment may rub off developing rootlets. When bulbs are in place, fill the pot with soil and press down firmly so that the surface is at least ½ inch below the rim. If the soil beneath the bulbs is packed too hard, and that above too loose, the growth of the roots may force the bulbs out of the pot. After the bulbs are planted give the soil a *thorough watering,* either by repeated sprinklings or by standing the pots in a tub or pan containing a few inches of water, leaving them there until moisture shows on the surface.

The treatment from now on has a most important bearing on the success or failure of the bulbs. An old rule says: Provide a temperature of 40° F. for rooting (a period of six weeks or longer), 50° for three weeks or so for growth of stem and leaves, and 60° for flower production. These ideals are usually impossible of attainment under home conditions, but you should approximate them as closely as you can and at least keep them in mind.

There are several ways of arriving at the same destination. The plunge pit is one. A well-drained location is selected in the coolest part of the garden—perhaps in the shade of a building or at the edge of a vegetable plot. A trench or pit is dug a foot deep, large enough to accommodate the pots. Three inches of pebbles or small stones or broken pieces of flowerpot are placed in the bottom to provide drainage and to discourage worms from entering the pots. Sprinkle a thin layer of sand (or peat moss) on the surface of the soil in pots; this will make it easier to separate covering material cleanly from the pot soil when the bulbs are brought in. Stand the pots on the drainage layer and fill in between and over them with the soil removed in making the pit, forming it into a mound. Leave it this way until the surface freezes ½ inch deep and then put on a layer of straw, hay, or something similar in sufficient thickness to prevent the soil around the bulbs from freezing solid. Not that this would harm them, but it might make it impossible to get them out of the pit without much labor and breakage of pots when the time comes to bring them indoors. A variation of this method is to use peat moss or leaf mold in place of soil for covering.

A method that may be the best for the average house-plant enthusiast is to stand the pots on a 2-inch layer of pebbles in a box about the size of a bushel basket—a deep fruit box or possibly an empty wine bottle carton. Leave a space of 2 inches between the pots and the side of the box and fill this with moist peat moss, which should also be packed between and over the pots, filling the box. Place the box (or several stacked closely together) outdoors in a cool place; and, when severe weather threatens, cover top and sides of the boxes with a thick layer of straw or its equivalent. Even if the peat moss does become frozen, it is a comparatively easy matter to bring the entire box indoors to thaw out so that the pots of bulbs can be removed without breakage. In boxes, it is easy to protect the bulbs from rodents by covering all possible entrances with ¼-inch mesh hardware cloth.

If you are lucky enough to have a cellar entry on the north side of the house, the box or boxes of bulbs may be placed there and covered with burlap bags if the weather becomes so cold that they are likely to freeze.

An unheated house cellar or a root cellar where the temperature stays between 35° and 45° F. is a good place to store bulbs during the rooting period, but it is rare to find such conditions today except in old country houses.

If a variety of bulbs is planted, it is necessary to label them so you will know what you are bringing in; and unless you have so few pots that all are brought in at the same time, you will also want to arrange them in the plunge pit so that it will not be necessary to open it up in its entirety to find the kinds you need.

One method of labeling is to write the names on wired wooden tree labels (obtainable from garden centers) and affix them to the top of 15-to-18-inch plant stakes. These are pushed into the pots when the bulbs are potted (take care not to spear any of the bulbs) and will project above the plunge-pit covering so that you know where to dig to get what you want. If the bulbs are placed in a storage cellar, ordinary 4-inch wooden pot labels can be placed directly in the pot; or you can write an abbreviation of the name with a grease pencil on the rim of the pot. There is no chance for Junior to transpose the labels when your back is turned if this last method is adopted; but if the same pots are to be used the following season, be sure that the name is erased if a different variety is planted.

Arrange the bulbs in the plunge pit in the order in which they are to come out so you can open one end and remove as many pots as are needed without disturbing the remainder. If you follow the plan of putting them in boxes, the selection of kinds in each box can be a forcing unit. The regulation 1⅛-bushel fruit box will hold two 5-inch pots and four 4½-inch; or three 6-inch and two 4-inch, which is as many pots as most of us want to bring in at one time.

When the pots are filled with roots, which will be in five to eight weeks, depending on kind, the bulbs are ready to be brought indoors to make their top growth. Remember the nearer it is to the natural flowering season, the easier it is to achieve success; and it will do no harm to leave the bulbs in the plunge pit (in northern climates) until January or February. But if you want early flowers, take a chance in late November or December. If the roots are making their way through the drainage hole in the bottom of the pot, they are sufficiently advanced. When no roots are outwardly visible, their condition can be determined by turning the bulbs out of the pot. This is done by placing the left hand (if you are a right-handed person) with fingers spread on the surface of the soil and, inverting the pot, tapping its rim on the edge of bench or table. There should be a generous mat of whitish roots in evidence. Do not spend too much time admiring them—return them gently to the pot as soon as you have satisfied yourself as to their condition.

When they are brought indoors, follow the pattern set by nature—increase the temperature gradually. Keep them in a temperature of 45° to 50° F. for ten days to three weeks before exposing them to greater warmth—if you can possibly manage it. During this period the light should not be too intense. When they have made a few inches of top growth, they can be placed in a sunny window, preferably in a temperature of 60° F. and certainly not over 70°. When the flowers are opening, and until they fade, you will, of course, want to keep them on view in living-room temperature during the daytime. It is quite all right to do this, but you will find that the flowers will last longer if, every night, you put them in a cool place (40° to 50° F.) just before going to bed.

From the time the bulbs are potted until the foliage withers (if you are planning to plant out the bulbs), the soil must be kept constantly moist; and during the time the tops are in active growth and until the flowers fade it is important that ample supplies of water are provided.

These methods are applicable to hardy spring-flowering bulbs in general. Crocus, snowdrop, and winter-aconite will not tolerate severe forcing, and it is better to bring these along to the flowering stage in a temperature not in excess of 50° F.

Water culture: The once common practice of forcing hardy bulbs, especially hyacinths, in water, is again popular. Hyacinth glasses, obtained from mail-order bulb specialists, are used. Enough water is put in them to barely touch the base of the bulb set on a constriction near the top of the vase. Then keep in a cool, dark, airy place until roots reach the bottom of the glass. (See also paper-white narcissi in the tender bulbs part of this section.)

Few plants are capable of supplying so much color and beauty in the home with so little effort as the hardy spring-flowering bulbs; and, although they are only transients, they are nonetheless welcome.

*NONBULBOUS SPRING FLOWERS:* It is possible to get a preview of spring by hurrying along certain hardy plants that normally bloom outdoors early in the spring. Among them are: *Astilbe, Claytonia, Convallaria, Dicentra, Epigaea* (trailing-arbutus), *Hepatica, Sanguinaria* (bloodroot), *Shortia, Tiarella, Trillium* and *Viola* (violet). Those who are interested in native plants and have access to wild areas in which they can dig without violating conservation laws or property rights doubtless will enjoy trying other kinds such as *Anemonella, Aquilegia* (columbine), et cetera.

The general practice to follow is to dig up the plants in the fall, taking care not to injure the root systems more than is necessary. Pot them in soil similar to that in which they are growing, water thoroughly, and plunge them in a cold frame. When several hard frosts have been experienced, mulch them with salt marsh hay, pine needles, or something similar, and forget about them until near the end of February. Then bring them indoors and keep in a well-lighted position in a temperature of 50° F. until their flower buds show, when they can be brought into the living room or plant room.

Roots of *Astilbe,* called "spirea" by florists, can be purchased in fall for forcing from a few dealers. The root mass should be soaked in a pail of water, potted in general-purpose mixture, watered thoroughly, and stored as cold as possible for six to eight weeks. Then bring indoors in a well-lighted window (60° F. temperature) and keep soil *wet*—stand pot in a saucer constantly filled with water.

Ordinarily, retarded "pips" of lily-of-the-valley *(Convallaria),* specially grown and prepared for forcing (use no other), are available from dealers in fall and early winter. These can be potted in sand or almost any material that will hold moisture (one grower who forced them by the million used sawdust) after the tips of the roots have been trimmed with a sharp knife. Space them 1 to 2 inches apart with the pips (buds) just above the surface. Water thoroughly, keep in a dark moist place (a closed ventilated box will do) for ten days at 70° F., and then gradually expose them to light. You should have blooms within three weeks after planting—if all goes well.

Two species, at least, of *Dicentra* have been used for forcing: Dutchman's breeches *(D. cucullaria)*—which does not really belong here because it has tubers—and bleeding heart *(D. spectabilis).* Doubtless others, such as fringed bleeding heart *(D. eximia),* could also be used. The bleeding heart will not stand for hurry-up tactics. As an example, one plant, dug up and potted September 25, was left outdoors until the end of January when it was brought into a cold room. A month later it was transferred to the living room, where it proceeded to grow apace, the pastel coloring of the young shoots and the gray-green ferny foliage giving much pleasure. But the flowers blasted—

*Cyclamen—a beautiful pot plant for cool, humid interiors.*

never a one getting beyond pinhead stage. I'm inclined to believe it was too much heat too soon.

Hepaticas (and possibly others) do not demand a long rest period. I knew of a plant used in a small plant arrangement which was dug up on November 17 and three weeks later bloomed in a Greenwich Village apartment!

If you have no cold frame, or don't want to be bothered with the care of hardy plants in fall and winter, it is possible to hunt around in the fields and woods for early-blooming plants, to be dug up and potted as soon as new growth is visible, and brought indoors to get a few days' jump on the season. Marsh-marigold, many violets, and bluets respond well to this treatment. So does the fast-spreading Confederate violet *(Viola sororia)*; digging some clumps for indoors is one way to reduce the outdoor population. It deserves repeating that good sense in regard to conservation should be observed when digging these native plants.

The plants in this section can be planted outdoors as soon as their attractiveness wanes, with the exception of lily-of-the-valley, which, as it makes no new roots when forced, is of no further use.

*TENDER WINTER- AND SPRING-FLOWERING BULBS:* These are mostly plants that cannot endure freezing. Generally they are not forced to bloom out of their natural season; therefore, when grown in good soil in a greenhouse, they may be rested and used another year. In the house, however, it is seldom that good enough conditions can be provided so that, with the exceptions noted below, it is usually better to buy new bulbs annually—bulbs that have been grown outdoors in a favored climate.

**Narcissi** of the paper-white type, such as 'Grand Soleil d'Or' and the so-called Chinese sacred lily, are included in this section because they cannot endure severe freezing. Usually these bulbs are grown in fiber obtained from garden centers or bulb specialists or in water with pebbles in the bowl to keep them stable. The method is to plant them so that about ⅚ of the bulb is above the rooting medium. Don't attempt to start them before the middle of October, then place them in a cool, dark place for two or three weeks, or until growth starts, when they should be brought into a sunny window and a temperature of 60° to 65° F. Keep the growing medium moist; and, if grown in pebbles, maintain the water at a level that is just below the base of the bulb. Although the paper-white narcissus is almost foolproof, lanky leaf growth and blasting or nondevelopment of the flowers are likely to occur if they are started too early and kept all the time in temperatures above 70° F. Buy the bulbs from a reputable source to be sure of getting good ones. They should be discarded after flowering.

*Cyclamen:* We may as well face it that cyclamens *(Cyclamen persicum)* are not easy to grow for most. If your rooms are kept at a temperature of 70° F. in the winter, you had better just cross them off your list and forget about them. They are gloriously beautiful, and it is well worth while to try to provide their rather exacting requirements. It is encouraging to know that there are some house-plant enthusiasts who are able to grow them either from seeds or as tuberous perennials persisting year after year.

First, as to its care when you receive a cyclamen as a flowering plant from the florist: Remember it was grown in a humid greenhouse in which the night temperature was maintained around 50° F. with a rise of 10° during the day. Try to give approximately these conditions indoors. You will not be able to match them exactly, but perhaps you have a cool room with an east window or a room in which the window area is considerably cooler than the rest of the room in which the plant may be stood; or an underheated room with plenty of light but with shade from bright sunshine except early in the morning. Never allow the soil to become dry during the time the plant is in bloom.

A *Home Garden* magazine reader sent in the following account of a six-year-old plant which produced as many as thirty blooms at a time. Her method:

Gradually reduce the water supply after growth wanes toward spring. Then the pot is stored in a cool room until the weather warms up outside, when it is placed outdoors in filtered shade. During all this ripening time the soil is lightly moistened about once in two weeks.

Early in August the corm is lifted and the soil replaced by a fresh mixture—rich loam and compost, 2 parts; sand, 2 parts; and oak leaf mold, 1 part. Then the corm is reset, high in the *same* pot, if possible, and the plant watered and placed under filtered shade again, where little headway is made until cool weather sets in near the end of the month. Early in September the cyclamen is brought in to a window with morning sun where 3½- to 4-inch leaves soon develop.

Here the plant stands on a thick block of wood in a deep bowl always filled with water, which is replaced daily with more *at boiling temperature.* This often rises to cover the pot base for 1 inch with no harm to the plant from the heat, if it is in need of moisture. The humidifying effect is marvelous, of course. Subsequently all the moisture needed reaches the roots via the wooden block. Weak liquid fertilizer is given monthly. Leaves reach a fine size and do not discolor. Flowers first open soon after the turn of the year and many buds continue to appear.

There is considerable deviation in the living-room temperature—a variation from 45° F. at night to 65° during the day. Still my cyclamen lives and blooms for some three months each winter and continues to do so *year after year.*

Notice particularly the temperatures 45° F. at night to 65° in the day. Notice, too, how the watering is done. While I am dubious about the necessity of using *boiling* water, the method is otherwise admirable.

September is considered the best month for sowing when raising them from seeds. While you must usually figure on a wait of fifteen to eighteen months before you get blooms from the florist-type cyclamens, there are now faster-blooming hybrids. The seeds should be sown in a well-drained bulb pan or seed flat in the mixture advocated for seed sowing (Chapter 15). Moisten by standing the pan in a container of water until the surface soil seems moist, then cover with a piece of glass or plastic shaded with paper. Remove covering when the seeds germinate; keep in a well-lighted place but shade from direct sun during the hottest part of the day. When the seedlings have two leaves, transplant them an inch apart in a flat of soil—loam, 1 part; sand, 1 part; leaf mold or peat moss, 2 parts.

Transplant again to give them more room when the leaves begin to touch. Throughout the winter try to keep the temperature within the 50° to 55° F. range. In April pot them in small individual pots and shift into progressively larger pots whenever the roots become crowded. For the second and subsequent pottings use the general-purpose mixture. Always be sure that the pots are well drained and raise the corm so that it is half in, half out of the soil. Five- or 6-inch pots will be large enough for the final potting, but when these become filled with roots and the first flower buds are to be seen, an occasional watering every three or four weeks with liquid fertilizer is beneficial, though be careful not to allow it to touch the crown of the plant. One way of avoiding this is to apply it by subirrigation as described above— actually it is a good plan to water by this means all the time the plants are indoors.

From midspring until fall the plants should be kept in a cool, well-lighted spot outdoors, shaded from bright sunshine during the hottest part of the day. When they are brought indoors, give them, if possible, an east window and stand them on pebble-filled trays containing water to increase the humidity. Ventilate as much as you can without drafts and without reducing the temperature to less than 45° F.

Here are some more of the most important tender bulbs to be grown in soil recommended for bulbs in Chapter 6, except where otherwise indicated. If acid, add about 1 tablespoon of ground limestone to about 4 quarts of soil mixture.

**Freesia:** The ever-popular, sweet-smelling freesia is native to South Africa and is grown in quantity in California to provide bulbs for culture in greenhouses and homes. Today freesias are obtainable in many color forms in tones of white, yellow, orange, pink, and violet. They should be potted in the fall, six bulbs to a 5-inch pot, at intervals of three or four weeks if a succession of blooms is required. Cool culture and plenty of sunshine are essential, so it is a good plan to give them a start in a sunny cold frame, bringing them indoors when frost threatens. Go easy on the watering until top growth is visible, then soak them whenever the surface appears to be dry. In the house give them a sunny window and a temperature as near 50° F. as possible. They will need some support, which can be given by placing three or four 1-foot slender bamboo stakes or stout wires around the edge of the pot and connecting them with thin twine.

**Amaryllis:** The plant commonly known as amaryllis *(Hippeastrum)* provides almost the largest flowers it is possible to grow indoors. The old-time *Hippeastrum,* itself a hybrid, has been superseded by improved varieties in a great range of colors. Dormant bulbs may be purchased from local outlets and mail-order bulb specialists during the fall and winter. When received they should be potted singly, with ⅔ of the bulb above the surface. Do not use pots whose diameter is more than 3 inches greater than that of the bulb.

*Correct way to pot an amaryllis.*

Keep them in a temperature between 60° and 70° F. and do not water until the flower bud is visible, and then only sparingly until the leaves start to develop, after which they should be watered freely. The treatment accorded after flowering will determine whether or nor flowers will be produced the following year.

Give them outdoor culture during the summer with special attention to feeding and watering so the foliage continues to grow. The pots can be sunk to their rims in the ground in a sunny area.

After flowering is past in winter or spring, the pots should be kept in a sunny window, watered regularly, and given a dose of weak liquid fertilizer every two or three weeks. When danger of frost is past, put them outdoors, preferably plunged in their pots as described above. In the fall, when weather begins to cool, bring them indoors and gradually reduce the supply of water at the roots, giving only enough to prevent the leaves from wilting. Some varieties will go completely dormant, losing all their leaves; others may retain some of theirs. These last must be kept in a light situation and watered occasionally. It is not necessary to repot annually unless the bulbs are becoming too crowded in their pots. Merely remove, when new leaf growth is beginning, as much of the topsoil as you can without disturbing the roots and replace with a 50-50 mixture of loam and thoroughly rotted manure or rich compost with a teaspoonful of bone meal—or superphosphate to each 5-inch pot.

**Cape-cowslips—***Lachenalia:* The ones commonly used, varieties of *L. bulbifera,* grow from 6 to 10 inches high with spikes of pendent flowers (somewhat after the manner of the English bluebell), which are usually coral red tipped with green or purple. The bulbs may be potted just below the surface, about 1½ inches apart, in 6-inch bulb pans. They must be grown under cool conditions, and could well be kept in a cold frame until frost threatens to penetrate it, when they should be brought into an unheated, frost-free, sunny room or, lacking that, a cool window.

*Babiana, Ixia, Sparaxis,* and other "Cape bulbs" are available for those who want to experiment with this class of plants. My best successes with the "Cape" bulbs have been with *Ixia,* treated the same way as *Freesia,* and with *Veltheimia viridifolia.* Many of the Cape bulbs are difficult to locate in catalogues but *Veltheimia* (I know of no common name for it!) is growing in popularity and is usually offered by bulb specialists in their fall catalogues. It is an excellent cool-window subject, doing best with at least a few hours of sun and in a wide temperature range from 50° to 65° F. The flowers, yellowish or tinged with red, and reminiscent of those of the hardy *Kniphofia,* are clustered on a main stalk that rises from a rosette of fresh green leaves about 12 inches long. Potting is the same as for amaryllis, but the bulbs must have a rest in summer without water, best accomplished by turning the pots on their sides. As soon as new leaf growth starts in late summer or fall, resume watering. Bulbs can remain in the same pots for years, but eventually will form offsets and need division.

**Easter Lily**—*Lilium longiflorum:* Not reliably winter hardy in most northern climates. The bulbs should be potted singly in 5- or 6-inch pots with 1 to 2 inches of soil under them (they are "stem-rooters," hence the deep planting) in September or October. If the weather continues mild, keep them in a shaded cold frame for a month and then bring indoors and give a 60° F. temperature. Keep soil moist, give all the light available, and watch out for aphids. After flowering, keep the foliage growing, and when frost danger is over, bulbs can be planted outdoors.

Some of the remarkable lily hybrids of the last decade or so are now being offered as pot subjects. The bulbs, available in the fall, are precooled and after potting should flower in about two and a half months. Heights for these hybrids range from 1 to 2 feet and colors from red and pink to yellow and white. Cultural treatment is as for the Easter lily, or follow the special instructions sent with the bulbs.

*Oxalis:* The group to which the Bermuda-buttercup belongs contains several species and varieties with a more or less floppy habit suitable for hanging containers. All the commonly grown kinds have three-parted cloverlike leaves. The Bermuda-buttercup *(O. pes-caprae)* has yellow flowers; *O. bowiei* is pink with lush foliage; 'Grand Duchess' is lavender and there is also 'Grand Duchess White'; *O. hirta* has violet or purple flowers and mosslike foliage. These bulbs start into growth with fragile shoots—whether or not they are planted— so it is desirable to obtain and pot them as early as possible in the fall to avoid damage. They may be set 1 inch deep, singly in 3-inch pots; or six in a 5- or 6-inch pot which must be well drained. Add enough limestone to the soil to make it slightly alkaline. Water sparingly until growth shows above the soil, and then water normally, but don't keep the soil sopping wet all the time. A sunny window is essential, and a temperature around 60° F. is desirable.

**Calla-lily:** The best known calla-lily is *Zantedeschia aethiopica,* which has large white, trumpetlike flowers in winter. There is a dwarf form known as 'Compacta' or 'Godfreyana' that is more suitable for most indoor gardens. The yellow calla *(Z. elliottiana)* is not so robust as *Z. aethiopica* and has yellow spathes ("flowers") and white-spotted leaves. The pink calla *(Z. rehmannii),* about a foot tall, has rose-colored spathes. Tubers of all these kinds are obtainable in the fall, when they should be potted in general-purpose mixture. Apply weak liquid fertilizer every three weeks when pot-bound. (Some growers recommend keeping the tubers of the yellow calla in a warm, dry place for a few weeks prior to potting them.) The tubers may be started in 4- or 5-inch pots and given larger sizes when they become pot-bound. Water sparingly at first but when growth is well above the surface keep them constantly wet. Grow them in a sunny window and give a 68° to 70° F. temperature during the day. After flowering, allow the foliage to mature, gradually reducing water, and finally allowing the tubers to rest for about two or three months. Then repot and start the cycle over again.

**Devil's Tongue:** Occasionally one sees devil's tongue recommended for house culture. This is the plant variously known as sacred lily-of-India (though it is not a lily and is native to China), snake-palm (not a snake and not a palm), umbrella arum, or voodoo plant and botanically as *Amorphophallus rivieri* (sometimes listed as *Hydrosme rivieri*). Granted that this plant of many aliases can be grown in the house, and admitting that its large purplish-maroon and spotted inflorescence (up to 6 feet in height) is arresting in its appearance; and that its enormous single leaf, 4 feet in diameter, is definitely ornamental—I submit that it should never be brought into the house during the time its flowers are discharging their offensive carrion odor, or perhaps my sense of smell is overdeveloped!

Kept at room temperature, the dormant tubers ordinarily throw up their inflorescences in March. If it were possible to keep them at a low temperature (say around 45° to 50° F.), it is likely that their flowering could be delayed until the advent of warm weather, which would enable us to place them outdoors where they could be seen and not smelled. This ought to be feasible, for in spite of their tropical origin I have known them to survive a New York winter when planted outdoors and mulched with about 6 inches of leaves. If dormancy is prolonged by low temperature, amorphophallus then becomes a house plant only in the sense that its tubers are stored indoors during the winter, for its real growth is made when planted in rich soil in a large pot or in the open ground in a sheltered location outdoors as soon as the ground has warmed up in spring and there is no longer any danger of frost. As a pot plant, it makes a tall, unusual leafy accent for a summer terrace.

**Monarch of the East, Red-calla, or Lizard-arum—***Sauromatum guttatum:* This is similarly foul-smelling but has a tailed, green-yellow spathe with black-purple spots. Its smaller size makes it a better bet as a house plant. It is also hardier when planted outdoors, and may be expected to withstand freezing temperatures if the tubers are planted 6 inches deep and mulched.

Both of these oddities are capable of producing their inflorescences without benefit of soil or moisture provided their tubers are of flowering size—4 inches or more in diameter for *Amorphophallus;* 3 inches for *Sauromatum.* Immediately after flowering, however, the tubers must be planted out, or, if the weather is not sufficiently warm, put in large flowerpots with rich soil to develop their umbrellalike leafy growth, which lasts all summer.


*SUMMER-FLOWERING BULBS:* With outdoor activities in full swing and with so many annuals and hardy plants to enjoy, there is, perhaps, less incentive to try to ensure a supply of flowering house plants for the summer months. However, often something is needed to take the place of the plants that are summering outdoors, and some of these "bulbs" are so beautiful that anyone interested in plants can hardly forgo the pleasure of growing them. Many can be grown in tubs, hanging containers, and planters or window boxes and used to decorate outdoor areas, provided they are sheltered from strong sunshine, wind, and heavy rainstorms. Caladiums and tuberous begonias, especially, make elegant accents for terrace areas.

**Achimenes:** The plants known as *Achimenes* have flowers somewhat reminiscent of those of gloxinia *(Sinningia speciosa),* to which they are related. The flowers are produced in great abundance on slender 8- to 15-inch stems for several weeks, usually in summer. The length of the blooming period depends to some extent on the variety and the care the plants receive. Of velvety texture, the ½- to 2½-inch flowers exist in a wide color range, from mauve, blue, and violet to pink, salmon, coral, and crimson. The opposite leaves sometimes show attractive bronze tints but may "burn" if they become wet in bright sun. The plants tend toward floppiness in growth habits and are therefore excellent subjects for hanging containers. Many named varieties are now available, mostly of hybrid origin.

The scaly rhizomes or tubers, which look like catkins or miniature pine cones, are planted ½ inch deep in shallow flats of moist sand and peat moss from January to March. When the shoots are from 1 to 2 inches tall, they are carefully dug up and potted in bulb pans, in begonia soil, using about six plants to a 10-to-12-inch container. Keep the soil moist and shade from bright sunshine, but give them plenty of light. When the pots are filled with roots, water them occasionally with liquid fertilizer, such as a fish emulsion. As soon as they are through flowering, gradually reduce the supply of water; and when the foilage has withered, keep them entirely dry. Before winter the tubers should be removed from their pots and stored in dry sand or in plastic bags in a temperature of 50° to 65° F. until it is time to start them again. The rhizomes will tell you when they have had enough rest by starting into growth without water or your help! They are profligate propagators—the five or six rhizomes of the previous season will have multiplied tremendously and must be separated and shared with deserving friends.

**Begonias—tuberous-rooted kinds:** The tuberous begonias are among the showiest of all plants, with flowers varying in size from 3 to 8 inches in diameter—and their culture is not difficult, especially in those regions favored with a cool summer climate. There are various types available with colors ranging from white through pink to rose, scarlet, and crimson; and from pale yellow to salmon, orange, and apricot. They may be single or double with plain petals, or frilled and ruffled, or decorated with a contrasting color on the edge of each petal. The double types may exhibit the exquisite form of the camellia-flowered varieties, look like a rosebud, or have the congested, frilled, and serrated petals similar to a carnation. Multiflora types have smaller flowers produced abundantly all summer. Then there are those with trailing stems (suitable for the front edge of planters or window boxes or hanging containers). Usually these begonias are sold under types and colors, and within these groupings there are a few named varieties.

Their culture is much the same as that of *Achimenes.* The tubers may be started in March or April in peat moss and sand, or in one of the soil-less mixes. Cover with ½ inch of soil. When growth begins, lift them carefully

*Tuber of tuberous begonia, showing buds, ready for starting into growth indoors in spring.*

*Early growth of a tuberous begonia. Tubers can be planted individually as here or several tubers can be set in flats.*

and pot them singly in 3- or 4-inch pots to be transferred later to larger sizes (use soil recommended for begonias, Chapter 6), or they may be put directly into the containers in which they are to bloom—6- or 8-inch bulb pans or pots. As with all begonias, drainage is important, so don't fail to put an inch or so of flowerpot chips in the bottom of each pot. Shade them from constant bright sunshine and keep soil moist but not soggy. In the fall, when they show signs of going to rest, gradually withhold water; and, when they have completely died down, remove the tubers and store at 50° to 60° F. in dry sand or peat moss or in plastic bags. While the usual practice is to purchase tubers, the adventurous can raise tuberous begonias from seeds and may get blooms the same year if they are sown in February; but it is a ticklish proposition for the beginner.

*Caladium* x *hortulanum*—**Fancy-leaved Caladiums:** Caladiums do not really belong here, for their flowers are insignificant; but the fancy-leaved kinds have much the same color effect as flowers, so here they are. There are many hybrids of *Caladium bicolor,* a native of tropical America, with long-stalked, arrowhead leaves, which in some varieties are almost transparent. Their coloration is immensely varied, as may be deduced from the few varieties described below. The plants range in height from 1 to 2½ feet. A popular caladium is 'Candidum', which has white leaves with green edges and veins. This is one of the best for an early display—it can be had in full leaf in January. 'Lord Derby' is translucent rose, with green veins and edges; 'John Peed' is bright red and green; 'Mrs. W. B. Halderman', pink with greenish veins and margins; 'White Christmas', white and bright green; 'Frieda Hemple', red leaves bordered green.

Preferably the tubers should be started in early spring in a warm temperature (70° to 85° F.) in shallow boxes of peat moss and sand, covering them about ½ inch deep. When the roots begin to grow, pot them in 3-inch pots in 3 parts peat moss, 1 part loam, 1 part sand. As soon as these pots are filled with roots, shift them to 5- or 6-inch sizes and use 2 parts loam, 2 parts peat moss, 1 part dried manure, 1 part sand. Or use one of the soil-less mixes throughout, following directions as to fertilizing on the bag. Shade from bright sunshine and water freely. When the leaves begin to fade, gradually reduce water until soil is dry. Store in the soil in their pots or in dry sand or peat moss in plastic bags in a temperature not less than 60° F.

**Gloxinia:** There are not many flowers that can beat the gloxinia *(Sinningia speciosa)* in size and variety of coloring. The flowers are broadly tubular, with flaring petals which may extend their diameter to 5 inches. Some are dark-spotted on a light ground; some have white throats with the remainder of the flower pink, blue, purple, or red; and some have their petals margined with a broad band of contrasting color. Although most commonly sold in mixture, many named varieties are also available from American and European hybridizers. The method of growing them is practically that of tuberous begonias except that it is wise to avoid getting water on the fuzzy velvety leaves. During the winter they may be stored as suggested for begonias or kept dry in their pots. If this last is done, it is possible to get by without repotting them for a year or two if some of the surface soil is scraped off and replaced by a 50-50 mixture of soil and dried manure, with a teaspoonful of bone meal or superphosphate.

I once gave a friend in the country a small plant of gloxinia, which was proudly displayed for my admiration a few years later. And she had a right to be proud, for that year the plant, in a 6-inch pot, had produced thirty-five blooms, it was 26 inches in diameter, and many of the leaf blades were 9 inches long. It was kept in a south window shaded by curtains and, from the west, by a porch.

Gloxinias can be propagated from seeds in spring (flowers in about seven months) or by inserting leaf cuttings. A propagating case is desirable but not absolutely necessary. One year, being in an experimental mood, I put one leaf in a glass of water in the house and another in a pot of soil in the shade of a building outdoors. Both produced tubers—the one started in soil being the larger.

*Sinningia pusilla* **and offspring:** There are other sinningias worth the attention of house-plant enthusiasts. The very popular miniatures such as 'Doll-baby', 'White Sprite', 'Little Imp', and many others are hybrids of *Sinningia pusilla* and other species (see Chapter 19) and form dainty foliage rosettes from which rise the perky little flower trumpets. Their flower stems rarely exceed 2½ inches in height, and they do best in brandy snifters or terrariums—or if you can maintain high humidity around them, keep them in the smallest pots (1½- to 2½-inch sizes for most). These are not necessarily summer bloomers, and many are considered virtually ever-blooming. They do well under fluorescent lights.

*Gloxinia tuber should protrude above soil surface.*

*Sinningia cardinalis,* formerly classified as *Rechsteineria cardinalis,* is considerably larger and may reach a spread and height of 12 or more inches. Its tubular scarlet flowers may appear from summer through fall and even into winter, depending on when plants renew growth after their dormancy. Culture is about the same as for achimenes and gloxinia.

*Smithiantha:* Attractive for its large velvety foliage mottled with maroon shades and its spikes of nodding yellow and red flowers is *Smithiantha zebrina.* The rhizomes can be planted whenever available but are usually started in midwinter. The plants develop slowly and may not start flowering until late summer or fall, but during this time you can enjoy their handsome foliage. The flowers are quite long lasting once in bloom, with new ones developing well into winter. Then the plants must be rested by gradually reducing their water supply. There are several named hybrids. Smithiantha's common name is "temple bells," which seems appropriate for a well-grown plant in full bloom.

Other summer-flowering bulbous plants available for pot culture include *Gloriosa, Hymenocallis, Lycoris,* and *Zephyranthes.*

## 4. CACTI AND SUCCULENTS

The plants included under the above very general terms include some of the most useful and popular of all for indoor culture. Most of them are specially adapted in nature to survive under conditions of extreme drought and atmospheric dryness, a characteristic that makes them particularly suitable for sunny windows of hot, dry rooms. No other group offers so many inducements to the collector. Many of the cacti remain small even when mature so that a large number of species and varieties can be accommodated in a limited space such as under a small fluorescent light fixture; and the same is true of certain genera included in the succulents. But before going any further it would be well to define what is meant by cacti and succulents.

Cacti are plants belonging in the cactus family, their position being determined by their floral characteristics. With very few exceptions all cacti are succulents but not all succulents are cacti. "Succulent" is the term applied to plants that have thick fleshy stems or leaves; and they are to be found in a large number of different plant families, including the fig-marigold, stonecrop, euphorbia, milkweed, thistle, and many others. Purslane, that pernicious weed of the vegetable patch, is a succulent, and so is the snake plant *(Sansevieria trifasciata),* although neither is to be considered in this chapter.

Contrary to popular belief, not all spiny succulent plants are cacti, though some—certain euphorbias, for example—look more like cacti, until you come to examine their flowers, than do some true cacti, such as *Pereskia,* which is a spiny, scrambling, climbing shrub with rather everyday leaves and is nothing at all like the usual conception of a cactus. Yet its relationship is

*The peanut cactus* (Chamaecereus silvestri) *has bright-orange-red flowers and dwarf, trailing stems.*

clear to the initiated, not alone on account of its flower structure, but because it can be used as an understock on which other cacti are grafted. It is interesting that similar environmental conditions in different parts of the world should have brought about drought-resisting adaptations, resulting in superficially similar appearances in widely separated (botanically) plant families. But this is a book on house plants, and I should not get involved in abstruse discussions.

While the structure of cacti and succulents is such that they are adapted to endure drought, not all of them are desert plants. Some, such as the orchid cacti and the mistletoe cactus, grow wild perched on the trees in tropical forests; hence they require more atmospheric moisture and different cultural conditions than most cacti. I have seen huge masses of mistletoe cactus growing wild on trees in Trinidad in a Turkish-bath atmosphere.

Cacti is an extremely diverse group. Some, such as the giant cactus, or saguaro, may reach a height of 60 feet and weigh many tons; others, such as certain *Lobivia,* may never be more than 1 or 2 inches high. There are some that hug the ground; others climb trees and clamber over walls if any are nearby. The flowers may be a foot long and almost as much across in some of those to which the name "night-blooming cereus" is given, or no more than ¼ inch in diameter as in some of the mistletoe cacti. Many of the smaller types bear flowers that are larger than the plant from which they spring. In general, cacti have no true leaves, their functions being carried on by the globular, cylindrical, triangular, quadrangular, or flattened stems.

There are some house-plant enthusiasts to whom cacti appeal because of the adaptability of most of them to culture in hot, dry rooms; others consider them ideal plants to put in small pots to stand on a window shelf; and to some the gorgeous blooms of the orchid cacti and Christmas cacti are more alluring. Still others are content to do without flowers while admiring the bizarre shapes and interesting spine patterns offered by many species. Those who are interested in plants as a means of "doing something" will turn to cacti because of the ease with which they can be grafted or the possibilities they offer for the construction of desert scenes in miniature gardens.

The cactus family is a large one, with more than two thousand species divided among about two hundred genera. Their nomenclature is a nightmare. The genus *Cereus* has been split up into dozens of genera, and those who learned about cacti under the old dispensation have difficulty in finding their way around among the new names—which doubtless are all to the good in the long run. Often the descriptions in the commercial catalogues do not tally with those given in botanical reference works.

The selection of species and varieties that follows consists for the most part of those especially recommended by experts for house culture. It is less than a tithe of those offered in one commercial catalogue alone, so those who feel that the species and varieties described here limit their capabilities will find no difficulty in adding to the list.

The plants below are grouped in three sections: (1) those of small size especially suitable for culture in small pots to be displayed on window shelves or on shelves under fluorescent lights, (2) those of greater stature, including climbing and scrambling forms, (3) the orchid cacti and similar kinds requiring a moist atmosphere.

*SMALL CACTI:* While all cacti can be grown in small pots when they are babies, it is better, when the objective is the cultivation of an extensive collection, to restrict oneself to those that never become large. Most of the plants included in this section may be expected to bloom—some of them when they are no more than 2 inches in diameter.

*Astrophytum*—**Sand Dollar, Bishop's Cap, Star Cactus:** The sand dollar *(Astrophytum asterias)* has a flattened, spineless body, 1 inch high, 3 inches across, pale green divided by the ribs into about seven sections shaped like pieces of pie. The flowers are 1 inch long, yellow in color. Bishop's cap or bishop's hood *(A. myriostigma)* is more or less globose, about 2 inches high, with five prominent ribs or ridges and no spines. A striking species, especially when the large yellow flowers are seen against the white body. There are several varieties of this. Star cactus *(A. ornatum)* may grow to a foot in height, but it blooms when small. It has clusters of inch-long spines on the ridges; the body is flecked with white dots. The flowers are lemon yellow and up to 3 inches broad. This, too, has many varieties.

*Chamaecereus silvestri*—**Peanut Cactus:** This species quickly forms clumps made up of peanutlike joints about 2 inches long covered with soft white spines. It must be handled gently, for the joints snap off very easily; any that are knocked off can be planted to start a new colony. This is an intriguing little plant with orange-scarlet flowers 3 inches long. If these cacti are required for display in 2- or 3-inch pots, it is wise to keep a supply of young stock coming along to take the place of the pots whose occupants have overflowed the container.

*Echinocereus*—**Hedgehog Cereus:** These, in general, are charaterized by large flowers on a comparatively small plant, but *E. delaetii* may make a cluster up to 8 inches tall covered with white curly hair. The flowers are pink. A lone wolf, *E. fitchii* makes a solitary body up to 4 inches tall with large pink flowers. *E. pulchellus* forms an upside-down cone, blue-green or gray-green in color and pink flowers. The lace cactus is *E. reichenbachii,* which has light purple, fragrant flowers on a stem which may get up to 8 inches tall. The rainbow cactus, *E. rigidissimus,* can hardly be seen for its variously colored interlocking spines. It has yellow flowers with white centers.

*Echinopsis*—**Sea Urchin Cactus, Easter-lily Cactus:** These have for the most part globular bodies and white flowers sometimes tinted with pink, purple, or green. *E. eyriesii,* which will flower from seed in about two or three years, has large white flowers. *E. multiplex,* with fragrant pink flowers 6 to 8 inches long, may grow to 6 inches or more tall.

*Espostoa lanata*—**Snowball Cactus:** Although this columnar species may grow up to 15 feet tall, it is included here because even young plants are covered with white cottony hair, which gives them a unique appearance, something like that of the old man cactus.

*Ferocactus* (syn. *Hamatocactus*) *setispinus*—**Strawberry Cactus:** So called, presumably, because of its red fruits, which really look more like cranberries. It has yellow flowers with a conspicuous red throat, produced when the plant is no larger than a ball 2 inches in diameter. Old specimens may get to be 6 inches high.

*Gymnocalycium*—**Chin Cacti:** These are generally small globular cacti with large flowers. *G. leeanum,* the yellow chin cactus, forms a small globe and has very large yellow flowers. The striped chin cactus, also a midget, makes a flattened, ridged globe with a rippled effect along the ridges. The flowers may be white, pink, or yellowish. Its botanical moniker is *G. mihanovichii.* The name "chin cactus" comes from a chinlike protuberance below each cluster of spines.

*Lobivia*—**Cob Cactus:** The name *Lobivia* is an anagram of Bolivia, where many of this genus grow wild, though they are also found in Argentina and Peru. *L. aurea* (now more correctly listed as *Echinopsis aurea*) has large lemon-yellow flowers on globular or cylindrical stems up to 4 inches tall. *L. cinnabarina* has scarlet flowers nearly 2 inches across on a plant broader than it is high. Hertrich's cob cactus *(L. hertrichiana)* is a flattened globe which may reach 4 inches across but is seldom more than 2 inches under cultivation. It has scarlet flowers almost 3 inches across, produced in great profusion.

*Lophophora williamsii*—**Peyote, Sacred-mushroom, Mescal:** This plant with dull, bluish-green, flattened globes up to 3 inches in diameter is not much to look at even when displaying its white or pink 1-inch blooms, but it is an interesting plant to grow because of its former association with the religious ceremonies of the Indians of the Southwest. It has a thick taproot and should be grown in a deep pot.

*Mammillaria*—**Pincushion Cactus:** This genus contains some of the most delightful cacti for growing in small pots, though many of them, when given room, may make large clumps. The powder puff cactus *(M. bocasana)* has globes 1½ inches across. The slender green tubercles are set on a pink body and topped with tufts of silky hairs and hooked brown spines, which, however, are not in the least bit vicious. The bird's nest cactus *(M. camptotricha)* ultimately makes clumps of globes 2 inches in diameter with large tubercles surmounted by four to eight conspicuous, flexible spines. The flowers are small, white, and greenish on the outside. *M. carnea,* which blooms all summer with pink flowers up to 1 inch, has cylindrical stems up to 3½ inches high and quadrangular tubercles. There are several varieties of the golden lace cactus *(M. elongata),* sometimes called golden stars from the harmless yellow spines which radiate from the tubercles. This is a fast grower with small white flowers, quickly making clumps of 4-inch-long cylindrical stems. Thimble cactus *(M. fragilis)* makes a short cylindrical stem with clustered globes at the top which readily break off to start new plants. Each tubercle has twelve to fourteen white spines radiating from it. The flowers are small, white and pinkish on the outside.

The old lady cactus is *M. hahniana.* It has a globular stem up to 4 inches high covered with white hair when old. It has rose-carmine flowers. *M. microhelia* is a cylindrical type up to 6 inches long, bedecked with white wool at the top. The flowers are white, ½ inch long. The fishhook pincushion *(M. wildii)* is a clustering type, with cylindrical or globelike stems and slender tubercles, each tipped with a hooked spine. The ½-inch white flowers are freely produced in a circle around the top of the body.

There are over three hundred species of *Mammillaria* and many varieties, all with something to commend them. The above selection, in the main, represents free-flowering kinds.

*Notocactus*—**Ball Cactus:** This genus has several free-flowering species including *N. apricus,* about 2 inches in diameter with yellow flowers larger than the plant. *N. haselbergii* makes an 8-inch globe, with white spines and numerous red flowers 1 inch across. A shining green globular stem with the central spines more than ½ inch long and 1½-inch yellow flowers with contrasting scarlet stigmas, sometimes produced four or more at a time, are the chief characteristics of *N. mammulosus.* It has the reputation of being easy to grow. Silver ball cactus *(N. scopa)* may grow up to 1½ feet. Young plants are globular, blooming while still small, clothed with white bristles, each tuft interspersed with longer red spines. The lemon-yellow flowers are 2½ inches across with pale anthers and a scarlet stigma. A striking plant in bloom and out.

*The bunny or rabbit ears cactus* (Opuntia microdasys).

*Opuntia*—**Prickly-pear, Cholla, Tuna:** The members of this genus are, in general, too large for culture in small pots, but there are two at least that are satisfactory for the purpose. Rabbit or bunny ears *(O. microdasys)* has small "pads" with no spines, but plenty of golden glochids (barbed bristles) in dense tufts arranged in diagonal lines. Then there is *O. ramosissima,* which, although capable of attaining 6 feet, is very attractive because of its habit of branching when still small. It then reminds one of a miniature edition of saguaro.

*Rebutia:* A group of small South American cacti with large flowers produced from the side or base of the plants. *R. minuscula* makes a globe about 2 inches in diameter with spiraled tubercles and bright crimson 1½-inch flowers around the base of the plant body. *R. senilis,* also globose, is usually only about 3 inches tall with bristly spines to 1¼ inches long and bright carmine 2-inch flowers. These rebutias should be shaded from bright sunshine and given more water than the general run of cacti.

*LARGE CACTI:* These are the cacti that are capable of reaching larger dimensions and appeal to those who appreciate bulk and need something more massive than the tiny varieties. While these big ones can be used as shelf plants when they are young, they are more impressive when they are grown up and most of them do not bloom until they attain a good size.

*Aporocactus flagelliformis*—**Rattail Cactus:** This has long flexible stems about ½ inch in diameter covered with bristly hairs and crimson flowers 3 inches long. It can be grown as a trailer or trained up on a support; but it is more commonly seen grafted at the top of a straight stem of another cactus. Its stems are so limp that they can be trained in any way that fancy dictates. It is an easy species to grow and showy in bloom.

*Cephalocereus*—**Old Man Cactus, Woolly Torch Cactus:** The name old man cactus is applied to *C. senilis,* characterized by the shaggy white hair with which the cylindrical stems are covered. It is a slow grower, and, although capable of reaching a height of 40 feet, pot-grown specimens in excess of 2 feet are rare. The flowers (I have never seen one in bloom!) are rose-colored, about 2½ inches long. A similar species, but less common, is known as woolly torch cactus *(C. palmeri).* Crushed limestone should be mixed with the soil for these.

*Cereus*—**Night-blooming Cereus:** The plants to which the name night-blooming cereus is commonly applied have been ejected from the genus *Cereus* and are now to be found under *Harrisia, Hylocereus, Nyctocereus,* and *Selenicereus.* They are mostly climbing or scrambling plants with comparatively thin stems which need a support of some kind. Their growth is inclined to be gawky, and the real reason for growing them is their fragrant flowers, which are spectacular enough to justify throwing an evening party to enable your friends to enjoy them.

Red-tipped dogtail is the strange name given to *Harrisia tortuosa,* which has six-ribbed erect or sprawling stems 2 inches in diameter. The flowers are about 7 inches long, white-petaled with numerous gold-tipped stamens. They open in the evening and close late the following morning.

Perhaps the best known of the plants to which the name night-blooming cereus is applied is *Hylocereus undatus,* also known as Honolulu queen cactus. This one has triangular stems which may climb or clamber to a distance of 40 feet when planted out in the tropics. Its flowers may be up to a foot long, yellowish green outside and white within. It has red edible fruits. The snake cactus *(Nyctocereus serpentinus)* may grow to a height of 8 feet but blooms when it is smaller than this. The stems are fluted, with needlelike spines. The flowers, with slender petals which open in the evening and do not close until noon of the following day, are fragrant, white, and about 7 inches long. Queen-of-the-night *(Selenicereus macdonaldiae)* is a high-growing climber with angled stems about ½ inch thick. The flowers are enormous, up to 14 inches across, with white petals, reddish or yellowish sepals, and conspicuous stamens and pistil.

Some of these plants are extremely tenacious of life. I knew of one (probably *Hylocereus*) which remained alive for many months though deprived of contact with the soil and hanging on a wire attached to the greenhouse roof. It had been inadvertently left behind when the main portion of the plant was removed. They need fairly good soil—in between cactus and general-purpose mixture—and rather dry conditons at the root during winter, but plenty of water when they are actively growing.

*Cleistocactus*—**Scarlet Bugler, Silver Torch:** Scarlet bugler *(C. baumannii)* has 1½-inch cylindrical stems (which may need support) up to 6 feet high. The spines are yellowish brown, but the striking feature is the slender, tubular, orange-scarlet flowers up to 3 inches long. The silver torch *(C. straussii)* has conspicuous bristly white spines on erect stems up to 3 feet high, and red to carmine-violet flowers, which may be nearly 4 inches long. This species is reputed to be able to endure a few degrees of frost.

*Echinocactus*—**Barrel Cactus:** The golden barrel cactus *(E. grusonii)* is attractive even as a small plant, but it may reach 4 feet in height and 2½ feet in diameter. There was a specimen in the Huntington Botanical Gardens, San Marino, California, about thirty years old whose weight was estimated at four hundred pounds. It is possible to buy specimens 1½ feet in diameter, but these are costly. The beauty of this plant depends mainly on the golden spines, arranged with almost mathematical exactitude, and the contrasting feltlike cushion at the top of the plant in which the red and yellow flowers are embedded.

*Lemaireocereus*—**Organ-pipe Cactus:** The organ-pipe cactus botanically is *L. marginatus.* Capable of reaching a height of 25 feet, it is commonly used in Mexico for making living fences. The common name is descriptive of its appearance, although its stems, unlike the pipes of an organ, are ribbed. It is one of those kinds that are sometimes embarrassing because of the height to which they grow. I was once in a greenhouse whose owner was compelled to append a "lantern" to accommodate it. If it gets too big for the home, the best plan is to cut off a section of suitable size from the top and root it, discarding the old plant.

*Opuntia*—**Cholla, Prickly-pear, Tuna:** One or two opuntias should be in every collection if only to represent what to many people is the typical cactus form with flattened oval joints resembling ping-pong paddles. Orange tuna *(O. elata),* which grows to about 3 feet, has almost spineless joints up to 10 inches long. The flowers, 2 inches across, are orange-yellow. *O. vulgaris* is perhaps best known in the form of its 'Variegata', sometimes called Joseph's coat because of the white, yellow, and pink splotches on the joints. These are oval and may reach a foot in length. The grizzly bear opuntia *(O. erinacea ursina)* grows to about 1½ feet, the plant body being almost completely hidden by shaggy bristlelike spines. The flowers are reddish yellow, 3 inches across. The paper-spined opuntia, *O. turpinii* (now reclassified as *O. articulata* 'Syringacantha'), has fat oval joints with prominent tubercles and long white flexible spines, something like white-pine shavings. A distinctive plant worthy of a place in any collection.

*Oreocereus*—**Mountain Cacti:** Coming from the Andes, these cacti can endure low temperatures. Old-man-of-the-Andes *(O. celsianus)* grows to 3 feet and has 3-inch branches covered with matted white hairs.

*Trichocereus spachianus*—**White Torch Cactus:** An easily grown species with cylindrical, prominently ribbed stems up to 3 feet tall. The flowers are pure white, about 6 inches across. It is frequently used as an understock on which crested or delicate cacti are grafted. It needs more water than most of its relatives.

Making a selection from many hundreds of large-growing kinds is difficult. Included are a variety of types distinctive in appearance and which should be listed in most specialists' catalogues.

Culture: The soil must be porous so that stagnant water does not remain about the roots. Most cacti require an alkaline soil which can be provided by mixing with it mortar rubble, limestone, oyster shells, or eggshells (if you have enough of them and want to go to this trouble), all of which should be crushed or pounded so that there are no pieces more than ¼ inch across.

Watering must be done with care. Although cacti are adapted to survive dryness (if you want to take a long weekend you can go away without worrying about them), during the time they are actively growing and in the summer months they can be watered as freely as you would a begonia. During the short days of winter they must definitely be kept on the dry side, giving them only enough water to keep the stems from shriveling. Avoid watering when the weather is overcast unless it is made necessary by shriveling stems.

Some types with globular or barrel-like bodies occupy so much of the soil surface that it is difficult to apply enough water from above to moisten the entire mass of soil. The pots of such plants should be partially submerged in a container of water until moisture shows on the surface. The way I have handled the small specimens is to stand them in small glass saucers, obtained from variety stores, which are filled with water whenever the soil seems to be getting dry. *Any water remaining in the saucer after an hour or two is poured off.*

Most cacti should be kept in a sunny window during fall, winter, and spring. Watch them especially in summer, and if there is any indication of sunburn shown by yellowing or browning of the body on the exposed side, provide light shade. If they are put outdoors for the summer, don't forget to keep them lightly shaded until they become acclimated to the more intense light. Any deviation from general care required by those listed is noted under the species or variety.

Cactus fanciers are interested in growing difficult kinds which sometimes thrive better when grafted on a more robust species. The fasciated or crested kinds also are usually grafted; and frequently one sees trailing or drooping kinds grafted on tall understocks in order to display them more effectively. While grafting is usually looked on as a means of increasing plants, it is primarily a cultural aid when applied to cacti, so it is described in this chapter rather than in the one dealing with propagation.

First, as to the understocks which will supply the root system and part of the stem of the completed plant. They must, of course, be kinds that are easily grown, and, generally speaking, there should not be too great a difference between the diameter of the understock and the grafted portion. In some cases it is desirable that the understock should be fairly closely related to the scion.

The shrublike *Pereskia* is often used as an understock for Christmas cactus, which, however, is very accommodating and can be grafted successfully on other diverse kinds such as *Selenicereus* and *Opuntia*. A plant of striking appearance can be constructed by inserting scions of *Schlumbergera* (formerly

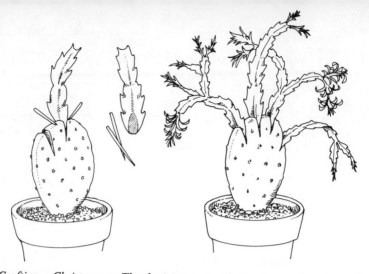

*Grafting a Christmas or Thanksgiving cactus* (Schlumbergera) *on* Opuntia.

known as *Zygocactus*) at 3-inch intervals around the upper edge of a large flat joint of an *Opuntia*. This is effective until the scions grow so much that they obscure the understock. An even stranger-looking plant can be created by grafting scions of the peanut cactus on each stem tip of a branched *Pereskia*.

*Trichocereus spachianus* is commonly used as an understock for allied crested varieties; for small globular forms, *Selenicereus* is among those favored.

The technique of grafting cacti is simple and the results relatively certain. If, for example, a high-grafted Christmas cactus is wanted, you obtain, or grow, a single-stemmed *Pereskia* a few inches taller than the desired height and cut off those extra inches squarely. Then split the stem to a depth of an inch. Take a shoot tip of Christmas cactus (some use one joint and some use two) and with a very sharp knife slice a piece off either side of the base to make a wedge which is inserted in the split of the understock and then pinned in place by a couple of slender cactus thorns thrust through stock and scion. If *Opuntia* is used as the understock, merely cut slits at 3-inch intervals across the edge of the upper half of the joint and insert the scions prepared as above and pin in place. The grafted plant should be shaded until union has taken place.

Another method that can be used, for example when grafting the rat-tailed cactus on *Selenicereus,* is to cut a wedge-shaped piece out of the under-stock and bevel the scion to fit in it. Pin in place with thorns and tie with soft twine. With some cacti it may be necessary to trim off some of the thorns to facilitate grafting.

The globular and crested types are usually grafted low, and fleshy-stemmed understocks (rather than the rather woody *Pereskia*) are used. The understock, rooted in a comparatively small pot, not more than 3-inch size, is cut off at the desired height with a single, clean, horizontal cut. The base of the scion is similarly cut, applied to the cut surface of the stock, and held in close contact by two rubber bands which pass below the bottom of the pot and over the top of the graft. The tension should not be too great—merely enough to press the scion gently against the stock. If necessary, a couple of thorns can be used to prevent the scion from slithering around. Two lengths of soft twine can be substituted for the rubber bands if something is used to prevent the twine from cutting into the scion. In this operation three hands, or even four, are desirable.

There is almost no limit to the fantastic creations made possible by grafting bizarre types of cacti.

When buying cacti, it is well to remember that those collected directly from the deserts of the Southwest are difficult to establish; and unless the plants are required for a temporary display only, it is better to obtain nursery- or greenhouse-grown plants.

## ORCHID CACTI

*Epiphyllum*—**Orchid Cactus**—are the plants some of which used to be rather generally known as *Phyllocactus*—meaning leafy cactus in reference to their flattened, leaflike stems, actually a misnomer because they have no true leaves. Of late years the botanists have been busy splitting them up into genera such as *Epiphyllum, Nopalxochia, Rhipsalidopsis* (Easter cactus), and *Schlumbergera,* syn. *Zygocactus* (Christmas cactus). The hybridizers have also been busy crossing the different sections so that it is difficult to know where we are. Thinking that most home gardeners are less interested in the fine points of botanical differences than they are in growing these plants, so spectacular when in bloom, and because they all need much the same cultural treatment, they are lumped together here under *Epiphyllum* except for the comparatively small-flowered *Schlumbergera.*

The plants themselves are awkward and ungainly, their flattened stems with scalloped edges seldom disposing themselves in a sightly manner. But they fully make up for their lack of grace when their colorful blooms, up to 10 inches in diameter in some varieties, are displayed, mostly in the spring and early summer, in glowing colors. Even unbranched specimens no more than a foot high will bloom, but some varieties are capable of developing into many-branched plants, 3 or more feet in diameter.

There are dozens and dozens of kinds available, including queen of the night *(Epiphyllum oxypetalum),* which is a night-bloomer and may grow to 6 feet with large, fragrant white flowers; red-orchid cactus *(Nopalxochia acker-mannii)* up to 3 feet tall with 8-inch flowers, scarlet on the outside, carmine within, and contrasting white stamens; and Easter cactus, *Rhipsalidopsis gaert-neri,* with drooping branches and scarlet flowers 3 inches long. Then there are the hybrids and named garden forms such as 'Elegantissimum', a dwarf form with bright crimson flowers, 'Gloria', with 8-inch flame-colored flowers, and 'Conway's Giant', 7-inch scarlet flowers.

These plants need different treatment from cacti in general except that, in common with all, the pots in which they are grown must be well drained. To ensure this, put at least an inch of flowerpot chips or something similar in the bottom. Use the soil recommended for begonias and do not pot too firmly. They must have abundant supplies of water at the root during the time they are actively growing, but it must run freely through the soil. They need moist air and should not be exposed to strong sunshine. Even during the winter, when they should be kept on the dry side at the roots, their branches should be sprayed on dry, sunny days. During the summer, keep them outdoors in the shade of a tree or building. In country districts one can often see excellent examples of orchid cacti growing in discarded cooking utensils, displayed on a shaded porch or apparently carelessly disposed on the lawn beneath a tree.

**Christmas Cactus** (*Schlumbergera* x *buckleyi,* sometimes listed as *S. bridgesii*) and its close relative, the Thanksgiving cactus *(S. truncata),* need much the same growing conditions as the preceding kinds except for a few differences which are given below. Both kinds have terminal branchlets made up of glossy, leaflike, flattened joints measuring about 2 inches by 1 inch. The flowers, about 2½ inches long, are typically rosy red. They are produced from the tips of the branches in late fall to midwinter. These are heirloom kinds of plants, lasting for years in the house and slowly increasing in size.

Before going into cultural methods for these two cacti, it might be helpful to dispel some of the fog that surrounds their nomenclature.

For many years these plants were generally lumped together as *Zygocactus truncatus* (and also as *Epiphyllum truncatum!*). The true Christmas cactus (*Schlumbergera* x *buckleyi*—and it is sometimes today erroneously listed as *S. bridgesii*) generally blooms at Christmas or soon thereafter and is an old hybrid (as the "x" in its specific name indicates) between *S. truncata* and *S. russelliana,* the last a rarely encountered species.

**Thanksgiving Cactus** *(S. truncata)* differs in having more pronounced "claws" on its flattened joints and less symmetrical flowers, which usually appear toward the end of November. It is also called the crabclaw or claw cactus.

Superficially, for most of us, there is not a great difference in the appearance of these two cacti, but if you wish to determine which you have, examine the edges of the leaflike joints, the flower shapes (*S.* x *buckleyi* is less "clawed" and has more regular-shaped flowers than does *S. truncata*), and notice the blooming time. Of course, to observe the last you must get the plant to bloom and this has been a problem for some people. Also, it must be admitted that blooming periods for the two overlap. There are also numerous color forms and hybrids involving the three species which are bound to alter flowering periods. One such form is 'White Christmas', which has attractive, waxy-textured white flowers and the clawed segments of *S. truncata.* Its blooming time so far seems to be closer to Thanksgiving than Christmas, despite its name. Commercial growers are also more able to manipulate and control flowering periods than are home gardeners.

Although they root easily from cuttings and grow well on their own roots, their drooping habits of growth have led to the practice of grafting them upon cacti with stiff, upright stems or on a *Pereskia* shoot, so that the flowers were displayed well above the pot. One of my earliest recollections was of the magnificent display made by a Christmas cactus grafted at intervals along a stem of *Pereskia* that extended from the eaves to the ridge of a greenhouse.

Many have been the recipes for bringing these two *Schlumbergera* cacti and their hybrids into flower. If you have been one of the successful ones, the chances are that your method has been one of the two that follow or even a combination of the two.

Short-day Method: This method takes into account that these cacti are short-day plants (the chrysanthemum is another) and so initiate flower buds when daylight decreases, as in the fall. Plants kept in rooms indoors in the fall that receive no artificial light at night can be expected to set buds. If there is to be light beyond the normal length of daylight during the fall months, few or no buds will form unless the plant is moved into a closet or protected from light by a black cloth covering or cardboard carton. Moving a plant out of the light in the evening and back in the morning to the necessary daylight can be a nuisance, but for apartment dwellers it is about the only way to have flowers year after year for the holidays.

Cool-temperature Method: Cool temperatures, as well as day length, seem to be a factor in bud set. Those who summer their plants outdoors in partial shade (the plants are attractive enough in foliage to decorate a terrace or patio) can simply leave the plants outdoors (and out of the glare of any outdoor evening illumination) as long as possible before frosts are due. The plants can safely survive 45° to 50° F. at night without suffering injury. If you live where frosts and subsequent really cold weather comes early, then you must rely on a cool but frost-free enclosed porch or similar area, where night temperatures range between 45° and 65° F. When buds have formed, the plants can be brought into warmer rooms for their flowering display. This cool-temperature method has been foolproof for me.

*OTHER SUCCULENTS:* The cacti circumvent their droughty environment by storing moisture in their thickened stems which take over the work ordinarily done by the leaves; and, in some cases, take on some semblance to them. These other succulents, for the most part, depend on their fleshy leaves, covered with an impervious cuticle, as moisture reservoirs. Unlike the cacti, which are native to North and South America, succulents are found growing in Europe, Africa, and Asia, as well as the Americas.

It has already been mentioned that succulents are found in a number of plant families; but the two that contain the most members suited for our purpose are the stonecrop family, represented in our gardens by such familiar plants as houseleek *(Sempervivum)* and showy sedum *(Sedum spectabile);* and the fig-marigold *(Mesembryanthemum)* family, represented by the ice plant *(M. crystallinum)* grown outdoors as an annual for the effect of the glistening pustules with which the plant is covered.

*Aeonium tabuliforme:* This close relative of the houseleeks is a strange-looking plant with overlapping leaves arranged in a rosette, 3 or more inches across, almost as flat as a table top. I have never grown it as a house plant, but it has been recommended by others for the purpose, and it is so distinctive that it should be given a trial if you can obtain it.

*Crassula*—**Jade Plant, Scarlet Paintbrush,** and others: The member of the stonecrop group most commonly seen is *C. argentea,* first introduced as Japanese-rubber tree and a name still occasionally used. Native to South Africa and having no connection whatever with rubber, the absurdity of this common name brought about the change to jade plant. Once considered by many a dreary plant with fat, uninteresting leaves and a stodgy habit of growth, the jade plant today, if not revered, has at least moved up in the house-plant world. It is undeniably easy to grow, tolerates a dry atmosphere and air conditioning, and occasionally, a venerable, pot-bound specimen will surprise you with sprays of small white flowers in winter. The angular, treelike growth of the jade plant can make a striking accent in modern interiors, an asset that has probably contributed to its rise in popularity.

In addition to the jade plant, this genus contains many plants of diverse form and habit. Among them is scarlet paint brush *(C. falcata),* which in favored regions may attain a height of 8 feet. As a pot plant it is usually a foot or so high with a flat head of bright crimson flowers. The grayish leaves are thick and fleshy, sickle-shaped, crossing at their bases.

*C. lycopodioides* has closely appressed, tiny, bright green leaves on slender branches. The general appearance, as implied by the specific name, is similar to that of some of the club-mosses and ground-pines *(Lycopodium)* of northern woods.

The name necklace vine *(Crassula rupestris)* could be applied to more than one species (though they are not exactly vines) with leaves united at the base so that they appear to be threaded on the stem. In addition to the one above, the ¾-inch leaves of which are glaucous with bright green spots, there is *C. perforata,* with slightly larger leaves, also spotted, which may grow into a shrub 2 feet tall. All these except *C. falcata* make excellent plants in small pots for shelf culture. *C. lycopodioides* does not mind a little shade.

*Echeveria* (sometimes called hen-and-chickens): The echeverias are rosette-forming plants often with bluish-white glaucous leaves and attractive flowers of coral or orange-red.

*E. elegans* makes 2-inch, blue-white rosettes with "chickens" around the base and long-lasting, small pinkish flowers with yellow tips rising 8 inches above the rosette. *E. gibbiflora* is one of the giants of the genus, reaching a height of 2 feet. The leaves are 7 inches long, glaucous with a pinkish tinge. The flowers are red. 'Metallica' has purplish leaves with, as the name implies, a metallic sheen.

One of the best known is *E. glauca,* often used as an edging to formal beds outdoors. The rosettes are 2 to 3 inches across and blue-green. This is a free-blooming species whose flowers are coral-colored without and yellow within. Chenille plant is the common name given to *E. pulvinata,* which

Kalanchoe uniflora *is a trailing plant with unusual rose-colored flowers that are long-lasting.*

has velvet-textured foliage rosettes tipped with red tints and stalks of yellow bell-shaped flowers in winter. Mexican firecracker is the name given to *E. setosa,* a species with fat, 2-inch-long hairy leaves in a globular rosette. The flowers are red tipped with yellow.

**Kalanchoe:** The plant variously known as miracle leaf, good-luck leaf, airplant, lifeplant, and floppers is *K. pinnata.* Not particularly beautiful, it is interesting because of the plantlets formed on the leaf margins—even if a leaf is cut off and pinned on a window curtain. It should be given general-purpose potting mixture, liberal root room, and light shade if you want 6-foot-tall plants. The flowers have green-yellow or purple-tinted inflated calyxes and reddish petals. Although not showy, a well-grown inflorescence is rather impressive.

Even more prolific of plantlets is *K. daigremontiana,* with curious mottled leaves which remind one of lizards. Although its height is sometimes given as "usually 1½ feet," it may attain 3 feet. Its flowers are not worth much.

The most popular species of all is *K. blossfeldiana,* grown commercially in enormous quantities for sale during Christmas and the winter, when it is covered with a succession of small scarlet flowers in clusters. Larger-flowered hybrids in yellow and pastel tints have been introduced. Although a perennial, second-year plants are not nearly so satisfactory as those grown from seeds or cuttings annually. General potting mixture should be used. It will take more water than the general run of succulents.

If you wish to reflower a kalanchoe for the holidays, summer the plant outdoors in full sun after cutting back faded flower sprays and straggly growth. In the fall, reduce daylight to about 9 hours a day (see Christmas cactus in the orchid cacti part of this section) and place the plant on a protected dark patio or move it into a closet each night. Buying new plants may be easier!

Panda plant (it does bring to mind a panda, though it is difficult to tell why), *K. tomentosa* (syn. *pilosa*), is a first-class window shelf plant. The 3-inch fleshy leaves, loosely arranged in a rosette, are blue-green, covered with a lush growth of short white hairs, except on the margins of the upper half, where they are rust red or sometimes almost black.

A species known as *K. uniflora* and sometimes called coral bells is an excellent plant for a hanging container. Its stems, clothed with 1-inch leaves, may trail over the edge to a length of 2 feet. The rose-colored inflated flowers are long-lasting and abundantly produced. It is rarely offered—watch for it. It needs moist conditions and a humusy soil.

There is one species that, if planted several together in a small pot, suggests a clump of miniature coconut palms. *K. verticillata* (sometimes listed as *K. tubiflora*) has almost cylindrical leaves (with plantlets at the tips) which are arranged in a cluster at the top of the stem with the lowermost ones drooping to give a palmlike effect. Although it is capable of growing to 3 feet, it is most effective when about 8 inches tall.

*Sedum*—**Stonecrop, Live-forever:** Among the subtropical sedums there are a number of interesting possibilities. Although many of them grow to a foot or more in height and as much across, it is practicable to use them as small pot plants for the window shelf or under lights because of the ease with which individual shoots will root when inserted as cuttings. Mature leaves broken off and left lying on the soil surface will often form roots and ultimately young plants.

The Mexican *S. adolphii* has fleshy, inch-long leaves, yellow-green with bronzy tints. The leaves of *S. allantoides* remind one of a shortened, curved baseball bat. In color they are gray-green as a result of the waxy "bloom" with which they are covered. *Sedum rubrotinctum* has red stems and green

¾-inch sausage-shaped leaves, tinged with red at their tips. Erect as a baby, it soon makes long stems which droop over the edge of the pot. Hairlike roots are produced along the stems. *S. guatemalense* is often confused for the preceding species and is actually quite similar. *S. stahlii* has chains of red football-shaped leaves in four ranks.

Doubtless, the hardy kinds, which have an important place in our rock gardens, could be grown indoors.

*Sempervivum*—**Houseleek:** The hardy sempervivums also can be grown indoors. If this is done, it would be a good plan to pot them in the fall and leave them in a cold frame until sometime in January so that they would get a part of the winter's rest to which they are accustomed. Among the interesting species are *S. arachnoideum* and its varieties and cultivars (cobweb houseleek); *S. tectorum calcareum,* whose leaves are tipped with red-brown; and *S. soboliferum,* which has globular rosettes.

*Mesembryanthemum*—**Fig-marigold;** also living stones, windowed plants, pebble plant, tiger's jaw, et cetera: This genus of upwards of 1,000 species has been split up into more than 100 genera, known collectively as Mesembryanthema.

The strong-growing kinds, especially the trailers, are widely planted in California to control erosion on banks and, ornamentally, for draping over rocks. It is the smaller species, however, with which we are concerned. They are among the most interesting plants in the vegetable kingdom. Coming from the Karroo and other desert regions in South Africa, they have developed protective mimicry to an amazing extent; and their adaptations to a hot, dry environment and brilliant sunshine are intensely fascinating. Some of them, mimicking the rocks among which they grow, are like chips of granite; some resemble water-worn stones.

To overcome their droughty environment, they store moisture in their thick, fleshy leaves which are covered with an almost impervious cuticle. If you want to demonstrate the effectiveness of this covering, pull off a leaf and split it open. After 12 hours compare it with another leaf pulled off at the same time but not cut open. The split leaf will shrivel to about half size; the other will be scarcely affected. Some species actually grow with their leaves buried beneath the soil, with only the more or less flattened tips visible. These are equipped with translucent "windows" through which light is admitted to the chlorophyll. Some of them never have more than two leaves on a stem at a time. Often they are so closely joined that they look like the solid body of a thornless cactus. Their flowers are daisylike (though, botanically, they are far removed from this family), often larger than the plant body and are usually brilliantly colored—yellow, orange, and magenta are common.

It is impossible here to do more than mention a very few of the genera to give a rough idea of the appearance of some of these plants. If you try a few and are successful with them, you are likely to want to assemble a collection; then, get the catalogues of specialists and make a selection.

*Cheiridopsis candidissima*—**Cigarette Plant:** It grows in tufts and has white leaves about ½ inch in diameter and 4 inches long, arranged in pairs. The flowers are 2 to 3 inches across, white or pale pink.

*Conophytum*—**Coneplant:** In this genus the growths consist of two leaves joined together, with a small orifice at the top from which a single flower arises that may be much larger than the growth from which it originates. A plant I received as *C. wiggetiae* had growths so closely aggregated in a rounded clump that the normal shape (an inverted cone, average dimensions about 1 by ¾ inch) of many of them was distorted by pressure. After probing gingerly into the clump, which was 5 inches across and 2 inches high, it seemed to me that the leaves were attached to a very short, branching stem system, completely invisible unless the growths were pried apart. This timid investigation also disclosed, to my horror, colonies of scale insects, attached out of sight, on the lower part of the growths. I had to break the clump apart and wipe off the insects by hand, for they were so well hidden between the plant bodies and the remains of the leaves of the preceding year that it was impossible to get at them with an insecticidal spray.

*Faucaria tigrina:* The tips of the leaves, seen in profile, look like the bow of a canoe. The leaves are in pairs, and the upper half of each leaf is furnished with recurving teeth, giving a fancied resemblance to the opened jaws of a tiger. There are about six pairs of leaves on the almost stemless shoots which grow to form a clump. The flowers, about 1 inch across and bright yellow, are produced in the fall.

*Glottiphyllum:* One occasionally sees these plants used in made-up miniature or florists' dish gardens. Their leaves in general are tongue-shaped, very fleshy, bright green, and cool to touch. *G. linguiforme* has leaves about 2½ inches long and yellow flowers about 2½ inches across.

*Lithops*—**Living Stones, Stoneface:** The plants in this genus grow somewhat in the same manner as *Conophytum.* In the wild the leaves of most species are partially or completely buried with only the flattened, often windowed top showing; and, when out of bloom, looking like pebbles strewn on the ground. Often the coloration on the growths (pairs of united leaves) forms interesting patterns. This is a large genus but plants must be obtained from a specialist. *L. pseudotruncatella* is one of the best with brownish growths marked with deeper brown lines and flowers of bright yellow which are up to 2 inches across.

*Pleiospilos*—**Living Rocks:** These, in general, have larger leaves than most of those previously mentioned. Those of *P. bolusii* look like 2-inch chunks of rust-colored stone. Its golden-yellow flowers are 3 inches across. The fat leaves of *P. simulans* are 3 inches long, gray-green with dark green spots, and look like chips of granite. The flowers, yellow or white, are 3 inches in diameter.

*Titanopsis schwantesii* is a plant of unique appearance. The leaves grow in small rosettes and their tips are densely covered with white warty tubercles.

The ¾-inch flowers are yellow in spring. Another species, *T. calcarea,* has rust-colored tips and larger yellow flowers.

*Trichodiadema densum* is very different in appearance from any previously described. It is a tiny shrub about 3 inches tall, its branches thickly clothed with cylindrical leaves ¾ inch long, each one tipped with a diadem of radiating white hairs. Each sepal tip is similarly adorned. The magenta flowers are nearly 2 inches across.

These "living stones," "windowed plants," and "mimicry" plants are reputed to be excellent subjects for house culture. My limited experience with them in my own home leads me to think that they are among the easiest plants to grow provided they can be placed in a sunny window (or close under fluorescent lights for 16 hours) and careful attention is given to watering. My own practice during the winter was to wait until the growths began to shrivel before giving any water, supplied by putting it in the saucer in which the plant was standing. At no time should the soil be kept wet, but when the new leaves are pushing up, it may be kept moist. Use cactus soil and be sure the pots are well drained.

Practically all these plants are small and slow growers, so they will not crowd you out of house and home unless you grow too many of them.

We turn now to the lily family and find there a number of xerophytic types and, among the haworthias, some with windowed leaves.

*Aloe spp.:* Many of the aloes are handsome plants and decorative in bloom when grown in regions where the climate permits outdoor cultivation; or when grown in greenhouses where there is plenty of room for their development. Those commonly seen as house plants (with the exception of *A. variegata*) always gave me the shudders because they were so dreary-looking. Some of them, maybe all, have a very bitter sap, which when dried becomes the "bitter aloes" of the drugstore, used medicinally and once commonly put on baby's thumb to prevent him or her from sucking it. Tiger aloe *(A. variegata)* is a neat little plant when young, with leaves spotted and banded in white. It is said to grow a stem about 9 inches high, with a foot-long flower stalk and red flowers 1½ inches long, but I never saw it do this.

*Gasteria*—**Warty-aloe, Ox Tongue:** These are the South African plants with thick, fleshy, tonguelike leaves closely arranged in two ranks. They may be smooth or warty, spotted or mottled with white, pale green, or copper. They vary in length from 4 inches to more than a foot. The flowers, while not especially showy, are long-lasting. *G. acinacifolia* has white-spotted leaves 14 inches long and a branching flower stalk up to 4 feet tall with reddish flowers about 2 inches long—the largest in the genus. A much smaller species is *G. brevifolia* with 2-by-4-inch leaves thickly spotted with white. Ox tongue is a name for a group of hybrids with green leaves that grow in spirals and take on purple shades. The warty-aloe is *G. verrucosa* with 6-inch grayish leaves decorated with pure white tubercles. The 2-foot inflorescence carries reddish flowers about 1 inch long.

*Haworthia*—**Cushion-aloe:** In this genus the leaves grow in rosettes and the plants are often cespitose—that is, the rosettes develop in dense tufts. The flowers are small, white or greenish, and not especially ornamental. There is a large number of species, but among the ones most commonly met are the following:

*H. cymbiformis* has pudgy leaves in close rosettes and "windows" in the flattened leaf tips. *H. margaritifera* makes a rosette of sharply pointed, stiff, fleshy leaves, decorated principally on the underside with white, warty tubercles which are probably responsible for its common name of white pearl or pearl plant. *H. setata* makes a rosette about 3 inches across. Its distinctive feature is the long slender "teeth" along the margins of the leaves which always reminded me of a movie star's eyelashes—except for the color.

*Agave*—**Century Plant:** The most important group of succulents in the amaryllis family is the one that includes the century plant. On an occasion when I was visiting a cemetery on the island of St. Thomas in the West Indies, I was amazed to see a metal century plant decorating a grave. For a while I could not figure out why anyone should use an artificial plant when wild ones of the same type were growing profusely all around. Then it occurred to me that size was the probable answer—the metal "plant" never got too large for its surroundings. This is the fly in the ointment for those who grow the century plant in the house—it invariably gets too big. I have seen century plants in the wild 12 feet in diameter; and, while they are not likely to get as large as this when grown as tub plants, they cannot be pruned to keep them in bounds and they grow much too big and awkward to handle long before they reach the flowering stage. These large tubbed plants do make striking accents for the sunny patio or terrace. Put the tubs on "wheels" so you can roll them indoors during winter in the North. (Most garden centers sell wheel-equipped platforms to set under large, heavy tubs.) Although there are many species, the only ones to consider as house plants are the striped forms of the century plant (*A. americana* 'Marginata') with yellowish stripes along the leaf margins; *A. americana* 'Medio-picta,' yellow-striped down the middle, accepted with the strict understanding that they are to be dispossessed as soon as they reach a diameter of 18 inches unless of course you live in a mansion; and *A. victoriae-reginae,* the queen agave, which never gets more than about a foot in diameter. Its leaves have pale gray or brownish margins and irregular stripings of gray or white on both upper and lower surfaces. The tips are armed with formidable, needle-sharp spines; but, unlike most agaves, the margins are free from the curved teeth that make one wary when handling them.

The milkweed family includes a large number of succulents, most of them contained in the group known as the Stapeliae. The number and importance of members of this tribe can be deduced from the fact that there has been a three-volume work devoted entirely to them. For the most part they have no true leaves. Their fleshy stems have a superficial resemblance to those of cacti but their flowers are like nothing else on earth. Of intricate construction and unique coloration, often very hairy, they range from the tiny flowers of some of the *Caralluma* species, only ⅛ inch in diameter, to those of *Stapelia gigantea,* which may sometimes reach almost 1½ feet across. The genera likely to be the most easily obtainable are *Caralluma, Hoodia, Huernia,* and *Stapelia.*

*Caralluma nebrownii* has angled stems up to 7 inches tall and very dark red-brown, starfish-shaped flowers 4 inches across. I have always felt a sentimental interest in this species, for it is one of many plants named in honor of Dr. N. E. Brown, who was one of my teachers when I was studying at Kew Gardens.

*Hoodia gordonii* grows to a height of about a foot, its erect, many-ribbed branches, 2 inches in diameter, set with numerous light brown spines. The flowers are about 3 inches across, nearly flat and almost circular, pale purple with greenish-yellow stripes. Other species are listed by specialists.

*Huernia penzigii* has angled stems up to 3 inches high and bell-shaped, black-purple flowers; *H. primulina,* the primrose huernia, also a low-growing plant, is perhaps the most attractive species with freely produced, creamy-yellow flowers an inch across.

*Stapelia* is known by the common names starfish flower and carrion flower, neither of which is particularly enticing nor as easy to say as its botanical designation. The name "starfish flower" comes from the shape of the blossoms and "carrion flower" from the vile odor emanating from them at times. Because of this last feature, it is fortunate that they are inclined to bloom in summer when it is possible to put them someplace out of the house where their perfume is less noticeable.

The giant stapelia, botanically *S. gigantea,* makes a sprawling plant with erect quadrangular stems up to 8 inches tall. The flowers are enormous, about a foot across under cultivation. They are yellowish in color, barred with numerous fine crimson lines.

*S. grandiflora,* in spite of its name, is not so large as *S. gigantea.* The flowers are up to 6 inches across, dark purplish brown, rather hairy with purple and whitish hairs.

One of the really hairy species, *S. hirsuta,* known as shaggy stapelia, in some of its forms has a dense cushion of hairs in the center of the flower which is about 4 inches across. The margins of the corolla lobes of all of them have a thick growth of long whitish or pale purple hairs. The flower color in general is purple-brown, marked transversely with yellowish or purple-brown lines. The flowers of *S. verrucosa,* about 3 inches across, have yellow ground color with red; in the variety *pulchra* the spots are purplish.

There are scores of additional species of *Stapelia,* all fascinating to those who enjoy their outlandish flowers. They are not difficult to grow in open sandy soil. They need plenty of sun, normal watering during most of the year, but dryness at the root in winter.

*Euphorbia*—**Medusa's Head:** This is a large and varied group belonging to the spurge family and containing such diverse elements as poinsettia, crown-

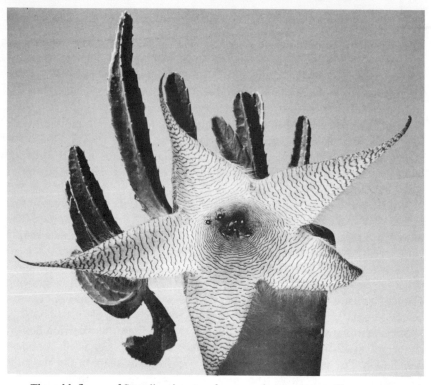

*The odd flower of* Stapelia gigantea *has an odor to attract flies necessary for pollinating the bloom. Flies are at work in center of this flower.*

of-thorns, and snow-on-the-mountain, which is grown as an annual in gardens. The succulent members, largely native to Africa, often closely resemble cacti of the cereus type. Personally, I never regarded them highly as house plants because of their vicious thorns and their possibly poisonous sap, capable of causing skin irritation. An exception might be in favor of Medusa's head *(E. caput-medusae),* which is sufficiently queer to warrant inclusion in any collection of oddities. It has a globular stem, surmounted by sinuous, slender branches which suggest the snaky hair attributed to the Gorgons of Greek mythology. In mature plants the branches may be up to a foot in length. (For the poinsettia [*E. pulcherrima*] and crown-of-thorns [*E. milii splendens*], see Section 6 in this chapter.)

The great thistle family contains a number of succulents of interest to specialists in the group. One that has appeal is *Senecio* (syn. *Kleinia*) *articulatus,* candle plant, which has joined fleshy stems covered with bluish-white waxy "bloom" and lobed leaves.

The culture of succulents in general is similar to that of cacti—porous soil, plenty of sunshine or about 16 hours under artifical illumination (use full-spectrum tubes), and very little water during the resting season. Most of them can tolerate coolness at night and the considerably warmer temperatures of the daytime—conditions that approximate their desert habitats.

Considerable space has been given to cacti and succulents because as a group they are well fitted for indoor culture and because they offer so much in the way of beauty and interest. Even so, there are many others in addition to those mentioned here. And there is the Cactus and Succulent Society of America, Abbey Garden Press, P.O. Box 3010, Santa Barbara, Calif. 93105.

## 5.  ORCHIDS

Orchids have been grown here and there as house (rather than greenhouse) plants for many years, but it is only in recent years that these glamorous plants have achieved wide popularity as subjects for window gardens or fluorescent lights. Although there are orchids difficult enough in culture so that their growing should be left to those with greenhouses, there are many, many kinds that are tougher than is generally believed and that if given good care are amenable to growing in the average house.

Some orchids are expensive compared to the costs of most house plants, but it is possible to get less expensive ones that have proved to be foolproof under indoor conditions with the right care.

Contrary to belief, many orchids do not require especially warm temperatures. Some do better in cool daytime temperatures (60° to 70° F.) and a drop to 55 ° at night; others require intermediate (65° to 75°) daytime temperatures with a drop to about 60° at night. Those preferring "hot" conditions, 70° to 80° during the day, tolerate a drop to 65° or lower at night.

Orchids need high humidity, at least 50 per cent, but so do many other house plants, and the measures taken for them should suffice for most orchids. Misting the foliage helps (but only on sunny days and when air circulation is adequate), and maintaining the pots above trays filled with moist pebbles is almost a necessity. However, it is best not to stand the pots directly on the pebbles, especially if they are of plastic, since good drainage is also a necessity. Rather, stand the orchid pots on inverted pots or suspend them from a rod (other house plants can stand directly below them on the pebbles), or build a slatted wooden frame or bench above the pebbles. Orchids should be watered when the potting medium becomes dry. It should never be allowed to remain soggy for day after day. This can become a problem with orchids in plastic pots—especially with long periods of rain when the plants are outdoors in summer.

Plenty of light is essential (although orchids do vary in their individual requirements) and about 4 hours of sunlight is about the minimum necessary for good growth and flowers during the winter. Orchids can be grown under artificial illumination. According to Richard Paterson of the American Orchid Society, either two sets of two 48-inch 40-watt tube fixtures or one 48-inch 4-tube (40 watts) fixture is needed to provide the 1,200 foot-candles necessary for flowers. The lights should be on about 14 hours a day, and the plants must be positioned from 6 to 12 inches from the tubes. The brightest light is at the centers of the tubes; orchids such as the cypripediums or "slippers" *(Paphiopedilum)* which require less light can be placed at the ends of the tubes.

In the North, when the weather becomes settled and warm, most orchids should be moved outdoors. They can be suspended from tree limbs, placed on benches in light shade (never dense shade), or those in flower (many orchids flower in the summer) can be displayed on the terrace.

Potting and repotting used to be something of a problem, particularly for the beginner. Today potting mixtures rely less on the old stand-by osmunda fiber (though it is still used) and more on shredded tree-fern fiber and fir bark or redwood chips in various sizes, perlite, and peat moss. Most mail-order orchid specialists provide mixes for various orchids, some complete with enough fertilizer for several weeks.

Beginners with orchids are advised to buy potted plants (preferably in bud or bloom) and then move on from there to repotting and division, neither of which in the normal course of events should be necessary for a year or more after purchase.

The following orchids are recommended for house culture—and for beginners:

*Cattleya:* *C. bowringiana,* which blooms in fall; *C. labiata,* fall; *C. mossiae,* early spring; *C. trianaei* (Christmas orchid). Except for the blush-colored *C. trianaei,* these are of that color generally known as "orchid." There are numerous hybrids, some with large true red (with no magenta) flowers that are deliciously scented.

*Laelia:* Members of this allied genus, *Laelia,* are not quite so showy, but their perky flowers can be long-lasting and welcome to the beginner. Ones to try include *L. anceps* and *L. autumnalis,* fall-blooming; *L. crispa,* white, summer.

The above are epiphytal orchids—and a mere handful of the possibilities for house culture—those that in nature grow perched on trees, where there is never any stagnant water about their roots. Under cultivation in the house they are best grown in flowerpots, although in greenhouses or outdoors in mild climates they may be grown in slatted baskets or on slabs of bark with osmunda fiber or sphagnum moss wired on in the vicinity of the roots. To secure free drainage and root aeration, the pots are filled half full of crocks—broken clay pots in ½-inch pieces. The potting medium can be the standard osmunda fiber packed firmly around the roots with a potting stick. Or various combinations of the materials mentioned above can be used: 1 part tree-fern fiber, 2 parts medium-size fir bark plus a handful of chopped (unmilled) sphagnum moss and perlite has been recommended. Water is applied to the roots only when the medium becomes quite dry, when a thorough soaking is given. Overwatering the roots is likely to be disastrous; but the foliage should be sprayed twice daily if the sun is shining. These epiphytes benefit from a summer outdoors, especially if they have spent the winter months under fluorescent lights.

*Cymbidium:* There are terrestrial orchids (those that grow in the ground) that have adapted to house culture. First are the cymbidiums, but it is important to select species or varieties among the miniatures whose leaves can be expected to remain within 10 to 30 inches in length and which have proved to be more tolerant of average indoor conditions. (Regular or standard-size cymbidiums have foliage up to 36 inches or more in length and eventually are simply too large for most dwellings.) Cymbidiums need cool temperatures and ample sunshine to initiate bud formation. Leave the plants outdoors late in the fall until just before heavy frost weather begins. Indoors they still need cool temperatures, such as on a wide window sill where the light is bright from several hours of direct sun. Under these conditions the flower sprays remain in good condition for weeks and weeks. Attention to watering and feeding is necessary, and the plants tend to produce more flower spikes when pot-bound.

*Paphiopedilum*—**Lady-slipper:** These terrestrial orchids include the kinds which, called green orchids, are often used in corsages. Most are of a convenient size for house culture and even out of flower are attractive with their leathery-textured, straplike leaves in rosettes or fans. Some have decidedly mottled leaves. *P.* x *maudiae* is a hybrid, usually blooming in spring. Its green-white slipperlike flowers can remain in good condition for months. Species worth growing are *P. concolor* (summer-blooming), *P. callosum* (spring to fall), and *P. insigne* (fall to spring). There are numerous hybrids.

Lady-slipper orchids need humidity and a cool temperature and should not be allowed to become dry at the roots. Great care, however, must be taken to avoid overwatering and creating a saturated growing medium, especially when the plants are newly potted, or in winter when temperatures are cool and the plants are in plastic pots. The plants should not be exposed to undiluted sunshine for more than a few hours, even in winter but do well under fluorescent tubes. They should not be placed outdoors in the summer except on a very protected terrace.

The preceding represents but the "bare bones" of the wide world of orchids. Although orchids are often plants for fanciers or hobbyists, it is quite feasible for the run-of-the-mill house-plant enthusiast to grow a few kinds or one or two plants among other house plants. The American Orchid Society publishes a monthly *Bulletin* and has many local chapters. For information write the society, care of the Botanical Museum of Harvard University, Cambridge, Mass. 02138. For books on orchids see Chapter 21.

## 6. SHRUBS AS HOUSE PLANTS

There are a number of plants of a shrubby nature suitable for indoor culture. Some of them have a tendency to grow too large and must be controlled either by selective pruning (see Chapter 13) or by renewing them from time to time by seeds or cuttings. The culture of the most important species and varieties is covered in this chapter. Some, you will find, are dealt with elsewhere—*Pelargonium* (geranium), for example, strictly speaking, is a shrub. When you come across these inconsistencies, remember it is convenience, yours as well as mine, and not ignorance, that inspired the arrangement.

*Abutilon*—**Flowering-maple:** More closely related to hollyhock than to maple, abutilons were in greater favor with Grandmother than they are with us—probably because she was able to grow them better as a result of being content (or was she?) to live in a house where the temperature, more often than not, was nearer 50° F. than 70° during the winter. Abutilons are characterized by maplelike leaves and hoopskirted, papery flowers very much like those of hollyhock. Most of those grown as house plants are of hybrid origin and are referred to as *A.* x *hybridum.* Named variants are 'Satin Pink Belle', with pink flowers; 'Souvenir de Bonn', salmon flowers with scarlet veins; 'Savitzii', with yellow flowers and leaves margined with white; and 'Crimson Belle', with deep red flowers. A package of mixed seeds might be expected to produce some, at least, of these color and leaf forms. Abutilons accorded the rank of species by the botanist are:

*A. megapotamicum,* differentiated from the general run in having rather small unlobed leaves and a very long, bright red calyx. Its petals are yellow and the stamens protude well beyond the corolla, giving a striking fuchsialike effect. Its drooping habit of growth makes it a favorite for culture in hanging containers. *A. striatum* 'Aureo-maculatum' has orange flowers veined with crimson and leaves variegated with yellow.

Seeds sown in the spring and grown along in pots outdoors until they are brought indoors in the fall will bloom in winter. Named varieties, and any exceptionally good forms originating from seeds, should be propagated from cuttings in the spring or fall. The tips of the shoots of young plants should be pinched out to promote a bushy habit. Old plants should be pruned in fall to encourage new growth for winter blooming. Give them a sunny window and a temperature of about 60° F. Use general-purpose potting mixture and when they are in pots as large as you care to handle and these have become crowded with roots, give them liquid fertilizer every four or five weeks.

*Camellia japonica, C. sasanqua*—**Camellia:** Camellias are worth growing for their rich, glossy foliage alone; added to this there are the gorgeous flowers, 2 to 6 inches in diameter and beautiful in form. These may be single, semidouble, or fully double in a wide range of color; some are all of one tone, and some are variously mottled and striped with another color. The most popular species is *C. japonica,* of which there are hundreds of named cultivars blooming mostly in winter and early spring. Recommended for indoor culture are 'Alba Plena', double white; 'Donckelari', semidouble, white petals margined with red; 'Professor Sargent', large red with crest; 'Purity', white, double; 'Debutante', peony-type, pink.

*C. sasanqua* is less compact than *C. japonica,* has smaller foliage, and blooms in the fall. Listed cultivars include 'Cleopatra', often double, cherry red; 'Hebe', single, brilliant pink; 'Mine-no-Yuki', semidouble, white with golden stamens.

A relative, sometimes listed as *Thea sinensis*, is *C. sinensis*. Although not a first-class ornamental because its white flowers are small and poorly displayed (but they possess some fragrance), it is perhaps worthy of room for its interest as the source of one of the great beverages—tea.

Camellias are very much worthwhile if you have a roomy, cool, well-lighted place in which to grow them in winter. They are not harmed by light frost (actually when planted outdoors, some have been known to survive temperatures down to zero), but grown as pot plants it is desirable to give them 45° to 50° F. during the winter months. Sunshine is supposed to be essential, but I was successful in carrying one (I don't know the variety) to flowering stage in a poorly lighted, unheated basement room. Perhaps they can endure more shade in winter than is generally believed—provided the temperature is kept sufficiently low. Camellias have the exasperating habit of dropping their unopened flower buds on the slightest provocation. Lack of light, too much heat, dryness of the air, and too much or too little water are all supposed to be contributory causes. Spraying the foliage with water every day helps to keep the plants clean and provide the humid atmosphere that is desirable.

The soil should have a reaction of about pH 5.5 to pH 6.5. Use a general-purpose mixture, substituting peat moss for leaf mold if the base soil approaches alkalinity. When repotting, avoid setting the old ball any deeper in the pot. Put at least a half-inch layer of broken pots in the bottom of the pot for drainage, because the plants should be watered freely but resent stagnant moisture at their roots. During the summer set them outdoors with the pots plunged in peat moss, in dappled shade. Very little pruning is necessary and should be restricted to shortening shoots which spoil the plant's symmetry. This should be done immediately after flowering.

*Chrysanthemum frutescens*—**Paris Daisy, Boston Daisy, Marguerite:** There are two forms of shrubby chrysanthemums sometimes grown as house plants. One is the white marguerite *(C. frutescens),* which has white flowers and glaucous foliage (meaning that the leaves are overlaid with "bloom," giving a blue-green cast). The second is the Boston yellow daisy (*C. frutescens* 'Chrysaster'). Perhaps the main reason for growing these daisies as house plants is as a source of cut flowers, although the plants, especially after being cut back in the fall, never flower as freely indoors as they do in the garden or in a cool greenhouse.

These marguerites begin to bloom more freely around Easter and are offered throughout spring for growing in gardens as annuals. Although old plants can be cut back after blooming and grown along to flower another year, it is better to raise new plants annually because marguerites have extensive root systems and are such voracious feeders that it is necessary to use pots inconveniently large. Old cut-back plants should be set outdoors about the middle of May and cutting of young shoots taken in June for the following winter. These, when rooted, should be potted in general-purpose mixture and shifted into larger pots when roots begin to crowd, until they are in "sixes" or "sevens." Then when these are filled with roots, start feeding with liquid fertilizer. Bring indoors before frost and keep in a sunny window preferably in a temperature between 50° and 60° F. (Cuttings can also be taken in the fall and throughout winter.)

**Poinsettia**—*Euphorbia pulcherrima:* Once a plant of uncertain temperament, rarely lasting through the Christmas season in decent condition, the poinsettia has been hybridized into a durable beauty that is undaunted by drafts and fluctuating interior temperatures. These hybrids, if given reasonable care—that is, watered when their soil is dry and kept in bright light—are often in as good condition at Easter as when received in December. The colored bracts which surround the small yellow flower clusters can be pink, white, or variegated as well as the traditional red.

Although plants can be brought into flower a second year, most people still treat them as transients, discarding them in spring when they finally begin to drop their foliage and bracts. If you wish to reflower your plant, cut back the stalks in spring to force new growth and repot in fresh general-purpose soil.

Water regularly but only as soil dries out, and after the weather warms, sink the pot outdoors in full sun. Pinch back new growth (can be used as cuttings to start new plants) in early summer to shape the plant. The poinsettia is another short-day plant (see also Christmas cactus), and while it will eventually bloom without special treatment, if you wish a holiday season display, the plant must be subjected to short days for about six weeks beginning in midfall. Bring the plant indoors and give it about 14 hours of darkness per day by placing it in a closet or unlighted room or by covering with a dark cloth or large carton. The plant must be brought back into good light each day after the dark treatment. During the day it should receive four or more hours of direct sun. Night temperatures of 50° to 65° F. and day temperatures of 60° to 70° F. are best.

**Crown-of-Thorns**—*Euphorbia milii splendens:* A shrub with tangled fleshy gray stems armed with fierce spines which warrant caution in handling it. The leaves are few in number on the tips of the branches and are soon shed if the plant is grown under arid conditions. The flowers are produced in greatest abundance in winter, but a well-grown plant is seldom without a few. It is the scarlet bracts (not petals) accompanying the flowers that make the plant bright and cheerful in spite of its spines and snaky branches. Give it all the sun possible; soil as for cacti and keep on the dry side during November and December.

*Fuchsia x hybrida*—**Fuchsia, Ladies' Ear-drops:** As many as two thousand fuchsias have been named over the years, believed to be derived mostly from hybrids of *F. fulgens* and *F. magellanica,* but far fewer than this number are likely to be available, even from a specialist. Although undeniably beautiful, the flowers of many varieties do not differ drastically from each other in color and form. The average grower of house plants can usually choose from several current favorites at garden centers and other local outlets or order rooted cuttings in early spring from mail-order sources. Those who want to make a hobby of growing fuchsias can join the American Fuchsia Society, Hall of Flowers, Golden Gate Park, San Francisco, Calif. 94122.

Fuchsias, in general, are summer-blooming shrubs in northern areas. They need cool conditions and shade from hot sun, but plenty of light. There are kinds to grow as upright shrubs or standard "trees," limited to one main trunk or stem, and as gracefully cascading plants in hanging baskets. The latter varieties are by far the most popular, especially with the interest these days in decorating outdoor-living areas. Such plants rarely do well over winter in overheated, dry interiors, and most people prefer to consider them transients to be discarded at the advent of cold weather. The instructions below, for those who want to "save" their plants for another year, show clearly that this program is a holding action only, since the plants are mostly dormant and therefore lack any ornamental value as house plants.

There are a few exceptions. The upright, shrubby fuchsias derived from *F. triphylla,* sometimes called the honeysuckle fuchsia, seem to adapt well to indoor conditions, such as a cool, bright window, after being outside all summer and often bloom cheerfully through most of the winter. 'Gartenmeister Bonstedt' is an old hybrid (ranging from 18 inches to 3 feet in height depending on age) with long, slender red-orange flowers and foliage tinged with red; 'Traudchen Bonstedt' has exceptionally long-tubed flowers in cream and salmon; 'Christmas Gem' has orange-red flowers and dark green foliage. Toward late winter, these triphylla hybrids can be pruned to shape them and force new growth, which, if all goes well, should bear flowers in summer through winter.

The following instructions are for cascade and upright varieties that have bloomed all summer into early fall. The plants are rested by keeping them cool—45° to 50° F.—during November and December, and giving them only enough water to keep the wood plump. In January they are brought into a day temperature of 60° to 65° F. (night 50°) and watered. As new growth develops, cut out dead and weak wood and trim to shape. Some growers shake the soil off the roots and repot at this time, using general-purpose mixture. Avoid overwatering until growth is well along, and spray tops with water at least once a day. Young plants can be raised by cuttings of young shoots cut off when they are about 4 inches long. They root very easily in peat moss and sand in a propagating case. A bushy habit should be promoted by pinching out shoot tips during the early stages of growth.

Fuchsias have so much charm and such beautiful and varied form and coloring that they merit the attention of all who can provide the cool growing conditions of winter and early spring.

*Gardenia*—Florists' Gardenia, Cape-jasmine: Those who conduct question-and-answer columns for gardeners come to loathe the sight of the name gardenia because the plant is provocative of more "Why does it drop its flower buds?" queries than any other house plant. The florists' gardenia, *G. jasminoides* 'Veitchii', is a cantankerous plant even when grown under what are supposed to be the ideal conditions of a greenhouse. It is not surprising,

*Cymbidium orchids on a summer terrace. Cymbidiums—the miniature types take up less space than the standard cymbidiums—are spectacular in flower but they require a sunny, cool window.*

therefore, that it is a bad actor when treated as a house plant. The old-fashioned Cape-jasmine *(G. jasminoides fortuniana)* is much easier to grow because it flowers during the summer months when it can be kept outdoors and can be induced to take a rest during the winter.

In spite of the gardenia's mean disposition, the glossy luxuriant foliage and beautiful waxen flowers impel thousands to attempt its culture in the house—and there are some who succeed! An acid soil, warmth, sunshine, moist air brought about by spraying the foliage daily, and the use of other humidifying devices are necessary. If the temperature falls much below 60° F., the foliage is likely to become yellow; if it goes much above 60° during the hours of darkness, the flower buds are likely to drop. An alkaline soil will also cause the leaves to turn yellow. This is provided against by using acid peat moss as a source of humus in the potting soil and by mixing a tablespoonful of iron sulphate to each bushel if the base soil is alkaline. (See mixture for acid-soil plants.) Keep the soil moist at all times but avoid waterlogging. Repot just before the plants are placed outdoors for the summer. When pots are filled with roots, water every four or five weeks with liquid fertilizer. Prune and pinch as described in Chapter 13.

The Cape-jasmine *(G. jasminoides fortuniana)* is a much more satisfactory plant to grow if you can forgo the pleasure of flowers in winter. It is admirable as a tub plant for patio or porch decoration or when placed at a strategic point in the garden. It can be stored for the winter in a light situation in a temperature of about 50° F. Give less water when it is resting.

*Hibiscus rosa-sinensis*—**Chinese Hibiscus, Rose-of-China:** Although reaching the dimensions of a large shrub (up to 30 feet) or a small tree in the tropics and subtropics, the Chinese hibiscus can be grown satisfactorily as a pot or tub plant because it does not resent hard pruning and produces its large blooms, reminiscent of hollyhock, to which it is related, on young shoots. (It is said that the flowers can be rubbed on the shoes in place of blacking when one needs a shine!) There are numerous cultivars available in the tropics. There is also one with variegated leaves and red flowers, 'Cooperi', commonly seen in greenhouses.

While one may be able to see flowers on greenhouse-grown plants of hibiscus at almost any season, they are primarily summer and fall bloomers. When grown as house plants, it is desirable to rest them during the winter in a temperature of about 50° F., keeping them on the dry side at the roots. At the beginning of March cut them back about one half, bring into a sunny window, repot in general-purpose mixture, and water freely when growth begins. A daily spraying of the tops will help new shoots to "break." They should be kept outdoors during the summer.

*Rhododendron*—**Azalea:** The rhododendrons forced by florists and commonly known as azaleas have evergreen foliage and generally resemble the winter-hardy azaleas we grow in gardens. Many of these tender azaleas are grown outdoors in mild climates, but most are not hardy in the North. They are hybrids of bewildering ancestry and new cultivars are constantly being introduced by commercial growers. Among those that retain their popularity are the large-flowered 'Albert Elizabeth', semidouble, white and deep pink, and 'Coral Bells', with pleasing coral-pink, "hose-in-hose" small flowers. This last is one of the azaleas offered by florists around Valentine's Day.

These azaleas can be grown as house plants if they are kept cool—40° to 50° F.—during November and December. While the florist with humid greenhouse facilities can force the earlier sorts into bloom for Christmas, it is usually fatal to attempt to do this under house conditions. When they are brought indoors in the fall just before frost, keep them in a light position in an unheated but frost-free room, and water the soil whenever it shows signs of becoming dry. Do not attempt to start them into growth before the middle of January; if you can curb your impatience until mid-February, so much the better. About five weeks at 60° F. will bring them into bloom. Spray the foliage daily during this time. Repot in a larger pot, if necessary, as soon as the flowers have faded, using the acid-soil mixture. If the roots are not unduly crowded, remove loose soil from the surface and replace with a 50–50 mixture of peat moss and rotted or dried manure and a teaspoonful of cottonseed meal, or dried blood. Or use a liquid fish emulsion every few weeks. When frost no longer threatens, place them outdoors in full sun or light shade, plunging the pots in peat moss to keep the roots cool and to lessen the need for watering, which, however, must be attended to during dry spells.

**Miniature Roses:** If properly handled, these offer opportunities for late winter, spring, and summer bloom in the house. These roses are miniature replicas of some of the hybrid teas and seldom exceed 8 to 15 inches in height, with flowers and foliage in proportion. There are several varieties available, including the one known to gardeners as *Rosa roulettii* (but correctly, *Rosa chinensis* 'Minima'), which started all the furor for them. This has an interesting story. It was found growing as a pot plant in the windows of cottages in the village of Mauborget, Switzerland, by a Dr. Roulet, who called it to the attention of his friend, the late Henri Correvon, a famous horticulturist of Geneva, who introduced it to general cultivation. According to Correvon, the peasants said it had been grown as a house plant in Mauborget for centuries. Included among other cultivars are 'Baby Gold Star', golden yellow; 'Midget', very dwarf, red; 'Red Imp', crimson buds, ruby red when open; 'Pixie', white; 'Starina', orange-red.

My own experience with these roses was disappointing, but others have reported excellent results. They should be obtained in small pots from dealers in January and immediately repotted in 3- or 4-inch pots in general-purpose mixture. Cut them back ½ to ⅔ and keep moist in a temperature between 60° and 70° F. (55° to 65° at night). Established plants should be rested by keeping them cool (40°) in November and December.

**Princess Flower—*Tibouchina*** (syn. *T. semidecandra*) *urvilleana:* The princess flower, or glory bush, has gorgeous royal-purple flowers, 4 to 5 inches across, produced over a long period in summer and fall. The hairy leaves take on a delicate "fall" coloring as they fade. When started from cuttings in spring, the shoots, as they attain a length of 8 inches to a foot, should have their tips pinched out until the required bushiness is obtained. The princess flower is best grown outdoors during the summer, and brought into a sunny window in the fall. When active growth ceases, the plant should be removed to a cool, well-lighted room and less water given. Cut back about ⅓ in the spring, give a higher temperature (65° to 70° F.), and keep soil moist. Use general-purpose mixture.

## 7.   FRUITS

Growing various tropical and subtropical fruits as house plants is an interesting project if one's bent lies that way, even though the possibility of obtaining edible fruit on such kinds as avocado, banana, date, and papaya is decidedly remote, unless conditions are exceptionally favorable and one has plenty of room to grow the plants. On the other hand, fig, lemon and a few other kinds of citrus, Christmas peppers, pomegranate, strawberry guava, and Surinam-cherry can be grown with a reasonable expectation of obtaining some fruit if given good culture. Then there are some grown solely for the beauty of their fruits with no utilitarian thoughts whatever. These include *Ardisia,* Jerusalem-cherry, Otaheite orange, and rouge plant or *Rivina.*

**Pineapple—***Ananus:* They are worth growing as foliage plants alone, though if this is the objective it would perhaps be better to use one of the more colorful varieties. *A. comosus* 'Nanus' grows only 12 to 15 inches high and bears a small edible "pineapple." *A. comosus* 'Variegatus' is similar but has ivory and pink variegated foliage.

It is easy enough to obtain a pineapple plant—of a kind. Merely buy a pineapple fruit when in season and slice off the crown of leaves at the top of the fruit, making the cut at the junction of fruit and leaf bases. Insert this in sand, keep it moist, and it will soon produce roots, when it can be potted in soil. Or suspend in a jar of water. Commercial growers do not use this method of propagation because it is said that such plants take longer to come into bearing—suckers originating at the base of the plant are used instead.

Like all bromeliads, pineapples need a well-drained, open rooting medium. Put at least an inch of broken pot pieces in the bottom of the pot for drainage, and use a soil mixture of equal parts fibrous loam, peat moss, thoroughly rotted or dried manure, sand, and granulated charcoal. Pot the plants on into progressively larger pots as they become root-bound if the objective is fruit production. Moist air, 60° F. minimum temperature, and ample light are necessary. A *mature* plant can be encouraged to fruit by enclosing the plant in a plastic bag with an apple for about five days.

**Coralberry—***Ardisia crenata:* The coral berry is famous for the lengthy period (two years) that it hangs on to its clusters of hollylike red berries. It is a first-class, tolerant house plant, and well-grown specimens are beautiful at all times because of their glossy crenulated leaves. Old plants become leggy and bare at the base and may then be air-layered (see Chapter 15). Perhaps a better plan is to raise new plants annually by inserting cuttings of nearly matured young shoots in a warm propagating case. Seeds can also be used, first washing off the pulp before sowing them in the spring. Seedlings, however, show a greater tendency toward legginess than do cuttings. Use general-purpose potting mixture. If possible, keep at 60° F. during winter. The chief enemy of ardisia is a brown scale insect which can be controlled by weekly forcible spraying with water. Do not, however, spray during the flowering period.

**Christmas Pepper—***Capsicum annuum:* It is grown as an annual by starting the seeds, which must be removed from the pods before sowing (in case you are using seed from your own plants), in May or June. The seedlings should be transplanted into small pots and shifted to larger sizes, up to 5 inches, as the pots become filled with roots. Use general-purpose potting mixture. Plunge the pots outdoors in a sunny situation in a bed of sand or peat moss to keep the soil from drying too frequently. Water during dry spells. Or they may be planted out and dug up with a ball of soil around their roots and potted in early fall. Keep well watered and shaded for a week or two. Bring indoors before cold weather and keep them in a sunny window. During winter, maintain a temperature of 55° F. (they will last better if kept cool) if possible, and do not allow the soil to become dry. The tiny, brilliant scarlet fruits are peppery and can be used as a condiment if they seem of greater value for this than for ornament.

**Papaya**—*Carica papaya:* The papaya grows too large for the average home. I have seen it more than 8 feet tall and 5 feet in diameter, growing in a large, enclosed porch heated in winter. It is easy to raise from seeds, but male *and* female plants are needed to obtain fruit, unless you happen to get a specimen in which both sexes are represented. Its foliage, something like that of castor bean, is ornamental. General potting mixture, routine care.

*Citrus:* Mention has been made elsewhere of the foliage value of citrus fruits when raised from seeds. If fruits are desired—and why not?—natural dwarfs or grafted plants of varieties adapted to pot culture should be purchased. These will come into bearing earlier than seedlings. A lemon (*Citrus* 'Meyer') is excellent for indoor culture and produces its fruits freely. 'Ponderosa', whose fruits are very large—up to two pounds—is another lemon often grown as a house plant. The dwarf or Otaheite orange (*C.* x *limonia*), often sold as fruiting pot plants by florists at Christmas, is decidedly ornamental when covered with small oranges, which, however, are very tart. Kumquats (*Fortunella* spp.), eaten skin and all, are pungent and palatable, though the plants are well worth growing for ornament, too.

All these citrus fruits have the added attraction of sweetly scented flowers and glossy foliage. None of them is likely to grow too big to be accommodated in the house with the exception of the 'Ponderosa' lemon, which will take several years before outgrowing its welcome. As to soil, the general-purpose potting mixture will suit them. In winter the temperature should be kept between 55° and 65° F. if possible. A weekly spraying, except when they are blooming, is desirable to help keep down scale insects. During the summer they should be placed outdoors so that the wood becomes thoroughly ripened.

**Surinam-cherry**—*Eugenia uniflora:* This, a Brazilian shrub related to the clove tree of commerce, has fragrant half-inch white flowers and small glossy leaves. The ribbed crimson fruits, about the size of gooseberries, ripen in winter and are quite palatable. Place outdoors during summer, but keep in a sunny window during the cold months. It will not be harmed if the temperature falls to 45° F. General potting mixture, routine care.

**Fig**—*Ficus carica:* Growing the fig is a challenge that some northern gardeners can't resist. Its fruits are produced on the new shoots so it can be pruned back in the spring if this should be necessary to keep the plant from becoming too large. It produces fruits, and, while they are not of first-class quality, there is some satisfaction in raising one's own fresh figs, even though living in a climate not suited to fig culture outdoors. This is one of those

*Steps in growing an avocado: The pit is suspended in water; then potted in soil and eventually becomes a small tree or branching shrub.*

shrubs that can be overwintered in a cool cellar and put outdoors when danger of severe frost is past if there is no room for it in the living quarters; or it can be started in the living room six weeks in advance of the time for setting outdoors. Plants that have started to grow should not be exposed to frost, and they should be shaded for a week or two to inure them gradually to more intense light. Use general-purpose potting mixture and water freely when growing; keep on dry side when they are resting in winter.

**Banana:** One would scarcely think of the banana as having house-plant possibilities, but the Chinese or dwarf banana *(Musa nana)* can be fruited when grown in a tub, and I have seen one almost of fruiting size grown in an enclosed plant room. Plants should be started as suckers in rather sandy soil in 8-inch pots. When the pot is filled with roots, transplant to a tub 24 to 30 inches in diameter and 24 inches high. As soon as the soil (general-purpose mixture) is filled with roots, give weak liquid fertilizer every two or three weeks. Warmth (60° F. minimum), moist air, and plenty of sunshine are required. The old trunk (it is not really a trunk, but rather a bundle of leafstalks) should be discarded after fruiting and a new plant or plants raised from the suckers appearing around the base.

**Avocado—*Persea americana:*** The avocado must be one of the most widely grown foliage plants in city apartments. Even if you don't see great beauty in the foliage, it is interesting to watch the germination of the large seed. If you have not already done so, the next time you have an avocado salad, save the seed, soak it in water to remove its outer covering, and then suspend it, large end down, with the base just touching some water in a wide-mouthed, clear-glass jar. Three toothpicks stuck into the seed at an equal distance apart will hold the seed at the right level. Sometimes this treatment will cause the seed to decay, but one has to take a few chances in life. If you want to *grow* an avocado, realizing that you are unlikely to get fruit from it as a house plant, start the seed a half inch below the surface in a 4-inch pot in sandy soil. It will grow no matter whether it is placed on its side or top side down, but you will save it the trouble of reversing the directions of root and shoot if it is placed with the small end up. To force the stem to branch, cut back about halfway when it reaches 6 to 7 inches. Keep the soil moist but not soggy. Bright light (some sun in winter, part shade in summer) is necessary for lush growth.

**Strawberry Guava—***Psidium littorale longipes:* Described as a "luscious tropical fruit" with "a delicious, sweet, and spicy flavor," the strawberry guava can be insipid and seedy. Its foliage is good, however, the 1-inch flowers are white and fragrant, and it has the merit of blooming and fruiting while comparatively small in size. General-purpose potting mixture, routine care.

**Pomegranate—***Punica granatum:* If you are ambitious to grow pomegranate in your home, you should get the dwarf single-flowered 'Nana'. The double-flowered one is more effective, but not likely to produce fruits. These dwarf forms make dense, twiggy little bushes clothed with small, narrow, shining leaves; the flowers are large and orange-red. The pomegranate should be placed outdoors in full sun during the summer months. Bring it in before frost (though light frost will not kill it) and keep in a sunny window in a cool room (50° F.) to rest with rather less water than normal at the roots. Start into growth by bringing it into living-room temperature in February and water it normally. Repot into larger pot whenever the roots become crowded, using general-purpose potting mixture. This has become a popular subject for indoor bonsai.

**Rouge Plant—***Rivina humilis:* The rouge plant is a relative of the pokeweed and grows wild in southern United States and tropical America. It is a weedy-looking plant (about 1½ feet tall) until it is redeemed by racemes of small but showy red berries which probably are not wholesome to eat. In the greenhouse it takes care of itself to the extent of developing plenty of self-sown seedlings in the gravel of the benches. I never grew it at home, but it is reported that it is a good house plant. If seeds can be obtained, it is worthy of a trial, needing no special treatment.

**Jerusalem-cherry—***Solanum pseudocapsicum:* If your rooms are hot and dry, there is not much use in bothering with Jerusalem-cherry, because under these conditions it quickly drops its leaves and berries. If you have small children who are inclined to eat anything of attractive appearance within reach, it might be as well not to allow Jerusalem-cherry in your home, for the fruits are poisonous. These plants are grown commercially in enormous numbers and sold at Christmas. The ornamental pepper *(Capsicum annuum)* bears edible fruits in various colors, but beware—they are very hot and only suitable for seasoning. Seeds may be sown indoors in February. Culture same as for Christmas pepper.

## 8. VINES AND TRAILERS

In addition to the pleasure given by their intrinsic beauty, climbing and trailing plants perform the function of adding height to the window garden. They can be grown to frame the window, or more likely today, be suspended in a suitable container to furnish the upper parts of the window. A few accessories are needed to accommodate the weak-stemmed habit which characterizes this group. The climbers will need supports of some kind or other. These can be elaborate or simple, depending upon taste and pocketbook. The simplest is a plant stake pushed into the soil of the pot, to which the shoots are tied or on which they climb of their own volition. A modification of this is a light wooden trellis attached to a section of board on which the potted plant is stood, as described in Chapter 13. One advantage of making a unit of plant and stand is that the whole can be removed from the window to a more convenient place if it should be necessary to spray against insect pests. Another method of supporting climbers is by means of light wire (picture wire is good) attached by hooks or screw eyes to the window frame. If the window is recessed, a simple trellis of wood or wire can be attached on blocks to the side framing so that it stands out an inch or two.

Droopers or trailers can be hung from brackets attached to the window casing or from rods placed horizontally across the window. Garden centers, hardware stores, and mail-order firms specializing in house plants will give you an idea of what is available. All sorts of hanging containers are offered, but indoors it is almost essential to use plastic pots with molded saucers to catch the drips that fall after watering.

There is considerable variation in size and vigor of trailing and climbing plants, ranging from the fragile grace of the Kenilworth-ivy to the massive solidity of the more robust philodendrons. Some trailers, such as abutilon, achimenes, coleus, fuchsia, oxalis, geranium, and sedum, have been disposed of elsewhere, either to avoid divorcing them from their families or removing them from a group to which they more appropriately belong. (And some of the trailing plants included here are more often thought of as foliage plants so really shouldn't be part of a section in a chapter devoted to flowering plants.) Sweet-potato, an excellent house vine, will be found in Chapter 10. Others that belong in this chapter are described below, but almost any plant can be displayed to advantage in a hanging container. For additional possibilities, check the General List of House Plants (Chapter 19).

*Cissus*—**Kangaroo Vine, Cape-grape, Grape-ivy:** These relatives of the grape provide excellent vines of good constitution for indoor conditions. The best known is grape-ivy *(C. rhombifolia),* whose leaves consist of three glossy toothed and pointed leaflets. It needs a fair amount of light, can endure heat and dryness, and may be used either as a trailer or as a climber. Of similar habit is *C. adenopoda,* which has tuberous roots and fuzzy leaves which are green above and red beneath. Its leaves also are divided into three leaflets. The Cape-grape (*C. capensis,* sometimes listed as *Rhoicissus capensis*) is more akin in appearance to the grape grown for its fruits. The developing leaves are particularly attractive, for they have a dense covering of pinkish-lavender hairs which disappear as the leaf ages. It, like *C. adenopoda,* has tuberous roots and is able to withstand drought and sun. The kangaroo vine *(C. antarctica),* native to Australia, has comparatively long and narrow leaves, shiny on the upper surface. It is rather awkward in appearance unless trained and pruned to the desired shape. It will grow well in poorly lighted situations and in air-conditioned rooms.

*C. discolor* might be worth a trial in a cool plant room (55° F.) in winter and not too hot and muggy in summer. Under cool greenhouse conditions it is a vigorous grower with exquisite oval or heart-shaped leaves up to 6 inches long, purplish beneath and velvety green above, marked with white, pink, and purple. Sometimes it is known as climbing-begonia, although in no way related.

All of these are of easy culture (except possibly *C. discolor*) in the average house in general-purpose potting soil. They should be kept constantly moist at the roots when they are actively growing. The tuberous-rooted kinds should be rested by keeping the soil fairly dry for a month or two after growth for the season is completed. All of them are subject to attacks by mealybugs, which should be watched for, especially in the angles made by junction of leaves and stems.

*Ceropegia woodii*—**Hearts Entangled, Rosary Vine, String of Hearts:** This is a plant that always excites interest with its thick, fleshy, heart-shaped, opposite leaves, about ¾ inch long, which are marbled white on green when grown in shade and white on coppery-bronze in sunshine. The undersides are pinkish overlaid with gray. Under favorable conditions its slender stems may trail to a length of 6 feet. The moisture contained in the leaves makes these stems surprisingly heavy. The small pinkish or light purple flowers add nothing decoratively, but they have an interesting structure. The plant produces tubers in the soil and along the stems, which can be used for propagating purposes. It is adaptable to varied conditions. It will grow in sun or shade and can be rested or not, according to its behavior—some plants will keep on growing throughout the year; others indicate their desire for a rest by wilting of the stems. When this happens, water should be withheld for a month or two. The soil recommended for cacti will suit *Ceropegia.*

*Cyanotis somaliensis*—**Pussy Ears:** This relative of the wandering Jew has trailing stems and triangular, fleshy, hairy leaves. It has bright purple and orange hairy flowers. Even though it may not be floriferous under house culture, it is worth growing for its unusual-looking leaves. Native to tropical Africa, it can stand plenty of heat and sun. Use general-purpose potting mixture and keep a little on the dry side in winter. *C. kewensis,* called the teddy bear vine (poor thing!), is similar.

*Cymbalaria muralis*—**Kenilworth-ivy:** This dainty little relative of the snap-dragon is rather commonly seen growing in chinks between brick and stone walls in England and seems to get along famously on the rather lean diet afforded by crumbling mortar. It has tiny lilac-blue, snapdragonlike flowers on fragile stems clothed with rounded, lobed leaves. There are color forms with white or pink flowers. It is admirable for use in a hanging container, and plants of good size can be grown in pots as small as 3 inches. It is easily raised from seeds sown in the spring, or old plants can be divided then. Its predilection for old walls suggests that it would not be amiss to include in the potting soil a handful of crushed limestone. Sun or part shade.

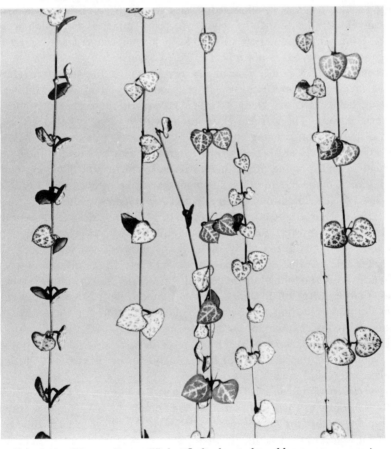

*Rosary vine* (Ceropegia woodii) *has fleshy, heart-shaped leaves, more conspicu-ous than its flowers. Another common name is string of hearts.*

*Ficus pumila (repens)*—**Creeping** Fig: Although the creeping fig can be grown as a trailer, it is more naturally a climber and should be so used whenever the right conditions present themselves. It attaches itself to its support by means of aerial rootlets (I have seen it cling tenaciously even to a painted surface) and in its climbing stage presses its small, heart-shaped leaves flat against the wall, post, or rock on which it is growing. When it has attained sufficient size and has reached the limits of its supports, it puts out an entirely different style of growth with leaves three times the size of those on the climbing shoots. This is known as the arborescent and fruiting stage, but it is seldom seen in the North except in large conservatories. The "figs" are said to be used in Japan for making preserves.

I once saw this fig ideally used in a friend's home, planted in a narrow border at the base of a wall (completely clothing it) that formed the inner boundary of an enclosed sun porch. It is an adaptable plant, enduring either warm or freezing conditions in winter with equanimity. If you haven't a wall on which to grow it, allow it to trail over the edge of the pot or insert vertically in the pot a slab of wood with bark attached on which it will climb. It is not particular as to soil; keep it well watered and spray the foliage occasionally. It is not much bothered by insects.

**Gesneriads:** This family (Gesneriaceae), of which the most universally known member is the African-violet, contains many plants with trailing or creeping habits that are being as much grown for these characteristics as for their flowers. The African-violet itself, with its long-petioled leaves, is often displayed in a hanging container.

Many gesneriads are better grown in greenhouses because of their need for high humidity while others have seasonal growth and flowering habits (for instance, many bloom in the summer) that make their culture a problem compared to the ubiquitous spider plant (*Chlorophytum comosum* 'Variegatum'). Nevertheless there is keen interest in this family on the part of hybridizers, commercial growers, and house-plant enthusiasts, and increasingly more and more gesneriads, especially of trailing habit, will be introduced that are better able to adjust to average house conditions. In the meantime species and cultivars of the following are generally available: *Aeschynanthus* (lipstick vine); *Columnea* (goldfish plant); *Episcea* (flame-violet); *Streptocarpus saxorum.* For the preceding, see Section 1 of this chapter; for *Achimenes,* see Section 3 of this chapter; for *Alloplectus nummularia,* see the General List of House Plants (Chapter 19). Other gesneriads, trailing and nontrailing, are available from specialists and increasingly can be picked up from local garden centers and greenhouses.

**Ivy**—*Hedera:* English ivy, Canary ivy, and Colchic ivy are the true ivies. Perhaps because of their low cost, they are among the most popular trailing or climbing plants for home use, even though they have a hard time of it and finally succumb, usually to an infestation of spider mites, if kept at 70° F. and over during the winter. The English ivy, *H. helix,* is an extraordinarily variable species with hundreds of named cultivars. The one once most commonly sold by florists (ironically enough sometimes as "old English ivy") is the Irish ivy, *H. h.* 'Hibernica', an exceptionally vigorous variety. It was in all probability this variety that "sported" and produced a dwarfish branching form, between 1915 and 1920, which was introduced under the name of 'Pittsburgh' ivy. This in turn sported freely and gave rise to cultivars such as 'Hahn's Self-branching', 'Long Point', 'Manda's Crested', 'Maple Queen', and 'Sylvanian', standard selections that have been joined by 'Fluffy Ruffles', 'Weber's Californian'—all rather compact, freely branching types, good for drooping over the pots but not much for climbing.

Distinctive forms with long, climbing shoots that can be obtained without too much difficulty are *H. h.* 'Scutifolia', heart-shaped, unlobed leaves, slow-growing; *H. h.* 'Discolor', which has small leaves variegated with white; *H. h.* 'Digitata', having five rather deeply cut lobes and gray veins; and *H. h.* 'Pedata', also sold as 'Caenwoodiana', which has a very long central lobe and is a rapid grower; 'Fan', which has dark green leaves veined in pale green, and 'Glacier', small-leaved, each leaf variegated in green, gray, and white with pinkish edgings.

*Creeping fig is the vine that fills this kitchen window.*

Although they are fairly enduring, keeping these ivies really happy means giving them moist, cool conditions (45° to 50° F. at night) during the winter. If you cannot do this, spray them with water as often as you can and give them a real shower bath once a week by spraying them thoroughly with water from the faucet, taking care to hit both sides of the leaves. This will prevent attacks by spider mites and scale insects, the worst enemies of the ivy.

Those who have a good planting of Irish ivy outdoors can cut shoots about 2 feet long in August or September and place the bases in water. They will root readily and remain in good condition for several months. Although ivies can endure winter sun indoors, they are better off if shaded from its direct beams, and are suitable for growing in a well-lighted north window. General-purpose mixture is satisfactory, and they should be kept moist but not soggy at the roots at all times.

The Canary ivy *(H. canariensis)*, native to the Canary Islands and, in geographical forms, to North Africa and Madeira (*H. canariensis* 'Variegata'), seems better adapted to survival in hot rooms than *H. helix* variants—perhaps because acclimated to warmer winters in its native home. The leaves are large, up to 6 inches across, and not so deeply lobed as those of most varieties of English ivy. Another variegated form is 'Gloire de Marengo', which has quite large leaves, beautifully marked with cream, yellow, or white.

For those who are interested in collecting ivies, there is the American Ivy Society, 128 W. Fifty-eighth St., New York, N.Y. 10019.

**Waxplant**—*Hoya carnosa:* An old-time favorite as a house plant, hoya is grown for its clusters of very fragrant, waxlike, white, pink-centered flowers which are produced in summer. The form 'Variegata', which has its thick, fleshy leaves irregularly margined with white, is attractive at all seasons. A few other variegated forms have appeared, some with puckery or distorted leaves that are more exotic than beautiful. (The miniature wax-plant [*H. bella*], reputed to be more free with its blooms, is recommended for hanging containers rather than trellises.) The waxplant climbs naturally with the help of aerial rootlets, and it is desirable to give it something in the nature of a bark-covered slab of suitable length to which it may become attached rather than to tie it to an ordinary plant stake. It should be potted in a humusy mixture such as that recommended for begonias; during late winter and spring, growth should be encouraged by keeping it warm (70° F.), moist at the roots, and by frequently spraying the top. Throughout late fall and early winter it should be rested by keeping the soil almost dry, watering it only when the leaves show signs of shriveling. During this time a temperature of 50° to 60° F. is preferred. The "spurs" on which the flowers are produced should not be cut off when the flowers have faded, for they will produce again. Partial shade is satisfactory.

*Ipomoea*—**Morning-glory:** Morning-glories, despite the fact that they may climb to 10 feet or more when planted outdoors, are adaptable to pot culture, and their cramped quarters have a tendency to force them into bloom earlier than is the case when their roots are unrestricted. Varieties of *I. nil* have long been favorite pot plants of the Japanese, who grow them from seed in 8-inch pots with constant pinching back to prevent vining growth. In this country they are usually sold in seed mixtures under the name Imperial Giant, Fringed, Double Mixed, and so on. The varieties of *I. nil* are characterized by flowers up to 6 inches across, single or double, variously ruffled, scalloped, and fringed, often mottled, flaked, or bordered with one or more colors. These morning-glories can be kept within bounds by pinching out the tips of shoots which seem likely to exceed the limits assigned them.

Other morning-glories that can be used are varieties of *I. purpurea,* the one known as 'Heavenly Blue Improved' being an especial favorite.

It takes these morning-glories from eight to twelve weeks to come into bloom from seeds, which may be started by planting three or four ½ inch deep in a 3-inch pot, afterward giving them a shift to a larger size; or by sowing them directly in the 5- or 6-inch pots in which they will bloom. Or sow two seeds in Jiffy pellet pots, later pinching off the weaker seedling and planting pot and plant into larger pot. Germination can be accelerated by soaking the seeds in lukewarm water for 24 hours prior to sowing them. Nicking or filing a notch in the seed coat serves the same purpose. The soil should not be too rich—use general-purpose mixture diluted by adding two extra parts of sand. They should be given a sunny window to ensure free flowering. Morning-glories climb by twining, so it is desirable to stretch three or four vertical wires up the window casing to serve as supports.

*Philodendron:* While all the philodendrons are climbers, there are some, noted in the chapter on foliage plants, that are too massive to be used for this purpose in the average house. There are two species, however, that may be considered first-class for either trailing or climbing. The heart-leaf philodendron (*P. scandens oxycardium,* formerly known as *P. cordatum*) is one of the most tolerant house plants and one of the most shade-enduring, growing well in a window in a north room. The leaves of this philodendron, in the juvenile stage, are about 4 inches long, heart-shaped and long-pointed. Another subspecies, *P. scandens scandens* (syn. *P. micans*), with leaves of similar size and shape, is much more beautiful because of the velvety appearance of the upper surface. But, unfortunately, it is also much more finicky and difficult to grow.

There is nothing much to be said about the culture of philodendron. Keep the soil moist but not waterlogged, and when the trailers get too long, snip off 6 inches from the tip of each one and either insert them in the soil of the pot in which the parent is growing (if it is bare at the base) or put them in the propagating case with a view to starting up a new pot filled with vigorous young plants to take the place of the old one.

*Plectranthus australis*—**Swedish-ivy:** This is not an "ivy" at all, but is a member of the mint family and closely related to *Coleus.* Its bright green, scalloped-edged leaves have a waxy, fleshy texture; the clusters of small white flowers are not very spectacular. The Swedish-ivy's value is in its trailing habit and its ability to quickly fill a hanging basket, requiring only minimum care along the way. As the stems lengthen, they can be pinched off to encourage a bushy, spreading habit. Such cut-off shoots can be rooted in sand and peat moss or in water to start new plants. In fact, Swedish-ivy remains in presentable condition for a long period while growing in water, such as in discarded wine bottles.

There are some attractive variegated leaf forms of Swedish-ivy. The leaves of *P. oertendahlii* 'Variegatus' are irregularly marked with cream white; its stems are purple in contrast to the bright green of *P. australis* and its flowers are pink. *P. coleoides* 'Marginatus' has leaves edged with white, and white flowers marked with purple. *P. purpuratus* has hairy-textured leaves that are purple underneath. Its flowers are lavender. A Swedish-ivy sold as 'Mint-leaf' has a decided mint fragrance, a pleasing attribute that seems to be lacking in other species of this genus. None of these requires any special attention other than the pinching back of overlong shoots, mentioned above. Give them bright light to some direct or diffused sunshine in winter and part shade in summer, moist but never overly saturated soil, and the coolish temperatures recommended for the majority of house plants.

*Saxifraga stolonifera* (syn. *S. sarmentosa*)—Mother-of-thousands; also strawberry-geranium, strawberry-begonia: It was difficult to decide whether to include this among the flowering plants, foliage plants, or trailers, for it could be put in any of these categories. It has panicles of white, long-lasting flowers in spring, carried well above the rounded leaves, which are reddish below and green above, veined with white. A characteristic feature is the numerous filiform stolons (runners), each carrying one or more plantlets after the manner of the strawberry. It is particularly effective when a single rosette is planted in a 3-inch pot with the runners trailing over the edge. This method implies starting a new pot annually. Of course it can also be grown with several rosettes in a larger container. While it is capable of surviving zero temperatures outdoors if planted in a sheltered nook, it can also get along in the living room, though it will be better off in a winter temperature of 50° F. Use begonia soil for potting, keep soil moist, shade from bright sunshine, and start new pots from runners annually. Watch out for aphids and cyclamen mites.

*Scindapsus*—**Ivy-arum:** The ivy-arum most commonly seen is *S. aureus,* native to the Solomon Islands, which for some unknown reason has been called the Ceylon creeper. (Its correct generic name is now *Epipremnum aureum.*) Built somewhat along the lines of heart-leaf philodendron, it gives a coarser effect, and its leaves are irregularly blotched with cream or yellow. A more refined character is *S. pictus* 'Argyraeus', which has small heart-shaped leaves spotted with white. A friend of mine had this growing for two years in the house in a 5-inch bulb pan. During that time it made shoots 15 feet long which were trained back and forth on a little trellis about 2 feet high. It is best when used as a climber; *S. aureus* can be used either to climb or to trail.

Both of these ivy-arums are sure bets in the house provided they are given reasonable care. They do not demand sunshine, but the variegation of the leaves will be more evident if they get three or four hours of sun daily. Use general-purpose mixture for *S. aureus;* begonia mixture for *S. pictus* 'Argyraeus'; keep moist and propagate from shoot tips when necessary.

*Sedum morganianum*—**Donkey's or Burro's Tail:** This plant should really be included among the succulents, but a well-known specimen is so striking as a trailer that it is discussed here. It makes trailing shoots 2 to 3 feet long, clothed from tip to base with closely crowded, gray-green, ¾-inch-long, cylindrical leaves with pointed tips. The flowers are red, produced at the ends of the shoots, but they are a minor matter compared with the decorative effect of the long, drooping shoots. Grow it in cactus soil in bright light; water less frequently during the winter, but often enough to prevent the leaves from shriveling.

*Senecio mikanioides*—**German-ivy:** This is an old-time house plant with thin, bright green leaves shaped like those of English ivy, and small, yellow composite flowers. It climbs by twining, but can also be used as a trailer, in which case the shoots should be occasionally shortened. Like so many house plants, it prefers to be cool (50° F.) during winter. Use general-purpose mixture for potting; keep in a light situation but shade from bright sun except in winter; normal watering. Slips from a neighbor will readily root if placed in water or in moist sand.

*Thunbergia alata*—**Black-eyed Susan Vine:** Although of perennial duration, the black-eyed Susan vine is usually grown as an annual. In spite of its name the flowers do not always have blackened eyes. In one variety the flower is pure white; in another it is orange with a white center. It is not so rampant as some climbers, and the shoots seldom exceed 4 feet in length. It may be trained up or allowed to hang down over the pot. It takes about three months from seed sowing to blooming, so if plants are desired for winter flowering, the seeds should be started in September or October. Sow about five seeds to a 5-inch pot, and after seedlings are well along, pull out all but the three strongest ones. Use general-purpose soil mixture; give the plants the benefit of a sunny window and water normally. If they become infested with spider mites, as they sometimes do, discard them.

*Tradescantia and Zebrina*—**Wandering Jew:** Plants known as wandering Jew, inch plant, "Tahitian bridal veil," purple heart, etc., continue to wander among various genera but even a rank beginner can spot the family (Commelinaceae) resemblances shared by all, no matter what genus they occupy at the time. (A few of the genera besides the two mentioned here are *Callisia, Cyanotis, Gibasis, Setcreasea.*) *Tradescantia* and *Zebrina* are among the more common and also the toughest in spite of their seeming fragility. Differing in rather obscure botanical characters, *Tradescantia fluminensis* and *Zebrina pendula* seem to the gardener to have much in common—similar habit of growth, great variation within each species, and ease of culture. The flowers are white in *T. fluminensis,* and the leaves are plain green, or striped with white or yellow, according to variety. In *Z. pendula* the flowers are purple; the undersides of the leaves are red-purple, the upper has a metallic appearance—in general, silvery with green or purplish markings on the center and margins. There are innumerable variations on this theme. One I had grew well in a 4½-inch pot, with a dozen shoots, most of them more than 2 feet long, clothed with leaves that were light red-purple beneath and bronze on the upper surface. It produced its purple flowers for several months. The cultivar 'Quadricolor' is striped with green, white, and red on green of a different shade. While the plants are likely to grow better when shaded, the color of the leaves is more intense when they are exposed to plenty of sunshine. They are not climbers but are among the best for hanging baskets—indoors and out on a terrace in warm weather.

Wandering Jew is not particular as to soil and will grow for lengthy periods in plain water. When the plants are approaching the limit of attractive growth (2 to 3 feet, according to variety, quality of soil, and size of pot), a few tips 4 inches long should be cut off, rooted in water or sand, and ultimately put in soil to start a new pot. It is a pleasure to be able to finish this section with a group of plants about which it is unnecessary to say "should be kept cool in winter"!

## 9.  GIFT PLANTS

Commercial growers make a practice of raising enormous quantities of showy flowering plants for the holidays—Thanksgiving, Christmas, Easter, et cetera. These often fall into the category of "gift plants" because they are frequently chosen for presentation to relatives and friends. Some of them are suitable for year-round house culture, but many are not, and the best we can hope for from them is that they will not collapse before blossoming has come to an orderly termination. It shouldn't be necessary to say that plants received as gifts must have the soil about their roots kept moist! (Evidently there are some who need this information: There are known cases of those who complain to the salesperson that their plant died after a couple of days in the house—something they couldn't understand, for they had done nothing to it!)

It is well to bear in mind constantly that these florists' plants were grown in well-lighted greenhouses, with temperature and humidity carefully controlled according to the varied needs of the plants. When they are received, we should try as nearly as possible to give them the same conditions; nonfluctuating temperature and moist air for poinsettias, coolness for primulas and chrysanthemums. As pointed out elsewhere, the plants experience a less abrupt change of conditions between greenhouse and home if they are obtained during the spring, summer, and early fall, when little or no artificial heat is needed, rather than in the depth of a northern winter. An azalea at Easter or Mother's Day has a much better chance of survival as a house plant

*A beauty and two beasts from the cactus-succulent world. The orchid*
*cactus (above left), while undeniably handsome in flower, is more like a huge*
*ungainly spider the rest of the time. The starfish flower (Stapelia*
*variegata) (below) is also known as toad cactus and carrion flower.*
*Its yellow and brown flowers, a few inches across, are intriguing.*
*The rattail cactus (above right) is an easily grown basket subject — more*
*pleasing than its name.*

*Bromeliads dazzle the eyes with their fancy leaf colorings and forms and exotic long-lasting flowers. The bromeliad shown here—the silver vase (Aechmea fasciata)—is popular as a house plant.*

*Coleus is one of the easiest plants to grow indoors from seed. These seedlings are becoming crowded and should be transplanted.*

A plant label makes an adequate tool for transplanting delicate seedlings. These pots are filled with one of the sterile soil-less mixes—handy for both seed sowing and later transplanting.

...pot of begonia seedlings is enclosed in a plastic ...g to prevent the growing medium from dry-...g out.

The roots of this geranium seedling penetrated the walls of its previous pot, so it is now being transplanted.

# Rooting a Pineapple Top

*The left-over tuft of foliage from a pineapple fruit can be induced to form roots and become a house plant.*

*Roots will form in soil. Fill a pot with one of the soil-less mixes. Insert the base of the foliage tuft, water, and enclose the pot and foliage in a plastic bag.*

Roots will also form in water —
which has occurred in this tumbler.
The rooted "cutting" should now
be placed in a pot.

Plants eventually may produce a "fruit" of sorts, but usually
not until they are a few feet tall. Enclosing the plant in
a plastic bag with a ripe apple for a week or so may speed
the fruiting process.

*In good light, such as in a sunny kitchen window, impatiens produces an abundance of bright flowers.*

*The coffee plant, which can be grown from seed (unroasted!), makes an attractive foliage plant. After a few years, plants may even produce sprays of fragrant white flowers.*

*'White Christmas' and 'Christmas Cheer' are two hybrids of the Thanksgiving and Christmas cacti. Here plants of the two hybrids have been set in one pot — the result being a living winter bouquet of red and white flowers.*

*Rex begonia 'Merry Christmas' shows the sharply defined color patterns that are typical of this special group. The color range of these fancy-leaved begonias is truly royal, with rich maroon, red, and pink shades contrasting with green and silvery zones.*

*Dieffenbachia 'Rudolph Roehrs' has large yellow or chartreuse leaves veined with dark green. Older specimens become treelike and can be grown in tubs. Good light is needed but these plants tolerate dry atmospheric conditions.*

than one obtained at Christmas. For one thing, it has not been debilitated by severe forcing.

Here is a look at some of these "gift plants" and what can be done with them. Except where otherwise indicated, living-room temperature is satisfactory.

*Acacia*—**Mimosa:** I was always skeptical regarding the possibilities of acacia as a house plant, until I once successfully brought *A. armata* (syn. *A. paradoxa*), the kangaroo thorn, through the winter to the flowering stage in March. This stupendous accomplishment (to me) was brought about by keeping the plant in an unheated room (45° to 50° F.) from September until toward the end of January, when it was brought to the plant room, where the temperature of the window area was around 60° F. except on warm, sunny days.

Acacias are those plants that you see in late winter with tiny yellow or pale to deep orange flowers arranged in decorative little pompons or spikes. The genus is a large one with about 450 species, but only a very few of them are grown commercially as pot plants, although many are favorite flowering shrubs or trees for outdoor planting in frostless regions. If you are fortunate enough to receive an acacia, place it in a sunny window in a cool room. When the flowers have faded, cut back the leading shoots and shift to a larger pot if the roots are crowded. Spray daily to encourage growth of new shoots and put outdoors when danger of frost is past. Bring indoors in the fall and keep in a well-lighted room between 40° and 50° F.

*Astilbe*—**Florists' Spirea:** *A. japonica* is a winter-hardy plant more often seen today in summer gardens, but it is still occasionally forced into early bloom. One of the few plants that do not resent overwatering, it should be stood in a saucer kept constantly filled with water. When the flowers have faded, it should be regarded as having fulfilled its function as a house plant, and can be planted outdoors in a humus-rich soil in the garden (see page 215).

**Christmas Begonia:** These are hybrids (*B. x cheimantha*) so smothered with panicles of pink flowers that the foliage is barely visible. Although they are improvements over the old Christmas begonia hybrids in their longevity and tolerance of house conditions, they are not to be considered as permanent house plants for most people. The flowers will last longer in the house if the plant is kept cool (50° F. at night) in a well-lighted window.

**Christmas Pepper**—*Capsicum annuum:* These plants should be given a sunny window, 60° F. temperature, soil kept constantly moist. For culture, see page 259.

**Cineraria**—*Senecio x hybridus:* The gorgeous blooms of cineraria fill almost everyone who receives one at Easter with the desire to keep it for another year. This is a vain hope, for although the plant is a perennial, it is almost impossible to carry it over under house conditions. In any case, better plants are obtained when seeds are sown annually. When plants are received from the garden center or florist, keep them as cool as possible (45° to 50° F.) if you want the flowers to last. Although it is said they are adapted to window-

Gesneria cuneifolia *is only a few inches tall and suitable for terrariums, where it produces a succession of orange and yellow flowers.*

garden culture, they are among the most difficult plants to raise successfully under the limitations of a house. Those who wish to make the attempt will find their culture described on page 208.

*Cyclamen persicum*—**Florists' Cyclamen:** Another difficult subject. Cyclamens require the same cool conditions as the preceding and plenty of water at the roots, which should be supplied by subirrigation. Stand the pot in a bowl of water until moisture shows on the surface to avoid getting water in the crown of the plant. There are some who are able to maintain this as a house plant; the "how to do it" is described on pages 217–19.

*Cytisus Canariensis*—**Florists' Genista:** Many have been disappointed because of their inability to keep alive the genista, with its sweetly fragrant, pealike yellow flowers, often available in the spring. It is *not* a good house plant, and about all one can do is to keep it cool and watered until the flowers fade.

**Easter Lily**—*Lilium longiflorum*—*and hybrids:* The Easter lily in its many varieties once headed the list of gift plants in point of numbers, but today it is beginning to get competition from some of the modern garden hybrids. Lily plants that have been made to bloom at Easter are useless for forcing another year, but they may be kept watered until danger of frost is past and then turned out of their pots and planted in the garden, where, if all goes well, they may produce another crop of blooms in the fall. In favored regions they may live indefinitely outdoors. Lilies are not among the easily grown house plants, but those who wish to give them a trial will find suggestions for handling on page 221.

**French Hydrangea**—*Hydrangea macrophylla:* This is still a popular plant at Easter and an extraordinarily thirsty one—it may need soaking *twice* a day. The colors may be white, pink, lavender, or blue. Pink varieties become lavender or blue when grown in acid soil which gives them access to the aluminum responsible for the change in color. Although recommended as a house plant, those who live in regions where it is hardy outdoors (New York City and south and similar regions) will probably prefer to plant it out when the flowers have faded. If you want to keep it as a house plant, cut the flowering shoots back to two "joints" when the flowers have faded and repot, using general-purpose mixture, bringing it up to pH 7 by the addition of ground limestone (try ½ pound per bushel to start with) if blue coloring in the flowers is not desired. Place outdoors, plunge pot in sand, and feed with liquid fertilizer when the pots are filled with roots.

After the first frost, store them in a cold cellar or garage and keep the roots on the dry side. Sometime in January bring them upstairs to a temperature of 50° F. for two or three weeks, then place in a sunny window and raise to 60° to 65° F., and don't neglect the watering. If smaller plants are desired, start them annually from cuttings made in February. These should be potted into progressively larger pots until the fall, when treatment should be the same as that accorded older plants.

**Heather** *(Erica):* The plants often sold as "heather," or even "Scotch heather," are not heather (which is *Calluna vulgaris*) at all. They are heaths (close relatives), and most of them are native to South Africa. The growing of heaths as pot plants is a ticklish proposition even when a greenhouse is available, and their culture is usually left to specialists. They are nigh to impossible as permanent house plants and unlike some of the hardy heaths, cannot even be planted outdoors in northern regions. All one can do is to keep them cool, water them normally, and hope that not all of the leaves will fall off before the flowers fade.

**Jerusalem-cherry**—*Solanum pseudocapsicum:* This is likely to be one of the most disappointing house plants when received from the florist at Christmas because when placed in a hot, dry room it sheds its berries and leaves in embarrassing profusion. The only way to prevent this is to *keep it cool*— 50° F.—and moisten the air as much as possible. Culture same as Christmas pepper (page 259).

**Primrose**—*Primula:* All types of primroses should be kept as cool as possible and watered freely. The culture of those commonly grown is given on page 207.

**Rose**—*Rosa:* Plants of hybrid tea, hybrid perpetual, and rambler roses are occasionally forced into bloom for the Easter trade. None of these is adapted for permanent culture in the home—in point of fact, their size puts them in the white-elephant class in small houses. They are winter-hardy in all but the most severe climates, and the best thing to do with them after the flowers have faded is to plant them outdoors. For miniature roses, see page 258.

Then there are the dish gardens, often sent as gifts. When made up commercially, they are likely to be overcrowded with roots squashed and mutilated in the endeavor to get more plants into the container than it can properly hold. More important, perhaps, is the probability that the arrangement will contain plants that are culturally incompatible. The best way to handle the situation is to keep the garden as is until you have had an opportunity to admire it and properly express your appreciation in the presence of the donor; and then take out and repot separately the plants that do not belong and rearrange the remainder.

The plants mentioned in this section do not, of course, exhaust the list of those you may receive as gifts. There are the hardy spring-flowering bulbs, useless for indoor growth another year, but which can be planted in the garden (if the soil in the pots is kept watered until it is safe from the weather standpoint to put them outdoors); and there are Marguerites (see *Chrysanthemum frutescens,* page 337) and a host of others that you will be able to locate by referring to the Index.

## 10.  FLOWERING HOUSE PLANTS THROUGHOUT THE YEAR

It is possible to have house plants in bloom all through the year provided one has sufficient room to accommodate the rather large selection of kinds desirable to make a real show, and provided the right treatment is given them.

Some plants are practically ever-blooming, such as African-violet and some of their relatives, wax begonia, and patience plant; and these, of course, appear high up in the lists of those who crave free-flowering plants. Some plants may be made to bloom at almost any time by giving the proper cultural treatment. Calla-lilies, for example, will start growing any time after their tubers have been rested by drying and still start to bloom in about eight weeks if given sunshine and a temperature of 70° F.

By making use of pre-cooled lily bulbs and lily-of-the-valley pips held in cold storage until needed for forcing, flowers can be had at will by giving the necessary cultural conditions and sufficient time for growth—about four months and three to four weeks respectively.

By changing the time of seed sowing, the normal blooming season for a given kind can be greatly varied. For example, cineraria seeds may be sown in May, August, and September, giving a blooming season from fall to spring. Far be it from me, however, to recommend growing cinerarias from seeds; their culture presents too many pitfalls without the use of a greenhouse. But you can buy blooming cinerarias from a florist. Many of the plants we ordinarily grow as summer-blooming annuals outdoors can be made to bloom in winter by starting the seeds during the summer or fall.

Some plants have their regular seasons for blooming regardless of how much they are pushed around by the gardener. Others are inclined to be erratic, so that it is difficult to predict with accuracy when flowers will make their appearance. Amaryllis bulbs, unless specially treated by the grower, may bloom any time from January to March—probably because of differences in the ripening of the bulbs.

The most important flowering house plants are listed in the following table. Not all of them can be considered good house plants. Some, marked by an asterisk, are best regarded as one would cut flowers—although ordinarily they last much longer. Perhaps it should be emphasized that the time of bloom as given is not necessarily natural for the species (e.g., sweet-alyssum), and that many of the plants listed can be flowered at a time other than that selected as most likely to be preferred by the grower.

The time allowed for bringing hardy bulbs into bloom is necessarily approximate. Much depends upon uncontrollable temperature variations which may be experienced under house conditions, sunshine or artificial light, and geographical location. Also it should be remembered that, as the natural blooming season approaches, less time is needed to produce flowers.

### Timetable for Flowering House Plants

#### KEY

* \*   Not recommended for permanent culture as house plants
* HB   Winter-hardy bulbs (or bulblike plants)
* TB   Tender bulbs (or bulblike plants)
* A   Annual

| Plant | When in Bloom | Special Treatment |
|---|---|---|
| *Abutilon*, Flowering-maple | Almost everblooming | Seeds or cuttings for new plants in spring. Prune old plants in fall for winter bloom. |
| *Acacia*, Mimosa, Wattle (\*) | Spring | Transitory as a house plant. Keep at 50° to 60° F. when received in bloom from florist. |
| *Achimenes* (TB) | Summer to fall | Start tubers in midwinter to early spring in milled sphagnum moss kept moist. |
| *Aechmea fasciata*, Silver Vase | Mostly summer to late fall | Mature plants usually bloom naturally but laggards can be hurried by enclosing in a plastic bag (empty "water cup" first) with a ripening apple for about five days. After bloom, offsets form; cut off and pot for next bloom. |
| *Aeschynanthus*, Lipstick Plant | Mostly spring and summer | Shorten stems after bloom. Young plants often bloom best so take frequent stem cuttings. |

| Plant | When in Bloom | Special Treatment |
|---|---|---|
| African-violet. See Saintpaulia | | |
| Alloplectus nummularia (syn. Hypocyrta nummularia), Miniature Pouch Plant | Summer | In fall and winter, becomes partly dormant; reduce watering during this period. Resume in spring. |
| Alyssum, Sweet-. See Lobularia | | |
| Amaryllis. See Hippeastrum | | |
| Anthurium scherzerianum, Flamingo Flower | Almost ever-blooming | Constant humidity important. |
| Aphelandra squarrosa, Zebra Plant (*) | Summer and fall, but pot-bound plants may bloom intermittently | Buy blooming plants from florist. Requires winter humidity and warmth. |
| Aporocactus flagelliformis, Rat-tail Cactus | Early to midwinter | Needs to be fairly dry and cool in winter (45° to 50° F.) to flower. |
| Apostle Plant. See Neomarica | | |
| Azalea. See Rhododendron | | |
| Begonia boweri | Spring | No special treatment needed to bring these into bloom at the time indicated, providing they are receiving sufficient natural or artificial light. Many, many other begonias of long-blooming habit are available. |
| B. 'Cleopatra' | Spring | |
| B. 'Lucerna' | Ever-blooming | |
| B. coccinea, Angel Wing Begonia | Spring | |
| B. corallina | Spring | |
| B. dregei | Winter | |

| Plant | When in Bloom | Special Treatment |
|---|---|---|
| B. x *erythrophylla* | Winter | |
| B. x *erythrophylla* 'Bunchii' | Winter | |
| B. *heracleifolia,* Star Begonia | Late winter to spring | |
| B. *metallica* | Spring | |
| B. x *ricinifolia* | Winter to early spring | |
| B. *scharffii* | Summer, but almost everblooming | |
| B. *semperflorens,* Wax Begonia (many, many cultivars) | Ever-blooming | Sow seeds anytime or buy plants. Seeds sown in winter and grown under fluorescent lights bloom in summer. A prolific self-sower with progeny well worth potting up and often retaining characteristics of parents. Caution: Do not overwater—allow soil to dry out between waterings. |
| B. *tuberhybrida,* Tuberous Begonia (TB) | Summer | Start tubers in moist peat moss in spring for summer flowers outdoors. |
| *Beloperone guttata,* Shrimp Plant | Virtually ever-blooming | Cut back to keep shapely. Take cuttings in spring |
| *Billbergia nutans,* Queen's Tears | Mostly winter | Pot up offsets produced after flowering. |
| Black-eyed Susan Vine. *See Thunbergia* | | |
| *Browallia speciosa* (A) | Winter to spring or summer to fall | For winter-spring bloom, sow seeds in summer. For summer-fall, sow in early spring. |
| *Calceolaria,* Slipperwort (*) | Mostly spring | Buy blooming plants from florist; keep in cool location to prolong bloom. |
| Calla-lily. *See Zantedeschia* | | |
| *Camellia japonica* | Winter to spring | Buy potted or tubbed plants in bud and bloom. To prevent bud drop, keep cool (45° to 50° F.) and moist in winter and spring. Take cuttings in summer, using |

| Plant | When in Bloom | Special Treatment |
|---|---|---|
| | | a root hormone; eighteen months to flowering size. |
| C. sasanqua | Fall | As above. Take cuttings in spring. |
| Campanula isophylla, Ligurian Harebell; Star of Bethlehem | Summer to fall | Cut back severely after flowering; take cuttings from new growth in spring. |
| Carissa grandiflora 'Nana Compacta,' Dwarf Natalplum | Mostly spring to fall | Needs daytime temperature of 65° F. or higher to flower. |
| Christmas Cactus. See Schlumbergera | | |
| Chrysanthemum frutescens, Marguerite or Paris Daisy | Fall to spring | Take cuttings in early summer for winter-blooming plants. |
| C. x morifolium, Garden or Florist Chrysanthemum (*) | Usually fall to winter | Buy budded plants; keep cool. Or plants may be dug and potted when buds have formed for indoor display. |
| Cineraria. See Senecio | | |
| Citrus, various kinds | Mostly late winter to spring (but intermittent in both flowering and fruiting) | Adequate natural or fluorescent light and moist soil needed for flowers and fruits. Feed liberally while fruits develop. |
| Clivia miniata, Kafir-lily (TB) | Spring | Keep rather dry at 55° F. during fall–early winter; raise to 65° F. in midwinter and water freely. |
| Coffea arabica, Coffee Plant | Usually late summer | Pinch stems to keep plants bushy. Blooming depends on age of plant—may take three to four years. |
| Colchicum autumnale, Meadow Saffron (HB) | Fall | Pot bulbs in late summer; plant outdoors when flowers fade. |

| Plant | When in Bloom | Special Treatment |
|---|---|---|
| Columnea, Gold-fish Plant | Ever-blooming to seasonal, depending on kind | Require a few hours of sun, then bright light; or grow under fluorescent lights. |
| Convallaria majalis, Lily-of-the-valley (HB) | Winter | Buy specially treated pips (roots); allow three to four weeks at 70° F. |
| Crocus, spring-flowering species and cultivars (HB) | Late winter to early spring | Pot corms in fall; keep in cold frame or trench until late winter; then bring indoors and grow at cool temperatures (50° to 60° F.). Or buy prepotted corms and follow directions on package. |
| Crocus, fall-flowering species and varieties (HB) | Early fall to early winter | Pot corms in late summer; can be planted outdoors after blooming. |
| Crown-of-thorns. See Euphorbia milii splendens | | |
| Cyclamen persicum, Florists' Cyclamen (*) | Early winter to late spring | Buy plants in bloom and keep in cool window. Seeds can be sown from summer to late fall; allow eight to eighteen months from seed to flower. |
| Cytisus canariensis, Florists' Genista (*) | Spring | Keep it cool when received in bloom from commercial grower. |
| Easter Cactus. See Rhipsalidopsus gaertneri. | | |
| Epiphyllum hybrids, Orchid Cactus | Mostly spring but varies | These epiphytes need careful attention to water needs—rather skimpy from fall to late winter; then more copious through blooming period to fall. |
| Episcia species and cultivars, Flame-violet | Mostly spring to fall, but some tend to be ever-blooming | Bright light increases flowering. Provide several hours of sun in fall and winter or twelve to fourteen hours of fluorescent light. Some tend to be shy bloomers. |
| Eranthis hyemalis, Winter-aconite (HB) | Mid- to late winter | Keep cold in cold frame or trench until midwinter. Grow indoors at 50° to 60° F. Bloom appears in about four weeks. |

| Plant | When in Bloom | Special Treatment |
|---|---|---|
| Erica melanthera, Christmas Heath (*) | Winter to spring | Keep in cool window (50° to 60° F.) when received from florist. |
| Euphorbia pulcherrima, Poinsettia (*) | Winter to spring | After flowering (colored bracts of new hybrids very long lasting), cut back; summer plants outdoors in good light. Bring indoors in fall. For holiday bloom, reduce day length to twelve hours or less by covering plant with box or black cloth; or move into dark closet. |
| E. milii splendens, Crown-of-thorns | Winter, but almost never out of bloom | Won't flower without adequate light—full sun for several hours or fluorescent light. Plants benefit from rest period in late fall to early winter induced by reducing water. |
| Flame-violet. See Episcia. | | |
| Freesia x hybrida (TB) | Winter to spring | Pot corms from late summer to late winter for succession of flowers (six corms to 5-inch pot). Allow three to five months for bloom at about 50° F. in cool cellar. |
| Fuchsia x hybrida | Spring to fall | Rest established plants in winter in cool but frost-free basement, garage, watering occasionally. In late winter, place in warmer room in good light and water regularly. As leaf buds swell, cut back to force new growth, repot and pinch new shoots for bushiness. |
| Gardenia jasminoides, Cape-jasmine | Mostly winter to spring | Plenty of sun (filtered sun in summer), humidity, and night temperatures between 60° and 65° F. in winter needed to form buds. |
| Genista. See Cytisus | | |
| Geranium. See Pelargonium | | |
| Gesneria cuneifolia | Ever-blooming | Bright light (filtered sun or fluorescent) and high humidity (50 per cent or higher). Popular terrarium subject. |

| Plant | When in Bloom | Special Treatment |
|---|---|---|
| Gloxinia. *See Sinningia* | | |
| Goldfish Plant. *See Columnea* | | |
| Grape-hyacinth. *See Muscari* | | |
| *Heliotropium arborescens,* Heliotrope | Summer to early winter | Buy greenhouse-grown plants. Or sow seeds in spring; or take cuttings in early summer; keep flowers pinched off until fall for indoor blooms. |
| *Hibiscus rosa-sinensis,* Chinese Hibiscus | Summer to fall | Keep at 50° F. in winter with reduced water; prune in early spring, increasing temperature to 70° F.; water freely. |
| *Hippeastrum* x *hybridum,* Amaryllis (TB) | Winter to early spring | Usually about ten weeks at 65° F. to bloom from time of planting. Keep leaves growing after blooming; sink pots outside and water as needed. Bring pots inside in fall; withhold water until bud tip shows in midwinter. |
| *Hoya carnosa,* Waxplant | Summer | Bright light such as four hours of sun daily or more of filtered light needed. Once buds form, do not move or turn plants; increase watering. |
| *Hyacinthus,* Hyacinth (HB) | Winter to early spring | Order specially prepared bulbs that will bloom by Christmas. Or pot regular bulbs in fall, place in cold frame or trench for two months, then bring indoors and grow on at 50° F. for three weeks; then four to five weeks at 65° F. Need four to six hours of sun. |
| *Hydrangea macrophylla,* French Hydrangea (*) | Spring | Keep plants (usually received as gift from florist) cool and well watered. After flowering discard; or in mild climates, plant outdoors. |
| *Impatiens wallerana,* Patience Plant, Patient Lucy | Almost ever-blooming | For winter bloom, start seeds in late spring, cuttings in summer. Needs several hours of sun or fluorescent light for winter flowers. |
| *Ipomoea purpurea,* Morning Glory (A) | Winter to spring | Ten to twelve weeks from seeds to first bloom. Needs sun. |

| Plant | When in Bloom | Special Treatment |
|---|---|---|
| *Jacobinia carnea,* Brazilian Plume | Late summer to fall | Remove faded flower heads. Cut back and repot after flowering; cuttings can be taken from new growth in spring. Needs bright light. |
| Jasmine, Star. *See Trachelospermum* | | |
| *Kalanchoe blossfeldiana* | Early winter to spring | Plants received in bloom at Christmas from florist need several hours of sun to remain in good condition. Avoid overwatering; let soil dry out thoroughly between watering. Begin in fall to allow only nine hours of daylight for flowers at Christmas. |
| *Lachenalia,* Cape-cowslip (TB) | Winter | Pot bulbs in late summer or fall; water and keep in cool room (about 50° F.). After flowers fade and foliage turns yellow, withhold water to permit bulbs to ripen. |
| *Lantana camara* | Winter | For winter window garden, take cuttings in spring; keep flowers picked off until fall. |
| *Lilium,* Easter Lily, and various hybrids | Winter to spring | Pot in fall; keep cool (60° F.) until rooted; allow thirteen to fourteen weeks at 60° F. after rooting. Precooled bulbs for growing at 65° F. usually available from late fall on and speed forcing process. |
| Lipstick Plant. *See Aeschynanthus* | | |
| *Lobularia maritima,* Sweetalyssum (A) | Winter to spring | Sow seeds in late summer. For spring bloom, sow in early to midwinter. |
| *Malpighia coccigera,* Miniature-holly | Mostly summer | Needs several hours of sun daily for flowering. |
| Marguerite Daisy. *See Chrysanthemum frutescens* | | |

| Plant | When in Bloom | Special Treatment |
|---|---|---|
| *Muscari,* Grape-hyacinth (HB) | Winter | Pot bulbs in fall; allow 6 weeks in cold frame or trench for rooting; then bring indoors to 60° F. for bloom in six to eight weeks. |
| *Narcissus,* Daffodil (HB), hardy species and cultivars | Winter | Pot bulbs early in fall; keep in cold frame or trench for six to eight weeks; then five to six weeks at 60° F. Bulbs can later be planted outdoors. |
| *Narcissus,* Paperwhite, Chinese Sacred-lily, 'Grand Soleil d'Or' (TB) | Winter | Grow in pebbles and water from fall to winter; allow six to eight weeks at 60°–70° F. |
| Nasturtium. See *Tropaeolum* | | |
| Natal-plum. See *Carissa* | | |
| *Nematanthus* (formerly *Hypocyrta*) *wettsteinii,* and other species and cultivars, Pouch Plant | Almost ever-blooming; others mostly spring to summer | Needs high humidity; for flowers, plenty of light in winter; filtered sun in summer. |
| *Neomarica* (formerly *Marica*), Apostle Plant, Walking-iris | Midwinter to spring | Keep at 65°–70° F.; divide after flowering. |
| *Nicotiana alata,* Flowering-tobacco (A) | Winter to spring | Dig seedlings in fall from self-sown seeds; or sow seeds in July. |
| Orchid Cactus. See *Epiphyllum* | | |
| *Ornithogalum arabicum,* Star of Bethlehem; *O. caudatum,* False Sea-onion; *O. thyrsoides,* Chincherinchee (TB) | Winter | Pot bulbs in fall; allow eight weeks at 60°–70° F. to bloom time. |

| Plant | When in Bloom | Special Treatment |
|---|---|---|
| *Oxalis cernua,* Bermuda-buttercup (TB) | Winter | Pot bulbs in fall; allow eight to ten weeks to bloom. |
| Patience Plant. *See Impatiens* | | |
| *Pelargonium domesticum,* Lady Washington Geranium | Spring | Take cuttings in spring; keep plants on dry side after flowering; prune and repot in late summer or fall; keep at 50°–60° F. |
| *P. hortorum,* Zonal Geranium | All year | Plenty of sun and cool temperature needed for winter bloom. Take cuttings in spring; keep flower buds pinched off until fall. |
| *P. peltatum,* Ivyleaf Geranium | Spring to fall | Cuttings in spring. |
| *P. tomentosum,* Peppermint Geranium; and other scented-leaf geraniums | Mostly spring to fall | Keep fresh supply of plants by taking cuttings in spring. Otherwise treat as *P. hortorum.* |
| Poinsettia. *See Euphorbia pulcherrima* | | |
| Pomegranate, Dwarf. *See, Punica granatum* 'Nana' | | |
| *Primula malacoides,* Fairy Primrose (*), *P. obconica,* Poison Primrose (*) | Winter to spring | Buy plants in bloom from florist; keep in cool window; discard when flowers fade. Or sow seeds from winter to spring. |
| *Punica granatum* 'Nana', Dwarf Pomegranate | Mostly spring to summer | Four or more hours of sun or fluorescent light needed for flower-fruit production. |
| *Rechsteineria cardinalis. See Sinningia cardinalis* | | |
| *Rhipsalidopsis gaertneri,* | Spring | Put plants outdoors in summer, watering sparingly; bring inside in fall to cool |

| Plant | When in Bloom | Special Treatment |
|-------|---------------|-------------------|
| Easter Cactus | | room (50°–55° F. at night); when new growth starts, water freely. |
| *Rhododendron* hybrids, Ever-green Azalea | Winter to spring | Summer potted azaleas outdoors in fil-tered sun, watering as necessary and fer-tilizing every two to four weeks. Bring indoors before heavy frost (azaleas need cool temperatures for even flowering) to good light and cool rooms (50° F.) for one to two months; then allow four to six weeks at 60° F. for bloom. |
| *Rosa chinensis* hybrids, Min-iature Rose | Winter to spring | Best blooms from potted plants kept in cold frame until midwinter; then brought into cool, sunny window. |
| *Saintpaulia io-nantha* and other species and cultivars, African-violet | Almost ever-blooming | Adequate humidity (stand pots on moist pebbles in trays) and bright light (several hours of sun in winter; filtered sun in spring and summer) or fluorescent light should guarantee flower production. |
| *Saxifraga stolo-nifera,* Mother-of-Thousands, Strawberry-be-gonia | Spring | Lots of sun in winter; cool windows; part shade in summer. |
| *Schlumbergera* x *buckleyi,* Thanksgiving Cactus, Claw C.; *S. truncata,* Christmas Cactus | Early to mid-winter | For flowers, requires a short day (about nine to ten hours—protect from artificial light at night during fall); keep plants outdoors until freezing weather arrives. After flowering, rest plants by watering less. Summer outdoors in partial shade. |
| *Senecio* x *hy-bridum,* Cineraria (*) | Late winter to spring | Buy budded plants from florist; keep in filtered sun in cool window; do not let soil dry out. |
| *Serissa foetida* | Mostly spring | Needs pinching to keep plants shapely, and bright light for flowers. |
| Shrimp Plant. *See Beloperone* | | |
| *Sinningia* (syn. *Rechsteineria*) *cardinalis,* Cardinal Flower (TB) | Summer to early winter | Treat as for gloxinia (below). |

| Plant | When in Bloom | Special Treatment |
|---|---|---|
| S. concinna, S. pusilla and other minia-ture sinningias (TB) | Summer or inter-mittent to ever-blooming | High humidity, as in terrarium; bright light (diffused sun or fluorescent light). Avoid overwatering, especially if tubers go into dormancy for a month or so (S. pusilla does not go dormant). |
| S. speciosa, Glox-inia (TB) | Mostly summer | Dormant tubers are usually available in late winter for potting; keep in warm room (70° F.); four months to bloom. Seeds sown in late winter bloom in seven months. In fall rest tubers by withhold-ing water. |
| Smithiantha cin-nabarina, S. zebrina and hybrids, Tem-ple Bells (TB) | Summer to early winter | High humidity and bright light (filtered sun in summer) for flowers as well as good leaf coloring. Tubers have about same growth cycle as gloxinia. |
| South African Cowslip. See Lachenalia | | |
| Spathiphyllum 'Clevelandii', White Flag, Spathe Flower | Mostly summer to fall | Shade in summer; diffused sun or bright light in winter. |
| Stephanotis flori-bunda, Madagascar-jasmine | Spring to fall | Keep soil barely moist—and cool in win-ter; increase water and feed from spring to fall. Being pot-bound seems to encour-age bud-set. |
| Sternbergia lutea (HB) | Fall | Pot bulbs in late summer; plant outdoors after blooming. |
| Streptocarpus hy-brids, Cape-primrose | Varies according to hybrid; some virtually ever-blooming | Buy blooming plants; keep in bright light (diffused sun or fluorescent lights). When plants stop blooming, usually in summer heat or at temperatures below 55° F., reduce watering until new growth shows. |
| Streptocarpus saxorum, Dauphin-violet | Intermittent, but mostly spring to summer | Needs bright light (diffused sun in sum-mer) for flowers; reduce soil moisture in winter. |
| Temple Bells. See Smithiantha | | |
| Thunbergia alata, Black-eyed Susan Vine | Winter—long-blooming | Starts blooming ten to twelve weeks from seed sowing. |

| Plant | When in Bloom | Special Treatment |
|---|---|---|
| *Trachelospermum jasminoides,* Star-jasmine | Mostly spring to summer | Needs bright light for flower production. |
| *Tripogandra multiflora,* Tahitian Bridal Veil | Intermittent to everblooming | Diffused sun in summer; bright light in winter. Prune straggly runners. |
| *Tropaeolum majus,* Nasturtium (A) | Winter to early spring | Start seeds or cuttings in midsummer for winter bloom. |
| *Tulipa* cultivars and species, Tulip (HB) | Winter to early spring | Buy budded plants from florist; keep in bright, cool window, 60° to 65° F. for best results. Or pot bulbs in fall; allow six to eight weeks in trench; lift, bring indoors two weeks at 50° F.; then four to six weeks at 60° F. for early vars., six to eight weeks for late vars. |
| *Veltheimia viridifolia* (TB) | Winter | Keep dry during summer. Start watering again in early fall or as soon as new growth shows. Flower color and longevity best in bright, cool window. |
| *Vriesia splendens* 'Major', Flaming Sword | Spring to summer | Bright light (will flower in north window) and high humidity. Keep leaf "vase" filled with water but allow pot soil to dry out between waterings. Beware of scale insects! Propagate from offsets that appear at base after flowering. |
| Waxplant. *See Hoya* | | |
| *Zantedeschia aethiopica,* Calla-lily; *Z. elliottiana,* Golden Calla-lily; *Z. rehmannii,* Pink Calla-lily (TB) | Almost anytime | Start well-ripened tubers eight weeks before blooms are required (tubers usually available in spring from dealers). *Z. elliottiana* tubers should be exposed in a warm, dry room for three to four weeks after receipt from dealer. |
| *Zygocactus truncatus,* Christmas Cactus. See *Schlumbergera* x *buckleyi* | | |

# CHAPTER 18

# *Foliage Plants*

THE SO-CALLED foliage plants are in general more tolerant than those grown primarily for their flowers. While they are not so cheerful as a pot of well-flowered tulips, African-violets, or poinsettias, many of them do exhibit striking coloration—not so brilliant, perhaps, as that of some flowers, but effective nonetheless. In some, the normal green of the leaves is striped, spotted, or mottled with white or yellow; in others, it is wholly or partly masked by other pigments, as in crotons and some of the begonias, which may also exhibit an iridescent sheen or have a metallic appearance. Often the colors are arranged in striking patterns, and sometimes the lower leaves are typically green while the newer ones are marked with carmine or other colors. Frequently it is the graceful form of the leaves as in palms and ferns that warrants the designation foliage plants.

There is certainly no lack of variety in form, size, and color of plants grown for their foliage, and it can be said of them that while on the whole they may not be so spectacular as some of the flowering plants, for the most part they function throughout the year. Exceptions are those such as the fancy-leaved caladiums which die to the ground and go completely dormant during the winter, but even these make a show over a much longer period than the general run of flowering plants.

Some of the bromeliads and begonias considered under flowering plants also have attractive foliage and are worthy of culture for their leaves alone.

For convenience in dealing with the cultural requirements and to avoid that "catalogue appearance," foliage plants are here grouped as far as possible according to their botanical affinities, starting with the group known as aroids.

## 1. AROIDS

These are plants belonging to the same family as the Jack-in-the-pulpit and calla-lilies—an enormous group which contains a large number of the toughest of our house plants.

**Chinese evergreen**—*Aglaonema* **spp.:** The most familiar Chinese evergreen hails from Borneo and the Celebes. For a while we were told to call it *A. marantifolium*, then its alias became *A. modestum*. (A similar species is *A. simplex*.) It is not specially beautiful or exciting—not even when it produces its greenish-white callalike inflorescence; but it grows almost equally well in water as in soil and can thrive in dim light and dry air. Better "lookers" are the dwarf (8-inch) *A. costatum*, whose broad, bright green leaves are spotted with white, and *A. commutatum elegans*, which reaches 2 feet with pale gray-green markings along the veins of its lance-shaped leaves. Mature plants may produce tight clusters of scarlet berries. These two are not quite so tolerant as the Chinese evergreen.

*A. crispum* reaches a height of about 18 to 36 inches, usually with several stems clothed with leaves, the blades of which are 10 by 4 inches, gray-green with featherings of deep green extending from the midrib. It is easy to grow. (This species was formerly listed as *Schismatoglottis roebelinii*.)

**Fancy-leaved caladiums** (See Chapter 17): They have a completely dormant period and are primarily suited for summer display, but by starting the tubers very early (January) or very late (June) it is possible to have them in good leaf in early spring and early fall respectively.

*Dieffenbachia* **spp. and cultivars:** The various species of dumb cane or mother-in-law plant (so-called because a piece of the stem placed on the tongue renders one speechless for three days), are characterized by thick, fleshy stems and large, handsome, broad leaves (up to 2 feet long and half as much wide, though usually less than this in the house) variously mottled, spotted, or striped with white, yellow, or greenish brown. These are handsome accents for warm interiors. Good ones are: *D. amoena;* 'Exotica'; *D. maculata*, in several forms such as 'Rudolph Roehrs'; and x *splendens*. As house plants they are at their best when 1½ to 2½ feet high; but, whether grown in home or greenhouse, dieffenbachias have the habit of becoming leggy and top-heavy. If so, they should be air-layered as described in Chapter 15.

*Monstera deliciosa:* There is a group of aroids that in nature climb on trees by means of aerial roots. Some of these are sufficiently stout to be grown as pot plants for a time without any support. One of the most striking is the Mexican breadfruit, sometimes called Swiss cheese plant, because of the holes naturally formed in the much-divided leaves—a development that, presumably, enables the large leaves, roundish in outline (up to 3 feet wide when planted out and given room), to withstand hurricanes without tearing. This is capable of standing much neglect and dim light. As a potted plant it is usually about 2 feet high. Its botanical name is *Monstera deliciosa*, but it is generally known to commerical growers as *Philodendron pertusum*.

*A collection of foliage plants showing their striking coloration patterns and varying shapes and textures. Included are crotons, bromeliads, ivies, ferns, and palms.*

**Philodendrons:** The best-known philodendron, all species of which are native to tropical America, is *Philodendron scandens oxycardium* (formerly listed as *P. cordatum* and *P. oxycardium*), the heart-leaf philodendron, a very enduring trailer which will not grow upright without a support. But there are others such as: *P.* x *corsinianum,* with leaves up to 2 feet long and 1 foot broad with purplish undersides; *P. gloriosum,* leaves 10 inches long with reddish margins and pale green veins; *P. mamei,* about the same size, with pinkish stalks, blade spotted with silver; *P. verrucosum,* 8-inch shiny leaves with paler lines, lined with salmon-violet beneath and red stalks covered with fleshy bristles. There is a vast difference between the juvenile and adult appearance of these philodendrons, especially in leaf size. *P. scandens oxycardium,* usually seen with 3-inch leaves as a trailer growing in a 4-inch pot, may have leaves up to 16 inches when planted out in rich soil in a greenhouse and allowed to climb.

There is almost no limit to the size of these climbers when given suitable growing conditions; most of them easily reach 20 feet or more, but in the house they range from 1½ to 2 feet unless given something on which to climb.

More bushy in growth habit and slower to climb, at least when grown as potted house plants, are various other *Philodendron* species and cultivars. *P.* 'Florida' has deeply lobed leaves, but it will show a tendency to climb if its growing tips are not frequently pinched. The fiddle-leaf philodendron (*P. bipennifolium,* formerly listed as *P. panduriforme*) has very large leaves and remains compact in habit before exhibiting a climbing tendency. *P. sel-loum* has large, deeply lobed leaves and remains within 3 to 4 feet in height under pot cultivation. However, it needs bright light to prevent the leaf stems from spreading sideways, eventually making it too bulky for most situations except automobile showrooms and similar roomy areas.

The botanists seem to have had no dearth of jawbreaking names when they came to naming members of this family (Araceae), as witness *Homalomena, Scindapsus,* and *Zantedeschia*—all good house plants, nevertheless.

*Syngonium:* One frequently sees *S. podophyllum* decoratively used in city restaurants and other places of business, though the owners probably don't know its name. It is sometimes known as nephthytis. The fact that it grows in the situations mentioned is an indication of its adaptability. It has arrowhead leaves on slender climbing stems and is usually given a bark support.

Another mouthful is provided by *S. angustatum* 'Albolineatum,' whose leaves are deeply lobed and marked with white. Small plants of this are often a component of the dish gardens made up by florists. Well-grown plants may attain a height of about 18 inches. Another species of similar size but different appearance is *S. auritum,* whose leaves consist of a large central lobe with two small lobes at its base. Its decorative value consists of the bright green, highly varnished character of the leaves.

*Xanthosoma lindenii:* This listing of worthwhile aroids could extend from A to Z were it not that *Zantedeschia* is included in the bulb chapter, so we will conclude with "X" for *Xanthosoma lindenii,* Indian-kale, which is native to Colombia. You may not be able to obtain this because it is slow to propagate and hence does not interest the commercial dealer, but it is an excellent house plant and you should keep your eyes open and, if you see one listed, grab it.

The cultural requirements of all these aroids are simple: fairly rich soil (general potting mixture); well-drained pots, so that they may be watered freely without danger of waterlogging; and a moderate amount of light. They succeed well in a north window—monstera and some of the philodendrons can get along in even less light. If the foliage can be sprayed with water daily, so much the better; if this is not done, wash the leaves at weekly intervals, using a sponge wet with lukewarm soapy water. The climbing types should be brought down to earth by air-layering if they get too tall for their location.

## 2.  LILY FAMILY

When we think of the lily family, it brings to mind the gorgeous flowers of tulip and lily; or perhaps, if we are gastronomically inclined, the succulent delights of asparagus and onion. But there are some well-known foliage plants in the groups, though they are not spectacularly beautiful.

**Asparagus-fern:** The asparagus-fern, which the florist often adds gratis to the package when you buy a half-dozen roses, can be grown as a house plant. *Asparagus setaceus* (syn. *A. plumosus*) is a tall-growing vine, but can be grown without support if the tips of the developing shoots are cut off. Emerald-feather (*A. densiflorus* 'Sprengeri') is really a vine, growing to a height of 10 feet or more if planted in rich soil and trained up on wires; but when grown as a pot plant, its shoots arch over and hide the pot. Exceptionally good specimens such as the one I once saw exhibited at a county fair may have had shoots 3 or 4 feet long hanging well below the pot. This species is the best asparagus for house culture, but its branches do not have the fernlike character of the preceding. Its tiny white flowers are attractive but not showy; they are followed by red berries if conditions are favorable. Both kinds need rich soil and plenty of water when growing; in winter it is desirable but not essential to provide a temperature near 50° F. Emerald-feather is a voracious feeder and should be given liquid fertilizer every two or three weeks when it is actively growing. Old mangy shoots should be cut away to make room for new growth.

*Aspidistra:* One of the most famous house plants, though not so popular as it was in Victorian days, is *Aspidistra,* the cast-iron plant, so-called because

*Aglaonema commutatum 'Treubii' and other equally attractive named forms are better looking than the more commonplace Chinese evergreen* (A. modestum) *and as durable under dim light conditions.*

of its ability to thrive almost anywhere. Its long, glossy leaves arising from the rootstock are heavy but decorative. The purplish-brown flowers are borne at the soil line and often pass unseen. The cultivar *A. elatior* 'Variegata' is striped green and white, but it is not as good-looking as the green-leaf type. Many homes used to have venerable specimens in 12- or 14-inch pots, but the plant is easier to handle if divided before it gets so large, and grown in 6-inch pots. Rich soil, ample watering, and a little light are all it needs, plus washing the leaves occasionally to shine them up and remove scale insects.

*Cordyline* **and** *Dracaena:* These plants are closely related, and many of the species have at one time or another been included in both genera. *Cordyline australis,* the fountain dracaena, has long, narrow leaves gracefully arching from a central stem. It was commonly used as the central plant in large plant vases during summer on estates or in formal gardens. It is easily grown as a house plant and can be raised from seeds. A New Zealand species, it can endure light frosts and is better off if kept cool in winter. An East Indian species, *C. terminalis,* which has stalked, lance-shaped leaves, is not so easy to grow, but if you have a room in which the air is moist, one or more of the dozens of its forms are worthy of a trial. The leaves, which have been used for hula skirts in Pacific islands, often exhibit remarkable coloration: 'Amabilis' is suffused with rose and white; 'Firebrand' is purple-red with red midrib. And so it goes; some have deep purple leaves; some are white when young, changing to green margined with rose when mature; and some are red all over. Strong light is needed to bring out the colors of the leaves.

The soil should be the general potting mixture; a moist atmosphere and daily spraying of the foliage are desirable; and abundant watering at the roots, but no waterlogging. When the stem becomes too long in proportion to the tuft of the foliage, the top can be air-layered; and after the layer has been removed, the stem remaining can be cut into 3-inch lengths, buried ½ inch deep in sand in a propagating case (70° to 80° F.) if more young stock is desired.

*Dracaena:* There are several species of *Dracaena* that make first-class house plants and that vary greatly in size and general appearance. *D. fragrans* is the one that often grows up so that it hits the ceiling and has to be discarded, or given to an institution, unless the owner has the foresight to air-layer it before it gets to the ceiling-touching stage. The arching, cornlike leaves may be 2 feet or more long and 3 inches wide. Occasionally this species and its varieties take it into their heads to throw up a panicle of flowers, which is just too bad, for the flowers—though fragrant—are not ornamental and their production destroys the symmetry of the plant. *D. fragrans* 'Massangeana' is the one most often offered commercially and is striped with yellowish green.

The gold-dust dracaena, *D. surculosa* (syn. *D. godseffiana*), has a branching habit and small, oval, deep green leaves irregularly spotted with yellow and white. It seldom reaches more than a foot or two in height. *D. sanderana* has leaves about 6 inches long and 1 inch broad, striped with white. Its stems rarely branch and, as they may reach a height of several feet, give an effect of slenderness. When I once worked for a New York florist and tended house plants in the houses of the affluent, I noticed that in neglected window boxes *D. sanderana* was the plant that survived after all the others had gone to their last rest. Another dracaena that is popular today, especially in modern settings, is *D. draco,* sometimes called the dragontree. As it ages it becomes treelike and is often used as a floor accent, giving an effect striking and artistic—or grotesque, depending on the viewer. No special treatment beyond ordinary routine care is needed by these dracaenas.

**Snake Plant:** The common snake plant, *Sansevieria trifasciata* 'Laurentii', is one of the most inelegant of all plants, with its stiff, 30-inch, upright leaves and the entire lack of form of the plant as a whole. Its yellow stripes, however, do provide a color note; but its chief claim to consideration is its toughness and ability to survive in darkish corners under conditions of neglect. It is erratic in its blooming habit, occasionally sending up its spike of fragrant flowers at unpredictable times. They are yellowish and not particularly ornamental, but their fragrance is welcome. *S. zeylanica* is similar in habit, but the leaves have transverse bands of light green. *S. trifasciata* 'Hahnii', which is occasionally seen as young plants in dish gardens, has its comparatively short leaves arranged in rosettes. 'Golden Hahnii' has yellow-striped leaves. The chief thing to avoid in growing snake plants is overwatering, especially in winter. The general potting mixture suits them; propagation is effected by division of the rootstock, and, except for 'Laurentii', leaves cut into pieces 3 inches long and inserted in sand.

**Ponytail-palm:** An oddity in the lily family is the ponytail-palm or bottle-palm *(Beaucarnea recurvata),* which can attract attention because of its grayish tapering trunk, bulblike and swollen at the base, and topped by a crown of cascading, narrow leaves. It is a plant that withstands some neglect and drought, since it stores moisture in the swollen trunk. Older specimens, from 3 feet on, can make striking accents in modern interiors, but they are usually expensive, since the plant is a slow grower. Give bright light (partial sun in winter) and allow the soil to dry out between watering. The plant grows so slowly it can remain in the same pot for years.

## 3.  MISCELLANEOUS PLANTS

We now come to a miscellaneous lot which cannot conveniently be grouped here by botanical affinities, so they are arranged alphabetically. They are followed by ferns and palms.

*Coleus*—**Painted Nettle:** In the days when summer bedding was the thing, dozens of painted nettles, chiefly varieties of *C. blumei,* were available. Then interest in them waned, perhaps because summer bedding (the massing of flowers in formal patterns) went out of fashion. Now the interest in potted plants for indoor as well as outdoor decoration has brought them back into the spotlight. Probably the best way to get a stock of these colorful plants is to buy a package of seeds, grow them indoors under lights or in a bright window, set the seedlings out in the garden in the spring, and rigorously select the best forms for propagation by cuttings. This last is easy, for tip cuttings make roots with rapidity if inserted in moist, sandy soil and covered with a glass or plastic and kept shaded for a couple of weeks.

If it were not for the brilliant coloring of the sometimes velvety looking leaves, coleus plants would give the impression of weediness because of their lush growth. In some, the leaves are clear yellow; in others, the green is veined or blotched with red, brown, yellow, or pink. In size they range from the 1½-inch leaves of small-leaved strains to the 8-inch leaves produced on specimen plants partly by culture (limiting the plant to one or a few shoots) and partly by selecting a naturally large-leaved variety. In some varieties, the leaves are deeply serrated, lobed, or fringed.

The chief drawback to coleus is the mealybugs' fondness for them. If a plant becomes badly infested, it is better to junk it, reserving a few cuttings, from which the bugs can be removed manually, to carry on the line. The foliage of coleus is sensitive to insecticides of sufficient strength to kill mealybugs. Use general potting mixture; keep soil moist; give enough light to bring out the leaf colors (choose the compact varieties to grow under fluorescent lights); and raise new plants annually from cuttings (they will root anytime) to replace mangy old ones.

**Fatshedera:** This plant is a bigeneric cross, its two parents being Irish ivy (*Hedera helix* 'Hibernica') and *Fatsia japonica.* Fatshedera has inherited the five-lobed leaf shape of its ivy parent but the large size—up to 10 inches across—of fatsia's leaves. In growth habit, fatshedera acts as though it can't decide whether to be a climber or a shrub so can be fastened to a bark slab or pruned to remain a shrub.

**Fatsia japonica:** It is naturally bushy and is easily kept to a height of 2 to 4 feet by pruning. It is even shown to advantage in hanging containers— the large, palmately shaped leaves on their long petioles droop gracefully, giving the effect of a trailing plant.

In addition to the temperatures as cool as can reasonably be provided, both fatsia and fatshedera require bright light, even some direct sun or diffused sun in winter and part shade in summer. Keep the soil moist but do not let it remain saturated.

**Ficus—Rubber Plant:** The fig family gives us several outstanding species for house culture including the India rubber plant *(F. elastica),* the plant for which Brooklyn was once famous; the fiddleleaf fig *(F. lyrata);* the weeping fig *(F. benjamina);* the Indian-laurel *(F. retusa);* and the creeping fig *(F. pumila).* The last named may be used as a climber or trailer (see page 266). The two first named, particularly *F. lyrata,* are handsomer when grown as single-stem plants. They can be air-layered if they become too leggy. The fiddle-shaped leaves of *F. lyrata,* which may be up to 18 inches long, have

*Rubber plant retains its popularity.*

much more character than those of the ordinary rubber plant, although an improved seedling with broader leaves, *F. elastica* 'Decora', is the form generally offered. There is also a variegated variety of rubber plant. Perhaps the weeping fig *(F. benjamina)* is the most popular fig today, especially older specimens that have developed into tall, graceful "trees." Mature specimens of the Indian-laurel are also used as treelike accents in tubs. General potting mixture; routine culture, plus occasional washing of the leaves. Bright light, except for long exposure to direct sunshine, especially in summer, is needed. Both the weeping fig and Indian-laurel will tolerate several hours of sun in winter in the north.

*Hedera helix*—**English Ivy:** We usually think of English ivy as a trailing or climbing vine (see page 266), but there are some forms of definitely upright habit and some which are sufficiently compact to be grown without support. In the first group we have *Hedera helix* 'Conglomerata', 'Minima', and 'Erecta'. These have stiff stems crowded with leathery, often ruffled leaves. Then there is the 'Pittsburgh' ivy, which "sported" so freely that many forms were selected and named. Among them are: 'Albany', with curious distorted leaves; 'Green Feather', somewhat laciniated; 'Hahn's Self-branching', 'Manda's Crested', 'Maple Queen', and 'Merion Beauty'. A collection of these and other forms, varied in leaf characters and habit, makes an interesting hobby for those who have none but north windows in which to grow their plants, more especially if it is a room which can be kept at about 65° F. during the day and 50° at night in winter. The chief enemies to be watched for are red spider mites, which flourish in heat and dry air, and scale insects. These can be prevented by thorough spraying of the leaves, both sides, at least once a week, using water from the hose or faucet applied with considerable force. Otherwise, care is routine.

*An example of an English ivy with ruffled leaves.*

*Maranta is popularly known as prayer plant because its leaves fold together at night.*

*Maranta*—**Arrowroot:** At one time considered capable of cultivation only in a warm, moist greenhouse, two species of *Maranta* have recently won their spurs as house plants. One is a variegated form (*M. arundinacea* 'Variegata') of the arrowroot of commerce, usually about a foot high as a pot plant with oblong leaves variegated with yellow. The other is *M. leuconeura kerchoviana,* dwarf, with elliptical leaves about 6 inches long, of velvety appearance, with large decorative spots. These should be potted in begonia mixture, kept moist, but not sopping wet, and given partial shade. Spraying the foliage daily with clear water is helpful.

*Pandanus*—**Screw-pine:** Screw-pines are beautiful as young plants, but one often sees heirlooms which are just the reverse, with browned leaf tips and a forest of suckers cluttering the base. Plants of this nature should have been discarded years before, and would have been were it not for a sentimental attachment to them, plus ignorance of the fact that they can easily be rejuvenated and perpetuated by sucker cuttings taken when the old plant is approaching unwieldy size. There are two species commonly grown as house plants—*P. utilis,* whose leaves are decorated with reddish spines, and *P. veitchii,* striped white and green, also armed with vicious spines along the margins. Both species have gracefully recurving sword-shaped leaves arranged spirally which causes everyone to wave his hand in circles when describing them. *P. baptistii* has no spines, which makes it ideal from the standpoint of no scratched hands, but unfortunately the leaves are not really strong enough to support their own weight, and some are certain to collapse in the middle, giving the plant a bedraggled appearance.

The screw-pines commonly produce "prop" roots from the stem which enables one to observe very easily the root cap, which is prominent in *Pandanus* and characteristic of all roots though not often so visible. Screw-pines can endure confined quarters for their roots, but when they become pot-bound they should be watered occasionally with liquid fertilizer; and, when the pot-bound condition is so extreme that they begin to heave themselves out of their pots, they should be shifted to a larger size. Use general potting mixture, keep them well watered, and give them a moderate amount of light.

*Peperomia:* Probably one of the commonest peperomias under cultivation is the one sometimes called watermelon–begonia (it has no connection whatever with watermelon or begonia!), which is *P. argyreia,* with pronounced silver stripes between the veins of the heart-shaped, fleshy leaves on red stalks. Its flowers are worthless decoratively. Another species which has become rather common in recent years is *P. obtusifolia,* a rather stodgy plant with fat green leaves on erect or semitrailing stems. There is a cultivar 'Variegata' with cream-colored markings on the leaves; it is a popular component of florists' dish gardens and terrariums. *P. caperata,* emerald ripple, is a neat little plant, 3 to 4 inches high, with bright green, deeply puckered leaves.

These plants require moist air and shade from bright sunshine. They are often used in terrariums but will grow in the open air of the living room. Use general-purpose potting mixture and keep it moist. Young plants can easily be raised from leaf cuttings inserted in sand in a propagating case or under a glass jar.

**Schefflera or Umbrella Tree—***Brassaia actinophylla:* This graceful, bushy plant, which eventually becomes treelike, bears glossy green leaflets in many compound rosettes, giving a lush, tropical effect. Young plants are known for their fast growth and eventually may reach 6 feet. Then they should be in tubs and used as floor specimens, if along the way they haven't lost their leaves because of lack of light or soggy soil. Despite its tropical appearance, the schefflera needs bright light—as much sunlight as available—and the daytime warmth of the average room. To prevent overwatering, allow the soil surface to dry between waterings. These precautions should not make the schefflera sound difficult. It is a phenomenally popular plant that is grown as a decorative accent in offices, showrooms, apartments, and houses.

*Soleirolia soleirolii—***Baby's Tears, Japanese-moss, Irish-moss** (syn. *Helxine soleirolii*): This little creeper is related to the stinging nettles (although it does not sting) and comes from the Mediterranean. Baby's tears, the name now generally accepted, does not seem particularly apt, but now that the botanical name has been changed from *Helxine soleirolii*—never easy!—to *Soleirolia,* it will probably be used more than ever. The tiny leaves are produced on slender, crowded stems to give the plant a mosslike appearance. Its shoots do not trail very far when deprived of contact with the soil, so in spite of its creeping habit, it is not very successful when it is desired to have the shoots trail below the level of the bottom of the pot. One of the best methods of displaying it is to build up a pyramid of soil-filled pots of diminishing size, sinking each pot an inch or two in the soil of the pot below. Small, rooted divisions set in the exposed soil of each tier will quickly grow so that the whole becomes merged in a green, fountainlike effect.

Baby's tears is sensitive to excessively dry atmosphere, but otherwise is easy to grow in ordinary soil in partial shade.

*Tolmiea menziesii*—**Pickaback Plant or Piggyback Plant:** The pickaback plant is native to the Pacific Coast from Alaska to California and is hardy outdoors, or nearly so, as well as durable in the house. Its flowers are green and not ornamental, so it is grown for its interesting foliage, which, while not especially beautiful, has a fresh greenness which is attractive. Its noteworthy feature, however, is the little plants which develop at the tip of the

*Emerald ripple* (Peperomia caperata) *is a small, compact plant with intriguingly puckered leaves.*

leafstalk, and these in turn may also produce plantlets of still smaller size, reminding one of Swift's jingle:

> *So, naturalists observe, a flea*
> *Hath smaller fleas that on him prey;*
> *And these have smaller still to bite 'em;*
> *And so proceed* ad infinitum.

The culture of pickaback does not present any special problems except its need for regular watering—merely give it reasonably good soil, water freely, and shade from bright sunshine, especially in summer. When the plants begin to look moth-eaten, as they will when aged, start new ones by potting up leaves with plantlets attached in sandy, humusy soil. It is well adapted to water culture, and leaves placed in a jar so that the water barely touches the leaf blade will soon grow.

## 4. FERNS

Many of the plants in the foliage classification are, technically, flowering plants, although their flowers may have little ornamental value. Aspidistra, a foliage plant if ever there was one, belongs to the lily family and has purple-maroon flowers an inch across. But many people grow it for years, never seeing the flowers even though it blooms annually, so modestly are they displayed. But there is no doubt whatever about the ferns; they definitely are flowerless plants and make up for it from our standpoint by the beauty and elegance of their fronds.

While many of the most desirable ferns are difficult (or impossible) for most interiors unless they are contained in a terrariun, bottle garden, or other enclosed case to give them the atmospheric moisture they need (maidenhair ferns in general, for example), there are enough amenable kinds to provide sufficient variety in size and form. Many ferns in nature inhabit shaded places, and their ability to thrive in a subdued light makes them particularly valuable in dimly lighted locations. It must not be inferred, however, that their use in sunny windows is prohibited. Most of them can be thus placed provided they are protected from direct sunshine by thin curtains or taller-growing plants.

Ferns are attractive from babyhood to maturity, and those which ultimately attain considerable size may be grown as infants even in small apartments, but gardeners whose hearts are wrenched when they have to discard a plant when it starts to crowd them out of house and home will want to know which species to avoid.

**Mexican Tree Fern:** One of these big ones is the Mexican tree fern *(Cibotium schiedei)* which may make a trunk 15 feet high with fronds 5 feet long. While it is hardly likely to grow so large under house conditions, specimens 6 feet in diameter and 3 or 4 feet high are not unknown. A well-grown specimen, about 3 feet in diameter, with its gracefully curving, much-divided, light green fronds, is exquisite, and can be recommended highly if you can bear to part with it when it gets too big for you.

**Sword Fern:** The sword fern *(Nephrolepis exaltata)* and some of the cultivars of the famous Boston fern (*N. exaltata* 'Bostoniensis'), more graceful than the first named, are capable of assuming huge proportions. The sword fern has fronds up to 5 feet long; and the same is true of Boston fern cultivars such as 'Rooseveltii'. But there are dwarf forms available for those who are cramped for space, such as 'Compacta', which grows to only a third of the size of this type and has very tough, long-lasting leaves. More than a hundred forms of Boston fern have had names attached to them at one time or another, ranging from once-pinnate types to those whose fronds are so much divided that they resemble moss. This would seem to offer plenty of scope for the "collector," but while probably many varieties are lost to cultivation, there are such commonly available cultivars as 'Fluffy Ruffles' and 'Whitmanii'. The drooping fronds of many of them hide the pots, which may be considered an advantage.

**Hare's-foot Fern:** The hare's-foot fern *(Polypodium aureum)* is distinctive with its massive glaucous (blue-green) fronds decorated on the undersides with clusters of golden spore cases. The cultivar 'Mandaianum' with ruffled pinnae (leaflets) is particularly attractive and in the greenhouse may make leaves 6 feet in length. Although not likely to be so vigorous as this in a house, it is on the large side as ferns go.

**Bird's-nest Fern:** There are plenty of ferns to choose from in the middle-sized bracket. One of the most striking, because it does not have the divided fronds characteristic of so many other kinds, is *Asplenium nidus,* the bird's-nest fern. This has machete-shaped leaves, often with wavy margins, arranged in circles around a central core of stem. Although these leaves may attain a length of 4 feet under very favorable conditions, they seldom exceed 2 feet when grown in the house. Young specimens a foot or less high are particularly attractive.

**Leatherleaf Fern:** I have always believed the toughest of all ferns to be *Polystichum adiantiforme* (syn. *P. capense, P. coriaceum*), the leatherleaf fern. (It is also classified as *Rumohra adiantiformis.*) I once had this thriving beautifully in a pot on the floor beneath a plant stand in a north window shaded by the porch roof. Under cultivation the fronds, triangular in outline, are about 1½ feet long and nearly as much broad, shiny and leathery in texture.

**Staghorn Fern:** The staghorn ferns are unusual in having fronds of two kinds. These plants are epiphytes (not parasites), attaching themselves to trees by means of sterile clasping fronds which, succulent and greenish when developing, ultimately become cinnamon-colored and parchmentlike. They flare outward at the top, leaving a space between them and the tree trunk which serves as a catchall for leaves and debris falling from the tree above. This debris decays and forms "soil" in which the roots ramify. The fertile

*The ever-popular, graceful Boston fern* (Nephrolepis exaltata *'Bostoniensis'*)
*and its many named forms show to advantage in a hanging container.*

fronds are grayish green, reminiscent in shape of the horns of the European reindeer.

The common staghorn fern *(Platycerium bifurcatum)* is a tolerant house plant and does not mind temperatures as low as 40° F. Usually these ferns are grown on a hunk of osmunda fiber wired to a board or a piece of tree trunk, and their watering presents a problem in a room where drips on the floor are anathema. I solved it in my own place by a Rube Goldberg contraption. On a shelf I placed a jam jar filled with water which was conducted to the surface of the fiber in which the fern was growing by means of a length of glass wick. The unabsorbed water dripped into another jar, and this, from time to time, was returned to the upper receptacle.

Once a week the plant should be taken to the bathroom or kitchen and thoroughly sprayed with water. This will keep it free from scale insects and moisten any part of the rooting medium missed by the drips. If you have an enclosed porch or plant room with a brick or stone floor which the daily watering will not harm, in which the temperature never falls below 40° F., with a north-facing wall on which *Platycerium* can be hung, you have an ideal spot in which to grow these ferns (at least those which are not strictly tropical); and you will have had something in the plant line that is distinctly out of the ordinary.

**Mother Spleenwort:** The mother spleenwort *(Asplenium bulbiferum),* beautiful enough with finely divided fronds, has an additional claim to consideration in the interest afforded by bulbils or plantlets which develop on the fronds. In nature these fall off and take root, thus serving as a means of propagation. It occurs in the wild from Malaya to New Zealand and is adapted to a wide range of temperatures—it can be grown either in the living room or in an enclosed porch provided the temperature does not go below 40° F. Its dimensions under cultivation are usually about 2 by 2 feet.

**Holly Fern** and **Green Cliff Brake:** Two species that are very much alike in general appearance when young but that can easily be distinguished by the color of the leafstalks are holly fern *(Cyrtomium falcatum),* green stalks, and green cliff brake *(Pellaea viridis)* with dark brown stalks. Both are handsome, with height and spread of about 1½ feet. The first named has hollylike pinnae (leaflets) and is more tolerant of house conditions than the cliff brake, which, however, has a little more distinction. Also distinctive is the button fern *(P. rotundifolia).* Its pinnae are round. Young plants can be put in terrariums. They are adaptable to a wide range of winter temperatures— 35° to 70° F.

**Brake Fern:** There are three species of brake fern suitable as house plants, all of which are represented by several cultivars. The Cretan or Mediterranean brake *(Pteris cretica—the P* is silent), that has fronds about a foot long, has forms such as ribbon brake *(P. cretica* 'Albo-lineata') with a white line through each leaf division; Riverton brake *(P. cretica* 'Rivertoniana'), whose pinnae are ruffled and lobed; and several other forms with tassled tips to the leaf divisions—Wilson brake (a compact variety) and Wimsett brake.

The sword brake *(P. ensiformis)* may get a little taller than the preceding. Its outstanding cultivar is Victoria brake, banded with white *(P. ensiformis* 'Victoriae').

Spider brake *(P. multifida)* has leaf divisions narrower than those of *P. cretica,* but otherwise similar.

**Tsus-sima Holly Fern:** Probably the smallest of the ferns commonly grown in the house is *Polystichum tsus-simense,* the Tsus-sima holly fern, which seldom attains a foot in height. It is tufted in habit with dark green upright fronds.

**Squirrel's-foot Fern** or **Ball Fern:** The squirrel's-foot fern or ball fern *(Davallia mariesii)* also is on the small side, with fronds up to 10 inches long. This is the species formerly imported from Japan in immense quantities in the guise of "fern balls" consisting of dormant rhizomes bound up with moss, which started into growth when kept moist. Even though it is deciduous (shedding its leaves annually), it is worth growing.

**Maidenhair Ferns:** It is generally conceded that the maidenhair ferns are among the most graceful and attractive. Unfortunately they have a sinister reputation as house plants, and most people fail with them unless they have a terrarium or enclosed case in which they can be grown. One species, however, the trailing maidenhair *(Adiantum caudatum)*, is quite conformable. It does not look much like a maidenhair, having drooping fronds which root and produce plantlets at their tips. It is attractive when displayed in a hanging pot or basket.

A typical maidenhair and the one most likely to succeed is the Delta maidenhair, *A. raddianum* (syn. *A. cuneatum*), which may have fronds 15 inches long, but usually they are shorter. In locations not too urban in charac-

*The Australian maidenhair fern* (Adiantum hispidulum) *in a terrarium with the terrestrial jewel orchid,* Anoectochilus sikkimensis.

ter, in a room where the air is humid and not contaminated with pollutants and kept from undiluted sunshine, this species and its many cultivars are worth a trial.

**Selaginellas:** While they are not true ferns, selaginellas may be considered here, for they are close allies. The ones most commonly grown as house plants are *Selaginella pallescens,* which looks like a fern, with closely branching stems, usually 6 inches long, clothed with very tiny leaves; and *S. kraussiana* 'Brownii', which, when well grown, looks for all the world like a cushion of bright green moss. This one grows exceptionally well even under adverse conditions. However, my enthusiasm was somewhat dashed when my young daughter scornfully asked, on seeing what I considered a beautiful mound of greenery completely filling a 6-inch pan, "Is that all it does?"

The resurrection plant, *Selaginella lepidophylla,* might be made to thrive if it were possible to obtain freshly gathered specimens. This is the plant, commonly sold as a novelty, which looks like a dried-up ball of moss. When placed in water the fronds unroll, revealing their green upper surfaces. Doubtless other selaginellas, some upright, some trailing, some exhibiting unique metallic coloring, could be successfully grown, especially in the humidity of a terrarium.

Years ago millions of ferns *(Cyrtomium, Polystichum, Pteris)* were raised annually to provide material for filling "fern dishes" to be put in elaborate

*Another terrarium grouping includes the small fern* Polystichum tsus-simense *(above, left), selaginella plants, and two miniature begonias ('Red Planet', center, and 'Bantam Gem', top right). All grow well under fluorescent tubes.*

filigreed silver holders and placed in the center of the dining table. Fern dishes are no longer the vogue, which, perhaps, is just as well, since a fern's expectancy of life in the cramped and crowded dish and dim surroundings was not a good insurance risk. These little ferns are very attractive, and the process of raising them from spores and watching their development is of absorbing interest, so you may want to try it. The process is described on page 165.

As previously mentioned, ferns in general are good bets when light conditions are not too bright. If the leaves turn yellowish green when grown in a south window and you are sure it is not due to lack of nutrients, give them more shade or move to a window with a north or west aspect.

Except for species such as the ball fern, which can endure drought when it is dormant, ferns must be kept constantly moist at the root. All ferns need ample watering when in active growth; however, avoid waterlogging the soil, though this is not likely to happen if the pots are well drained.

If the fronds become yellowish and you are sure it is not due to too intense light, it is usually a sign that nutrients are lacking. Feeding with liquid fish emulsion, nitrate of soda, or sulphate of ammonia (see Chapter 7) will correct this condition provided other environmental factors are favorable.

Repotting, if necessary, is done at the beginning of the growing season. Some kinds—as *Adiantum* and *Pteris*—may have to be divided at this time to prevent them from attaining unwieldy size. Boston fern varieties do not respond well to division—raise young plants from runners to replace specimens which have grown too large. (See Chapters 8 and 15.)

Keep a close watch for insect pests—particularly the fern scale, the males of which are slender and white, the females rotund and brownish. Learn, if you do not already know, how to distinguish between them and the spore cases which develop on the back of the fronds. You may feel insulted by this advice, but the receipt of many frantic letters asking for expeditious measures against scale insects when none were present may deter some from laboriously removing spore cases by hand under the impression they are destroying scale insects!

Ferns appeal more to some gardeners than to others. Their beauty of form compensates for lack of flowers; and there are varieties not devoid of coloring other than the normal green. In this chapter a baker's dozen or so of genera suited to house culture has been listed. Anyone who feels impelled to make a hobby of a collection of ferns could easily find dozens more equally tolerant.

## 5. PALMS

**Kentia Palm:** There was a time when palms as house plants were as much in evidence as the ubiquitous rubber plant. Palms are back in evidence today but perhaps not in such numbers as formerly, since they now have to compete

*Many foliage plants, such as this thatch palm* (Thrinax acantheacoma), *benefit from being put outdoors in summer and help decorate patio and terrace areas. Always expose them to the stronger outdoor light gradually to prevent burning of the foliage.*

with other imposing foliage plants. Still widely used is *Howea forsterana,* the kentia palm. Native to Lord Howe Island in the Pacific, kentias used to be in great demand as "rented" palms for use at balls, parties, weddings, and funerals; and to some extent as house plants.

The toughness of kentia was impressed on me many years ago when I worked in the design department of a New York florist. Dozens of these palms ranging up to 10 feet in height were used on any job of considerable size. Every time they left the store their leaves were bundled together with newspapers, the number of thicknesses depending upon the severity of the weather. Then, looking like wrapped mummies, they were stuffed in a horse-drawn wagon and taken to their destination, which might be a hotel, a drafty concert stage, or a private home. There they were unwrapped and the kinks shaken out of their leaves. The following day they were tied and wrapped again, packed in the cold, cold wagon, hustled into the dismal back room of the store, unwrapped and crowded together, pot touching pot, on the bench. Even with this program of rough handling, alternations of heat and cold and crowding, they survived for many weeks, but ultimately had to be discarded or sent to a greenhouse to recuperate.

Plants of kentia purchased from a florist usually are "made up"—that is, a large plant is set in the center of the pot with three smaller, younger ones around it to avoid the naked appearance of the base. They are admirable for porch decoration or outdoor-living areas in summer if room can be found for them indoors in winter.

One of the most beautiful and useful palms (because of its small growth) is the Weddell or Coccos palm, *Microcoelum weddellianum,* which used to be fairly common. Its graceful leaves made up of narrow, bright green, shiny pinnae are decidedly ornamental. It needs warmth and high humidity.

Its place has been taken to some extent by a relative of the date palm, *Phoenix roebelenii.* This perhaps is of even more elegant habit, but its leaves do not have the shiny brightness of the Weddell palm.

Of recent years, a dwarf palm from Guatemala, the parlor palm, *Chamaedorea elegans* (sometimes called *Neanthe bella*), has become very popular. In its natural habitat it grows in shade, in thin soil subject to rapid drying, so that it is tolerant of the dim light and dry air of our homes. A pinnate-leaved palm, it has the interesting feature of flowering when two or three years old; so if you are lucky enough to have both a male and a female (the sexes are produced on separate plants), it may be possible to enjoy the sight of its dark green, ultimately black fruits displayed on the

*A worm's-eye view of an episcia dramatizes the striking foliage patterns and texture of this African-violet relative.*

orange-yellow branches of the inflorescence. So dwarf is this palm that it is possible for it to reach its full development when growing in a 6- or 8-inch pot. The bamboo palm *(C. erumpens)* is taller growing and is an acceptable substitute for bamboo in rooms of oriental decor.

**Fan-leaved Palms:** These palms are not so well suited to house culture as the more graceful feathery types because their lateral spread is so great that they take up too much room in a house of average size. The Chinese fan palm *(Livistona chinensis),* however, takes up little room as a young plant and is worth getting if the opportunity presents itself. *L. chinensis,* when mature, has a trunk 30 feet tall with leaf blades up to 6 feet in diameter on stalks 6 feet long, and *L. rotundifolia* is capable of attaining a height of 80 feet, so don't expect them to grow to maturity in your home.

Palm seeds are occasionally offered in the catalogues of firms dealing with unusual seeds and of those featuring house plants, and there is no difficulty in obtaining seeds of the date palm during the winter months when the fruit is on the markets. The seeds are not difficult to raise if sown ½ inch deep in sandy, humusy soil, kept moist, in a temperature of about 70° F. Don't be too disappointed in the appearance of the seedlings. With the exceptions of species like the parlor palm and the Weddell palm, whose leaves early in life acquire the graceful character of adult specimens, most palms are very unattractive in the young state, with some leaves undivided and some just beginning to hint at what they will be like when they are grown up.

Palms, in general, should be potted in a fairly heavy, rich soil (general-purpose potting mixture), and when they become pot-bound (a condition they do not resent so long as it is not extreme), they should be watered with liquid fertilizer every few weeks during the active growing season.

They will endure reduced light and may indeed be injured if transferred from the home to undiluted sunshine outdoors.

If you find it possible to make yourself sponge the leaves every week with lukewarm soapy water, it will keep them free from scales and mealybugs and spruce them up generally. This time-honored chore, hated by all budding professional gardeners who were compelled to spend hundreds of weary hours sponging palms, is nevertheless a good practice and one that can be recommended for many foliage plants with tough, leathery leaves.

This does not exhaust the list of plants grown for their foliage; others will be found in the General List of House Plants. The bromeliads, members of the pineapple family, many of which have spectacular foliage, are discussed under Flowering Plants in Chapter 17 because their unique flowers seemed to justify their inclusion there. Many of the gesneriads (African-violet relatives) have foliage whose textures and coloration vie with their flowers for attention, two examples being *Smithiantha* (temple bells) and *Episcia* (flame-violet), discussed in Chapter 17. Other house plants with unusual or outstanding foliage are included in Vines and Trailers, also in Chapter 17.

# 4

## LISTS OF PLANTS

CHAPTER 19

# General List
# of House Plants

(Where few or no details are given after a plant's name, see Index for reference to discussions in previous chapters.)

*Abrus precatorius,* Rosary Pea, Crab's Eyes. A small vine, not particularly attractive, which has been recommended. Sow seeds (which are very poisonous) in general-purpose mixture; keep moderately moist in sunny window.

*Abutilon hybridum* and others, Flowering-maple.

*Acacia,* Mimosa. *A. armata,* Kangaroo Thorn.

*Acalypha hispida,* Chenille Plant. This is a difficult house plant in my experience. Raised from cuttings; general-purpose potting mixture; moderately moist; sunny window.

*Achimenes* spp. and cultivars. Tuberous, summer-flowering plants.

*Acorus gramineus* 'Variegatus.' A grasslike plant, 10 inches tall, related to sweet flag. Slow growing; young plants are often used in miniature gardens and terrariums. Division; general-purpose potting mixture; plenty of water; sun or shade.

*Adiantum* spp. and cultivars, Maidenhair Fern.

*Aechmea* spp. and cultivars, Pineapple relatives.

*Aeonium tabuliforme.* Succulent.

*Aeschynanthus* spp. and cultivars, Lipstick Plant.

*Agapanthus africanus,* African-lily. A blue-flowered, summer-blooming, bulbous plant, 3 feet tall. Grown in tubs for terrace, porch, and garden decoration; stored nearly dry in cool cellar or room over winter. Division; general-purpose mixture; moist when growing; sun or light shade.

*Agathaea coelestis. See Felicia amelloides.*

*Agave* spp., Century Plant and others.

*Ageratum houstonianum.* Bedding plant with small blue or white flowers in heads. Small plants may be dug up from garden in fall, potted and grown in sunny window. Subject to attack by white flies.

*Aglaonema* spp. and cultivars, Chinese Evergreen and others.

*Allium neapolitanum,* Flowering Onion. Small white flowers in umbels. Treat as hardy spring-flowering bulb, but don't expose to severe freezing.

*Alloplectus nummularia.* A gesneriad (African-violet relative) formerly known as *Hypocyrta nummularia.* Fibrous-rooted trailer with small, scarlet pouch-shaped flowers. Tends toward dormancy in late summer through fall when little moisture is required. Cuttings (when in active growth); lean humusy mixture; bright or fluorescent light.

*Aloe* spp., Aloes.

*Alternanthera amoena.* Dwarf plants, with varicolored leaves. Can be grown in terrariums (see Chapter 4).

*Alyssum maritimum. See Lobularia maritima.*

*Amaryllis. See Hippeastrum.*

*Amorphophallus,* Devil's Tongue.

*Anacharis canadensis,* Canada Waterweed, Elodea. Aquatic.

*Ananas comosus,* Pineapple.

*Anoectochilus sikkimensis,* Jewel Orchid. A small terrestrial orchid with bronze foliage and orange-red veins. Needs high humidity—best provided in a terrarium. The plants can be maintained in small pots filled with small pieces of fern bark and chopped sphagnum. Avoid overwatering roots.

*Anthericum. See Chlorophytum.*

*Anthurium* spp. and cultivars, Flamingo Flowers and others.

*Antigonum leptopus,* Coral Vine, Rosa de Montana. A vine with racemes of bright pink flowers; has been recommended. Seeds or cuttings; general-purpose mixture; moderately moist; full sun necessary for flowers.

*Antirrhinum,* Snapdragon.

*Aphelandra squarrosa,* Zebra Plant. Handsome foliage plant—its glossy leaves have white veins—with clusters of small yellow flowers surrounded by long-lasting yellow bracts in summer and fall. Difficult; requires high humidity. Cuttings in spring; general-purpose mixture, moist from midwinter to fall, then less moist until midwinter; diffused sun or bright light. Cutting back halfway after flowering helps keep plants shapely.

*Aporocactus flagelliformis,* Rat-tail Cactus.

*Araucaria heterophylla,* Norfolk Island-pine. A handsome pyramidal evergreen. General-purpose mixture, moist in summer—drier in winter; light shade. Best kept cool, 45° to 50° F. in winter, but tolerates warmer temperatures.

*Ardisia crenata,* Coral Berry.

*Areca. See Chrysalidocarpus lutescens.*

*Aristolochia elegans,* Calico Flower. A vine with 3-inch flowers, which has

*The gold-dust plant* (Aucuba japonica *'Variegata')* *is a handsome evergreen shrub suitable for cool rooms out of direct sunshine. The plant shown here remains outdoors all year on a patio sheltered from wind and extreme cold.*

318 ALL ABOUT HOUSE PLANTS

been recommended. Probably difficult except in greenhouse. Seeds in spring; general-purpose mixture; moist soil; sunny window.

*Asparagus* spp. and cultivars, Emerald-feather, Asparagus-fern.

*Aspidistra elatior,* Cast-iron Plant.

*Asplenium* spp., Birds-nest Fern and others.

*Astilbe japonica,* Florist's-spirea.

*Astrophytum* spp., Star Cactus, Bishop's Cap Cactus, Sand Dollar, et cetera.

*Aucuba japonica* 'Variegata', Gold-dust Plant. An almost hardy shrub, 2–3 feet tall as a tubbed plant, with gold-spotted leaves, suitable for a cool room but best in an unheated enclosed porch or plant room. Cuttings (will root in water); general-purpose mixture; moist; partial shade.

*Azalea. See Rhododendron.*

*Azolla caroliniana,* Mosquito Plant. A floating aquatic fern for aquarium or pool.


*Beaucarnea recurvata,* Ponytail-palm, Bottle-palm.

*Begonia* spp. and cultivars.

*Beloperone guttata,* Shrimp Plant.

*Bertolonia maculata.* A dwarf herb with handsome, velvety green leaves and purple-bordered veins. Suitable for terrariums (see Chapter 4).

*Beta vulgaris,* Beet.

*Billbergia* spp. and cultivars, Pineapple relatives.

*Bowiea volubilis,* Climbing-onion. Might appeal to those who like oddities. Twining, much-branched, bright green stems are produced from above-ground bulbs, 3–5 inches across. Division; cactus soil; rest in summer; sun.

*Brassaia actinophylla,* Schefflera.

*Brassica rapa,* Turnip.

*Brodiaea uniflora,* Spring Star-flower. *See Ipheion uniflorum.*

Bromeliads, a family which contains the pineapple, Spanish-moss and plants variously known as bromels, air-pines, et cetera.

*Bryophyllum. See Kalanchoe.*

*Buxus sempervirens* 'Suffruticosa', Dwarf Box. Hardy shrub. Young plants occasionally used in miniature gardens or terrariums. Cuttings; general-purpose mixture; sun.


*Cabomba caroliniana.* Aquatic.

Cacti.

*Caladium* spp. and cultivars, Fancy-leaved Caladiums and others.

*Calathea.* Tropical plants grown for their beautiful foliage. Although some might possibly thrive in the open air of the living room (a relative, *Maranta leuconeura* does), they are more likely to be successful in a terrarium. For this purpose dwarf kinds should be chosen, such as *Calathea micans, C. roseopicta,* and *C. undulata.* Division; begonia soil; moist conditions; partial shade.

*Calceolaria herbeohybrida,* Calceolaria. Has been suggested as a house plant, but I am ready to take off my hat three times to anyone able to grow it as such. Culture as for *Senecio cruentus* (cineraria).

*Calliandra haematocephala,* Red Powder Puff. Shrubby plant with fluffy flowers in late winter and spring. Full to part sun in winter; part shade in summer. Prune after flowering to keep bushy shape—12–36 inches in height.

*Callisia fragrans.* (Has also been listed as *Spironema fragrans* and is sometimes sold as *Tradescantia dracaenoides.*) A strong-growing relative of wandering Jew, with hanging stems terminated with rosettes of broad, oblong-lance-shaped leaves. Small, white fragrant flowers in clusters on tall branching stems. A tolerant house plant. Culture as *Zebrina.*

*Camellia* spp. and cultivars, Tea-plant, Camellia.

*Campanula isophylla,* Ligurian Harebell, sometimes called Star of Bethlehem. A plant with gray-green leaves and somewhat trailing stems; abundant pale blue flowers produced over a long period in fall. Cuttings; general-purpose mixture with handful of crushed limestone to a 6-inch pot; moderately moist; shade from bright sun; cool (50° F.) in winter.

*Capsicum annuum,* Christmas Pepper.

*Caralluma nebrownii.* Succulent.

*Carica papaya,* Pawpaw, Papaya.

*Cattleya* spp. and hybrids, Orchid.

*Cephalocereus senilis,* Old Man Cactus.

*Ceratopteris thalictroides.* Aquatic.

*Cereus peruvianus,* one of the Cacti.

*Ceropegia woodii,* Rosary Vine, Hearts Entangled.

*Chamaecereus sylvestri,* Peanut Cactus.

*Chamaedorea* spp. and cultivars, Dwarf Mountain Palms or Bamboo Palms.

*Chamaerops humilis,* Dwarf Fan Palm. From the Mediterranean region; can endure light frost. Try in enclosed unheated porch or cool room. See palms for culture.

*Cheiridopsis candidissima,* Cigarette Plant. Succulent.

*Chimaphila* spp., Pipsissewa. For terrariums.

*Chionodoxa luciliae,* Glory of the Snow. See section on hardy bulbs in Chapter 17.

*Chlorophytum comosum,* Spider Plant. A very common plant of easy culture, the striped-leaf form being in greatest favor. An excellent choice for hanging containers because of the cascades of numerous plantlets. Division; general-purpose mixture; moist; sun or partial shade.

*Chrysalidocarpus lutescens,* Golden Feather Palm, Areca Palm. Graceful, pinnate leaves with yellow stalks. See section on palms for culture.

*Chrysanthemum frutescens,* Paris Daisy, Marguerite.

*C.* x *morifolium,* Garden Chrysanthemum.

*Cibotium schiedei,* Mexican Tree Fern.

*Cineraria. See Senecio* x *hybridus.*

*Cissus* spp., Grape-ivy, Cape-grape, Kangaroo Vine.

Calathea argyraea *prefers the junglelike atmosphere of a terrarium, but since it grows about 8 inches high, it is too large for the average terrarium. However, it does well in a humus-rich soil that does not dry out and in a reasonably humid, warm situation out of direct sun. For terrarium use, select some of the smaller-growing calatheas.*

*Instead of displaying the spider plant* (Chlorophytum comosum) *in a hanging container, for a change suspend the pot in a tall vase.*

*Citrus* spp. and cultivars, Grapefruit, Otaheite Orange, Lemon, et cetera.

*Cleistocactus* spp., Scarlet Bugler, Silver Torch.

*Clerodendrum thomsoniae.* A twining vine having showy crimson flowers with creamy-white calyxes. Cuttings; general-purpose mixture; moist, except in fall when it should be rested by reducing the supply of water; sunny window. Prune after flowering to force new growth which bears the flowers.

*Clivia miniata,* Kafir-lily.

*Cobaea scandens,* Cup-and-saucer Vine. A strong-growing vine with large greenish or purplish flowers. Needs at least a 6-inch pot for good results. Raise annually from seeds sown in late winter; general-purpose mixture; moist; sun or light shade.

*Codiaeum variegatum pictum,* Croton.

*Coffea arabica,* Coffee Plant. An authentic source of the brew (two beans per berry!) but as a house plant most attractive for its foliage and shrubby growth habit. The white, fragrant flowers that produce the berries usually appear on mature plants only—three to four years old. Some sun and average room conditions. General-purpose mixture, moist but not soggy.

*Colchicum* spp. and cultivars, Meadow Saffron.

*Coleus* spp. and cultivars, Painted Nettle.

*Columnea* spp. and cultivars.

*Conophytum* spp., Cone Plant. Succulent.

*Convallaria majalis,* Lily-of-the-valley.

*Coprosma repens.* A New Zealand shrub (or small tree when planted out) with shining leaves blotched with yellow in 'Variegata', the one most commonly cultivated. Rooted cuttings useful in cool-room terrariums; as a tubbed shrub for frost-free, unheated, enclosed porches and cool rooms. Cuttings; general-purpose mixture; moist; cool in winter; sun or light shade.

*Cordyline terminalis,* Dracaena *(which also see).*

*Cotyledon* spp. Succulents suitable for sunny windows. Many plants formerly known as *Cotyledon* are now referred to as *Echeveria* and *Adromischus.* Cuttings; cactus soil; on dry, cool side in winter, moist when growing actively; sun or very light shade.

*Crassula* spp., Jade Plant, Necklace Vine, et cetera. Succulents.

*Crinum longifolium,* Bengal-lily, Milk-and-honey-lily. A summer-flowering bulb with large pink or white flowers for tubs on terrace or patio. Propagated by offsets from the bulbs; bulb soil, moist when growing; dry and cool in winter; sun. Pot as amaryllis—with neck of bulb protruding.

*Crocus* spp. and cultivars.

*Cryptanthus* spp. and cultivars, Pineapple relatives known as Earth-stars.

*Cyanotis somaliensis,* Pussy Ears.

*Cycas revoluta,* Sago "Palm." The processed leaves are used as a backing for funeral pieces. Seeds (when obtainable); general-purpose mixture; moist, but somewhat dry and cool in winter; sun or light shade.

*Cyclamen persicum,* Florists' Cyclamen.

*Cymbalaria muralis,* Kenilworth-ivy.

*Cymbidium* spp. and cultivars. Orchids.

*Cyperus alternifolius,* Umbrella Plant. A semiaquatic sedge with umbels of grasslike leaves on stems up to 4 feet. 'Gracilis' is only 12 inches tall and is preferred for house culture. Cuttings of umbels in water; general-purpose mixture; wet; sun or light shade.

*Cypripedium* spp., Hardy Lady-slipper Orchid. For the tropical lady-slipper orchids, see *Paphiopedilum.*

*Cyrtomium falcatum,* Holly Fern.

*Cytisus canariensis,* Florists' Genista, Broom.

*Daphne odora,* Fragrant Daphne. A small evergreen shrub with intensely fragrant white to purple flowers in late winter. Cultivar 'Marginata' has leaves bordered with yellow. Cuttings; equal parts loam, leaf mold, peat moss, sand; moist; 50° F. in winter; sun or light shade.

*Daucus carota sativa,* Carrot.

*Davallia* spp., Squirrel's-foot Fern and others.

*Dendrobium nobile* and others. Orchids.

*Dieffenbachia* spp. and cultivars, Dumb Cane, Mother-in-law Plant.

*Dizygotheca elegantissima,* False-aralia. This plant with the dizzy name is a shrub or small tree, but when grown in a pot is usually seen with a single stem about a foot tall, clothed with elegant compound leaves with slender, gracefully drooping leaflets. Cuttings; general-purpose mixture; moist soil and air; warmth (65° to 70° F. at night, 70° to 80° daytime); partial shade.

*Dolichos lablab,* Hyacinth Bean. Has been recommended. A climber with purple or white flowers and purple seed pods; often grown as a porch or patio vine outdoors. Seeds in late winter; general-purpose mixture; moist; sun.

*Dracaena* spp. and cultivars, Corn Plant, Dragon-lily, et cetera.

*Dyckia fosterana* (Pineapple relative). Terrestrial bromeliad with silvery spiny-edged leaves in a rosette about 8 inches high.

*Echeveria* spp. and cultivars. Succulents.

*Echinocactus* spp., Barrel Cactus.

*Echinocereus* spp., Hedgehog Cactus, Rainbow Cactus.

*Echinopsis multiplex,* Sea Urchin Cactus, Easter-lily Cactus.

*Epigaea repens,* Trailing-arbutus. Treat as other hardy native plants in terrariums.

*Epiphyllum* hybrids, Orchid Cactus. *See also Nopalxochia ackermannii.*

*Episcia* spp. and cultivars, Flame-violet.

*Eranthis hyemalis,* Winter-aconite. Hardy bulb.

*Erica melanthera,* Black-eyed Heath.

*Espostoa lanata,* Snowball Cactus.

*Eucharis grandiflora,* Amazon-lily. A tropical bulb with beautiful, fragrant

*Calceolaria is spectacular in flower. It should be obtained from a florist, then discarded after flowers fade. The flowers will last longer in cool rooms out of direct sun.*

white flowers in late winter, early spring. Requires warmth and high humidity. Division (after flowering); general-purpose mixture; partial shade.

*Eugenia uniflora,* Surinam-cherry.

*Euonymus japonicus,* Evergreen Euonymus. Near-hardy shrubs sometimes used indoors in miniature gardens and terrariums. Cuttings; general-purpose mixture kept moist; partial shade.

*Euphorbia* spp. and cultivars, Crown-of-thorns, Poinsettia, et cetera.


*Fatshedera lizei,* Aralia-ivy, Tree-ivy.

*Fatsia japonica,* Japanese-aralia.

*Faucaria tigrina,* Tiger's Jaw. Succulent.

*Felicia amelloides,* Blue Daisy, Blue Marguerite. (Sometimes listed as *Agathaea coelestis.*) Almost ever-blooming in sunny windows if fading flowers are removed. Seeds, sown in summer for winter bloom; cuttings; general-purpose mixture; moist; sun.

*Ferocactus setispinus,* Strawberry Cactus.

*Ficus* spp. and hybrids, Fig, Rubber Plant, et cetera.

*Fittonia vershaffeltii,* Nerve Plant, and its variety *argyroneura,* are suitable for terrariums. The former has oval leaves with red veins, the latter has white veins. Cuttings; general-purpose mixture. Can be grown without aid of a terrarium but needs high humidity (stand on pebbles in water-filled tray) and warmth. Cuttings; general-purpose mixture; partial shade.

*Freesia* spp. and cultivars, Freesia.

*Fuchsia* spp. and cultivars, Fuchsia.


*Galanthus nivalis,* Snowdrop. Hardy bulb.

*Gardenia jasminoides,* Cape-jasmine, Gardenia.

*Gasteria* spp. and cultivars, Warty-aloe, Ox-tongue. Succulents.

*Gaultheria* spp. Wintergreen and creeping snowberry are native woodland plants for terrariums.

*Gesneria cuneifolia,* Gesneria. An almost ever-blooming gesneriad of small stature that thrives in terrariums. Bright red tubular flowers. Division of underground runners, seeds, or leaves (slow); humusy (but well-drained) soil; feed sparingly—avoid overfertilizing; bright light but best under fluorescent lights.

*Gloriosa* spp., Glory-lily.

*Glottiphyllum linguiforme,* Tongue-leaf. Succulent.

*Gloxinia perennis.* A lesser-known gesneriad. (For the popular florist's gloxinia, see *Sinningia speciosa.*) A rhizomatous plant with large, heart-shaped leaves and pretty lavender flowers, bell-shaped, usually in summer. Plant the rhizomes in early spring—dormancy usually begins in late summer to late fall. Cuttings, division of rhizomes; humusy soil mixture, moist when growing; partial shade.

*Goodyera* spp., Rattlesnake-plantain. Hardy native orchid with attractive foliage, sometimes used in terrariums.

*Grevillea robusta,* Australian Silk-oak. A tree with fernlike leaves which makes a handsome pot plant when young. Seeds in spring; general-purpose mixture; moist; sun or light shade.

*Guzmania zahnii,* Pineapple relative.

*Gymnocalycium* spp., Chin Cacti.

*Gynura aurantiaca,* Velvet Plant. Its most striking feature is the egg-shaped leaves, densely covered with velvety violet or purple hairs. Cuttings; general-purpose mixture; moist; sun. Useful in hanging containers. *G. procumbens* (syn. *G. sarmentosa*) is similar; both are burdened with the common name Purple Passion Vine.

*Hamatocactus setispinus,* Strawberry Cactus. *See Ferocactus setispinus.*

*Harrisia* spp. and cultivars. Some of the Night-blooming Cereus belong here.

*Haworthia* spp., Cushion-aloe, Window Plant, et cetera. Succulents.

*Hechtia argentea,* Pineapple relative.

*Hedera* spp. and cultivars, English Ivy, Canary Ivy.

*Heliotropium arborescens,* Heliotrope.

*Helxine soleirolii,* Baby's Tears. *See Soleirolia soleirolii.*

*Hibiscus rosa-sinensis,* Chinese Hibiscus, Rose-of-China.

*Hippeastrum* spp. and cultivars, Amaryllis.

*Homalomena rubescens.* An aroid with broad, arrowhead leaves and reddish
  stalks. See Index for culture reference.

*Hoodia rosea.* Succulent.

*Howea forsterana,* Kentia Palm, Paradise Palm.

*Hoya* spp. and cultivars, Waxplant.

*Huernia* spp. Succulents.

*Hyacinthus* spp. and cultivars, Dutch Hyacinth, Roman Hyacinth.

*Hydrangea macrophylla,* French Hydrangea.

*Hydrocleys nymphoides.* Aquatic.

*Hydrosme rivieri,* Devil's Tongue, Voodoo Plant. *See Amorphophallus rivieri.*

*Hylocereus undatus,* Night-blooming Cereus.

*Hypocyrta nummularia. See Alloplectus nummularia.*


*Impatiens* spp. and cultivars, Patience Plant, Zanzibar Balsam.

*Ipheion* (syn. *Brodiaea* or *Triteleia*) *uniflorum,* Spring Star-flower.

*Ipomoea,* includes such diverse species as Morning-glory and Sweet-potato.

*Iresine lindenii,* Blood-leaf. A plant with reddish leaves commonly used for
  outdoor bedding. Has been recommended, but the plant I tried looked
  very unhappy in the house. Cuttings; general-purpose mixture; moist; sun.

*Iris* spp., including the many varieties of English, Dutch, Spanish, and Netted
  Irises. Those experienced in growing hardy bulbs in the house might like
  to try these. The netted iris *(I. reticulata)* is dwarf with deep violet flowers
  marked with orange. See Index for culture reference.

*Ixora coccinea,* a tropical evergreen shrub with clusters of small red flowers,
  has been recommended but failed for me. Cuttings; general-purpose mixture; moist air and soil; sun.


*Jacobinia carnea,* Plume Flower. *See Justicia carnea.*

*Justicia brandegeana,* Shrimp Plant. *See Beloperone guttata.*

*J. carnea,* Plume Flower, Flamingo Flower. Showy pink or crimson flowers
  in dense terminal clusters; unattractive leaves. A plant I once tried bloomed
  and got along very well until the heat was turned on, when it began to
  fail. Cuttings; general-purpose mixture, moist; sun or part shade.


*Kalanchoe* spp. and cultivars, Life Plant, Panda Plant, et cetera.

*Kleinia articulata. See Senecio articulatus.*

Eucharis grandiflora *(Amazon-lily) is not the easiest of*
*bulbs to flower under average indoor conditions, but the fragrant*
*white blooms are worth the struggle. The bulbs require a rest*
*after flowering, usually in spring. Withhold water; resume*
*watering as new growth starts.*

*Lachenalia* spp., Cape-cowslip.

*Laelia* spp. and cultivars. Orchids.

*Lantana camara,* Lantana.

*Laurus nobilis,* Sweet Bay Tree, Laurel. This shrub or tree, with aromatic
leaves used in cooking and perfumery, is popular, when trimmed to pyramidal or standard form, for outdoor display in summer and hallway or garden
room embellishment in winter. Cuttings; general-purpose mixture; moist;
cool in winter; sun.

*Lemaireocereus marginatus,* Organ Cactus.

*Leucojum vernum,* Spring Snowflake. Hardy bulb.

*Ligularia tussilaginea* 'Aureo-maculata', Leopard-plant. This has large rounded leaves blotched with yellow or white; usually 8 to 12 inches tall as a pot plant. Division; general-purpose mixture; moist; cool in winter (45° F.); sun or partial shade.

*Lilium longiflorum,* Easter Lily.

*Lippia citriodora,* Lemon-verbena. A shrub of mediocre appearance grown for its fragrant leaves. Cuttings; general-purpose mixture; moist when growing, on dry side and cool in winter; sun. (Sometimes listed as *Aloysia triphylla.*)

*Lithops* spp., Flowering Stones, Stoneface, Living Stone. Succulents.

*Livistona* spp., Fan Palms.

*Lobelia erinus,* Bedding Lobelia. Young plants can be dug up from the flower border, potted, and brought indoors in the fall, but usually with not much success.

*Lobivia* spp., Cob Cactus.

*Lobularia maritima,* Sweet-alyssum.

*Lophophora williamsii,* Peyote, Sacred-mushroom, Mescal. A Cactus.

*Ludwigia* spp. Aquatic.

*Lycopodium* spp., Club Mosses.

*Lycoris radiata,* Spider-lily. A bulbous plant with bright red flowers in umbels in the fall. Usually stored in pots in cellar during winter and used for patio or porch decoration in late summer. Offsets; bulb soil; moist when growing; dry in winter; sun.


*Malpighia coccigera,* Miniature-holly, Singapore-holly. The spiny evergreen leaves are responsible for the common names of this small tropical shrub. It bears little, starry pink flowers in winter-spring. Can be trained as indoor bonsai. Cuttings; general-purpose mixture; soak, then allow soil surface to dry before next watering; sun or bright light.

*Mammillaria* spp., Pincushion Cactus, Lace Cactus, et cetera.

*Maranta* spp., Arrow-root and Prayer Plant.

*Marica northiana,* Apostle Plant. *See Neomarica.*

*Mesembryanthemum,* Ice Plant. Most of the plants formerly known under this name have been transferred to other genera, collectively known as the Mesembryanthema. Those most likely to be of interest are described and discussed in the succulents section of Chapter 17.

*Microcoelum weddellianum,* Coccos or Weddell Palm.

*Mimosa pudica,* Sensitive Plant. A roadside weed in the tropics. The sensitivity of its leaves is always intriguing. Grow it as an annual outdoors, where its little pompons of pink blossoms are attractive, or indoors on a sunny window sill. Treat as an annual (seeds).

*Mitchella repens,* Partridge Berry.

*Monstera deliciosa,* Mexican Bread-fruit.

*Musa nana,* Dwarf Banana.

*Muscari* spp. and cultivars, Grape-hyacinth. Hardy bulbs.

*Myosotis* spp., Forget-me-not.

*Myriophyllum* spp., Milfoil, Parrot's Feather.

*Myrtus communis,* Myrtle. Aromatic evergreen shrub from the Mediterranean with white flowers and dark blue berries, usually from spring to summer. Several dwarf forms available, some with small or variegated leaves. Cuttings; general-purpose mixture; cool (55° to 65° F.), sunny windows or bright light.

*Narcissus* spp. and cultivars, Daffodil, Paper-white Narcissus, et cetera.

*Neanthe bella* (Palm). *See Chamaedorea.*

*Neoregelia* spp. and cultivars, Pineapple relatives.

*Nephrolepis exaltata* 'Bostoniensis', Boston Fern.

*Nephthytis afzelii. See Syngonium podophyllum.*

*Nerine* spp. and cultivars, including Guernsey-lily *(N. sarniensis).* Has been recommended, but it is doubtful if many would want to give it a cool, sunny window throughout the winter (when the leaves are active) for the sake of its admittedly showy blooms in late fall. The bulbs should be dried off in their pots from May to August. Bulb soil; sun.

*Nerium oleander,* Oleander. A shrub with showy pink flowers which can be stored in a cool, well-lighted cellar during the winter. See the section on shrubs in Chapter 17.

*Nicotiana alata,* Flowering Tobacco.

*Nidularium* spp., Pineapple relatives.

*Nierembergia hippomanica,* Blue Cup Flower. Has been recommended. Can be dug up from flower border in the fall.

*Nopalxochia ackermannii,* an Orchid Cactus species much used in hybridizing with *Epiphyllum* and others.

*Notocactus* spp., Ball Cactus.

*Nyctocereus serpentinus,* Snake Cactus.

*Nymphaeas* spp. and cultivars, Water-lily. Aquatics.

*Ophiopogon* spp. and cultivars, Lily-turf, Snakebeard.

*Opuntia* spp., Cacti, Prickly-pears.

*Oreocereus* spp., Mountain Cacti.

*Ornithogalum,* spp. and cultivars. Tender bulbs.

*Osmanthus fragrans,* Fragrant-olive. A shrub with tiny fragrant flowers in winter. Has been recommended for house culture. Needs to be kept cool during winter. Cuttings; general-purpose mixture; moist; sun or partial shade.

*Othonna capensis,* Little Pickles. A succulent trailer, with cylindrical fleshy leaves and small yellow daisies. Cuttings; cactus soil; rather dry in winter; sun.

*Oxalis* spp., Bermuda Buttercup, et cetera.

*O. rubra,* a summer-flowering species; can be dried off in winter (keep cool). Division; general-purpose mixture; moist in summer; sun.

*Pandanus* spp., Screw-pines.

*Paphiopedilum* spp. and cultivars, Lady-slipper Orchids.

*Passiflora* spp., Passion Flower. These vines have been grown successfully as house plants. Seeds and cuttings; general-purpose mixture; moist; sun or partial shade.

*Pedilanthus tithymaloides,* Redbird-cactus (not a true cactus), Slipper Flower. Succulent stems; 2 feet tall when grown in pots; oval, pointed leaves bordered with white in 'Variegatus'. Has been grown successfully in the house but probably difficult to purchase. Culture as for cacti and succulents.

*Pelargonium.* Geraniums of varied species and types.

*Pellaea viridis,* Cliff Brake Fern.

*Pellionia.* Two species, *P. daveauana* and *P. pulchra,* are grown in hanging baskets or as indoor ground covers in planters or for a time in terrariums where they must be restrained by pinching. Cuttings; general-purpose mixture kept moist; part shade.

*Peperomia* spp., Watermelon-begonia and many other fine foliage plants.

*Pereskia* spp. Cacti.

*Persea americana,* Avocado.

*Philodendron* spp. and cultivars.

*Phoenix roebelinii,* Pygmy Date Palm.

*Pilea cadierei,* Aluminum Plant, *P. involucrata,* Panamiga, and *P. microphylla,* Artillery Plant. Cuttings; general-purpose mixture; moist; partial shade. Useful in terrariums.

*Pittosporum tobira* 'Variegata'. A shrub with white markings on leaves. Young plants can be used in terrariums. Cuttings; general-purpose mixture; moist.

*Platycerium bifurcatum,* Staghorn Fern.

*Plectranthus australis,* Swedish-ivy.

*Pleiospilos* spp., Living Rocks.

*Podocarpus macrophyllus maki.* A tree related to conifers, with narrow leaves. Popular tub plant for cool rooms.

*Polypodium* spp. Ferns.

*Polyscias balfouriana, P. fruticosa* (Ming-aralia), and *P. guilfoylei* are shrubs with ornamental foliage, suitable when young for pot and terrarium culture. Can be trained as indoor bonsai. Easy to grow.

*Polystichum* spp., Leather-leaf Fern and others.

*Portulacaria afra.* A small succulent shrub of undistinguished appearance sometimes used in dish gardens. There is a variegated form.

*Primula* spp., and cultivars, Primroses of various kinds.

*Psidium littorale longipes,* Strawberry Guava.

*Pteris* spp. and cultivars, Brake Ferns.

*Punica granatum,* Pomegranate.

*Rebutia* spp. Cacti.

*Rechsteineria cardinalis. See Sinningia cardinalis.*

*Rhipsalidopsis gaertneri,* Easter Cactus.

*Rhipsalis* spp., Mistletoe Cacti. Epiphytic, with small white or creamy flowers. Culture same as Orchid Cacti.

*Rhododendron* spp. and cultivars, Evergreen Azalea.

*Rhoeo spathacea,* Three-men-in-a-boat, Moses-on-a-raft, Purple-leaved Spiderwort. A rather ungainly plant whose leaves are purple beneath. Small white flowers in boatlike bracts that appear intermittently. Culture as for *Zebrina.*

*Rivina humilis,* Rouge Plant.

*Rosa* spp. and cultivars, Miniature Rose.


*Sagittaria* spp., Arrowhead. Aquatics.

*Saintpaulia* spp. and cultivars, African-violet.

*Salvinia auriculata,* Floating Fern. Aquatic.

*Sansevieria* spp. and cultivars, Snake Plant, Bowstring-hemp.

*Sauromatum guttatum,* Monarch-of-the-East, Voodoo-lily.

*Saxifraga stolonifera,* Mother-of-thousands, Strawberry-geranium.

*Schefflera. See Brassaia actinophylla.*

*Schlumbergera truncata* (syn. *Zygocactus truncatus*), Crab-claw Cactus, Thanksgiving Cactus.

*S.* x *buckleyi* (syn. *S. bridgesii*), Christmas Cactus.

*Scilla sibirica,* Siberian Squill. Hardy bulb.

*Scindapsus* spp. and cultivars, Pothos.

*Sedum* spp. and cultivars, Stonecrop, Live-for-ever.

*Selaginella* spp.

*Selenicereus grandiflorus,* Queen-of-the-night. Cactus.

*Sempervivum* spp. and cultivars, Houseleek.

*Senecio articulatus,* Candle Plant. Succulent.

*S.* x *hybridus,* Cineraria.

*S. mikanioides,* German-ivy.

*Serissa foetida* 'Variegata'. A little shrub with ½-inch oval leaves bordered with yellow; single white flowers borne intermittently. There is a double-flowered form of *S. foetida* known as snow-rose. Used in dish gardens and as indoor bonsai. Cuttings; general-purpose mixture, moist; sun or part shade.

*Setcreasea pallida,* 'Purple Heart'. Culture as for *Zebrina.*

*Sinningia cardinalis,* Cardinal Flower.

*S. concinna.* A miniature gloxinia with tuberous root which is usually everblooming, at least under terrarium culture. Several small attractive hybrids available.

*S. pusilla,* Miniature Gloxinia. Popular terrarium plant and parent of many hybrids. This and above do well under fluorescent lights.

*S. speciosa,* Gloxinia.

*Smithiantha zebrina,* Temple Bells.

*Solanum pseudocapsicum,* Jerusalem-cherry, Christmas-berry.

*Soleirolia soleirolii* (syn. *Helxine soleirolii*), Baby's tears.

*Sparaxis* spp. and cultivars. Tender bulbs.

*Spathiphyllum floribundum* and others. An aroid with fairly showy white spathes. For culture see section on aroids in Chapter 18.

*Spironema fragrans. See Callisia fragrans.*

*Stapelia* spp., Carrion Flower, Star Flower. Succulents.

*Stephanotis floribunda,* Madagascar-jasmine. A shrubby climber with evergreen foliage and exquisitely beautiful, white tubular flowers in clusters in late spring and summer. The wax-textured flowers possess a powerful fragrance. Cuttings; general-purpose mixture, moist when actively growing in spring-fall, drier in winter; some sun in winter, part shade in summer.

*Sternbergia lutea,* Mt. Etna-lily.

*Strelitzia reginae,* Bird-of-paradise Flower. Stemless; leaves rising to 3 feet, 1½ feet long, ½ foot wide. Inflorescence purple, yellow, and blue. Culture same as *Clivia.*

*Streptocarpus* x *hybridus,* Cape-primrose.

*S. saxorum.* An attractive plant burdened with such silly common names as Dauphin-violet, false-African-violet.

*Fittonia, sometimes called nerve plant, thrives under fairly humid conditions. In dry rooms, grow it in a terrarium.*

*The aromatic-leaved myrtle* (Myrtus communis) *of the Mediterranean grows best as a house plant in a cool, sunny window. The white flowers are fragrant.*

*Swainsona galegifolia,* Swan Flower. A shrub with long, flexible stems and racemes of pea-shaped flowers—white, pink, red, or rose-violet according to variety. Seeds; general-purpose mixture; moist; sun.

*Syagrus weddelliana,* Coccos or Weddell Palm. *See Microcoelum weddellianum.*

*Syngonium* spp. and cultivars, Nephthytis.

*Tagetes patula,* French Marigold.

*Talinum paniculatum,* Flame Flower. Related to, but nothing like, portulaca. The variety *variegatum* is marked with white or pink. Small red flowers on branched stalks. Seeds; general-purpose mixture; not too moist; sun.

*Thunbergia alata,* Clock Vine, Black-eyed Susan Vine.

*Tibouchina* (syn. *T. semidecandra*) *urvilleana,* Princess Flower.

*Tillandsia* spp., Pineapple relative.

*Titanopsis calcarea,* succulent that resembles limestones. Needs rest in winter.

*Tolmiea menziesii,* Pickaback Plant.

*Torenia fournieri,* Wishbone Plant, Blue Wings.

*Trachelospermum jasminoides,* Star-jasmine, Confederate-jasmine. Shrubby vine, as a house plant usually more shrub than vine, with fragrant, star-shaped white flowers, mostly in spring and summer. Cuttings; general-purpose mixture; moist but allow soil surface to dry between thorough waterings; winter, sun; summer, part shade.

*Tradescantia* spp. and cultivars, Wandering Jew.

*Trichocereus spachianus,* White Torch Cactus.

*Trichodiadema densum,* one of the Mesembryanthema.

*Tripogandra multiflora* (syn. *Tradescantia multiflora*), Tahitian Bridal Veil. Fast-growing basket plant of airy habit with small white flowers—virtually ever-blooming. Culture as for *Zebrina.*

*Tropaeolum majus,* Nasturtium.

*Tulipa,* Tulip. Hardy bulb.

*Utricularia* spp., Bladderwort. Aquatics.

*Vallisneria spiralis,* Eel-grass. Aquatic.

*Veltheimia viridifolia.*

*Vinca major,* Periwinkle. A trailing evergreen with plain or variegated foliage. Often used in the foreground of outdoor window boxes and planters in summer, it can be brought into an unheated enclosed plant room or porch where it will survive and perform a decorative function if the temperature does not fall too much below freezing. Division; cuttings; general-purpose mixture; moist; sun or shade.

*Vriesia* spp. and cultivars, Pineapple relatives.

*Xanthosoma lindenii,* Indian-kale, Spoon Flower.

*Yucca aloifolia,* Spanish Bayonet. There are several forms of this plant with variously striped leaves which are good-looking but need careful handling because of their very spiky leaves. Culture as for succulents in general.

*Zantedeschia* spp. and cultivars, Calla-lily, Golden Calla, Pink Calla.

*Zebrina pendula,* Wandering Jew.

*Zygocactus truncatus,* Christmas Cactus. *See Schlumbergera* x *buckleyi* and *S. truncata.*

*Fleshy-leaved* Aloe vera *is a handy plant to have on the window sill, as its sticky sap is reputed to help heal minor skin burns and irritations.*

# CHAPTER 20

# *Plants for Special Conditions*

HERE is a selection from the main list of plants for various locations and purposes. There is no hard-and-fast dividing line between plants suitable for north, south, east, and west windows, which explains why the same plant may appear in more than one list. This versatility is also an indication of the plant's adaptability to varied conditions. Climatic factors, too, have a bearing on a plant's ability to thrive in any given location. A plant that demands all the sun available in a cloudy region could be expected to get along in an east, west, or even a north window in those favored sections where the sun is always shining, or nearly so, during the hours of daylight. I should mention that flowering plants in general, if grown in a north window, may bloom sparsely or not at all during the winter, but growing them under artificial light is a solution. Most house plants are benefited by all the sun available during the winter months, but some of them will need some shade as the days begin to lengthen and the sun gains power.

These lists are intended to be nothing more than a rough guide. Before making a final selection the cultural requirements for each plant should be considered.

**Easily grown plants:** None but the toughest kinds are represented here. Beginners would do well to start with a selection from this list.

*Agave* spp. (Century Plant)
*Aglaonema* spp. and cultivars (Chinese Evergreen)
*Aloe vera* (Bitter Aloe)

*Asparagus* spp. and cultivars (Asparagus-fern)
*Aspidistra elatior* (Cast-iron Plant)

Cacti, in general
*Chlorophytum comosum* (Spider Plant)
*Coleus* x *hybridus*
*Crassula argentea* (Jade Plant)
*Dieffenbachia* spp. and cultivars (Dumb Cane)
*Dracaena* spp. and cultivars (Dragon-lily)
*Ficus* spp. and cultivars (Fig)
*Howea forsterana* (Kentia Palm)
*Impatiens* spp. and cultivars
*Monstera deliciosa* (Mexican Bread Fruit)
*Neomarica northiana* (Twelve Apostles)

*Pandanus veitchii* (Variegated Screw-pine)
*Philodendron scandens oxycardium* (Heart-leaf Philodendron)
*Plectranthus australis* (Swedish-ivy)
*Sansevieria* spp. and cultivars (Snake Plant)
*Scindapsus* spp. and cultivars (Pothos)
*Senecio mikanioides* (German-ivy)
*Soleirolia soleirolii* (Baby's Tears)
*Syngonium podophyllum* (Nephthytis or Arrowhead Vine)
*Tradescantia fluminensis* (Wandering Jew)
*Zebrina pendula* (Wandering Jew)

**Plants for north windows** and locations away from the source of light in sunny or bright rooms. However, most of them will grow better in east or west windows where they receive from four to several hours of sunshine.

*Aglaonema* spp. (Chinese Evergreen)
*Araucaria heterophylla* (Norfolk Island-pine)
*Aspidistra elatior* (Cast-iron Plant)
*Begonia* spp. and cultivars
Bromeliads
*Caladium* spp. and cultivars
*Chlorophytum comosum* (Spider Plant)
*Cissus rhombifolia* (Grape-ivy)
*Dieffenbachia* spp. and cultivars (Dumb Cane)
*Dizygotheca elegantissima* (False-aralia)
Ferns
*Ficus* spp. and cultivars (Fig)
*Fittonia* spp. (Nerve Plant)
*Hedera* spp. and cultivars (Ivy)
*Maranta* spp. and cultivars (Prayer Plant)
*Microcoelum weddellianum* (Coccos Palm)
*Monstera deliciosa* (Mexican Bread Fruit)

*Pandanus* spp. (Screw-pine)
*Pellionia* spp.
*Peperomia* spp. and cultivars (Rubber Plant)
*Philodendron* spp. and cultivars
*Pilea* spp. and cultivars
*Saintpaulia* spp. and cultivars (African-violet)
*Sansevieria* spp. and cultivars (Snake Plant)
*Saxifraga stolonifera* (Mother-of-thousands, Strawberry-geranium)
*Scindapsus* spp. and cultivars (Pothos)
*Selaginella* spp.
*Soleirolia soleirolii* (Baby's Tears)
*Spathiphyllum* spp. and cultivars (Spathe Flower)
*Syngonium podophyllum* (Nephthytis)
*Tolmiea menziesii* (Pickaback Plant)
*Tradescantia fluminensis* (Wandering Jew)
*Zebrina pendula* (Wandering Jew)

Saxifraga stolonifera *'Tricolor'* has leaves marked with cream, pink, and green and is sought for terrariums because of its compact habit.

*A hanging basket displays the silver-marked leaves of episcia to full advantage.*

**Plants for south windows:** Most of these will grow almost as well in east or west windows.

*Abutilon* x *hybridum* (Flowering-maple)

*Acalypha hispida* (Chenille Plant)

*Ageratum houstonianum*

*Beaucarnia recurvata* (Bottle-palm)

*Begonia* spp. and cultivars (in winter)

*Beloperone guttata* (Shrimp Plant)

*Brassaia actinophylla* (Schefflera)

Bromeliads

Cacti, in general (Orchid and Christmas Cactus types should not be exposed to strong, undiluted sunshine over long periods, especially in summer)

*Camellia* spp. and cultivars

*Ceropegia woodii* (String of Hearts)

*Chrysanthemum frutescens* (Marguerite Daisy)

*C.* x *morifolium* (Florists' Chrysanthemum)

*Citrus* spp. and cultivars (Lemon, Orange, et cetera)

*Clerodendrum thomsoniae* (Bleeding-heart Vine)

*Coleus* x *hybridus*

*Cyanotis* spp.

*Cyperus alternifolius* (Umbrella Plant)

*Episcia* spp. and cultivars (Flame-violet)

*Euphorbia pulcherrima* (Poinsettia)

*E. milii splendens* (Crown of Thorns)

*Freesia* x *hybrida*

*Fuchsia triphylla* (Honeysuckle Fuchsia)

*Gardenia jasminoides* (Cape-jasmine)

*Gynura aurantiaca* (Velvet Plant)

*Heliotropium arborescens* (Heliotrope)

*Hippeastrum* spp. and cultivars (Amaryllis)

*Hyacinthus* cultivars (Hyacinth)

*Ipomoea batatas* (Sweet-potato)

*I. tricolor* (Morning Glory)

*Iresine lindenii* (Bloodleaf )

*Iris* spp. and cultivars

*Kalanchoe* spp. and cultivars

*Lachenalia* spp. and cultivars (Cape-cowslip)

*Lantana camara*

*Lilium longiflorum* and others (Lily)

*Lobularia maritima* (Sweet-alyssum)

*Malpighia coccigera* (Miniature-holly)

*Narcissus* spp. and cultivars (Daffodil)

*Neomarica northiana* (Twelve Apostles)

*Nicotiana alata* (Flowering Tobacco)

*Oxalis* spp. and cultivars

*Pelargonium* spp. and cultivars (Geranium)

*Plectranthus* spp. (Swedish-ivy)

*Rosa* cultivars (Miniature Rose)

*Senecio mikanioides* (German-ivy)

Succulents, in general

*Tagetes patula* (French Marigold)

*Thunbergia alata* (Black-eyed Susan Vine)

*Tibouchina urvilleana* (Princess Flower)

*Tropaeolum majus* (Nasturtium)

*Tulipa* spp. and cultivars (Tulip)

*Veltheimia viridifolia*

*Zantedeschia* spp. and cultivars (Calla-lily)

**Plants for east and west windows:** Can be grown in south windows if shaded by taller plants or thin curtains when necessary.

*Acalypha hispida* (Chenille Plant)

*Achimenes* spp. and cultivars

*Acorus gramineus* 'Variegatus' (Miniature Sweet Flag)

*Aeschynanthus* spp. and cultivars (Lipstick Plant)

*Anthurium scherzerianum* (Flamingo Flower)

*Bambusa glaucescens* (Bamboo)

*Begonia* spp. and cultivars

*Beloperone guttata* (Shrimp Plant)

*Brassaia actinophylla* (Schefflera)

Bromeliads

Cacti, Orchid and Christmas types

*Caladium* spp. and cultivars

*Campanula isophylla* (Ligurian Bellflower)

*Carissa grandiflora* (Natal-plum)

*Cissus* spp. (Grape-ivy)

*Citrus* spp. and cultivars (Lemon, Orange, et cetera)

*Coffea arabica* (Arabian Coffee)

*Columnea* spp. and cultivars

*Cyclamen persicum*

*Cymbalaria muralis* (Kenilworth-ivy)

*Cyperus alternifolius* (Umbrella Plant)

*Dieffenbachia* spp. and cultivars (Dumb Cane)

*Dracaena* spp. and cultivars (Dragon-lily)

*Episcia* spp. and cultivars (Flame-violet)

*Eucharis grandiflora* (Amazon-lily)

Ferns, most kinds

*Ficus* spp. and cultivars (Fig)

*Fuchsia triphylla* (Honeysuckle Fuchsia)

*Gesneria cuneifolia*

*Grevillea robusta* (Silk-oak)

*Hedera* spp. and cultivars (Ivy)

*Hippeastrum hybridum* (Amaryllis)

*Hoya* spp. and cultivars (Wax Plant)

*Hydrangea macrophylla* (French Hydrangea)

*Impatiens* spp. and cultivars

*Ligularia tussilaginea* '*Aureo-maculata*' (Leopard Plant)

*Neomarica northiana* (Twelve Apostles)

Orchids, most kinds

Palms, most kinds

*Pandanus* spp. (Screw-pine)

*Pittosporum tobira*

*Podocarpus* spp. and cultivars

*Polyscias* spp. and cultivars

*Primula* spp. and cultivars (Primrose)

*Rhododendron* cultivars (Evergreen Azalea)

*Saintpaulia* spp. and cultivars (African-violet)

*Senecio mikanioides* (German-ivy)

*Serrisa foetida*

*Sinningia pusilla* (Miniature Gloxinia)

*S. speciosa* (Gloxinia)

*Smithiantha zebrina* and hybrids (Temple Bells)

*Spathiphyllum* spp. and cultivars (Spathe Flower)

*Stephanotis floribunda*

*Streptocarpus* x *hybridus* (Cape-primrose)

*S. saxorum*

Succulents, in general

*Torenia fournieri* (Wishbone Plant)

*Trachelospermum jasminoides* (Star-jasmine)

*Tradescantia fluminensis* (Wandering Jew)

*Tripogandra multiflora* (Tahitian Bridal Veil)

*Veltheimia viridifolia*

*Zantedeschia* spp. and cultivars (Calla-lily)

*Zebrina pendula* (Wandering Jew)

**For cool temperatures:** The following do best with cool nights (50° to 60° F.) and cool days (55° to 68° F. range), but many other house plants will tolerate such cool temperatures for short periods (two to three weeks) without suffering damage. Avoid overwatering under these conditions.

*Acorus gramineus* 'Variegatus' (Miniature Sweet Flag)

*Araucaria heterophylla* (Norfolk Island-pine)

*Aspidistra elatior* (Cast-iron Plant)

*Aucuba japonica* 'Variegata' (Golddust Plant)

Cacti, Christmas types especially

*Camellia* spp. and cultivars

*Campanula isophylla* (Ligurian Bellflower)

*Chrysanthemum* spp. and cultivars

*Coprosma repens* (Mirror Plant)

*Crocus* spp. and cultivars

*Cyclamen persicum*

*Cymbalaria muralis* (Kenilworth-ivy)

*Daphne odora*

*Eranthis hyemalis* (Winter-aconite)

*Euonymus* spp. and cultivars

*Freesia* x *hybrida*

*Hedera* spp. and cultivars (Ivy)

*Hyacinthus* cultivars (Hyacinth)

*Laurus nobilis* (Sweet Bay Tree, Laurel)

*Ligularia tussilaginea* 'Aureo-maculata' (Leopard Plant)

*Myosotis* spp. (Forget-me-not)

*Myrtus communis* (Myrtle)

*Narcissus* spp. and cultivars (Daffodil)

Orchids, many kinds, especially *Cymbidium*

*Osmanthus fragrans* (Fragrant-olive)

*Pelargonium* spp. and cultivars (Geranium)

*Pittosporum tobira*

*Primula* spp. and cultivars (Primrose)

*Rhododendron* cultivars (Evergreen Azalea)

*Rosmarinus officinalis* (Rosemary)

*Saxifraga stolonifera* (Mother-of-thousands, Strawberry-geranium)

*Senecio* x *hybridus* (Cineraria)

*Soleirolia soleirolii* (Baby's Tears)

*Tolmiea menziesii* (Pickaback Plant)

*Veltheimia viridifolia*

*Vinca major* (Periwinkle)

# CHAPTER 21

# *Some Sources for Plants, Supplies, and Other Information*

Below are some suggested books for further reading about the many aspects of indoor gardening. If you have been unable to find certain house plants or supplies you want, a list of some companies from which you can order by mail is also provided.

### *Books*

*A House Plant Primer.* Brooklyn Botanic Garden, Brooklyn, N.Y., 1972.

*All About African Violets,* by Montague Free. 2nd ed. Revised by Charles Marden Fitch. Doubleday & Company, Garden City, N.Y., 1979.

*Beginner's Guide to Hydroponics,* by James Sholto Douglas. Drake Publishers, Inc., New York, N.Y. 1973.

*Bonsai for Americans,* by George F. Hull. Doubleday & Company, Garden City, N.Y., 1964.

*Bonsai for Indoors.* Brooklyn Botanic Garden, Brooklyn, N.Y., 1976.

*Bromeliads,* by Victoria Padilla. Crown Publishers, Inc., New York, N.Y., 1973.

*Cacti and Other Succulents,* by Jack Kramer. Harry N. Abrams, Inc., New York, N.Y., 1977.

*Complete Book of House Plants Under Lights, The,* by Charles Marden Fitch. Hawthorn Books, Inc., New York, N.Y., 1975.

*A long planter filled with philodendron, sansevieria, dracaena, and other foliage plants of tough constitutions serves as a divider between kitchen and living room.*

*Discovering Hydroponic Gardening* by Alexandria and John Dickerman. Woodbridge Press, Santa Barbara, Calif., 1970.

*Exotic Plant Manual,* by Alfred Byrd Graf. (4th ed.). Roehrs Company, East Rutherford, N.J., 1976.

*Facts of Light About Indoor Gardening, The.* Ortho Books, Chevron Chemical Company, San Francisco, Calif., 1975.

*Fern Growers Manual,* by Barbara Joe Hoshizaki. Alfred A. Knopf, New York, N.Y., 1975.

*Ferns,* by Philip Perl and editors of Time-Life Books. Time-Life Books, Va., 1977.

*Flowers When You Want Them—A Grower's Guide to Out-of-Season Bloom,* by John James. Hawthorn Books, Inc., New York, N.Y., 1977.

*Fun with Terrarium Gardening,* by Virginie and George Elbert. Crown Publishers, New York, N.Y., 1973.

*Gardens in Glass Containers,* by Robert C. Baur. Hearthside Press, Great Neck, N.Y., 1970.

*Hanging Plants for Home, Terrace and Garden,* by John Philips Baumgardt. Simon and Schuster, New York, N.Y., 1972.

*Herbs to Grow Indoors,* by Adelma Grenier Simmons. Hawthorn Books, Inc., New York, N.Y., 1969.

*Home Orchid Growing,* by Rebecca Northen. Nostrand-Reinhold, New York, N.Y., 1970.

*House Plant Decorating Book, The,* by Virginie F. and George A. Elbert. E. P. Dutton & Co., Inc., New York, N.Y., 1977.

*House Plants for Five Exposures,* by George Taloumis. Abelard-Schuman, New York, N.Y., 1973.

*Indoor Gardener's How-to-Build-It Book, The,* by Jack Kramer. Simon and Schuster, New York, N.Y., 1973.

*Little Plants for Small Spaces,* by Elvin McDonald. M. Evans and Co., Inc., New York, N.Y., 1974.

*Miracle Houseplants—The Gesneriad Family, The,* by Virginie F. and George A. Elbert. Crown Publishers, Inc., New York, N.Y., 1976.

*Orchids as House Plants,* by Rebecca Tyson Northen. Dover Publications, Inc., New York, N.Y., 1976.

*Six Ways to Grow House Plants,* by Muriel Orans. Countryside Books, A. B. Morse Co., Barrington, Ill., 1976.

*Terrariums.* Brooklyn Botanic Garden, Brooklyn, N.Y., 1975.

*Terrariums and Miniature Gardens,* edited by Kathryn Arthurs. Sunset Books, Lane Publishing Co., Menlo Park, Calif., 1973.

## *Plants and Supplies*

Abbey Garden
176 Toro Canyon Rd.
Carpinteria, Calif. 93013

(Cacti and succulents)

Alberts and Merkle
2210 S. Federal Highway
Boynton Beach, Fla. 33435

(Orchids and tropical plants)

Arthur E. Allgrove
Wilmington, Mass. 01887

(Terrarium and bonsai plants and supplies)

Buell's Greenhouses
P.O. Box 218
Weeks Rd.
Eastford, Conn. 06242

(African-violets and other gesneriads; supplies)

Burgess Seed and Plant Company
Bloomington, Ill. 61701

(Plants and supplies)

De Jager Bulbs, Inc.
188 Asbury St.
South Hamilton, Mass. 01982

(Bulbs for indoors)

Desert Dan Cactus
W. Summer St.
Minotola, N.J. 08341

(Cacti)

Edelweiss Gardens
54 Robb-Allentown Rd.
Robbinsville, N.J. 08691

(General list of plants)

Fennell Orchid Company
26719 S. W. 157 Ave.
Homestead, Fla. 33032

(Orchids, bromeliads, ferns)

Fischer Greenhouses
Oak Ave.
Linwood, N.J. 08221

(African-violets and relatives, orchids, etc., supplies)

George W. Park Seed Company
Greenwood, S.C. 29647

(Seeds, plants, supplies)

Homeland Industries
95 Evergreen Ave.
Brooklyn, N.Y. 11206

(Hydroponic units)

House Plant Corner
Box 5000
Cambridge, Md. 21613

(African-violets, orchids, etc., lights, supplies)

John Scheepers, Inc.
63 Wall St.
New York, N.Y. 10005

(Bulbs for indoors)

Jones and Scully
2200 N.W. 33rd Ave.
Miami, Fla. 33142

(Orchids)

K & L Cactus Nursery
12712 Stockton Blvd.
Galt, Calif. 95632

(Cacti and succulents)

Kartuz Greenhouses
92 Chestnut St.
Wilmington, Mass. 01887

(General list including gesneriads, begonias, dwarf geraniums, succulents)

Lauray of Salisbury
Salisbury, Conn. 06068

(Begonias, cacti, gesneriads, fuchsias, succulents)

Logee's Greenhouses
55 North St.
Danielson, Conn. 06239

(General list, with extensive offering of begonias)

Mellinger's
2310 West South Range Rd.
North Lima, Ohio 44452

(Plants and supplies)

Merry Gardens
Camden, Me. 04843

(General list, but emphasizes rare and unusual)

Orchids by Hausermann, Inc.
Box 363
Elmhurst, Ill. 60126

(Orchids and supplies)

Peter Paul's Nurseries
Canandaigua, N.Y. 14424

(Terrarium and carnivorous plants;
terrarium supplies)

S & G Exotic Plant Company
22 Goldsmith Ave.
Beverly, Mass. 01915

(Orchids, most species)

Shoplite
97 Carlton Ave.
E. Rutherford, N.J. 07073

(Light garden equipment and supplies)

Tinari Greenhouses
2325 Valley Rd.
Box 190
Huntington Valley, Pa. 19006

(African-violets)

Wilson Brothers
Roachdale, Ind. 46172

(Geraniums, African-violets and
relatives; supplies)

# *Photographic Credits*

We gratefully acknowledge the cooperation and assistance of the following sources of black-and-white photographs in this book:

Robert C. Baur: pages 19, 52, 55

The Bettmann Archive: page 20

Jonathan Bodge: page 48

Charles Marden Fitch: pages 23, 33, 45, 46, 47, 60, 63, 64, 67, 79, 92, 104, 113, 115, 116, 117, 120, 132, 136 (top), 156, 157, 159, 160, 161, 162, 164, 186, 201, 224, 228, 241, 248, 274, 292, 307, 308, 317, 320, 326, 333, 336 (top)

Homeland Industries: page 106

Margaret C. Perry: page 16

Judy Sugar: pages 61, 299, 300, 302, 311, 323, 331

George Taloumis: pages 18, 22, 24, 25, 26, 29, 30, 35, 84, 88, 98, 101, 112, 122, 123, 136 (bottom), 140, 147, 148, 149, 155, 168, 169, 170, 171, 194, 205, 211, 216, 232, 256, 265, 267, 294, 298, 305, 310, 332, 336 (bottom), 341

Terrarium Association: pages 44, 50, 51, 53, 57

# Index

**(NUMERALS IN BOLDFACE INDICATE ILLUSTRATIONS)**